MAGGIE

Her Fatal Legacy

Also by John Sergeant

GIVE ME TEN SECONDS

JOHN SERGEANT

MAGGIE

Her Fatal Legacy

MACMILLAN

First published 2005 by Macmillan
an imprint of Pan Macmillan Ltd
Pan Macmillan, 20 New Wharf Road, London N1 9RR
Basingstoke and Oxford
Associated companies throughout the world
www.panmacmillan.com

ISBN 1 4050 0526 2 HB
ISBN 1 4050 4734 8 TPB

1 3 5 7 9 8 6 4 2

A CIP catalogue record for this book is available from
the British Library.

Typeset by SetSystems Ltd, Saffron Walden, Essex
Printed and bound in Great Britain by
Mackays of Chatham plc, Chatham, Kent

For Mary

PICTURE ACKNOWLEDGEMENTS

Camera Press: 17; Corbis: 4, 7, 15, 21, 22, 24;
Getty Images: 2, 3, 5, 8, 9, 11, 12, 20, 27, 28, 29, 31;
PA Photos: 1, 10, 16, 19, 23, 25, 26;
Courtesy of the author: 6, 13, 18, 30.

Contents

Acknowledgements ix

1. *Maggie and me* 1

2. *'The prime minister will see you now'* 12

3. *Heart versus head over Europe* 26

4. *The assassin with the golden hair* 39

5. *Into battle with sets of initials* 52

6. *The diva and the bear* 64

7. *'My God, that man is so German'* 76

8. *'Maggie, Maggie, Maggie; out, out, out'* 88

9. *Mrs Thatcher goes too far* 101

10. *Murder through the front door* 113

11. *'I fight on; I fight to win'* 125

12. *One more triumph – because it's the last* 137

13. *Anyone but Heseltine* 149

14. *The nice Mr Major* 161

15. *Managing without Maggie* 173

16. *Finding a plumber, and a new role* 184

17. *Missing the buzz at Number 10* 196

18. *'Game, set and match'* 208

19. *'Not enough oomph, enough whizz, enough steam'* 221

20. *The bitter taste of victory* 234

21. *The unlucky prime minister* 246

22. *The end of the beginning* 258

23. *Maggie backs unity – but not for long* 270

24. *In the foothills, with Mr Major* 283

25. *Enter Mr Blair* 296

26. *'No change, no chance'* 309

27. *'Were you up for Portillo?'* 322

28. *The Mummy returns* 334

29. *'I am an ism'* 347

30. *The fatal legacy* 360

Index 373

Acknowledgements

I never realized, until recently, how important computers would be to my work, particularly those I can operate at home. In writing this book I have had access to a number of information retrieval systems which have been invaluable, but I would particularly like to mention Lexis Nexis. Their newspaper archive has been enormously helpful in reminding me of how my journalist colleagues covered critical events, and the powerful search facility allowed me to make all sorts of enquiries, some of which were so straightforward I would have been embarrassed to have discussed them with a competent researcher.

I have also drawn heavily on a host of political memoirs from the key political figures of this period; all the most important quotes are attributed directly in the text. My particular thanks go to those who have allowed me to interview them in depth about their experiences. In every case they were generous with their time, and in many instances were prepared to provide corrections and additions to the transcripts of what they said.

The following is not an exhaustive list of those who provided me with their version of what happened as some of those who helped me insisted on remaining anonymous, but I would like to give special thanks to: Lord (Kenneth) Baker, Tony Blair, Gordon Brown, Bill Cash, Lord (Peter) Carrington, Kenneth Clarke, Iain Duncan Smith, Frank Field, Lord (Ian) Gilmour, John Gummer, William Hague, Lord (Douglas) Hurd, Lord (Michael) Heseltine, Michael Howard, Lord (Geoffrey) Howe, Sir Bernard Ingham, Neil Kinnock, Sir Brian Mawhinney, John

Acknowledgements

Major, Sir Christopher Meyer, Mo Mowlam, Lord (Norman) Lamont, Lord (Cecil) Parkinson, Chris Patten, Michael Portillo, Lord (Charles) Powell, Stephen Shelbourne, Lord (David) Steel, Lord (Norman) Tebbit, Sir Andrew Turnbull, John Whittingdale, Michael Mates and Lord (John) Wakeham.

I also owe a great debt to my wife Mary, who conscientiously corrected the first drafts of each chapter; and special thanks are due to my skilful editor and friend at Pan Macmillan Georgina Morley and my literary agent Mark Lucas, who made sure the project did not falter.

1

Maggie and me

'JOHN, NOT ALL OF THEM LIKED YOU,' Pauline confided over
lunch. She smiled and I tried not to look too concerned. We
were among a group of six who regularly ate together in a vast
dining room, served by ever-attentive waiters mostly from the
Philippines. I had given my first talk on a cruise ship, and
inevitably it was my references to Margaret Thatcher which
had caused some concern. Most of the elderly passengers were
on a trip round the world, which no doubt they felt was their
just reward for a lifetime of hard work. They did not want
their peace disturbed by unexpected attacks on Lady Thatcher.
Pauline's husband Terry had made a good living out of selling
fire extinguishers to hotels and schools – 'squirters' he called
them – and if the conversation took too serious a turn he
would deftly move us into shallower waters. Printed notes
awaited me in my cabin and I was slightly surprised to learn
that on board the pride of Fred Olsen's fleet, the *Black Watch*,
we were not expected to engage in discussions about politics
and religion. It is reasonable to ask: what on earth was I doing
there?

'No,' had been my response when the agent responsible
for providing the ship's entertainment had phoned me at home.
'But, John . . .' he tried to interrupt. 'No. Certainly not,' I
went on. He didn't give up. 'But, John, you would start in
Tahiti.' He paused, dramatically. 'Oh,' I responded. 'Then you
would go to the islands of Bora-Bora, Samoa, Tonga, Fiji;
then Auckland, and you'd fly back from Sydney.' Sometimes,

particularly in phone conversations, it is best to admit when you've got something completely wrong. I announced gravely, 'When I said "Certainly not" that didn't necessarily mean no.' All those years listening to politicians had not been wasted. My wife Mary could not get away from her teaching job; so when I swapped the cold and rain of London in February for the balmy tropical paradise of Tahiti, it would be my elder brother Peter who would join me for the three-week cruise. As a former actor, he would be my perfect agent, floor manager and all-round companion.

He could not help me much, though, in tackling the most difficult problem. As we made our royal progress across the South Pacific at a stately seventeen knots, helped by a gentle breeze from the trade winds, wasn't it up to me to provide some insight and wisdom? Not all the seven hundred passengers could be expected to attend my talks – they had bridge to play and deck quoits to throw – but given a straight choice between me and staring out to sea, I managed to attract a few hundred. But could I provide some enlightenment or even a sense of purpose to our magical journey on the other side of the world?

This was early 2004, British spring turned into southern hemisphere high summer by a day-long flight. I had spent a good deal of the previous eighteen months preparing a book on Margaret Thatcher. Now I was meeting a group of people – most of a similar age to the former prime minister – who might not take kindly to my less than reverent approach to the subject. Pauline, my companion at lunch, confirmed what I had already guessed. 'I met a lady coming out of your talk who wasn't at all sure about you,' she said. 'She couldn't work out where you were coming from, as regards Lady Thatcher; and there was some muttering from others.' Fortunately, the majority of those who attended the talk had been interested, and at times amused, by my rambling account of my life as a political correspondent being dragged along in the wake of the most controversial prime minister in recent British history.

For years, my party piece – very definitely not a Conservative party piece – has been my account of her final days. It includes some explanation of how I stood outside the British embassy in Paris on a dark, cold November night in 1990 solemnly telling thirteen million television viewers to the BBC six o'clock news that Mrs Thatcher would not be coming out to comment on her disastrous showing in the leadership election. My earpiece, which was meant to connect me with the backstage team in London, was not working so I did not hear the newsreader, Peter Sissons, warn me: 'John, she's behind you.' A large part of the audience immediately sensed this was a great moment of political pantomime, and to judge from the comments I have subsequently received, it appears that thirteen million people also shouted at me, 'She's behind you.' This could, in other circumstances, have been a career-threatening moment, particularly as I had only recently been appointed chief political correspondent. But such was the genuine confusion at the heart of government that my role in bringing this incident live to homes across the country elevated rather than depressed my reputation.

I was greatly helped by the behaviour of the prime minister's press secretary Bernard Ingham and another official from Number 10, who appeared to be pushing me aside as they searched for a microphone. It was this other official who had earlier told me she would not be coming out. I wrongly assumed they were looking for my microphone, and in my usual, helpful way I said, rather plaintively, 'Here is the microphone,' thrusting mine forward. This seemed to make them angrier and it has even been suggested – though I have always denied it – that at this point Mrs Thatcher hit me with her handbag. The truth is that they were looking for another microphone, which had been set up across the courtyard near the main gate. It had been placed there so that Mrs Thatcher could speak to a small but high-powered delegation from the British press – who were none too pleased with my BBC exclusive.

Mrs Thatcher was so keen to be rid of the distasteful task of admitting she had failed to win the first round of the leadership ballot that she gave her comment to me, and then disappeared back into the embassy. She thanked those of her MPs who had supported her in her battle against Michael Heseltine, and she promised to put her name forward for the second ballot. But it was not to be. Two days later she announced her resignation. What made the 'handbagging incident' in Paris an award-winning event on television was that the prime minister looked as if she had lost her grip on power; and indeed she had lost control, but not in the way the pictures suggested. This trivial misunderstanding outside the British embassy had taken on the power of a political cartoon. Unwittingly, Mrs Thatcher, with a little help from me, had provided a tableau which could have been entitled, *The Great Fall*. I couldn't resist giving my elderly cruise-ship audience one of my oldest lines: 'It made my career, and it finished hers.'

For many years after Mrs Thatcher resigned this was my view: that when the Conservative party turned against her – after eleven years as one of the most dominant figures ever to occupy Downing Street – her power had been broken. The Thatcher era was over. But after writing my memoirs during a final three-year stint at Westminster, as political editor of ITN, I had more time to reflect. The conclusion I came to – and this is the theme of this book – is that Mrs Thatcher's power to influence events did not end with her resignation. She was to have an extraordinary Indian summer to her political career; and even now it is impossible to understand the present state of British politics without a clear grasp of the part she played after her departure from Number 10. Partly this was because of her early successes in government. She had built up an amazing following across the world; as Britain's first woman prime minister, fully determined to dress the part, she had become the most famous politician in the world. I covered her first visit to see the Russian president, Mikhail Gorbachev, in Moscow in 1987 and the trip ended with a visit to Georgia. Two million people stopped work to line the route her motorcade took to the airport at Tbilisi. She was a superstar.

For many of my audience on the *Black Watch* Lady Thatcher had kept her aura; indeed she had regained much of the popularity she had lost at the end of her time in office. In the autumn of 1990 no doubt many of those now relaxing on the cruise had been appalled by the poll tax, annoyed that inflation had crept back into double figures, and might have accepted that she had become an electoral liability to the Conservative party. In modern politics it is hard for any prime minister not to look shop-soiled after two terms in office, let alone someone who soldiers on deep into their third term. So much news coverage – now twenty-four hours a day – is devoted to the all too human inhabitants of Number 10 that it is not surprising that voters simply get bored with the same character. Once relieved of the necessity of taking unpopular decisions ex-prime ministers have the opportunity to polish up their image, and nearly fourteen years later in the promenade lounge of this luxury cruise ship it seemed there were few who did not feel that Margaret Thatcher had been Britain's last great political leader.

It was not that they were all Conservative voters – some voted Labour or Liberal Democrat – but I think my jokes at her expense were only tolerated because they were funny. Any real attack on the former prime minister would not have gone down well. As they put on their evening dress for dinner –

dinner jackets every third night was the rule – you felt a collective longing for order and respectability. These were not Thatcher's children we have heard so much about, but Thatcher's brothers and sisters; and if that BBC chap was a bit iffy, they could take comfort in the fact that the lecturer taking over in Sydney would be Sir Bernard Ingham himself. From Cape Town, on the final leg, those of a right-wing persuasion would have even more of a treat. The lecturer on the way back to Southampton was the former prime minister of Rhodesia, Ian Smith, still going strong at the age of eighty-four. Sergeant, Ingham and Smith; for the true blues things could only get better.

When we returned home, Bernard and I compared notes. I had come to know him well during the eleven years he had served as Mrs Thatcher's press secretary. He did not like being called a spin doctor, but he became the first civil servant who increasingly filled that role, putting the best possible gloss on the government's activities. And I suppose if he was a spin doctor, I was one of his patients. Often twice a day I would sit among a group of reporters at his off-the-record briefings, taking the medicine from Bernard. With his prominent eyebrows and jutting chin, he skilfully turned himself into the alternative voice of Margaret Thatcher, and was a personality in his own right, a cross between a Yorkshire terrier and a British bulldog. With him, as with Mrs Thatcher, the best kind of argument could only be expressed in straight lines, and if alternative representations were offered he would often react by repeating his catchphrase, 'Bunkum and balderdash.'

He agreed with me that the passengers on the *Black Watch* held Baroness Thatcher in high regard. 'They must do,' Bernard insisted, 'otherwise why would they want to hear from me what it was like working with her – after nearly fourteen years?' In his view it was not a matter of whether they were Conservative or voted for other parties; she represented 'common sense' not the 'nonsense we have to put up with nowadays'. But I then tackled him on the central, most disturbing question for anyone who takes that view. If she was so admirable, how can they come to terms with the fact that she was ditched by her own party? 'They can't understand it,' Bernard retorted, 'and that is why people have become cynical about politics and politicians.' He spoke with passion on a point which he must have reiterated many times in the pastel-coloured lounge high above the waters off the coast of Australia. The downfall of Margaret Thatcher had been an event so bewildering to ordinary people, he argued, that it had driven a wedge between the public and Parliament which had yet to be removed. And as for the Conservative party itself: 'All these years later, they have still not got over it.'

When visitors are guided round Parliament, the highlight of the tour is the chamber of the House of Commons. Most people are surprised that it is not larger, and grander. There are not nearly enough seats for the 659 MPs. Seen on television it suffers from the same distorting effect as the Centre Court at Wimbledon: the cameras make it seem bigger than it is. Many parliaments have their seats arranged in a semicircle; this makes it easy to see which parties are on the left wing, and which are on the right. The small, oblong shape of the House of Commons encourages quite a different view of how politics is conducted. On a guided tour you are likely to be told about the apocryphal new MP being shown round by an experienced colleague. 'It must be difficult,' the new member suggests, 'having to make your speeches not to your friends, but across the chamber to your enemies.' The older MP shakes his head. 'No, you've got that wrong,' he says. 'Your opponents sit in the benches on the other side of the chamber. Your enemies are on your own side.'

The way that Mrs Thatcher was removed from office by her own side is the most dramatic recent example of the way

battles within a party can be far more important than the
set-piece jousting across the chamber. These internal conflicts
are likely to be more vicious, bloodier affairs; and, as in a civil
war, they can give rise to personal antagonisms on a grander
scale, as well as having much longer-lasting effects. The reason
for this is fairly obvious: in a conventional war combatants
have little choice but to fight for their country; in a civil war
most of those involved can choose on which side to fight.
Votes in Conservative leadership elections are conducted by
secret ballot, but enough of the argument has to be fought out
in public for the battle lines to be clearly drawn. For Conservative MPs the question had to be answered: 'Are you with
us, or against us?' And the answers were not forgotten.

If you are not a Conservative supporter, you may be
thinking, 'Well, why should I care? The Tories got themselves
into a mess; if they spend years trying to sort it out, that's
their problem.' But, of course, it is not as simple as that.
The devastating effect on the Conservative party of the divisions which led to Mrs Thatcher's departure and the long
struggle which took place after she'd gone weakened British
politics as a whole. The landslide Labour victories in 1997 and
2001 against an enfeebled opposition hardly strengthened the
democratic process. The Conservative foreign secretary Francis
Pym greatly annoyed Mrs Thatcher at the start of the general
election campaign in 1983 when he said on television, 'Land-
slides on the whole don't produce successful governments.'
She thought it hardly the sort of confident rallying cry she
would expect from a leading member of the cabinet, and after
the Conservative landslide only a few weeks later – they had a
majority of 144 – she sacked him. It was not, in her view, his
only offence; it was simply the last straw. But he was right.
Landslide victories are not usually good for the country. In the
British parliamentary system the strength of the opposition
matters, as does the vital question of who is leader of the

official Opposition. Weak oppositions weaken governments; they severely reduce the chances of ministers listening to sensible argument and advice.

For nearly two years I had been trying to work out the best way to approach the subject of Margaret Thatcher. I could not escape her; we had spent too long foraging in the same pastures. From the moment she had become leader of the Conservative party in 1975 I found her impossible to avoid. I covered her first visit to Brussels, where she met officials from the European Commission, a group who would later join the ranks of her least favourite people. On the same trip she went to the headquarters of NATO to meet the military leaders of the alliance, with whom she felt very much more at home. During her first election campaign, in 1979, I had been diligently present at all her major speeches; and when she won the election I even crawled through the feet of a large crowd of her supporters at Central Office in order to obtain her first radio interview as prime minister. When she arrived in Downing Street, having kissed hands with the Queen, I was, of course, waiting outside Number 10, microphone in hand. During her years in power, until the very end, she was never far from my professional thoughts.

Having retired from political journalism at the end of 2002, I was in a position to produce, if not a magisterial tome on the Thatcher years, at least a more reflective assessment than is possible during the hand-to-mouth life of a reporter. I had many advantages over more distant observers. As well as a direct memory of the key events and often some inside knowledge picked up at the time, I was able to draw on contacts at the highest levels. Many of the most senior members of her governments had become friends who would be ready to help with their comments. I would also be able to talk in detail with those who had followed Lady Thatcher to Number 10. Both John Major and Tony Blair put aside time to give me their assessments of the prime minister who one way or another had helped them reach the highest office. What was lacking before I started this quest was a theme. Winston Churchill once complained about one of the drafts of his own speeches. 'It's like a pudding,' he said. 'It lacks a theme.' Oxford University Press have produced a CD-Rom which contains all of Lady Thatcher's public statements in the forty-five years before she resigned as prime minister. It is a splendid compendium, but anyone hoping for an easy read should give it a miss. The compact disc contains more than seven thousand statements and a total of more than fourteen million words. But there is not one sentence in it which constitutes a theme.

I was increasingly drawn to the idea that I should concentrate, not so much on the glory years, but on what happened after she resigned: the aftershock from which the Conservative party has still not yet recovered. Up until the time that Michael Howard became Conservative leader, late in 2003, Lady Thatcher was still a force to be reckoned with; she took a direct hand in all the leadership elections before that date and her role was crucial in determining their outcome. I was just finishing an interview for this book with Douglas Hurd, now Lord Hurd, in the tea room of the House of Lords when I came across another former foreign secretary, Lord Carrington. I have long appreciated his briskness and no-nonsense approach, and so I did not hesitate to ask him a direct question: 'How much influence did Lady Thatcher have on leadership elections after she'd gone?' He immediately replied, 'She intervened in all of them, and always with disastrous results.' He then grinned broadly, enjoying the surprise on my face.

Slowly it was beginning to dawn on me that perhaps I had a theme. It would not take away from Lady Thatcher her main achievements. She was, without doubt, one of the greatest prime ministers of modern times. But I would also not shrink from pointing out how much she was disliked, and how much she was bitterly resented by those – like the miners – who felt her victories had been at their expense. But I wanted to try to explain what happened after her downfall: how Lady Thatcher tried to come to terms with being rejected by Conservative MPs, her deep sense of betrayal, and her determination neither to forgive nor forget. The consequences, not just for her but for British politics in general, were profound; and if I could clear up some of the bewilderment felt by the passengers on the good ship *Black Watch* maybe that would be good too.

I was acutely conscious of the need to establish contact with the small number of people who had direct experience of how Lady Thatcher operated, both in and out of government. If my advances were rejected by any of the key witnesses, the whole project would be in jeopardy. It would take time, and luck would play its part. Not only was it important to speak to those who had held prominent positions, it was vital to have some idea of the line they would take. Hours spent with people merely prepared to repeat what they had already said in public would not be of much use. Social events involving those who inhabit the Westminster village were my most useful hunting ground, and I got lucky when the broadcaster James Naughtie and his wife Ellie gave a joint fiftieth-birthday party at the London Welsh Rugby Club in Richmond. I found myself queuing up for food with the former Conservative chairman and eminent Brussels commissioner, Chris Patten. I explained how I was writing a book about Margaret Thatcher and was hoping to talk to him. 'Oh, yes,' he replied, smiling broadly. 'She destroyed the Conservative party.'

At last I had my theme.

2

'The prime minister will see you now'

FOR A PRIME MINISTER to spend more than half an hour with a journalist is unusual; if it is for an interview which will not be broadcast or published in a newspaper that is really quite something. This was one of the thoughts buzzing through my head as I made the oh-so-familiar trudge up Downing Street one afternoon, towards the end of July 2002. I was on my way to talk to Tony Blair about Margaret Thatcher. The policeman on the gate greeted me in his customary way: 'Hello, Mr Sergeant. Can I check your identity?' I was never sure whether he realized he was being funny, but it always cheered me up. If you appear on television regularly, you inevitably have identity problems. People often believe you are an old friend; a woman once gave me a puzzled look and finally asked, 'Are you *someone*?' It was a relief to reply, 'Not really.' I found it oddly relaxing to have a policeman who knew me well look at my Westminster pass to see if my face matched the photo.

Prime ministers sometimes pretend they are not mesmerized by the media. Clement Attlee allowed a telegraph ticker tape machine to be installed at Number 10, but that was only, he insisted, to keep an eye on the cricket scores. When political pressures threatened to overwhelm him, Harold Macmillan would ostentatiously read a Jane Austen novel. Tony Blair never pretended that the media were not vitally important: from the moment he entered politics he knew that the script – sometimes rather portentously called the narrative – of his career could only be written by the media; and his task was to influence it as much as possible.

One of Mr Blair's first appointments as Labour leader was to take on Alastair Campbell as his press secretary. Tall, witty and with a scowl as his default expression, Mr Campbell, like Bernard Ingham, had the great advantage of usually knowing what was in Mr Blair's mind; and if, on some issues, he was not sure, then just as Bernard might guess at Mrs Thatcher's thoughts, Alastair would chance a view on Mr Blair's behalf. I had always got on well with him, although sometimes in a fairly rough way. Once, on his way into the regular meeting of political correspondents called The Lobby, Alastair – in a jovial way – kicked me on the leg. I immediately kicked him back. Despite this, without his help I would not have been given an interview with the prime minister to talk about Lady Thatcher.

Prime ministers have a certain amount of fellow feeling for each other, especially if they have not been rivals. James Callaghan was once in a small gathering of former inhabitants of Number 10 and wondered how they might be described. He thought the most appropriate collective noun would be a 'denial'. But that tells you more about his period in office than he perhaps intended; he was almost always on the defensive. A 'pride' of prime ministers is what most of them would like to be, lions able to take on the world, and improve it as well. Mr Callaghan, and later John Major, were both severely constrained by their dwindling and finally vanishing parliamentary majorities. Towards the end of their periods in office they could barely manage a roar between them.

Mr Blair, having recently won his second landslide victory – in the election of 2001 – was often compared with Mrs Thatcher. He had done better in terms of seats in his two elections than she ever had, but the effect was the same. Both of them had enough MPs not to have to worry too much about backbench opinion. Both of them had exceptional flair and vote-winning appeal. What surprised me during my interview with Mr Blair was the extent to which he was prepared to acknowledge Margaret Thatcher's strengths, and to make it clear that he wanted to emulate her. From the leader of a party which had spent years vilifying the former Conservative leader, it came as quite a surprise.

We met in the cabinet room and Mr Blair then ushered me through the French windows into the garden. 'It'll be quieter here,' he said. The garden is quite large – Mr Major used it to hold news conferences – but the lawn is hemmed in by a brick wall which cuts it off from Horse Guards Parade. I looked in vain for any signs of the IRA mortar attack of some years earlier – the bombs landing in the garden smashed windows and sent Mr Major and his colleagues diving for cover under the cabinet table. The garden now looked cared for and peaceful, and this mood was matched by Mr Blair's demeanour. But he had aged considerably during his five years in office. It was hard to see how anyone could have compared him with the frisky young cartoon character Bambi. He looked greyer, and contrary to my own experience of getting older, seemed to have lost weight.

Mrs Thatcher suffered in a similar way from the strains of her premiership. When she first arrived at Number 10, she exuded a kind of healthy radiance; she gave the impression of being a natural in the job, totally confident that she could overcome the challenges and merely irritated that there were only twenty-four hours in each day. At a Downing Street party she told my wife how she got over the excitement of winning the election: 'Oh, you can't stay on cloud nine for ever – you have to settle down to a routine.' But after eleven years that routine of punishing days and short nights had taken its toll. When I met her at a Downing Street reception shortly before the end the old radiance had gone. On that occasion she appeared to be lecturing her guests on anything she had decided was safe and reasonably relevant. When she spoke to me, with the veins showing in her tired eyes, I thought for a moment she was addressing someone behind me. Like a faulty two-way radio she was able to transmit but not to receive.

In Mr Blair the change was not very noticeable to begin with. During the election campaign of 1997 he had worried privately about his receding hairline, but that had not struck me as being at all significant. He was young and confident; in America he would have been a perfect candidate for president. The big change came with the devastating effects of the Iraq crisis: he quickly began to look his age, and the stress of office was no longer disguised. But that was some way in the future. At the time of my interview he was still enjoying one of the longest political honeymoons in British political history.

He had retained his directness and – quite rare in senior politicians – his ability to engage in discussion. Many of his similarly overworked colleagues were already finding real conversation a bit of a strain. But there was still plenty to concern Mr Blair in the summer of 2002; he was worried about the need to give his period in office a sense of direction, about how his narrative might appear to future historians. The comparison with Mrs Thatcher may well have been troubling him. His first term in office – apart from the dramatic decision to grant the Bank of England independent control of interest rates – looked cautious if not timid. Most of his more controversial moves, including devolution with separate parliaments for Scotland and Wales, had been carried out on the back of strong public support. Indeed there were times when it seemed Mr Blair could not decide policy until his faithful polling expert Philip Gould had given him the nod. The most notable exception was his decision to take on the Serbs and their leader Slobodan Milošević, who were forcing thousands of ethnic Albanians out of Kosovo. With his friend and close ally, the

American president Bill Clinton, it was decided to attack the Serb forces from the air in a joint US–British operation. After some very difficult weeks and a concerted international campaign against the bombing, the air raids succeeded and Mr Blair was able to keep his promise that the refugees would be 'home by Christmas'.

Surprisingly, it seemed that Lady Thatcher had played a part: Mr Blair revealed that he had talked to her 'reasonably regularly' since becoming prime minister and they kept in touch, particularly over international issues. 'I found her immensely helpful over Kosovo,' he said. I wondered whether this was simply because this was an issue on which they agreed. 'We were,' Mr Blair admitted, 'on the same side of the argument. But she was not just very supportive; she was very kind personally. She understood the pressure. She was very good about advising me on how to take the military advice on board, and how to use it.' Much is often made of loneliness at the top; how when the big decisions have to be made there is no one to lean on, you are on your own. One of Mr Blair's virtues in the early part of his premiership was that he was prepared to be open about this and not try to shroud his own feelings in mystery. It was only later when his more messianic side came to the fore – particularly over Iraq – that he found it difficult to admit to mistakes, or even weakness.

'It worked out in the end,' Mr Blair continued. 'But there were points when it was very rocky indeed, and I thought at one point that we were really pretty extended, in terms of our political credibility. And she was just very, very supportive at those times.' 'And her advice to you on this occasion was to trust your instinct?' I suggested. He nodded and smiled, as he recalled what she had said: 'You are doing the right thing; don't pay any attention to the critics. Go on and get it done.' When I read the transcript of the interview later, I thought back to those occasions when Mrs Thatcher had taken delight in urging a course of action on an American president. There was the famous occasion when George Bush was said to have 'wobbled' over the possible US response to Saddam Hussein's invasion of Kuwait; that was until Mrs Thatcher had provided some necessary stiffening to the president's resolve. Her advice to Mr Blair was, as I had suspected, vintage Thatcher. She was never, it seemed, happier than when she was involved in a fight which could be portrayed as virtuous.

MR BLAIR TOLD ME about his first encounter with Mrs Thatcher, which had occurred one day during prime minister's question time in the House of Commons. The young Mr Blair had had the temerity to suggest that the government was not taking responsibility for providing people with jobs, in stark contrast with the policy outlined in the 1944 White Paper on full employment. 'At which point,' Mr Blair recalled, 'she put her handbag up on to the Dispatch Box, opened it, and drew out the White Paper. She then proceeded to slaughter me with various selective quotations.' Mr Blair was amazed that she had been able to produce the right document without any apparent warning. How had she or her advisers made sure she was so well prepared? 'I have never known to this day how they knew,' he told me. 'But I think that is where the term "handbagging" came from.'

This encounter with the first woman prime minister had made a strong impact on Mr Blair. His respect for her grew. 'She was a very fine intellect,' he told me. 'She had a really uncluttered mind, a very clear mind.' When he was researching the speeches she made when she spoke for the Conservatives on Treasury matters, back in the 1970s – to look for ammunition to use against her – he had been impressed. 'Her speeches then were really good, detailed forensic speeches; she had a clear way of expressing herself.' Mr Blair was speaking as one former lawyer about another, but as a politician what he most admires is the way that Mrs Thatcher set a course for her party in government which radically changed the history of Britain. That is the aim of any prime minister, and – apart from the post-war Labour government of Clem Attlee – the way her government responded to the challenge puts her ahead of any other British leader since Winston Churchill.

When I travelled with her during the election campaign of 1979 a great deal of attention was given to the mere fact that she was a woman. There were even serious commentators who believed that she would not be able to overcome this supposed disadvantage. There was a widespread feeling that, in the secrecy of the ballot box, the electorate would baulk at the prospect of a woman leader. Now – in large part due to her period in office – this seems hopelessly old-fashioned. She was determined to remain feminine, and this was one of her great strengths. She came over as a real person. To some she seemed like a pushy parent – Conservative MPs would often refer to her as 'mother' – to others she was bossy and objectionable, to still others she wore interesting clothes and was even sexy. For me her big attraction was that she provided an endless stream of stories: she was invariably good copy.

One of her major political advantages in 1979 was that James Callaghan's Labour government had so obviously run out of steam; the election was caused by the loss of a vote of no confidence in the Commons, and the preceding six months had been dominated by strikes and industrial unrest which had come to be known as 'the winter of discontent'. But Mr Callaghan had personal qualities which suited Number 10 including an avuncular style and a commanding way in the Commons; he would confidently trounce Mrs Thatcher at prime minister's questions, making her seem almost girlish. Usually she would ask only one question, which added to the impression that she was out of her depth. Fortunately for her this was long before the Commons was broadcast on television.

Margaret Thatcher's greatest strength was in her policies. Looking back at the manifestos on which the election was fought, it is clear that the spirit of the times was on Mrs Thatcher's side. In her manifesto foreword, she wrote, 'There has been a feeling of helplessness, that we are a once great nation that has somehow fallen behind and that it is too late now to turn things round. I don't accept that.' She had 'no magic formula' nor did she make 'lavish promises', but she was determined that the balance of power between the individual and the state, which had increasingly been tilted towards the state, should be reversed in favour of individual freedom. The power of the unions, which had brought the country close to disintegration during the winter of discontent would be reduced; wealth creation and enterprise would be encouraged; income tax would be cut, and inflation would be kept in check by exercising financial discipline – by controlling the money supply. People would be given the legal right to buy their council homes. Attempts by Labour to directly control prices and incomes in the private sector would be abandoned and what came to be known as privatization of state assets would get under way. The Conservatives were, of course, opposed to any further nationalization of firms or industries.

Labour's manifesto, in comparison, seems a backward-looking document, merely recycling policies already past their sell-by date. Their industrial strategy was based on yet another attempt to build what they called a 'constructive national partnership' with unions and management. They boasted of having 'hammered out' a new framework with the unions as represented by the Trades Union Congress. Governments, the party manifesto insisted, should step in to help create employment, to limit price rises and to assist industry to modernize itself. They accused Mrs Thatcher of wanting to gamble the people's future on a return to the nineteenth-century free market. Labour proposed to negotiate planning agreements with the major industrial companies, 'with the necessary back-up statutory powers'. To achieve full employment it would be necessary, they believed, to have longer holidays, earlier voluntary retirement and to move towards a thirty-five-hour working week. Only in their acceptance of the need to sell off some council houses to tenants did they seem to realize that the days of old Labour socialism were numbered. It is not surprising that Mrs Thatcher described the 1979 contest as 'the most crucial election since the war'.

To anyone who followed closely the events of the 1970s it was clear that this was a turning point. The mood of resignation, sometimes despair, which had culminated in the winter of discontent is hard to exaggerate. The effect on Britain's standing in the world was obvious. There was endless talk about the 'British disease' of poor industrial relations and strikes, and of low productivity producing low wages. Sometimes it led visitors to reach erroneous conclusions about the general state of the country. I saw a group of Americans on a tube train travelling into London from Heathrow Airport. On spotting some allotments alongside the track, they leaped to completely the wrong conclusion. 'Look,' one of them said, pointing to the rows of carefully tended vegetables, 'subsistence farming.' I remember going to a reception for eminent businessmen in London at about the same time; one of them turned to me and said, 'Do you think this country is governable?'

Mrs Thatcher's first term in office was far from easy. One of her early moves, with her chancellor Sir Geoffrey Howe, was to double the rate of Value Added Tax, from 7.5 to 15 per cent. Indirect taxes would be allowed to rise; direct taxes, particularly income tax, would be cut. I was making a television film for BBC2 in a brush factory near Bristol which Mrs Thatcher had visited during the election campaign, and when the news was announced the chief executive nearly knocked his radio off the table. He was astounded that a Conservative government was prepared to put up taxes, a strategy which would obviously affect his business.

The budget of 1981 was even more controversial. In the teeth of a recession, the government decided to increase taxes. It was the most dramatic example of the importance placed on monetarist economics by Mrs Thatcher's government as a way of defeating inflation. The housewife determined to 'balance the books' – as Mrs Thatcher had portrayed herself during the election campaign – was made flesh. An amazing 364 leading economists, one for nearly every day of the year, signed an advertisement condemning the policy. A leading Conservative in the Whitby constituency of the Treasury chief secretary, Leon Brittan, actually fainted during an interview with me for *Newsnight* on BBC2. She was desperate to appear loyal even though the budget, which led to an increase in fuel prices, badly hit the rural economy in areas such as hers. But the overall effect, long term, was beneficial; and my hapless interviewee soon revived. The 1981 budget became the foundation for Mrs Thatcher's claim that her economic policy helped to 'save the country'.

The economy did indeed begin to pick up as the election of 1983 approached, but there was an extra, completely unexpected factor. Every successful prime minister needs some luck, even if that involves being lucky with your enemies. For Mrs Thatcher the incompetence and unpleasantness of the military junta which ruled Argentina in retrospect seems heaven sent. It was a series of classic British mistakes, including the suggestion from Nicholas Ridley, then a minister at the Foreign Office, that Britain might be prepared to give up sovereignty of the Falkland Islands, which encouraged Argentina to resolve its long and bitter grievance by carrying out an invasion. It was

Mrs Thatcher's fortune that, thanks to the bravery and skill of the British forces, with vital help from the Americans, the islands were triumphantly recaptured.

Mrs Thatcher had even more luck with her enemies at home. Labour's initial reaction to her success was to turn in on itself; the left wing of the party, led by among others Tony Benn, convinced itself that what was needed was not less but more old-fashioned socialism. At the very moment when the country was moving firmly to the right, the Labour party found itself fighting a rearguard action to try to keep itself even roughly in the centre. Labour's civil war ruled it out of contention for the duration of the Thatcher period and beyond. They would be in opposition for eighteen years. The 1983 Labour manifesto, which called for more nationalization and a withdrawal from the European Community, was famously described by one of the party's senior members, Gerald Kaufman, as 'the longest suicide note in history'.

With her landslide victory in 1983 Mrs Thatcher was finally able to dominate her cabinet. She had spent her first term complaining that some members of her team, including Christopher Soames, Jim Prior and Ian Gilmour, had been insufficiently radical; they had been cautious when she had wanted them to be bold, particularly on economic policy. She described them as 'wet', while the rest were happy, for a time, to be known as the 'dries'. The wets were worried about the effect on the social fabric of the nation of policies which seemed to be intent on increasing the differences between rich and poor, between those who owned property and businesses and those who did not. Mrs Thatcher was more concerned that unless the government acted quickly to reduce the power of the state and encourage enterprise her mission would fail.

Once again Mrs Thatcher was helped by her choice of enemies. If victory over General Galtieri of Argentina had boosted her popularity in her first term, during her second period in office she had good reason to thank the president of the National Union of Mineworkers Arthur Scargill. She once inadvisedly, referred to him as 'the enemy within' but, at least within Conservative circles, Scargill was as disliked as Galtieri. The confrontation with the militant miners was the bitterest industrial dispute of modern times; it still scars the memories of many of those involved and might have turned out very differently if Mr Scargill had obtained the wholehearted sup-port of the miners through the ballot box. For Mrs Thatcher it sealed the success of her second term. Coupled with her privatization programme, which had been an enormous popu-lar success, she reached the peak of her power with her second landslide win in 1987.

FOR TONY BLAIR this high point in the Thatcher ascendancy contains much to be admired, although he is fully aware of the divisive effects of many of her policies. That 1987 election triumph had long since passed when he and I met, but he told me he was particularly impressed by her 'tremendous clarity of objective, matched by huge determination and vigour'. Com-promises along the way were acceptable, but on certain key policies she never lost sight of her objective. As Mr Blair put it, 'She never yielded her ultimate goal.' The examples he gave included her epic struggle with the miners. The first time she was confronted by strike threats from the National Union of Mineworkers, she did back down; but when the real fight with Mr Scargill was joined she was able to ensure there were sufficient coal stocks, police countermeasures were in place, and she did not have to yield. Mr Blair was not commenting on the tactics she had used, but he spoke approvingly of the way she had pursued trade union reform over a period of eight years, little by little, not giving up.

Mr Blair, unlike many in the Labour party, is able to accept that Mrs Thatcher's clearly defined philosophy of rolling back the state, putting greater emphasis on individuals and curbing trade union strength was an inevitable reaction to the growth of state and trade union power. 'She was a considerable prime minister,' he told me. 'It is foolish for anyone, left or right, to deny that. She understood the importance of putting trade unions into a proper legal framework. And she understood the need to take an axe to some of the things in the public sector that were out of date.' But it was not entirely a paean of praise. Under Mrs Thatcher, Mr Blair contended, there had been 'massive under-investment in public infrastructure' and an 'indifference towards social division, because, she argued, people could stand on their own two feet'.

Without Mrs Thatcher, it is often argued, Mr Blair would not have become Labour leader, or indeed prime minister. The changes she made to British politics paved the way for New Labour. Union leaders being chosen through a ballot of members is one example of many. In this context it is perhaps not surprising that Mr Blair should have been so ready to heap praise on the former prime minister. I asked him bluntly, 'When people say she is the founder of New Labour, what do you say to that?'

'I think that's . . .' He paused.

'Going too far?' I suggested.

'Yes,' he went on. 'The fact is we were so badly beaten in the eighties that we finally realized that fundamental reform and not tinkering were necessary to get us back into power.'

For Tony Blair there is no doubt that the success of his government's military involvement in Kosovo – backed by Lady Thatcher – was a turning point in his attitude to the United States, and encouraged him to seek ways of working with the Americans to solve major international problems; it led perhaps inevitably to the joint invasion of Iraq. There is a clear parallel between Iraq and the Falklands War in that the vital if discreet part played by the American alliance strengthened Mrs Thatcher's determination to be Washington's most important ally. But the parallel breaks down when you consider the domestic political consequences: the success of the Falklands War helped produce a landslide for Mrs Thatcher in 1983. The far more complicated and controversial intervention in Iraq has become Mr Blair's millstone, with many of his former supporters deciding that he can no longer be trusted.

In classical Greek tragedy the future is ordained. Pride comes before a fall; hubris is followed by nemesis. Even at the height of a leader's success a fatal flaw of character can emerge, and the seeds of failure are sown. For Mrs Thatcher the last electoral triumph would occur in 1987; she would never again win the formal support of British voters. But what happened in the last period of her rule would help set the tone of British politics until the present day; and it would take another political generation to understand why the glory days came to an end, and to appreciate what a disaster would befall the Conservative party.

3

Heart versus head over Europe

EUROPE IS THE ISSUE at the centre of our story. It was by no means the only reason for Mrs Thatcher's downfall, but it was the question on which she found herself in a minority within her own cabinet. It was also the issue she chose to highlight in the last part of her career; and its effect on the Conservatives was so damaging that it helped remove their chances of government for many years But for a leader renowned for her consistency, the way she tackled the subject varied enormously during her time at the forefront of British politics. It is hard to imagine Baroness Thatcher now having much positive to say about an 'ever closer union' in Europe, but those were the words used in the original Treaty of Rome which Britain signed up to, and she supported British entry.

As prime minister her role was crucial in extending the power and the scope of the European Union: she joined the leaders of other member states in supporting moves which led eventually to the euro and an institutional structure she would later complain had laid the foundations for a European superstate. For some of her colleagues it was always a matter of 'heart versus head'; she never wanted Britain to go down the path she would later believe led, at the very least, towards a European federation, but she sometimes judged it unwise to object. She also changed her mind.

Mrs Thatcher was a child of her times. As the daughter of a shopkeeper in the small market town of Grantham in Lincolnshire she had direct experience of German aggression.

She was not quite fourteen when the Second World War began and nearly twenty when it ended. Her home town was surrounded by American airbases and was sometimes the target of German bombs. There were more than twenty raids; seventy people were killed and about two hundred injured. Margaret Thatcher spent a good deal of her time preparing for her School Certificate exams hiding under the kitchen table. Her husband Denis served in the war, and it is not surprising that her political hero was Winston Churchill. Previous Conservative leaders had had far more experience of fighting, but Mrs Thatcher was still profoundly affected by her wartime memories, which were all the more vivid because these events took place when she was barely out of her childhood.

I am nearly twenty years younger than she is, but through my own experiences I can catch something of the atmosphere in which she was brought up. As a child in the 1950s I lived in a family of similar means – and much the same ambitions – at Great Tew in Oxfordshire; its thatched cottages built in honey-coloured stone provided perfect picture postcards for sale at the village shop. My father was the vicar. The war cast a long shadow and many of the common assumptions which surrounded Mrs Thatcher's upbringing were still very much in evidence. The simple pleasure we took in the fact that Britain had won the war came with an assumption that Britain was best. We may have been busy disposing of our empire, but that was for the good of the former colonies not through any weakness of the mother country. 'Made in England' was a guarantee of quality; if we travelled abroad it was assumed that the standard of the plumbing and other facilities would not be as good as we had at home. Not being able to drink water from the tap without fear of illness seemed particularly strange. What could be more straightforward than filling a glass with water?

I spent a couple of hours in a London restaurant in 2003

discussing Mrs Thatcher's views on Europe with one of her former political secretaries, Stephen Sherbourne, who helped write many of her speeches. An archetypal back-room figure, very clever and rather shy, he later became Michael Howard's chief of staff when he took over as party leader. Mr Sherbourne believes that Margaret Thatcher's attitudes to the politics of the continent were largely instinctive. He told me: 'She had a tremendous belief, which may have come from her father, that England was better than other countries.' It stemmed from her experiences as a child in Grantham. 'A phrase she used all the time about the European countries was, "We either beat them, or rescue them." Britain had neither been beaten, nor did it need to be rescued.'

Like Mrs Thatcher I managed to get into Oxford University, but there our paths diverged. Whereas I studied politics, philosophy and economics, the future prime minister had been stuck in a chemistry lab. But we both conformed in different ways: I became a middle-of-the-road student of the 1960s – supporting radical left-wing ideas – she had soon been a junior member of the Conservative party. I went on to become a journalist and eventually a BBC reporter; after a spell as an industrial chemist, she had been chosen as a Conservative parliamentary candidate in a winnable seat. She also married a wealthy man, and qualified as a lawyer. When our paths crossed she was already leader of the Conservative party, and the differences between us were immense. But this did not prevent me from enjoying being with her, and catching some of the excitement of her political advance. She was different, and not just because she had broken the men-only rule. She was prepared to speak her mind, answer questions and delight in her role as the woman in blue who had stormed the male citadel. I also found her overly serious manner rather amusing.

When I interviewed Tony Blair he spoke with admiration of the way Mrs Thatcher had climbed to the top of the

Conservative party. He thought she must have found it 'very stuffy, old-fashioned and patronising, and not a very pleasant place to operate', and she must have been very tough to have survived. He believes there were two sides to her personality: in some things she was 'incredibly conservative' and that is why she was a Tory; in other ways she could be radical, and she spent a lot of her time battling the traditional elements within the Conservative party. Certainly in her early days as leader it was her conservative side which seemed to dominate. It was quite enough for them to accept her as a woman, without frightening the party with her radicalism. This was particularly true in relation to her attitude to Europe.

It was sometimes said that she became leader because she was the only one in the party who had the balls to stand up to Edward Heath. A strong sense of loyalty had prevented William Whitelaw, one of Heath's obvious successors, from standing against him. Mr Heath never forgave Mrs Thatcher for deciding to take him on; he had not considered her a possible threat even though she had reached the cabinet as education secretary. The fact that he had led the Conservatives to ignominious defeat in 1974 – after choosing to fight an early election on the dubious issue of whether the unions or the government ran the country – was not a matter Mr Heath was keen to dwell on. Mrs Thatcher's alleged treachery was, for him, a far more compelling subject. I had got to know him during his two election campaigns of 1974, both of which he lost, and on the few occasions I went to see him – usually to record an interview – he would speak off camera in an exasperated way about 'that woman'. He found it difficult to find anything complimentary to say about her. Their relation-ship – if that is the right word – became known as the longest grudge match in history.

But when she succeeded him as leader of the Opposition Mrs Thatcher treated Edward Heath with caution and respect.

Within months she had to decide how the party should campaign in the Common Market referendum, which had been sprung on the public by the prime minister Harold Wilson as an ingenious way of preventing the Labour party from splitting on the European issue. In an amazing deviation from normal practice, the cabinet was openly divided: ministers were allowed to campaign on either side of the issue, with Tony Benn and Barbara Castle among those calling for a 'No' vote. Britain had been taken into the European Economic Community in 1973 when Mr Heath was prime minister, an achievement of which he was inordinately proud; the referendum, following a brief and fairly feeble attempt at renegotiation two years later, would decide whether membership should be confirmed.

It was a curious campaign, with senior Labour figures, led by the home secretary Roy Jenkins, standing shoulder to shoulder with their usual opponents in the Conservative party such as the shadow chancellor Geoffrey Howe, urging the public to vote 'Yes'. I remember covering campaign meetings and staring in wonder at what seemed the unnatural line-up on the platform. Cynics would point out later that the only time Britain would be allowed a vote on Europe was when all the major party leaders were in agreement and there was little chance of upsetting the European apple cart. Mr Wilson portrayed the ballot as a chance for voters to decide on the most important policy issue since the Second World War. But it was really a skilful manoeuvre designed to see off Labour's anti-marketeers, the Euro-sceptics of their day, who were threatening to undermine the government. The result was a massive endorsement of membership by a two to one majority. For a time it looked as if the issue had been settled. Britain had made an historic choice; it had chosen to join Europe.

Mrs Thatcher did not play a prominent part in the 'Yes' campaign. She was happy to leave that to her predecessor Mr

Heath, who was given the task of leading the Conservative campaign. It seems a remarkably generous move on her part, given that he was already highly critical of her leadership in private. She made a number of conventionally pro-European speeches, and firmly stamped on newspaper speculation that she was cool on Europe. Whereas half the Labour MPs were in the 'No' camp, only a small minority of Tory MPs joined them; in the main the Conservatives considered entry into the EEC one of their greatest achievements.

In one of her speeches during the referendum campaign – at Hendon – Mrs Thatcher argued that Britain must stay in Europe, not least because of the need for partnership in the political, military, social and economic fields. 'The paramount motive for doing so is political – the warranty for peace and security. The countries of western Europe, by working ever more closely together in economic and social concerns, are building bridges of reconciliation and understanding between peoples long divided by rivalry and conflict.' Despite later attempts by Mrs Thatcher and her supporters to claim she was simply endorsing an economic arrangement, this speech under-lines the importance she gave to the political argument for joining. For most of those prominent in the 'Yes' campaign there was no doubting the political significance of membership; and the idea that there could be a tariff-free market for goods within Europe without tough regulations to enforce it now seems hopelessly naive. If member states could no longer decide for themselves what tariffs would be placed on imported goods there would necessarily be some loss of sovereignty.

As I followed Mrs Thatcher around the country as part of a group of correspondents covering her election tour in 1979, Europe was not a big issue. The main complaint the Conservatives had about the Labour approach to Europe was that they were not sufficiently pro. The Tory election manifesto positively glowed with Euro-enthusiasm. 'The next

Conservative government,' it said, 'will restore Britain's influence by convincing our partners of our commitment to the Community's success. This will enable us to protect British interests and to play a leading and constructive role in the Community's efforts to tackle the many problems which it faces.' Edward Heath had succeeded in his aim of making the Conservatives the party of Europe, and Mrs Thatcher had no intention of appearing to change course. At her opening news conference she said, 'You are going to get nowhere if you join a club and you spend all your time carping and criticizing it.'

Much of the campaign revolved around Mrs Thatcher's personality. She played up the stereotypical image of a woman who could sort men out, who kept the household budget, and who did not waste money. That she was married to a millionaire and sent her children to expensive private schools was glossed over. Instead she was portrayed as the battling house-wife who stood up for freedom and knew about the real world. She endlessly visited shopping centres and factories. She took every chance to show that she could be kind as well as bossy. Someone fainted at a railway station; she immediately rushed to see if she could help. The coach carrying her and the press party was stuck in a field in Scotland; she ordered us all out to push. And there was the celebrated incident when she cradled a new-born calf for the cameras at a farm in Suffolk. Her campaign was dominated by American-style photo opportunities which quickly became the norm in British elections. James Callaghan and the Labour campaign looked tired and old in comparison.

MRS THATCHER was eager to learn. She appeared to defer to her senior colleagues: she would not even rule out Edward Heath joining her cabinet if she was fortunate enough to win the election. She denied any wish to confront the unions or anyone else and tried to soothe fears that electing her would be the jump in the dark it undoubtedly was. When she won the election – with a handsome majority of forty-four seats – and I pushed forward my microphone in front of Number 10 it was not too surprising that she came out with the lines from the supposed prayer of St Francis of Assisi which begin, 'Where there is discord may we bring harmony.' The words were provided by one of her speechwriters, the playwright Ronald Millar, who was also responsible for 'The lady's not for turning' – her famous response much later when pressure built up for a policy U-turn across the board.

Her eagerness to accept advice from media advisers and senior colleagues was a great strength. It also reflected her genuine feelings that climbing to the top of the tree and staying there was not going to be easy, and that she had a lot to learn. Foreign policy, in particular, is notoriously difficult to master if you do not know any of the personalities involved, nor how to position yourself on the international stage. To begin with she relied heavily on her foreign secretary Lord Carrington, whose well-cut suits and brisk, upper-class ways gave off a super-confident air. Her first European trip as prime minister was to Italy, where attention to protocol – and perhaps a bit of theatricality – seems to matter. Mrs Thatcher made the mistake of attempting to leave the British embassy in Rome too early for her visit to the Italian president. The team of motorcycle outriders, glad their long wait was over, leapt onto their machines and engines roared. I heard Lord Carrington coolly advise Mrs Thatcher that there was a danger they would arrive before they were expected. A firm thumbs down was given to the outriders; engines were stilled and Mrs Thatcher leaned across to her accompanying reporters without any hint of embarrassment, and said, 'Well, let's have a chat.'

On this occasion I did not want to reveal to my colleagues what was on my mind, so I did not jump in with a question. I wanted to ask Mrs Thatcher about her determination to ensure that Britain received more from the European budget. It was the first sign of steel in her relations with the other member states of the EEC but I was anxious to cover it exclusively in the interview it had been agreed I would have for Radio 4's *The World at One*. Later, sitting in plush armchairs inside the embassy, I was given the interview as arranged. In fairly forceful language she laid out the points which would dominate her European policy during her first term in office. This was the beginning of her campaign to see that Britain should not have to pay into the EEC budget nearly £1,000 million more than the country received from the Community. This came to be known as the battle for 'Maggie's billion'. Incidentally, none of her close associates ever called her Maggie to her face; she was always Margaret or Prime Minister, but she was quick to see that the name was useful for headline purposes and made her more of a public personality. There was always a populist streak in her approach to the media, and when she was speaking in public she would sometimes self-consciously refer to herself as Maggie.

The public argument, which seemed to start almost casually during the interview in the British embassy in Rome, was to have a profound effect on Mrs Thatcher's approach to Europe. It would also add one more policy difference to the chasm which had opened up between her and Edward Heath. After she had won the 1979 election, she sent the former prime minister a message saying she did not want him to become foreign secretary, a post he might have accepted; when she subsequently offered him the chance to become British ambassador to Washington he brusquely turned it down. Prime ministers cannot avoid making enemies and these early decisions helped set the scene for the drama that would finally engulf her many years later.

Her attitude to the budget problem highlighted traditional differences between Britain and the other member states. With other European leaders there was always an emotional side to their attachment to the European project. It embodied their hopes of finally putting to rest the violent animosities which had frequently pulled the continent apart. They were determined to reduce the strength of nationalism which had contributed to these disasters and they saw the EEC as a way of transcending national boundaries. Every attempt was made to reduce the importance of nationality in the organization of the European club. It was not meant to matter where people were born, or what language they spoke. Officially Europeans were now pulling together as one, and the budget was meant to be simply the way that the club paid its bills. The revenues came from the customs dues each country collected and a small proportion of their VAT receipts, and the system was designed to provide an automatic fund for running the EEC. Individual countries were not expected to complain if they set their economists to work calculating exactly what they put in and what they received, and discovered that it compared unfavourably with the position of other member states.

It is greatly to Mrs Thatcher's credit that she was unimpressed by what she would later refer to as 'misty Europeanism'. For a variety of highly technical reasons Britain was paying far more than other countries in relation to its wealth; the fact that Germany paid even more was in Mrs Thatcher's eyes simply another sign of the Germans' guilty conscience for what they had done in the earlier part of the century. A test of any political system is to be able to address complaints of unfairness by individuals, communities or in this case member states. She was right to fight for British interests in this way; and subsequent governments were in no doubt about the importance of the rebate which she eventually negotiated.

But Mrs Thatcher's blunt, pragmatic approach was received with horror by those who saw her approach as fundamentally anti-European. In the French phrase, which dominated discussions of this sort, she had shown herself to be totally unsympathetic to the *ésprit communautaire*, which only loosely translates as 'community spirit'. Diplomats at European gatherings were quick to point out if any delegate appeared not to be *communautaire*. There was also the simple point, disguised by this high-flown rhetoric, that if Britain was to put less into the EEC budget, other countries would have to contribute more. Complaints that the British prime minister – a newcomer at European summits – was restarting an argument which had been settled long ago were hardly without financial motive; the other leaders were also fighting in the interests of their national budgets.

At a news conference after a European summit later in 1979 in Dublin she declared, 'I am only talking about our money, no one else's; there should be a cash refund of our money to bring our receipts up to the average level of receipts in the Community.' Most of the other heads of governments made little attempt to disguise their feelings. They were irritated by the way she lectured them; the German chancellor Helmut Schmidt responded by falling asleep at one of the private meetings of the Community leaders. Mrs Thatcher relished an argument, particularly when she felt completely confident that right was on her side, but she acknowledged later it was a strain. In her memoirs she says she knew the summit was going to be hostile and unpleasant. 'I went to Dublin with a newly tailored suit,' she writes. 'Ordinarily I would have enjoyed wearing something new on an occasion as important as this, but I thought twice: I didn't want to risk tainting it with unhappy memories.' The new suit was not worn.

It would take five years before the argument over Maggie's billion was settled and the budget question finally resolved. First, she had to grapple with the Falklands War and her re-election in 1983. Fortunately for her the Labour party had swung dramatically against Europe and in their election manifesto even argued for Britain to withdraw, so on this issue Mrs Thatcher found widespread support at home. But at a string of European summits there were clashes with the leaders of the other member states. Soviet propaganda had dubbed her the 'Iron Lady' and this image of her became a fixture on the European scene. Finally, in 1984, at a summit hosted by France at Fontainebleau, Mrs Thatcher settled the budget issue. She accepted a deal whereby two thirds of the British deficit would be refunded. It was generally regarded as a victory, but in consequence she found it harder to find allies among European leaders on other key issues and it reinforced her distrust for what she later called 'that un-British combination of high-flown rhetoric and pork-barrel politics which passed for European statesmanship'.

One of the most important figures in Downing Street during the Thatcher years was Charles Powell, the civil servant who became her private secretary in 1984 and was her chief adviser on foreign affairs. With Bernard Ingham he formed the dynamic duo that – to the irritation of many members of her cabinet – ran the Number 10 machine. His younger brother Jonathan Powell, also from the Foreign Office, became Tony Blair's chief of staff and formed a similar partnership with Alastair Campbell in support of Tony Blair. It seems that no dominant prime minister in recent years can do without a Powell, although they tend to pronounce their surname in different ways. Charles, who became Lord Powell, would call himself 'Po-ell'; his brother, as a Labour adviser, adopts the more ordinary 'Pow-ell'.

I met Charles in the summer of 2003 at his offices in Berkeley Square where he works as an adviser to international companies. He is still the impeccable civil servant, the loyal official, but he also has an independent way of thought and a streak of irreverence characteristic of the higher levels of the civil service. Tall and confident, he has a restlessness that appealed to Mrs Thatcher and was eager to answer questions about her, particularly on Europe. The years of wrangling over the European budget, he is convinced, had a dramatic effect on her views about the EEC. 'It started to erode her commitment to the concept of European union,' Lord Powell told me, and he believes it lost her the chance to make real friends of key figures in Europe. She became the outsider at European summits, and her growing friendship with President Reagan and their determination together to take on the Soviet Union helped to set her apart. Her close association with the new American president emphasized the importance she attached not to Europe but to Britain's historic alliance with the United States. She appeared to have made a choice; and it was in favour of the Anglo-American alliance.

4

The assassin with the golden hair

TOO MUCH ATTENTION may have been given in recent years to the famous remark made by Harold Macmillan when asked what tested him most as prime minister. He replied, 'Events, dear boy, events.' It neatly encapsulates the pressures of Number 10, and the sense that, however clear the skies, at any moment a storm might be brewing which could drive the government off course. How a prime minister responds immediately and instinctively to events can be far more important than hours spent studying official papers, weighing up options and consulting colleagues. But there is perhaps another answer which could be given if prime ministers are honest about the difficulties they face. The most awkward problems, the ones that last for years and are sometimes never resolved, are those which involve a clash of personalities.

Some years ago it was fashionable when describing history to attach little importance to the character of the principal protagonists. However, those who have watched the political process at close hand are never in doubt that personalities matter. I remember at the height of the plotting against Mrs Thatcher a bewildered Conservative MP grabbing me by the arm and saying, 'But are we really in a Shakespeare play?' I nodded vigorously and replied, 'The only question is: which play is it, and who will win?' The temper of the times and the issues politicians face are relevant too, but the disruptive effects of human nature and the ability some politicians have to rise above events should never be underestimated.

MAGGIE

To understand the fall of Margaret Thatcher we have to name names, and, however much he may sometimes play down his role, there is one prime suspect: Michael Heseltine. He might prefer other titles, including The Man Who Would Be King, but among those proud to call themselves Thatcherites, there is only one: the Assassin. When he toppled their queen in 1990 they called it regicide, and many of them were only half-joking when they said, 'Off with his head.' Personally, I have to admit that I like him; over the years I have watched him with interest, sometimes confidently stirring crowds, at other times proving surprisingly vulnerable. I am not going to say that he would be a brilliant prime minister – that is too big a question to settle in a phrase – but he is certainly someone with whom I would be happy to go into the jungle.

HE HAS LONG SINCE come to terms with his Tarzan nickname, an inevitable consequence of his golden hair, dashing style and public school good looks. Throughout most of his career he was one of the big beasts in politics. It was almost inevitable that he and Mrs Thatcher would find that the cabinet was not large enough for them both. Opposite poles of a magnet attract; like poles repel. They were so alike it is surprising they managed to get on at all.

In politics of all sorts, at Westminster or anywhere else where power is pursued, those with unusual abilities have an extra burden to carry. To be noticed as the coming man or woman, to be marked out for higher office, can be a serious disadvantage. Rivals are alerted, jealousies aroused, and smaller fry combine if they sense a common threat. For Michael Heseltine, dressed immaculately in an expensive suit, simply to walk into a room with a file under his arm and swing his long legs under a table was often enough to create a stir. I remember a female member of John Major's cabinet telling me she enjoyed watching Mr Heseltine. 'I just like to see what he's up to.'

It's usually assumed that someone like Mr Heseltine is up to something; he must have a clever plan, a personal agenda, and his actions were invariably judged in that light. Stories were told to support this view. As a student at Oxford he was said to have sketched out on a piece of paper his future career in the most confident terms: '1950s, millionaire; 1960s, MP; 1970s, minister; 1980s, cabinet; 1990s, Downing Street.' As he progressed inexorably along that path – and as it turned out every one but the last was faithfully accomplished – his denials that he had ever written such a note were easily dismissed. From early on Mrs Thatcher was in no doubt that Michael Heseltine was someone to watch, and she did not look upon his progress kindly.

The fact that they were not attracted to each other may not seem particularly relevant to those who view politics as a game of chess where the placing of each piece on the board determines the outcome. But for those like me, who have watched so many Westminster dramas in close-up, politics without emotion is not politics at all. You do not have to be an expert in body language to know what is going on, but it certainly helps. With some politicians, Tony Blair and Gordon Brown being the obvious current examples, it is sometimes the only way of knowing that they are finding life together rather difficult. With Mrs Thatcher and Mr Heseltine, the plain fact is they didn't fancy each other; in fact, they did not even like each other. To employ the phrase that she used to distinguish her real friends from her political allies, he was never 'one of us'.

IN JUNE 2003 I spoke to Lord Heseltine, as he now is, about Margaret Thatcher. As the founder of Haymarket Press he maintains a top-floor office at their modern headquarters in

Hammersmith. His desk faced a large rack of magazines and I could not resist pointing out that it was like a newsagents. 'It's different,' he smiled, 'when you own them.' I was reminded of a recent estimate of his fortune which put his total wealth at about £60 million. He had retired from politics, but there was still part of him that longed to be back in the front line. 'I would like to do one more big conference speech,' he mused. Tarzan was missing the jungle.

When Edward Heath was challenged for the leadership of the Conservative party in 1975 Mr Heseltine first abstained and then openly supported William Whitelaw, who was beaten by Mrs Thatcher. At her first meeting with Tory MPs the new leader announced that she would be accessible to all and open to any approaches. 'And besides,' she said, 'I want to be made a fuss of by a lot of chaps.' Mr Heseltine told me how appalled he had been. 'I sat at the back of the room and shook my head in disbelief.' Part of Mrs Thatcher's charm for many men was that she did have a flirtatious side. She would put her hand on your arm long before it became a standard technique for women bosses in the BBC. In those days it could provide quite a heady moment for a supposedly hardened political journalist; and I was not immune to the effect, which was – dare I say it – almost sexy.

But the Thatcher charms did not work on Mr Heseltine. Unlike John Major, for example, he is not a tactile politician. He does not naturally kiss babies in public, throw his arms round supporters or give people a gentle nudge in the ribs. He expects to dazzle from a distance, and he admits to finding Mrs Thatcher difficult to deal with as a woman. He told me of embarrassing meetings where he found himself having to behave in a way quite out of keeping with the way he had been brought up. As a former public schoolboy, he expected to treat women with 'a certain deference'. Seats had to be offered to them on buses; they should be allowed to have their say without interruption. But up against this woman prime minister, there were times he felt that a totally different, ungentlemanly approach was needed to ward off a surprise attack. 'You suddenly found that if you behaved in any way that allowed a chink of light to emerge in your defences, you'd have her tanks through it,' he told me. 'You just had to realize that she'd always interrupt you. So you waited for her to stop, and you'd start again. And you had to start again, and again, and again, until she listened; otherwise you'd just get flattened. And I found this acutely uncomfortable.'

I was determined to hear from those more favourable to Mrs Thatcher who had been close to events at the time, and one of my key contacts was Norman Tebbit. A couple of months after seeing Lord Heseltine I spent an hour in a small interview room at the House of Lords, tape-recording Norman's recollections. He used to frighten me when I first met him; it was not so much his 'bovver-boy' image, carefully played up by the model-makers of television's *Spitting Image*, more the impression that he could not wait to take you to pieces in argument. Coupled with a black cloak and a pair of fangs, he might easily decide to drain your blood as well. When he knows that you appreciate the sharpness of his humour and his genuine smile, mellowness takes over; but you can never be certain this mood will last. Discussing Mr Heseltine was not difficult; he just did not want to make it too obvious he was putting the knife in. Norman Tebbit argued that Mr Heseltine's attitude towards Mrs Thatcher involved much stronger emotions than simple embarrassment. He told me that welling up inside Mr Heseltine was his anger and humiliation at having to serve a woman as prime minister, particularly this woman. It is obviously a charge that Mr Heseltine would reject.

What is undoubtedly true is that there was a clash of personalities which started early on in Mr Heseltine's period as a minister under Mrs Thatcher. She openly admitted that her relations with him had never been easy, but this did not prevent her seeing the benefits of having him in the cabinet. Even after they had totally fallen out she was prepared to describe him as 'one of the most talented people in politics'. To begin with he was given promotion and even allowed to shine. First he was secretary of state for the environment, and then he was given his big chance as defence secretary with the high-profile task of mounting a propaganda battle against the Campaign for Nuclear Disarmament and the Labour left. Never too shy to wear a flak jacket when the press cameras were about, he loved this form of combat. Soon the Conservative party began to be impressed, if not always to warm to this rising political star.

But the more successful he was, the more the tension grew between him and the prime minister, and they had their first serious battle within the cabinet. What made it particularly serious was that Mr Heseltine won. Winning against a prime minister is always hazardous, winning against Mrs Thatcher carried the clear danger that she might see it as a contest, and would therefore, at some point, insist on retribution. The battle was over a government defence order and was not particularly significant in itself, but it was the vital precursor to the row that led Mr Heseltine to storm out of the cabinet. It also helps to explain exactly why the prime minister and her eventual assassin found working together so difficult.

Mrs Thatcher's ally Norman Tebbit, as trade and industry secretary, was responsible for helping the ailing British ship-building industry. Two nationalized yards, Cammell Laird on Merseyside and Swan Hunter on Tyneside, both desperate for orders, were competing to build two frigates for the Royal Navy. Mr Tebbit decided that Cammell would only be allowed to bid for one of the contracts; Swan could bid for both of them. Mr Heseltine complained that this was unfair and broke the established rules. Swan would be able to spread the cost of overheads over two contracts so could offer a much lower price. Cammell would therefore automatically be out of the running.

The matter was discussed in a cabinet committee and Mrs Thatcher supported Mr Tebbit. It was decided that Swan should win the competition to build the two frigates. Mr Heseltine flatly refused to accept the decision. He was adamant that Mr Tebbit should not be allowed to interfere with contracts in this way. The matter was unresolved. A grumpy Mr Heseltine returned to the Ministry of Defence only to be told on arrival that the prime minister had already sent a conciliatory message. She accepted that a solution agreeable to him would have to be found. In the event the two yards were allowed to build a frigate each at an extra cost to the taxpayer of £7 million. The details are not as important here as the fact that, faced with open opposition from Mr Heseltine, Mrs Thatcher had backed down.

Lord Tebbit told me that he had initially won the argument in the cabinet committee with the support of the prime minister, and it was only reversed after the intervention of Lord Whitelaw, the leader of the House of Lords. Willie Whitelaw's rather bumbling, patrician air disguised a sharp practical skill at settling disputes. After failing to become leader himself, he had decided to be totally loyal to Mrs Thatcher. He became her chief fixer behind the scenes. 'Everyone needs a Willie,' Mrs Thatcher once declared, oblivious to the double entendre. And Willie Whitelaw had another obvious advantage in her eyes. He was not fond of Mr Heseltine, whom he once described as 'the sort of man who combs his hair in public'.

'Willie asked me,' Lord Tebbit recalls, 'if I would be willing to back off in cabinet and concede it to Michael. "Otherwise," Willie said, "I fear he's going to use it as an excuse to resign and we can't let him do that."' Lord Tebbit added, 'Willie was determined not to let him play that game again.' And so was Mrs Thatcher. It was not a defeat she cared to remember, but almost exactly a year later – in 1985 – she was pleased to get her revenge. This came in the storm which blew up over the future of the only helicopter company in Britain. It took the political world by surprise, led two cabinet ministers to resign, and left Mrs Thatcher severely weakened and badly rattled. It became known as the Westland Affair.

Once again the argument was over a technical matter involving defence procurement. The West Country firm of Westland was hoping a bid from the giant American helicopter company Sikorksy would prevent them from going under and throwing thousands of people out of work. But there was also the possibility that a European consortium could save the company. Mrs Thatcher firmly backed the American option; Mr Heseltine was ready to risk his whole political future on promoting a European solution. In retrospect this can be seen as the dramatic emergence of the fault line which was to split the Conservative party for a generation: the extent to which Britain should play a part in the political and economic integration of Europe. But some of those closely involved in the argument also see this as a clash of wills. A senior Conservative MP, Michael Mates, who became one of Mr Heseltine's closest allies, is convinced that for Mrs Thatcher it was a deeply personal affair. In an interview granted especially for this book, he told me, 'It was guns at noon.'

An easy way to determine the level of emotion is to consider the pettiness of some of the issues which brought so much anger and pain. For Mr Heseltine one of the most serious charges against Mrs Thatcher is that she did not hold a cabinet discussion on Westland on one particular occasion when he should have been allowed to make his case. One of the disputes, which continue to this day, is whether that cabinet meeting was actually promised. Another way to see how matters were blown out of all proportion is to consider what actually happened to the company. Westland never came down firmly on the American or the European side. As a small helicopter company heavily dependent on military orders, it did what it had done before and relied on support from both sides of the Atlantic. It became a British company linked to an Italian company, and for a time was controlled by the American firm Sikorksy. There was no simple solution.

This analysis will not satisfy those still prepared to take up cudgels on behalf of the chief protagonists. In the Heseltine camp his view is seen as essentially practical and far-sighted. In the other camp there is a strong feeling that Mrs Thatcher was faced with nothing less than a rebellion, an attempt to undermine her government. The row went on for weeks and, as often happens, in the short term it was only the political journalists who benefited. My wife soon got over the surprise of picking up the phone to hear Michael Heseltine ask to speak to her husband. Mrs Thatcher's press secretary Bernard Ingham wrestled behind the scenes trying to limit the damage. It was nerve-racking to find that my every little sentence was being closely examined by those involved; it seemed as if everyone at Westminster had become obsessed with the twists and turns of the affair. Some people would be badly hurt, that much was obvious, but for weeks it was not clear who they would be.

One of the joys of working at Westminster compared with being a war correspondent is that, despite all the nail-biting suspense, in the end no one gets killed. But it can be a fearsome environment nevertheless. The fate of one of those involved in the Westland Affair, the trade and industry secretary Leon Brittan, who had taken over from Mr Tebbit, is the nearest Westminster gets to the military epitaph KIA – killed in action. Mrs Thatcher was determined to use him in her battle with Mr Heseltine. As Mr Mates puts it, 'She chased Brittan all over the place saying "What are you doing? The man's walking all over you." ' According to this account it was after one such fierce row when she gave Mr Brittan 'an enormous bollocking' that he decided that part of a letter from one of the law officers should be leaked to the Press Association news agency.

One of the conventions of British politics is that the advice of the law officers, the ministers holding judicial positions, should not be made public. It's a convention that is often questioned. It came up again in the controversy over the Iraq War and whether Tony Blair was legally entitled to order the invasion by British troops. The solicitor general Sir Patrick Mayhew had said in a private letter that Mr Heseltine had been guilty of 'material inaccuracies' in his submission over Westland. Once the news agency published this juicy titbit, a media frenzy ensued. Mr Heseltine was, of course, livid. It was only one of many breaches of normal procedure from both sides in this argument. It was not in itself particularly important; it just added to the general atmosphere of crisis.

Mr Brittan might have been able to hang on, even though his department had leaked the law officer's comments, but eventually he was forced out following a particularly unpleasant meeting with backbench Tory MPs. He had become the official scapegoat in the affair, taking the heat off the prime minister herself. Found guilty of losing the confidence of his colleagues, there was even a whiff of anti-Semitism in the complaints made against him. A Tory of the old-fashioned sort, John Stokes, announced that Mr Brittan should be replaced by a 'red-blooded, red-faced Englishman, preferably from the landed interests'. Fortunately Mr Brittan, one of the cleverest men in politics, went on to a highly successful career as a member of the European Commission in Brussels. But his Westminster career was over.

The obvious question is whether, given their particular temperaments, an almighty clash between Mrs Thatcher and

Mr Heseltine was bound to happen? On the morning he resigned, when the Westland Affair came to a head on 9 January 1986, Mr Heseltine had told his ally Mr Mates that he had no intention of taking that step. When the news came out later Mr Heseltine's wife Anne was taken completely by surprise. Her comment went into the quotes of the week columns: 'Oh, my God.' It is clear that by the time the argument had reached this stage Mrs Thatcher was determined to be rid of Mr Heseltine. She announced to the cabinet that the only way to prevent any further escalation of this row in public was for all statements on Westland to be authorized by the cabinet secretary Robert Armstrong. Mr Heseltine was told firmly he could not even repeat comments he had made in the past without authorization. He was being told it was time for him to shut up.

Mr Heseltine recalls in his memoirs that she read out this policy from a note produced from her *handbag*. His italics make the Thatcher handbag seem as ridiculous as the bag in Oscar Wilde's play *The Importance of Being Earnest*. Finding the policy in a handbag, Mr Heseltine implies, is as absurd as finding the baby Ernest in a handbag. He also sees it as a clear sign of a plot. The policy had been worked out by Mrs Thatcher before the meeting took place and she was forcing him to make a choice: submit to her will or leave the cabinet. He still maintains there was no choice at all. He had to go.

In keeping with the farcical air which surrounded so many events in the Westland Affair, members of the cabinet were not sure what Mr Heseltine meant when he stood up and said that he must leave it. The position was only clarified when Mr Heseltine told a startled BBC cameraman outside Number 10 that he had resigned. His walk to the Ministry of Defence, across the road from Downing Street, turned into one of the longest walks in politics; it looked as if he would never return to government. Most of the cabinet could not believe that he had been prepared to risk all in his shoot-out with Mrs Thatcher. Some of the most important decisions are taken by the prime minister acting alone or with a small group of ministers. Britain's decision to start production of an atomic bomb, and the less dramatic but some would say equally momentous move to join the European Exchange Rate Mechanism were never even discussed in cabinet. Mrs Thatcher's behaviour over the Westland Affair was not that unusual; prime ministers are usually determined to get their way, and cabinet ministers, however bloody minded, cannot always stop them. The drama of the Westland Affair can only be understood in terms of a spectacular personality clash between a prime minister who felt threatened, and a cabinet minister pushing his luck.

Mrs Thatcher's verdict is uncompromising. She says in her memoirs, 'I knew from Michael's behaviour that unless he were checked there were no limits to what he would do to secure his objectives at Westland. Cabinet collective responsibility was being ignored and my own authority as Prime Minister was being publicly flouted. This had to stop.' But her reputation was badly dented. It looked as if she had lost control. The Westminster village had been shaken by weeks of tension, and it would be a long time before the government regained its composure.

Mr Heseltine is still in no doubt about the correctness of his behaviour. 'There are certain very clear conventions about the rights of cabinet ministers,' he told me in the interview I recorded with him at his Haymarket headquarters. 'And if you allow yourself to be trodden over, bypassed, ignored, silenced artificially, denied the right to put a case to the cabinet, that is the beginning of the end for you. You must never let yourself be put in that position, especially as defence secretary.'

Close colleagues of Mr Heseltine are convinced that if he had not resigned over Westland another issue would have set him and Mrs Thatcher at each other's throats. One of the items the cabinet discussed that morning, after Mr Heseltine had left, was the poll tax, which more than any other policy would contribute to Mrs Thatcher's downfall. Mr Mates is convinced that on this issue Mr Heseltine would have resigned anyway, and he adds, 'Perhaps that would have been a better issue.' This former army officer, often referred to as the Colonel, became part of a very small team devoted to promoting Mr Heseltine's ambition to return to Number 10 as prime minister. It did not take long before Mr Heseltine was fighting a brilliant, unorthodox campaign for the leadership which in the end would succeed in toppling Mrs Thatcher. But he could not have done it without the help of powerful individuals and fortuitous circumstances. He may have had the motive, but he needed the means and the opportunity. This was not a job for a lone assassin.

5

Into battle with sets of initials

WITH ALL THE FIREWORKS over Westland dominating the news, far less attention was given to one of the most important milestones in the development of the European Union, the dull round of talks leading to the historically important Single European Act which came to a conclusion in Luxembourg in December 1985. European negotiations reach a level of dullness which only those who have tried to report on them can fully appreciate. American journalists have an acronym which they use when even the most conscientious of their number cannot stay awake, MEGO, standing for 'My eyes glaze over.' In Brussels they have a factory which makes MEGOs and also DBIs, those stories which are 'dull but important'.

ONE CAN ONLY marvel sometimes at how a large number of highly intelligent people, often with astonishing abilities in foreign languages, with comfortable offices and salaries to match, put up with all this impenetrable prose and these interminable meetings. Matters at that time were made even harder for the journalists involved because the European commissioner responsible at the Luxembourg summit was a Thatcher appointee, Lord Cockfield, who wore black-framed glasses with very thick lenses which seemed to cut him off from the rest of the world, and had a ponderous manner which made broadcast interviews extremely difficult. His background gave no clue to his difficulties with the media: he had been managing director of Boots in the 1960s; he switched to politics in the 1970s and was trade secretary before accepting the post in Brussels in 1985. He did more than any other commissioner to create the EU of today; and not surprisingly he fell out badly with Mrs Thatcher.

I spent two years covering the monthly sessions of the European Assembly, from 1979 until 1981, and after a week in Strasbourg my head would be buzzing with Euro-jargon. Even the leader of the Labour MEPs, Barbara Castle, who had had one of the sharpest tongues at Westminster, could not resist slipping into Euro-speak. I had appreciated her down-to-earth manner when we were once stuck in a lift with a television crew when she was secretary of state for health and social security. The lift went out of control, roaring up and down the seven-storey building where she worked. Cool as could be, she ordered one of us to press the red emergency button and when the lift stopped, briskly instructed us to get into the other lift. One of the crew could take no more and stumbled off into the darkness of the basement; the rest of us continued to her office at the top of the building. But even the formidable Mrs Castle succumbed to Brussels jargon. At our convivial lunches in Strasbourg she would find it impossible not to refer at some point to *rapporteurs* – the people who write the committees' reports, or *porte-parole* – the spokesmen for the European commissioners; and then there were all those sets of initials. Anything from the Common Agricultural Policy, or CAP, down to a special method of voting could have an acronym. If you did not know your Euro-speak your invitation to lunch might be turned down; and, believe me, in Strasbourg whom you have lunch with is very important. With Mrs Castle you also had to be aware that she had hoped to become the first woman prime minister; that the Conservative Mrs Thatcher had destroyed this ambition was an uncomfortable though undeniable fact. It is also true that at that time Mrs Castle, who had supported the 'No' campaign in the referendum, was much more Euro-sceptic than Mrs Thatcher.

When it came to the negotiations over the Single European Act, the acronym which really mattered was QMV, which stands for qualified majority voting. What made this method of voting so important was that it removed the right of member states to exercise a veto. QMV meant that another layer of national sovereignty was removed. For some Euro-sceptics a vital line had been crossed. If you were a true believer in the nation state, they argued, QMV was the devil's own work. But for the British team who sat down at the Luxembourg summit it was simply a way of ensuring that the original plan for a common market under the Treaty of Rome could be put into practice. This voting system had actually been set out in the treaty, but it had never been applied. Each country was allotted a certain number of votes and for most important negotiations a two-thirds majority was the minimum required. This was a qualified majority. However, it did not prevent arguments over the allocation of votes, and the issue resurfaced when the EU was enlarged and there were complaints that Poland had been given the same number of votes as Spain.

The main aim of the Single European Act was to make it much harder for countries to act in a protectionist manner by stopping goods coming into their countries; they would not be able to dig in their heels when the trading rules were being drawn up. The Single European Act is now seen by many as the vital precursor to the Maastricht Treaty. It is also the negotiation, undertaken personally by Mrs Thatcher, which she looks back on with the most regret. To her Euro-sceptic supporters it is the most embarrassing blot on her record. This was the moment, they believe, when she should have said no; this was in their view when the federal character of the European project was laid bare. However, at the final news conference at the Luxembourg summit Mrs Thatcher was upbeat. She was pleased with what she had achieved.

From my long experience of European summits, this optimistic mood is not unusual; I cannot remember a summit when the British prime minister did not claim to be pleased with the outcome. I would sometimes tease the press secretaries by asking them with mock seriousness whether it would be all right if I used the word 'triumph'. It was midnight when the final news conference was held. The heads of government had spent the day fussing over the details and delighting in any small changes they had been responsible for in the final text. Mrs Thatcher was particularly gratified that she had been able to insert a line confirming the right of member states to keep control of immigration from outside the EEC and act on a national basis to fight crime and terrorism. It hardly seems much of a victory now.

She was little more successful in trying to remove the commitment to economic and monetary union, although she did manage to change the wording so that the treaty speaks only of 'cooperation' in this field. The implication was still clear: this was an agreement to start the drive towards a single currency, although its creation still seemed a very long way off. Mrs Thatcher was totally in agreement with the main thrust of the treaty, which was to make sure that there really was free movement of goods and services within the EEC. Business-friendly free trade was a goal she could readily accept. But it was already obvious that for some of the most powerful figures in Europe this could only be completely achieved with a common currency. It was also significant that the treaty would change the name of the European Assembly; it was given more formal power over the EEC budget and henceforth would be described officially as the European Parliament.

To 'complete the single market', as the objective behind

the Single European Act became known, required a dramatic change in the way that controversial decisions were taken. It is easy now to take free trade within the EU for granted. Cash machines in the member states obediently churn out currency when we are on holiday and no one seems to care that it was banking directives at European level which made that possible. The deep-seated protectionism of many countries, particularly France, is also easily forgotten. Two years before agreement was reached on the Single European Act the French government was so determined to reduce the number of imported Japanese videos they insisted that before they could reach shops in France they would have to be sent for customs checks to a warehouse in the town of Poitiers. The piles of VCRs and the angry customers led to the incident being called the Battle of Poitiers. Within months the move was reversed; if the French authorities had persisted they could have been taken to the European Court.

In order to fashion new agreements for free trade it was necessary to introduce qualified majority voting by member states when decisions were made in the Council of Ministers. Countries could no longer unilaterally introduce trade restrictions; if they did Brussels would step in with the backing of European law, which had precedence over national law. A whole raft of regulations, hundreds upon hundreds, spewed out of Brussels, more than ever before; and a target year, 1992, was set for the completion of the single market. It was a triumph for Lord Cockfield, whose main task was to implement the policy, but Mrs Thatcher soon regretted his zeal. She had seen him as a successful businessman and tax expert. Other members of the cabinet got annoyed when she repeatedly said, 'Let's ask Arthur what he thinks; he's a businessman.' They did not think this made him uniquely qualified to comment on economic policy. At the time of his appointment she had no idea that he would 'go native' in

Brussels and reveal himself as an ardent European. Lord Cock-field was soon speaking of the 'great adventure' of the internal market project. He compared it with the European reconstruction programme which followed the Second World War. But his biggest mistake – in Mrs Thatcher's eyes – was that he came out strongly in favour of tax harmonization. He was even prepared to argue against Britain's insistence on keeping its zero VAT rating on food, children's clothing and new housing. Only Ireland maintained a zero rating of this sort; all the other member states charged VAT in these areas. To ram the point home Lord Cockfield insisted he was above nationalism. 'We have to look ahead to a time when we will owe allegiance to Europe as well as to Britain,' he said in a speech which annoyed the prime minister. She looked with increasing dismay at the way he pushed forward the 1992 project. He had started his career with the European Commission full of praise from Mrs Thatcher; in 1989 she refused to grant him a second term.

Mrs Thatcher's record over the Single European Act is still a matter of considerable controversy. To her it mattered deeply that looking back over her time in government people would be able to say, 'She always stood up for Britain.' She became greatly attached to the phrase she used to sum up her attitude at her last European summit, 'No, no, no,' and she was never prepared to admit that during her premiership she had been responsible for increasing the power of European institutions to the detriment of Westminster. It may have suited her self-image to appear unbending and at times ideologically committed to a particular cause, but this is not a rounded picture of Mrs Thatcher as prime minister. She was essentially a practical politician, not an ideologue. She may have given the impression of doggedly following a single course, but she would duck and weave like any other successful politician. And sometimes she regretted what she had done. In an interview for this book, the former foreign secretary Lord Hurd told me, 'Perhaps she would say now that unwittingly, poorly advised or whatever, she gave the green light to a lot of Brussels interference in the name of the single market which she certainly didn't envisage when she accepted the Single European Act.'

In the autumn of 1990, in her brilliant last speech to the House of Commons as prime minister, Mrs Thatcher was given one more chance to extol the virtues of her leadership, and it is significant that she chose to highlight the effects of the Single European Act. Right to the end of her period in office she could be surprisingly pro-European in some of her public comments. She told the Commons, 'During the past eleven years, this government has had a clear and unwavering vision of the future of Europe and Britain's role in it. It is a vision which stems from our deep-seated attachment to parliamentary democracy and commitment to economic liberty, enterprise, competition and a free market economy.' And she referred directly to the battle for the single market: 'For us, part of the purpose of the Community is to demolish trade barriers and eliminate unfair subsidies, so that we can all benefit from a great expansion of trade both within Europe and with the outside world. The fact is that Britain has done more to shape the Community over the past eleven years than any other member state.'

In the House of Lords interview room, where I met him in 2003, Norman Tebbit was unrepentant about the support he gave Mrs Thatcher over the Single European Act negotiations. He believed Britain had made strictly limited concessions in order to create the single market. 'If we had not conceded a great deal on majority voting,' he told me, 'the French would have been able to block every attempt to open their markets.' He rejects the idea propounded by some of Mrs Thatcher's supporters that she did not understand the implications of what was being proposed. Lord Tebbit accepts that she perfectly understood there would have to be more majority voting. 'What we didn't understand is that legal disputes would be decided on the basis of the European view of law as opposed to the British view of law.' Lord Tebbit believes it was the way the European Court interpreted the law that caused problems later. The British view, as he put it, is that law is something written down, whereas judges in the European Court tend to come out in favour of arguments which further the cause of European integration.

Cecil Parkinson was one of Mrs Thatcher's closest colleagues, and his old-fashioned good looks and soothing manner also made him one of her closest friends. She would have appointed him foreign secretary in 1983 to replace Francis Pym but he admitted to having an affair with his secretary Sara Keays, and she decided to give him a less prominent role; he became trade and industry secretary before being forced to resign anyway when the scandal came out. Mrs Thatcher brought him back into the cabinet, as energy secretary, four years later. I also met Lord Parkinson in the House of Lords, in one of the vast receiving rooms where huge wall paintings dwarf tiny desks. He told me that Mrs Thatcher had never been enthusiastic about the Single European Act and felt she had been 'taken for a bit of a ride'. It had seemed like a good business idea; she once said to him, 'You know we buy the Germans' motor cars, why won't they buy our insurance?' But the way the act allowed Brussels to interfere with other matters such as health and safety was quickly a source of intense dissatisfaction.

Lord Parkinson views the act as contributing towards her growing distrust of other European leaders. He was particularly struck by her own description of the way her attitude hardened following her experience with the Single European Act: 'If you put your hand in the oven and burn it, you don't stick your head in it next time.' She felt that what had started as an economic issue was turned into a political weapon to hasten the drive towards a federal Europe. She was determined not to make that mistake again. But she did precisely that when she agreed in 1990 that Britain should join the Exchange Rate Mechanism. However, we must not get ahead of ourselves; there would be plenty of drama and excitement before that decision was taken, and Mrs Thatcher would fall out with not one but two of her chancellors. Yet before we leave the effects of the Single European Act, signed with great ceremony in 1986, it is worth considering the view of the man who would become Mrs Thatcher's third chancellor, John Major.

When I first thought about this book I knew that talking to Mr Major would be vital. He holds the key to any understanding of what happened to the Conservatives before they lost their grip on power. He worries that historically he will be overshadowed by the dominant figures who preceded and succeeded him at Number 10, but Mr Major's rise to the top and his seven years in Downing Street cannot be easily dismissed. He certainly had enormous problems with the European issue – some would say it almost destroyed him – and the extraordinary pressures he had to withstand have to be taken into account when drawing up the balance sheet of his premiership. On a personal level I have always liked him, but getting him to talk publicly about Mrs Thatcher was not a simple matter.

I was anxious not to be rebuffed; much could depend on how the initial approach was made. Fortunately, in the summer of 2002, while I was still working as political editor of ITN, I met him by chance walking down Piccadilly. He appeared to be delighted to see me, and, to the obvious consternation of the plain-clothes policeman who was accompanying him, stopped to engage me in animated discussion. While the policeman anxiously scanned the small crowd which immediately began to form, Mr Major gave the impression that he had all the time in the world. He looked more relaxed and less careworn than I had ever seen him at Number 10: he was a striking advertisement for the joys of not being in office. And yes, he would be happy to talk, although some of it might have to be off the record. His female assistant gave me a fax number, and asked me to send a written request.

I was struck once again by Mr Major's charm. On television he often looks rather strained, as if he would prefer to be somewhere else, and the sound of his voice seems to come from a higher register. In ordinary life he can strike up an instant rapport, usually helped by a firm handshake or a tactile gesture of some sort. I remember how when I met him at a lobby party at Westminster soon after he became prime minister he responded to my suggestion that he should give us the details of his speech the next day. Throwing an arm round my back and grabbing me by the neck, he smilingly declined, 'even for an old friend like you'. It was an unusual but effective way of demonstrating his warmth. As a politician it was Mr Major's fate to be underestimated: he could be very formidable indeed.

Even out of office, though, his diary was very full and his new business links frequently took him abroad. It was only in April the following year that we would finally meet for the promised chat; and even then he would not agree to his remarks being on the record until we had gone through the transcript some months later. He was anxious not to add to the problems of the current Conservative leadership, but he was conscious too that in the past he had pulled his punches about Mrs Thatcher. He does not hate her – that is not Mr Major's style – but he is highly critical of the destabilizing effect she had on his leadership. This is a matter we shall return to in much more detail, but of relevance here is his determination to destroy the impression built up by the Euro-sceptics that when Mrs Thatcher was in charge she never bowed to the federalist ambitions of other European leaders.

Mr Major is still provided with intensive police security. We met at his new flat, which from the sixth floor looks out over an impressive sweep of the River Thames. I mentioned that he had an even better view than the one from his old friend Jeffrey Archer's flat at a different point on the river bank. We had both been to parties there so I knew the comparison would be relevant, but Mr Major only smiled. With Jeffrey still in jail – and with his view therefore inevitably restricted – it was not perhaps the most tactful of remarks, but Mr Major was not embarrassed about his connection with the peer whose ennoblement he had personally recommended. When Lord Archer was subsequently released Mr Major was one of the friends who refused to drop him.

If Mr Major has regrets about his time in office, many of them stem from disagreements in the party which he believes were not helped by the many occasions when Mrs Thatcher intervened, and were in his view sometimes made far worse. When he was at Number 10 he could not express his annoyance too forcefully without giving these disagreements even more publicity, but six years after his departure from Downing Street he was prepared to tell me how she and her supporters had made his life extremely difficult. He had been particularly annoyed at the way they would claim she had been a consistent Euro-sceptic. 'In government,' he told me, 'she was infinitely more pragmatic than her oratory. Her oratory was often unremitting and unbending, but what she did was not.'

Mr Major gave her acceptance of the Single European Act as an example. This was, he insisted, an obvious move towards closer European integration. 'There were gains in it,' he said. 'Installing the single market was a big gain, but it remained an integrationist measure. Without the single market you could not have had the other moves towards integration, towards a single currency or anything else. No single market would have meant no single currency.' In his view the Single European Act gave birth to the Maastricht Treaty. 'Nothing that followed later would have happened but for the Single European Act.'

I put to Mr Major the argument Mrs Thatcher would employ, that the problem with the Single European Act was the way it was interpreted. The moves towards a single market were fine, but what was objectionable was the way it was used by the European Court and the European Commission to bring about closer integration. Mr Major conceded that the European Commission had stretched its powers beyond what was expected; they put forward health and safety measures to be voted on under QMV which had nothing to do with free trade. But, Mr Major then added, with obvious feeling, 'Are we to believe that the prime minister who negotiated the Single European Act did not know what it meant?' He was clearly irritated by the way that on this and other European issues Mrs Thatcher had been prepared to blame the advice she had received at the time. 'She had the same gift,' he told me 'that Elizabeth the first had: of shifting the blame for unpopular things onto other shoulders.'

The rift which grew between Mr Major and Mrs Thatcher is the subject of later chapters. So too is Mr Major's view that Mrs Thatcher was responsible for Britain joining the Exchange Rate Mechanism. But it is now time to consider the breakdown in relations between Mrs Thatcher and the two other men who would serve her as chancellors of the exchequer, Nigel Lawson and Sir Geoffrey Howe. As with Mr Heseltine and with Mr Major, once again Europe was the issue at the heart of these disputes.

6

The diva and the bear

THE PRIME MINISTER is the 'First Lord of the Treasury'; it says
so on the polished brass plate on the door of Number 10. Most
of those who have occupied the post have no doubt wished
the inscription was in larger letters, and that their neighbour,
the chancellor of the exchequer, paid it more attention. Those
with a recent interest in politics might imagine that it is only
since Tony Blair became prime minister and his undeclared but
obvious rival Gordon Brown came to operate from next door
that the occupants of these posts have appeared to be at each
other's throats. But the struggle between the head of government and the minister charged with looking after the nation's
finances has an almost timeless air. It is as if the very nature of
these two jobs has a way of pitting one against the other.

For the skilful prime minister there can be a straightforward
way round the problem: never appoint a rival to Number 11.
Mr Blair did not have that option. Whatever else may have
been agreed at that famous dinner at the Granita restaurant in
Islington in 1994, Mr Brown was certainly promised the keys
to Number 11 if Labour won the general election. In return
he gave Mr Blair a clear run in the leadership contest. Mrs
Thatcher was more fortunate. Of her three chancellors, Sir
Geoffrey Howe, Nigel Lawson and John Major, the first two
never looked like serious candidates and Mr Major was only in
the running after she had fallen. Mrs Thatcher did not believe
that any of them could pose a real threat; she never doubted
her superior abilities in the top post.

Of the relationships, the strangest and in a way the most important was the one between Mrs Thatcher and Sir Geoffrey Howe. In personality and temperament they could hardly have been more different: if she could be compared to an operatic diva, capable of hitting the highest notes, he was more like a bear with a big brain, treating emotions like honey, not something to be shared with strangers. Over the years he put up with Mrs Thatcher: when she was cross, he did not hit back; when she raged, he looked mildly displeased. The only times he deeply resented her behaviour was when she was rude to him in front of officials; he hated being made to look foolish in front of his subordinates. They were together for fifteen years and Sir Geoffrey tells friends, 'That is longer than most marriages.' He is proud of their partnership, and sees it as by far the most rewarding part of his professional life; and as with many politicians whose personalities have never impressed the public, he is disappointed that his work on policy is not more widely recognized.

Sir Geoffrey is a very British politician; you could not imagine him flourishing outside the conventions of Westminster politics. He has plenty of abilities, but only a few of those that Americans regard as essential in a politician. He does not relish being out on the stump; kissing babies, he would consider, is a matter for parents, close relatives or friends, not for politicians after votes. Having lunch with him can be a strain, if only because he speaks so softly. When he was out of office he once told me how much he was in favour of Britain joining the euro, but he said it so quietly I could not tell whether he was really committed.

The Labour politician Denis Healey, who was for some years Sir Geoffrey's opposite number as shadow chancellor, famously described being attacked by him as 'like being savaged by a dead sheep'. Yet beneath his woolly exterior Sir Geoffrey Howe was a formidable force. He was one of the key figures behind the ism which became known as Thatcherism, and in the early part of Mrs Thatcher's period in office without him the whole edifice might have crumbled. His controversial budget of 1981, when he put up taxes despite the country being in the middle of a recession, was a brave achievement, and he does not object to Margaret Thatcher taking much of the credit for putting the public finances in order. He remembers that for forty-eight hours she was the only one of his colleagues who spoke up publicly in favour of the budget.

An extraordinary insight into the early relationship between Mrs Thatcher and Sir Geoffrey is provided by Michael Portillo, who for a long time was one of her favourites and would never publicly criticize her. But in July 2002, when he was coming to the conclusion that he did not want to stand again for Parliament, I talked to him as part of the preparation for this book, and in his office at Westminster, in one of the maze of rooms near the top of the building, he regaled me with Thatcher stories.

Michael Portillo was a young member of the Conservative research department during Mrs Thatcher's first election campaign in 1979. His job was to keep her informed of what the press was saying. In private her reactions were often rather wild, but these would later be modified for public consumption. Mr Portillo got used to this. He learned that from him a friendly positive reaction was what she wanted; a sentence beginning 'yes' would often do the trick. 'Yes, Mrs Thatcher,' the twenty-two-year-old Mr Portillo would say, and then make sure that his written advice on the line she should take was far more sober than the angle she had suggested. He was surprised that Geoffrey Howe would adopt a quite different, and to Mrs Thatcher very irritating, response. 'No,' he would say firmly, risking an immediate confrontation. The men she liked tended to be dashing and glamorous – Cecil Parkinson fitted the bill perfectly – 'Whereas,' Mr Portillo told me,

'Geoffrey was kind of mumbling, and in a funny kind of way sort of old womanish; she hated that.' Often she found him boring, and when there was tension between them he found her difficult to handle.

Mr Portillo remembered an occasion in that same election campaign when they were amused to learn that Karl Marx's granddaughter, still alive and living in London, had decided to vote Conservative. Her picture appeared in the papers and provoked one of the rare moments when Mrs Thatcher tried her hand at being funny. She seized his glasses from Sir Geoffrey's nose, placed them on her own, and said, 'Doesn't she look like me?' Mr Portillo admits that she did slightly resemble Karl Marx's granddaughter, and Geoffrey Howe, blinking without his glasses, undoubtedly looked funny, but in Mr Portillo's view making him look foolish was also rather cruel.

Europe, and in particular linking the pound with the other EEC currencies, was their greatest policy difference. The plan had first been proposed in the dying days of the Labour government of James Callaghan. The prime minister had gone for a walk in St James's Park with his young foreign secretary David Owen, who would later form the breakaway Social Democratic party and the alliance with the Liberals. The Germans and the French were supporting a plan for what was then called the European Monetary System, or EMS, the latest in a series of suggestions for linking the European currencies. How, Germany and France argued, could there be a real common market if the rates of exchange for the different currencies floated up and down at will?

James Callaghan decided with David Owen that as far as Britain was concerned the idea was a dead duck. Britain did not join the EMS, and this policy was confirmed by Mrs Thatcher's incoming government, although her chancellor, Sir Geoffrey Howe, was convinced that sooner or later Britain would have to join. Looking back on this lengthy saga Sir Geoffrey is convinced that, as with Britain's belated membership of the EEC, it would have been far better to have been in at the beginning. If Britain had joined what was to be called the Exchange Rate Mechanism in 1985, he believes the dire consequences of Britain's membership five years later could have been avoided. However, in 1979 the official policy was that Britain would join when the time was right, or ripe. No one could be sure where these particular words came from, or whether ripeness or rightness was the vital test. In practice, Mrs Thatcher implied the answer was definitely 'No' and would stay 'No' if she had anything to do with it.

After the election landslide in 1983 and the sacking of Francis Pym, Sir Geoffrey Howe, to his delight, was promoted to foreign secretary. His keenness that the pound should link up with other European currencies was no longer directly relevant, but his successor at the Treasury Nigel Lawson adopted the same view, much to Mrs Thatcher's annoyance when she found out. To begin with, the relationship between Mrs Thatcher and her new chancellor had a familiarity which she had never managed with Sir Geoffrey. She fussed over Mr Lawson like a mother hen. She liked his intellectual brilliance and his capacity to take risks.

There was a streak of the gambler about Mr Lawson, and in his younger days he had been thought good-looking. The years had taken their toll, his girth had widened, and there was often a certain untidiness about him which Mrs Thatcher did her best to rectify. She would be heard telling him to have his hair cut; and Michael Portillo tells the story of Mr Lawson about to set off for a ceremony at Buckingham Palace being called back by Mrs Thatcher and forced to change his shoes. The prime minister lent him a pair belonging to her son Mark. Unlike Sir Geoffrey, Mr Lawson did not seem to mind being fussed over in this way. He took it, correctly, as a sign of approval.

As the election of 1987 approached, Mrs Thatcher was increasingly prone to treat Sir Geoffrey in a patronizing way. I was in the press party which accompanied her to Moscow just before the general election of 1987, in many ways the high point of her whole period in office. She was at the peak of her career domestically, following the success of the privatization programme and her triumph over the miners; and partly through her close alliance with Ronald Reagan she had become the most famous woman politician in the world. It was the first time the reforming Soviet president Mikhail Gorbachev had welcomed her to Moscow. He was the Russian leader with whom she had declared she could 'do business'. Like many famous Thatcher phrases this was thought up by someone else, in this case her press secretary Bernard Ingham, who had been trying to summarize the mood of talks with Mr Gorbachev at Chequers during an earlier visit to Britain. Mrs Thatcher liked the phrase and it became a convenient cliché to describe the relationship between her and the man who helped to bring about the end of the Soviet empire.

The Moscow trip started badly for me. Aboard the VC-10, Bernard Ingham told us that she would not be coming to see the press party for a while and so we could tuck into the luxurious meal provided for us by the RAF. With splendid wines, napkins and proper cutlery – not the plastic utensils provided on commercial flights – we were beginning to enjoy ourselves. Suddenly Mrs Thatcher arrived at my elbow. I stood up as a mark of respect, throwing all my food and crockery onto the floor. The prime minister immediately insisted on clearing up the mess. She loved being able to upstage the press. 'You stay where you are,' she cooed. 'I'll sort this out.' The implication was clear: you are just another foolish man who has to be rescued by a competent woman. Flustered RAF staff rushed forward to help.

The real embarrassment was, however, reserved for Sir Geoffrey Howe. As foreign secretary he had a difficult role to play. In his case too Mrs Thatcher was suggesting that a competent woman was needed, to sort out Mr Gorbachev. Soon after the mess-on-the-carpet incident, the prime minister returned to the part of the plane reserved for the press, literally pulling the foreign secretary after her. 'Look,' she said, clinging to his casual sweater. 'What do you think of Geoffrey's new jumper?' It could hardly have been more tactless; the foreign secretary was being treated like a dummy. With Mrs Thatcher it seemed to have become a habit, even in cabinet meetings.

One of their cabinet colleagues Lord Hurd, in an interview for this book, told me she treated Sir Geoffrey with a 'total lack of perception'. There were times in front of colleagues when she was 'sort of vindictive towards him'. He went on: 'He is such a gentle creature; he did nothing to offend her, yet she lashed out at him. And when you consider how he helped her in the early days and how faithful he'd been to her, I think that was very surprising.' Lord Hurd believes there were certain people, including Sir Geoffrey, who simply irritated her, and the older she got the more irritated she became. Years later, on a foreign trip a friendly MP asked Sir Geoffrey how badly he had been treated by her. 'It was simply dreadful,' he replied.

I myself incurred Mrs Thatcher's wrath during the trip to the Soviet Union when I accused her of electioneering. Mobbed while touring a housing estate in Moscow and clearly delighted, she accepted bunches of flowers and signed lots of autographs. It was as if the Tories were fighting a by-election in 'Moscow North'. When I put this to the prime minister, she became very angry indeed. I thought she was going to knock me down the seven flights of stairs to the bottom of the apartment block. 'I am simply doing my duty,' she snapped, implying that I certainly was not. It is perhaps worth pointing out that the general election was called within a few weeks, and that much of Mrs Thatcher's first election broadcast was taken up with pictures of her being lauded in Moscow.

The cabinet split over European policy surfaced in a dramatic way after Mrs Thatcher won the 1987 election. For some time Mr Lawson had decided that if the pound could not be formally linked with the Exchange Rate Mechanism he would plump for the second best option: he would secretly ensure that the pound shadowed the German Deutschmark, the two currencies maintaining the same exchange rate whatever the movements of other currencies. If this policy succeeded it would then be possible to say that, were Britain to join the system, little would have to change. The only difficulty was that Mr Lawson omitted to inform the first lord of the Treasury. A group of journalists from the *Financial Times* told Mrs Thatcher what was happening at an informal meeting in November 1987. She was horrified and said later of Mr Lawson, 'How could I possibly trust him again?'

It took time for this extraordinary rift between Mrs Thatcher and Mr Lawson to become public knowledge. I know when it hit me. I was sitting in the gallery of the House of Commons some months later, on 10 March 1988, listening to a standard session of questions to treasury ministers, normally a very dull way to spend the afternoon. Mr Lawson said that any further significant rise in the value of the pound against the Deutschmark was 'unlikely to be sustainable'. The foreign exchange markets took this to mean that the Treasury would intervene to keep the value of sterling down, and so the pound dropped. Within half an hour the prime minister, also asked about the pound, said, 'There is no way in which one can buck the market.' The pound quickly regained its previous level on the assumption that the prime minister's view would prevail and the Treasury would not intervene in the market.

But the strong suspicion that Mr Lawson and Mrs Thatcher disagreed on exchange rate policy – a central plank in the government's approach to the economy – could not be dispelled.

Two months later, in May, Sir Geoffrey Howe stepped into the argument. As the years had passed, with the economy and the pound going through almost the full range of possibilities, it had become increasingly difficult to argue that Britain was simply waiting for favourable conditions before joining the Exchange Rate Mechanism. Sir Geoffrey Howe found audiences inclined to laugh when the 'time is right' formula was used. To sound more credible he would tack on the phrase 'and we know we can't go on saying that for ever'. On this occasion he went further, saying, 'We cannot forever go on adding that qualification to the underlying commitment.' Journalists were quick to ask whether there was an underlying commitment.

Only the day before, the prime minister had been challenged by the Labour leader Neil Kinnock to say whether she agreed with her chancellor on the way he was dealing with the pound. Mrs Thatcher would only say that Mr Lawson ran the economy extremely well; there was no question of her referring to an underlying commitment to join the ERM. To the delight of political journalists, the story of a serious cabinet split was now up and running. It seemed that Mrs Thatcher's authority was being openly flouted by two of her most senior ministers. The government made strenuous efforts to deny there was any rift, but the speculation could not be quashed completely for the simple reason that it was true.

Sir Geoffrey phoned Downing Street to suggest that the three of them should meet and try to sort out their differences. He received a stinging reply, as she later recalled: 'I told him three times – since he did not seem to take it in and persisted in his attempt to contrive a meeting at which he and Nigel could get their way – that the best thing he could do now was to keep quiet. We were not going into the ERM at present and that was that.' Despite her tough talk, Mrs Thatcher was not prepared to risk a direct confrontation with her colleagues and no meeting took place. But she had been given a clear warning that unless joining the ERM was put into effect at some point, she might have to remove one or both of her senior colleagues. She decided to bide her time.

European politics was moving on. The following month, at a summit in the German city of Hanover, there was a development which alarmed the Euro-sceptics. It was agreed that Jacques Delors, the French president of the European Commission, should head a high-powered committee to look into the prospects for economic and monetary union, in effect a single European currency. The committee would report formally in one year's time. This was a policy Mrs Thatcher had tried to block on many occasions, and Mr Delors, the leading thinker on the future of the EEC, was increasingly depicted as Mrs Thatcher's chief opponent in matters European.

Lord Powell, Mrs Thatcher's friend as well as her former foreign affairs expert, believes that she was deliberately misled about the importance of this committee by the German chancellor Helmut Kohl, whose relationship with Mrs Thatcher was never warm and at times seemed to break down completely. On this occasion, when Lord Powell was present, he apparently gave her the impression that the committee was a way of putting the issue into cold storage, and that he was personally not interested in the idea. Instead, as Lord Powell told me, the single currency plan came back with a vengeance; the committee put forward very specific proposals which the German chancellor then endorsed. The drive towards the euro accelerated. Lord Powell told me Chancellor Kohl's behaviour at the Hanover summit was 'a source of disillusion to her'. I think that is putting the matter rather mildly: Mrs Thatcher felt she had been double-crossed.

With his short stature, academic manner and painfully slow English, Jacques Delors tried to appear reassuring on his regular visits to Number 10. He was keen to counter the image, given to him by the British tabloid newspapers, of a devil incarnate. I once asked him, as he went into a meeting, about moves towards economic and monetary union. 'Slowlee, slowlee . . .' he said, moving his arm in an undulating fashion oblivious to the rather sinister impression this would create on the British television audience. Mrs Thatcher liked his cleverness – and she liked sparring with him – even though she agreed with the *Sun* and the *Daily Mail* that he was a dangerous European federalist who would dearly love to see a United States of Europe. The *Sun* made clear its opposition with the headline UP YOURS DELORS, and Mrs Thatcher was enticed by one of her speechwriters into a tabloid-style riposte, accusing the Commission president of trying to introduce 'socialism by the back delors'.

Having defeated the trade unions over the closed shop and restrictive practices, the prime minister did not intend to see the position reversed by new labour laws emanating from Brussels. For her a seminal moment came when Mr Delors was the guest of honour at the TUC conference in Bournemouth in September 1988. She was not impressed by the way the union leaders warmed to Frère Jacques; and when Mr Delors called for a European government and forecast that in ten years' time 80 per cent of new legislation would come from Brussels, she began preparing for a speech in the Belgian city of Bruges which she hoped would throw him off course. It was the most Euro-sceptic speech she had ever made and it caused consternation among establishment politicians across Europe. For the first time she spoke openly about her fears that a European super-state was being created: 'We have not successfully rolled back the frontiers of the state in Britain only to see them reimposed at a European level, with a European super-state exercising a new dominance from Brussels.' This speech set out her considered view that Britain would not accept further moves towards a federal Europe. It was her most important speech on Europe during her last few years in office, and it produced a split within the Conservative party which has still not completely healed. The Bruges Group dedicated to keeping the flame of Euro-scepticism burning would soon be created, based on the principles laid out in her speech. For years afterwards the issue was simple: were you in favour of a European super-state or not? As so often in her career, Mrs Thatcher had set the terms for the debate. This particular dividing point, within the Conservative party, would remain for years to come.

7

'My God, that man is so German'

MARGARET THATCHER had a blind spot about Germany, and this was part of the reason she got on so badly with Helmut Kohl. It would be wrong to say she did not like foreigners, or that she was so obsessed by her relationship with Ronald Reagan that she could only see the world through the eyes of the wartime Anglo-American relationship. She had a close relationship with Mikhail Gorbachev; they seemed to like arguing with each other, often about the principles of good government. When they met for the first time in Moscow I went with a group of British journalists to see a performance of Tchaikovsky's *Swan Lake* at the Bolshoi Theatre; the second act was held up for fifteen minutes because the two leaders were so deep in conversation that they delayed their return to the splendidly ornate box at the back of the stalls. Later she revealed to me the point at issue, which she had been determined to hammer home: the need for the Soviet Union to learn to respect the rule of law.

The prime minister was a sensation when she travelled to Eastern Europe, especially to Poland where her much declared attachment to freedom and her green suit – chosen to represent hope – established her as the most exciting politician from the West. And there were other European leaders, particularly the French president – François Mitterrand, with whom she established bonds of respect and admiration. She was grateful for the support he gave Britain during the Falklands War. Mr Mitterrand once said, 'She has the eyes of Caligula and the lips of Marilyn Monroe,' but I think we should take this as a joke, otherwise the reference to Caligula seems peculiarly insensitive. This Roman emperor, who was murdered in AD 41, is customarily portrayed as an incestuous, insane tyrant, who made his horse a consul and declared himself a god; even Mrs Thatcher's worst enemies could not accuse her of that.

With Helmut Kohl, though, the electricity never flowed, or if it did it went in the wrong direction. It may seem trivial, but the sheer size of the German leader did not help. Every year he would go on a strict diet for a few weeks, but for most of the year he still weighed nearly twenty stone, and with his height of well over six feet towered over the other European leaders. Mrs Thatcher often seemed to treat him, not as a gentle giant in a fairy story, but more the angry troll who, though frightening, should not be appeased; she reserved the right to play Goldilocks. Chancellor Kohl dominated many of the summits, not least because Germany was easily the biggest contributor to the European budget. She hated the way he sometimes banged on the table and shouted that if Germany was going to pay, Germany should get its way. Lord Powell, who speaks fluent German and almost invariably travelled with Mrs Thatcher, told me, 'It reinforced her instinctive prejudices about Germany as a sort of bullying nation.'

Chancellor Kohl did try to get on with Mrs Thatcher. Before their formal meetings he would always arrive with a generous present, a brooch or some other item which he had selected personally. In the spring of 1989 he invited her to spend a weekend with him and his wife at their home near Ludwigshafen, close to the French border. He wanted to convey, in folksy terms, that he was as much a European as a German. One of the highlights of the visit was lunch at an old, half-timbered local inn where they cooked traditional food. Chancellor Kohl's favourite meal was duly served: potato soup, pig's stomach, sausage, liver dumplings and sauerkraut. He asked for a second helping while Mrs Thatcher tried to conceal the fact that she had lost her appetite. Lord Powell told me the pig's stomach was clearly not to her liking. 'She chased it rather reluctantly round the plate with her fork and then tried to hide it.' The mood of the formal talks was no better. Neither side could agree on the main issue of the time: how to deal with short-range nuclear weapons in Europe. When Mrs Thatcher got back to her plane for the trip home, she kicked off her shoes and told Charles Powell, 'My God, that man is so German.'

Mrs Thatcher was unimpressed by the desire of German politicians to subsume their national identity into some kind of federal Europe or European union. She saw this as a hangover from the Nazi period. Good Germans, as they were sometimes called, were desperate to throw off the image of extreme nationalism bequeathed by Adolf Hitler. For Chancellor Kohl, with direct memories of the Second World War – his brother was killed in the closing stages – it was a sign of progress and renewal. But Mrs Thatcher considered that to argue from the special case of the Germans, trying to shake off memories of the Nazis, to the idea that no European country should behave like a sovereign state was simply wrong-headed and dangerous. This generation of German leaders might be nervous of governing themselves and want to see the nation state fade away, but that was certainly no argument for allowing a federal Europe to be established. It would not suit Britain or most of the other member countries. The pro-European case argued with such consistency and fervour by German politicians was therefore rejected by Mrs Thatcher; and she was increasingly determined to stand up to those arguing for the same future at home.

The immediate question in the spring of 1989 was whether Britain would join the Exchange Rate Mechanism as part of a move towards European economic and monetary union. Mrs

Thatcher was determined to say oppose membership and was still smarting from the way her chancellor Nigel Lawson had secretly tried to shadow the Deutschmark as a prelude to entry. She even publicly complained – in a BBC interview broadcast on 19 May – that as a result of this policy inflation had picked up. Privately, Mr Lawson threatened to resign. The clear division between Mrs Thatcher, on the one hand, and her two most powerful lieutenants was complete. Both the chancellor and Sir Geoffrey Howe were convinced that Britain should join the ERM. The tension at the top of the government was clear for all to see.

Mockery is one of the strongest weapons a politician can use, and if you are in opposition and the blows strike home it can be the most valuable weapon of all. The economy is almost always at the centre of the national debate; it connects to people in the most basic way. Labour's shadow chancellor John Smith was an expert in mockery and he knew there was nothing worse for Margaret Thatcher than to be treated as if she was not a serious person. Mr Lawson, too, liked to be regarded as an intellectual heavyweight, and in those days, before he went on his diet, he had an appropriately ample figure. During a debate on the economy in June 1989 the two of them had to sit close together on the government front bench of the House of Commons listening to Mr Smith make them look foolish.

It was one of the funniest occasions at Westminster I can remember. Mr Smith looked like a traditional bank manager, short and well filled out in his dark suit and glasses; people tended to respect and believe what he had to say, and his mischievous sense of humour took them by surprise. On this occasion his approach was hardly sophisticated, but some of the best jokes are reminiscent of the classroom, with po-faced adults being made fools of by children. Making all he could of the fractious atmosphere in Downing Street, the shadow chancellor suggested, with mock seriousness, that a spirit of good neighbourliness was the only answer to the confusion and disarray which lay at the heart of government policy. To heighten the absurdity of his suggestion, he quoted from the words used in the theme tune of the Australian TV soap opera *Neighbours*. The lyrics start in a fairly lofty way, pointing out that everybody needs good neighbours; the mood then becomes more practical. 'Just a friendly wave each morning helps to make a better day,' Mr Smith repeated, trying to keep a straight face. 'Neighbours need to get to know each other. Next door is only a footstep away.' He peered over his glasses to see if Mrs Thatcher and Mr Lawson were taking note. They squirmed in discomfort. With a helpful air Mr Smith stressed the words of the final verse: 'With a little understanding, you can find a perfect blend. Neighbours should be there for one another. That's when good neighbours become good friends.'

The Commons erupted with gales of laughter; even the Tories could not hide their amusement. Mrs Thatcher employed her special look of grown-up disdain when MPs were fooling about. She was not angry; she was above it all but she was certainly not amused. If she had made a comment it would have been along the lines of, 'Boys will be boys,' followed by a forced laugh. But inside the apparently unaffected prime minister the determination grew that she would be rid of Mr Lawson before long. Mrs Thatcher usually regarded jokes at her expense as something others would have to pay for. She was determined not to have major decisions hijacked by two of her colleagues, however senior. But before this matter came to a head, there was a campaign to fight – for the elections to the European Parliament.

Mrs Thatcher wanted to make sure her new advocacy of Euro-scepticism was fully reflected in the style and wording of Conservative advertisements. She personally approved the most controversial poster, which read, 'Stay at home on June 15th and you'll live on a diet of Brussels.' The former Conservative party chairman Norman Tebbit, who was usually happy with caustic comment on British membership of the EEC, described it as 'the worst election advertising in living memory'. It certainly did not help the party in the polls. In those days public opinion was mainly pro-European and the Tories were certain of a hard fight to get anywhere near their support in the previous Euro-election in 1984, but the result was still a shock to the government. The number of Conservative MEPs was reduced from forty-eight to thirty-five, and the pro-Europeans were quick to blame the party's negative campaign.

The result encouraged the chancellor and the foreign secretary to take on Mrs Thatcher over the question of British membership of the ERM. The issue was due to come up at the Madrid summit at the end of June. At a tense, formal meeting at Number 10, Sir Geoffrey Howe and Nigel Lawson both told Mrs Thatcher that unless they could secure a serious commitment to join the ERM, they were both prepared to resign. Mrs Thatcher did not respond directly, and indeed it was not until Sir Geoffrey was sitting in the council meeting in Madrid and listening to her outline the British position that he knew she was prepared to give way. 'I can reaffirm today,' she declared, 'the United Kingdom's intention to join the ERM.' She laid out the conditions that Sir Geoffrey and Mr Lawson had agreed to: that British inflation should be lower, that exchange controls should be abolished within Europe, and that further progress should be made on the single market, the much vaunted free trade area within Europe which had still not been fully established. 'It was,' Sir Geoffrey commented later, 'as close to the outcome for which Nigel and I had been pressing as we might have hoped.' Mrs Thatcher took some comfort from the fact that she had avoided resignations and had failed to give any date by which ERM entry would be achieved. She also did little to stop the persistent rumours of continuing disagreement with her chancellor and foreign secretary. Talk of a reshuffle, with either or both of them heading for the chop, soon began to surface.

When the reshuffle came, the following month, I stood in Downing Street puzzling over why it was taking so long. In the event Mrs Thatcher had settled for half a loaf. Nigel Lawson would stay as chancellor, but Sir Geoffrey Howe was moved away from the foreign office to be demoted to leader of the House of Commons. But those bald facts hid a day of dramatic negotiations behind the scenes. Sir Geoffrey had no warning he was about to be sacked. At one stage he was offered the job of home secretary, and he was only persuaded not to resign from the government when he was promised the position of deputy prime minister, the post once held by Willie Whitelaw. The relatively young and inexperienced John Major, who had impressed Mrs Thatcher by his willingness as Treasury chief secretary to cut public spending, was appointed foreign secretary.

The reshuffle did not solve Mrs Thatcher's problems. Nigel Lawson had thought he might be sacked or forced to resign. We had lunch together just before the reshuffle at a select restaurant called Mijanou in Victoria. He was extremely discreet. It is one of the myths of these off the record lunches that guests cannot resist blurting out secrets. All too often the guest is more interested in finding out what other senior politicians are up to than giving any hint of their own plans. In these circumstances it sometimes pays to suggest the action your guest might be prepared to take and see how they react. I suggested to Mr Lawson that he would like to leave office on a high note, and only if that were possible would he contemplate resignation. In other words, if Mrs Thatcher wanted him out she would have to sack him. He nodded in agreement.

At the 1989 Conservative party conference there were more opportunities to guess what was really going on. The party chairman Kenneth Baker attended a dinner with BBC correspondents and asked us each to suggest one word to sum up the prospects for the conference. I suggested 'survival', which got an easy laugh, but when he left, he stopped to whisper to me, 'Nothing wrong with survival.' His main task was to try to paper over the cracks between Mrs Thatcher and her chancellor. We were invited to film them together as they swept down the stairs of the Imperial Hotel, but the sequence only added to the speculation that they were finding it difficult to overcome their differences.

They differed, not only about policy but also over who should be allowed to advise the prime minister. Professor Sir Alan Walters had returned to Downing Street after an absence of five years and Mrs Thatcher made no secret of the fact that she increasingly relied on his advice about the economy. When John Smith mocked the neighbours of Downing Street he had suggested that the real chancellor was Alan Walters and Mr Lawson merely the post holder. Professor Walters was a radical monetarist, not reluctant to say what level of interest rates was appropriate and very much in tune with Mrs Thatcher's European views. He dismissed the ERM as 'half baked', and what made his position so controversial was that this assessment was published. Mr Lawson decided that the choice of who should advise the prime minister was simple: 'Him or me?'

After the party conference he felt that the only way to restore confidence in the financial markets was for Professor Walters to resign, and he knew that Mrs Thatcher would be very unlikely to allow that. He went to see the prime minister on 26 October 1989, and told her that Alan Walters would have to go. Mrs Thatcher listened intently and then, as expected, dug in her heels. 'If Alan were to go,' she said, 'that would destroy my authority.' But she was clearly very upset at the thought of losing Mr Lawson. She asked him at least to reflect. When he returned later that day, his mind made up, she begged him to stay. 'I handed her my resignation letter,' Mr Lawson says. 'At first she refused to take it; but then she took it and popped it into her handbag, unopened, saying that she did not wish to read it.' She flattered, she pleaded, but she refused to say the one thing he wanted to hear, that Alan Walters would go. The die was cast.

As it happens I was having lunch that day with the new foreign secretary John Major. I was sympathizing with the hard time the press had given him when Mrs Thatcher had over-ruled him at the Commonwealth conference in Kuala Lumpur. We ended the meal, at Mijanou again, with a bizarre moment when Mr Major asked me for my advice. I was taken aback, not realizing this was one of his ways of tempting journalists to look at the situation from his point of view. 'Be brave,' I said, not knowing he would be thrown further into the fire that very evening. Just after six o'clock it was announced that the new chancellor of the exchequer would be John Major.

On the surface it looked as though Mrs Thatcher had won the struggle for power. In reality she had been badly weakened. She had missed the chance of leaving office in triumph. Even some of her closest supporters now argue that 1989 was the best time for her to have resigned. After ten years as prime minister, she could have left to the cheers of a largely grateful nation; but she much preferred to listen to the voices of the Thatcher loyalists at the party conference who had shouted, 'Ten more years.' Long-serving prime ministers cling to the hope they will leave office at a time of their choosing. They feel their experience is particularly useful in foreign affairs; and with dramatic events unfolding in Europe it would have been out of character for Mrs Thatcher to give any serious thought to resignation.

When the Berlin Wall came down in November it seemed that the tough stance she had taken with President Reagan during the Cold War had dramatically paid off. The virtually bloodless revolution which swept through Eastern Europe happened so quickly it was difficult to take in. So many preconceptions had to go as well, particularly the image of implacable communist regimes which would never succumb. Suddenly, it seemed, the nightmare grip of the Soviet Union had disappeared. Mrs Thatcher felt vindicated as well as elated, but she was not happy at the prospect of a reunited Germany. Pro-Europeans, including the new foreign secretary Douglas Hurd, were shocked at the way Mrs Thatcher's relations with Chancellor Kohl sank to rock bottom. Lord Hurd, in the interview for this book, told me there were times when Mrs Thatcher and Chancellor Kohl refused to speak to each other. He told me that vital business had to be conducted at foreign minister level, between himself and Hans-Dietrich Genscher. Lord Hurd described the way the relationship deteriorated: 'She let personal feelings destroy her relationship with the German leader and that was a big mistake.' She got on well with Mr Genscher. 'She has natural good manners, and she used them to very good effect. It was just with Kohl that she couldn't manage it, and nor could he.'

Chancellor Kohl's main complaint was Mrs Thatcher's opposition to any rapid move towards German unification. It would, she argued, make President Gorbachev's position difficult, because a united Germany would be against the interests of the Soviet Union. But she was also concerned about the effect of Germany's increased power on British interests in Europe. Chancellor Kohl wanted to be remembered as the statesman who had unified Germany and persuaded Europe that his nation no longer wanted to dominate the continent. His differences with Mrs Thatcher were too great to be bridged; and her stance on German unification was, for pro-Europeans, another example of her lack of understanding of the best way forward in Europe. At Westminster an unlikely challenge was prepared by the pro-Europeans, which would only later look like the writing on the wall for Mrs Thatcher. She would be forced to fight her first leadership election while still in office.

A STUDIED LACK of concern was Mrs Thatcher's response to the leadership challenge, which came a year before the one that finished her off. For fourteen years the provision for a contest of this sort had lain dormant. Most Conservative MPs did not even know that the relevant clause in the party's rule book existed. And then along came the wispy, rather grey figure of Sir Anthony Meyer, a Conservative MP who was convinced that Mrs Thatcher was completely wrong over Europe. Michael Heseltine was already firmly established as the real potential danger to the prime minister, and he too strongly disagreed with her policy on Europe, but he was careful not to have any direct contact with Sir Anthony. One of those who worked ceaselessly for the former defence secretary during the time he was playing the King over the Water was the Conservative MP Keith Hampson. He did meet Sir Anthony, who asked him whether it would hurt Mr Heseltine's prospects if he stood against Mrs Thatcher. The answer was no but Mr Heseltine insists this was on Mr Hampson's authority not his own.

None of this stopped Sir Anthony being referred to throughout the contest, and ever since, as the stalking horse. This description slipped so quickly into the political vocabulary that hardly anyone bothered to research its origin. Stalking horses were used from the 16th century onwards to deceive deer or game birds. Horses did not alarm game so hunters could hide behind them until they got within range. Some hunters, lacking horses, rigged up painted screens to look like them. The old Etonian baronet Anthony Meyer fitted the role, but which hunter was he trying to conceal? Mrs Thatcher and her loyal colleagues insisted there was no real threat but when the vote took place thirty-three Conservative MPs voted for Sir Anthony and nearly the same number abstained. It was ominous for Mrs Thatcher that about sixty of her MPs were not prepared to support her. 'A shot across the bows' was the phrase used by John Cole, the BBC's political editor, and myself; unfortunately we both used it in recorded pieces for the same news programme. 'At least,' the editor commented dryly, 'you were not in disagreement.'

Even when she came to write her memoirs Mrs Thatcher still did not seem to appreciate the seriousness of this event. 'The results,' she says, 'were by no means unsatisfactory,' although she records her campaign manager George Younger telling her that there was 'a certain amount of discontent'. She does not refer to a far more dramatic warning delivered by another of her campaign team, one of the most consummate backstage politicians of the period, Tristan Garel-Jones: 'There are a hundred assassins lurking in the bushes, Prime Minister.' Her supporters at the party conference had shouted 'Ten more years' but in reality her life at Number 10 would be over in little more than ten months.

8

'Maggie, Maggie, Maggie; out, out, out'

RIOTING, MOB RULE and anarchy are hardly conditions Mrs Thatcher would like to have associated with her period of government, but they were an unexpected consequence of the policy she was keen to promote as the flagship of her third term. Anger over the poll tax was expressed in many different ways; there was nothing, though, to match the explosion of hatred and bitterness which took over the centre of London on 31 March 1990, the day before the tax was introduced in England and Wales. There was a riot which stands comparison with some of the most violent scenes in the capital's history. The organizers estimated that 200,000 took part in the peaceful protest march; Tony Benn made a speech and feelings were vented in the now traditional shouts of 'Maggie, Maggie, Maggie; out, out, out.' Then the mood turned nasty. In Whitehall and Trafalgar Square well over a thousand people, mainly young militants convinced of the justness of their cause, engaged in running battles with the police, who fought desperately to regain control. The riot spread across the West End. Cars and buildings were set on fire and shops looted. It was the worst assault on police and property for more than a century.

Amazingly, no one was killed, but about five hundred police officers were hurt following a series of tactical blunders. The police had failed to appreciate the seriousness of the situation and moved in too late. At one stage seven police officers were trapped in their vehicle as rioters tried to remove the petrol cap in order to set the van on fire. One of the officers inside said, 'It was a baying, screaming, yelling, spitting, swearing mob. I don't think they would have worried too much about killing us.' More than four hundred people were taken to hospital. The organizers of the march maintained that only a very small percentage of the protestors had been to blame. The chairman of the All Britain Anti-Poll Tax Federation, Tommy Sheridan, said, 'We utterly condemn the mindless idiots who climbed onto scaffolding and threw lumps of metal, concrete and fire extinguishers into the crowd. The majority of those who became embroiled in running battles had nothing to do with our protest.' The official police enquiry stated that 1,985 crimes had been reported and there were 531 arrests. Because the police had been unable to contain the riot, Scotland Yard had to pay out more than £3 million in compensation under the 1838 Riot Damages Act.

The poll tax was meant to be a fair and simple means of raising revenue for local authorities. Instead of money being paid through rates from each household assessed on the basis of wildly outdated property valuations, the tax would be levied on individuals. Everyone would pay, and everyone would therefore be keen to ensure that their local council was delivering worthwhile services. No longer would a large pro-portion of the population, exempt from paying rates, be indifferent to the raising of local taxes. It would also be possible for easy comparisons to be made with people living in other areas; extravagant councils would be clearly identified, and their ruling parties could expect to suffer in the subsequent elections. Accountability, the holy Grail of local government reform, would finally become a reality.

But the basic unfairness of the new system could not be ignored. The wealthy landowner would pay as much as the landless tenant. The duke and the dustman would be charged the same amount. The argument that about half of local government expenditure was covered from general taxation, which did take account of people's ability to pay, may have impressed economists but carried little weight with the public. It also became obvious that differences between councils would not merely reflect their extravagance or thrift; the way national funds were distributed left some local authorities better off than others for no apparent reason. I was able to film a street in London on the boundary of two local authorities and point out that those on one side of the road would pay over £100 a year less than those on the other for no apparent reason. The system had quickly become as complicated as the rates. With a group of journalists I was taken to the hideous tower blocks inhabited by the Department of the Environment in Marsham Street only to be told that the one person who really under-stood how the tax was arrived at was off sick. Many councils took the opportunity to increase spending, knowing that the government would get the blame because they had introduced the new tax. For individuals and households there were far more losers than gainers. Endless exemptions were created, and the system soon came to be seen as chaotic as well as unfair. Before long Mrs Thatcher was the only member of the government ready and able to argue passionately for the poll tax, officially known as the Community Charge.

The Community Charge was the flagship programme of Mrs Thatcher's third term and a year after the 1987 election she was determined to 'put my own stamp on it'. At a local government conference in London she expressed her complete confidence that the system would weed out overspending councils, and she made clear it was Labour councils she had in mind. 'Believe you me,' she declared, 'this is going to trans-form inner cities because no longer are they going to be able to spend, spend, spend.' One of her key objectives was to expose the Labour left – council leaders like Derek Hatton in Liverpool – who had become a dominant force in local government. She made it sound like a crusade: 'While Neil Kinnock and his colleagues try to slap on another layer of make-up to conceal the face of the Labour left, it is actually there for all to see in Labour councils up and down the land.'

In 1989, after the poll tax had been introduced in Scotland, Mrs Thatcher was aware that her flagship had run into stormy seas. She replaced Mr Ridley, whose upper-class, eccentric manner put off many voters, with the far more credible figure of Chris Patten. But unlike Mr Ridley he did not believe in the policy; all Mr Patten could do at this stage was try to get another non-believer, the chancellor Nigel Lawson, to dish out more money from central funds to alleviate the problems. It was not enough. Apologists for the poll tax argue that it might have succeeded if the average payment could have been kept at a reasonable level. When the plans were being worked out in 1985 it was thought the tax would be levied at under £100 a head. By the time the scheme was implemented, five years later, the average was heading towards £400. At the time Mr Patten loyally tried to defend the tax, but in his interview for this book, he admitted ruefully that it was 'like a heat-seeking missile homing in on floating voters in marginal constituencies'.

The Conservatives were taking a beating in the opinion polls, and in the first by-election in England where voters had the chance to comment on the introduction of the Community Charge, on 22 March 1990, there was a swing of more than 20 per cent against the Tory candidate and the Conservatives lost the supposedly rock-solid seat of Mid-Staffordshire. By the time the great London riot took place at the end of the following week the poll tax was already looking as if it might wipe out the chances of Mrs Thatcher winning the next election, and this point began to weigh heavily on the minds of Tory MPs. An opinion poll taken a week after the terrible scenes in London suggested that just over 30 per cent of voters believed the riot was 'understandable' and 7 per cent thought it had been 'justified'.

Even as the disorder took place Mrs Thatcher was still trumpeting the benefits of the tax. She insisted that people would come to appreciate the advantages of knowing whether their councils were being extravagant. To cut down their poll tax bills, they could vote Conservative. On the same afternoon as the rioters progressed up Whitehall, she told a party conference, 'It costs £96 more for the privilege of living in Labour Warrington than in neighbouring Tory Trafford; £108 more in Labour Liverpool than in next-door Tory Wirral; and an appalling £399 more in Labour Camden than in adjoining Tory Westminster.' The prime minister said this in the comfort of Regency Cheltenham and seemed blind to the fact that the areas of high poll tax she referred to were far more deprived than the Tory areas she selected. The great majority of the people who lived in these poorer areas were unable to up sticks and move and saw little prospect of their councils suddenly switching to the Conservatives. Mrs Thatcher and her government appeared completely out of touch.

The anarchy in London and the many demonstrations in other parts of the country should have alerted Mrs Thatcher to the extreme political danger she faced, but after years in office it had become increasingly difficult for her to admit she might be mistaken. Members of her cabinet complained she had become more autocratic. Chris Patten believes Mrs Thatcher made the worst mistake of her career by introducing the poll tax because 'Her eye was off the ball.' Instead of concentrating on domestic issues – and the poll tax was by far the most important – she was obsessed by the problem which had captivated the leading members of the government: the twisted, tortured argument over the European Exchange Rate Mechanism. 'She was completely focused on the disagreements over ERM with Lawson and Howe,' Mr Patten told me. 'She was involved in a power play with her two most senior ministers. She wasn't actually thinking about the policy which had made her most unpopular, and that was the poll tax.' If there was a single cause for Mrs Thatcher's fall, it has to be this ill-conceived plan to reform domestic rates, and the reason she failed to give it a higher priority was yet again Europe. All roads, it seems, lead to Rome.

PRIME MINISTERS often seek solace in history; whatever problems they may be facing, they are slight in comparison with the great issues of war some of their predecessors had to confront. Anniversaries are often occasions when the occupant of Number 10 can afford to spend some time at least contemplating the good fortune of the present. In April 1990 I travelled with Mrs Thatcher to Turkey to commemorate the seventy-fifth anniversary of the disastrous Dardanelles campaign, the most serious mistake of Winston Churchill's career. On the plane Mrs Thatcher leafed through some letters from soldiers at the front. As she related the horrors of Gallipoli, seen through the eyes of those who had taken part, she was far more relaxed than usual. She was at her best with the veterans, all in their nineties. During a ceremony by the beach where they had landed one of the old soldiers found it difficult not to cry and she reached out to hold his hand. But it was only a brief respite from her problems at home. When she returned, the European issue was still waiting to be resolved.

WHAT MADE HER POSITION particularly difficult was that on the crucial question she was in a minority; almost all the other members of her cabinet were in favour of Britain joining the ERM. The only one who was deeply opposed to the idea was Nicholas Ridley, now the trade secretary; and he would be forced to resign in July in circumstances bordering on the farcical. His crime was to be rude to the Germans, even though his views were close to those of the prime minister. His mistake was to allow his remarks to be tape-recorded by Dominic Lawson, who happened to be the son of the former chancellor Nigel Lawson; more relevantly he was also the editor of the *Spectator* magazine, which published Mr Ridley's remarks in full.

This Conservative-supporting publication made every effort to highlight the insensitive nature of Mr Ridley's views. On the front cover a cartoon depicted Mr Ridley, paint bucket and brush in hand, running away from a portrait of Chancellor Kohl, whose features had been altered to include a Hitler moustache and a shock of black hair. The message was obvious: the trade secretary was convinced the Germans were back on the march. In his interview Mr Ridley described the drive towards economic and monetary union as 'a German racket designed to take over the whole of Europe'. He went on: 'It has to be thwarted. This rushed takeover by the Germans on the worst possible basis, with the French behaving like poodles to the Germans, is absolutely intolerable.' Mr Ridley was particularly scathing about the prospects for a European central bank to oversee the single currency. 'I am not against giving up sovereignty in principle, but not to this lot. You might as well give it to Adolf Hitler, frankly.' Dominic Lawson suggested that Chancellor Kohl was preferable to Hitler, adding, 'He's not going to bomb us, after all.' Mr Ridley was in no mood to agree. 'I'm not sure I wouldn't rather have the shelters and the chance to fight back, than simply being taken over by economics. He'll soon be coming here and trying to say this is what we should do on the banking front and this is what our taxes should be. I mean, he'll soon be trying to take over everything.' Mr Lawson asked Mr Ridley if his views were coloured by the fact that, at sixty-one, he could remember the Second World War. 'Jolly good thing, too,' Mr Ridley replied, effectively nailing down the lid on his own political career.

For the next two days Mrs Thatcher tried to resist the wave of calls for her trade secretary to resign, some of them from Conservative MPs. The problem was that in private she shared most of Mr Ridley's views, but if she backed him a serious diplomatic incident would be unavoidable. It was Saturday lunchtime on Radio 4 when I had the unenviable task of saying whether I thought he would be forced to go. I concluded that he would. Fortunately, by the time I made that broadcast the decision had already been taken: Mr Ridley was forced to resign even though he withdrew his remarks 'unreservedly'. The son of a viscount, he had an unworldly manner which could be charming or irritating, depending on whether or not you agreed with him. With his love of paradox and his rather patrician air, he liked to cut through conventional thinking.

I was once interviewing him about the poll tax when the lights went out in the studio at Westminster. I suggested, wrongly as it turned out, that we continue to talk because the audience would not notice. This was, after all, a radio interview. Surprisingly, the then secretary of state for the environment agreed. 'The poll tax,' he told me, 'will be a vote winner.' But hearing him say this in the blacked-out studio, it did seem as if he was whistling in the dark. He carried on regardless, having accepted the logical argument that the audience would not notice, and in doing so demonstrated one of his political weaknesses. Logic is not always the politician's best friend. His career would have advanced if he had relied more on common sense. He should have waited for the lights to go back on; and then he might have sounded more convincing.

About two weeks after Mr Ridley resigned Mrs Thatcher confessed that some of the things he had said in his interview with the *Spectator* were in tune with the feelings of people in Britain. It was also revealed that earlier in the year the prime minister had held a private seminar at Chequers to hear what six experts thought about the likely future role of the Germans in Europe. Again this caused a row because the summary of their proceedings, written by Mrs Thatcher's loyal foreign affairs expert Charles Powell, was leaked to the press. He described how the participants had noted some of the less flattering attributes of the German character in the past: angst, aggressiveness, assertiveness, bullying, egotism, an inferiority complex, sentimentality, self-pity and a longing to be liked. He then summed up their fears: 'The way in which the Germans used their elbows and threw their weight about in the European Community suggested that a lot had still not changed . . . No one had serious misgivings about the present leaders, but what about 10, 15 or 20 years from now? Could some of the unhappy characteristics of the past re-emerge with just as destructive consequences?' What made the leaking of this memo so embarrassing is that the ideas clearly chimed with what Mr Ridley had said, and — it was now hardly a secret — with Mrs Thatcher's own views.

ONE OF THE PRINCIPLES of good foreign policy is that there is no point carrying out an attack unless you can see it through. President Mitterrand was once asked why he did not mount a crusade against Colonel Gaddafi, the Libyan leader, who was for years the bête noire of the West. The French president shook his head and replied, 'I could put a stick in his eye and make him angry, but I could not remove him.' Mrs Thatcher, in her last year in office, managed to annoy the Germans but could do nothing to prevent the realization of two of their most important aims in the post-war period: the drive towards the single European currency, and their country's reunification. On 3 October the new united Germany was proclaimed, and two days later, as the move towards the euro gathered momentum, Britain finally joined the Exchange Rate Mechanism.

From the spring of 1990 Mrs Thatcher had regular discussions with her new chancellor, John Major, about whether Britain should soon join the ERM. Their talks were much easier for her than the brittle, sometimes brutal exchanges she had endured with his two predecessors at the Treasury: Nigel Lawson, now out of government, and Sir Geoffrey Howe, safely parked, it seemed, as leader of the House of Commons. The fact that Sir Geoffrey was also deputy prime minister did not seem to trouble Mrs Thatcher; he was no longer a member of the inner circle, and at no point was he even consulted. She found Mr Major far more congenial. He had nothing like the knowledge of economics which Mr Lawson had and was far less inclined to argue, but to her annoyance he too was in favour of joining the ERM. Mrs Thatcher's position was also weakened because her close adviser on these matters Sir Alan Walters, whose reappointment had triggered the final row with Mr Lawson, was no longer working with her at Number 10. He had felt obliged to resign at the same time as Mr Lawson, despite Mrs Thatcher's pleas that he should stay on.

Mrs Thatcher believed that Mr Major had become far too keen on appeasing other European governments, who were pressing for Britain to join, and was not impressed by his argument that entry to the ERM was a way of keeping the Conservative party together. But she finally acquiesced. One of my best scoops as a political journalist was to reveal on the BBC *Today* programme on Radio 4 that a senior member of the cabinet had told me that Britain would soon join the ERM. As he put it, 'The Rubicon has been crossed.' I made the broadcast a few weeks before the announcement. Because I had been given this information in confidence, I could not reveal that my source was none other than the chancellor of the exchequer, John Major. Having pushed aside her two previous chancellors, Margaret Thatcher could not afford to get rid of a third. And there were powerful forces arrayed against her. The only argument for the ERM she found attractive was that it would bring an immediate fall in interest rates, which were up at the startling level of 15 per cent. In my interview with Mr Major in 2003 I suggested that he had managed to persuade Mrs Thatcher of the case for joining. 'Are you suggesting,' he replied with mock surprise, 'that we have a young, inexperienced chancellor of the exchequer who in some mysterious way overrules, outmanoeuvres and outbids a dominant prime minister eleven years in office?' His gentle satire could not conceal his bitterness at the way he has been made to take most of the blame.

For Mr Major the decision to join the ERM remains the greatest mistake of his political life. It destroyed his government's credibility when during his premiership in 1992 the pound was forced out of the mechanism, and he is determined that Mrs Thatcher should not escape the consequences of what was ultimately her decision. He rejects the suggestion made by Thatcher loyalists that in some way, 'She did not know what she was doing.' As he made his argument Mr Major only just managed to contain his temper, throwing out his points like bullets from a gun. 'We are told on the one hand that Margaret was a master of detail and knew exactly what she was doing; yet here is a subject that she had been discussing for six years with her foreign secretary Geoffrey Howe, her chancellor Nigel Lawson and his successor as chancellor John Major. And after six years this titan of British politics did not understand the subject. Is that a credible proposition?'

Mr Major prefers to base his argument on a series of propositions he does not agree with, but the rising tone of his voice and the baleful glare from behind his glasses made me want to take cover. 'Are people suggesting,' he goes on, 'that on an issue that was the central plank of economic policy, the first lord of the Treasury, who'd been discussing it with her three most senior economic advisers for six years, did not understand what it was about? Such a suggestion is quite simply preposterous.'

He seemed to be daring me to contradict him. I did not do so, but I did suggest that Mrs Thatcher believed the ERM would not be such a rigid system as it later became, that there would be greater leeway for the pound. He dismissed the idea. 'Of course she knew that,' he said. 'Not a shadow of doubt that she knew that. And indeed if it wasn't rigid what would be the point of it? The whole purpose of going into the ERM was that we had tried interest rate policy to curb inflation and we had been forced to give way.' He scoffed at the implication that Mrs Thatcher was in favour of devaluation. 'Devaluation? Margaret? You can't be suggesting she thought devaluation was right?'

Mr Major told me Mrs Thatcher could easily have stopped him going ahead, but she never even tried. Inflation to her was one of the great evils, hitting the weakest hardest, and in particular small businesses – like her father's shop in Grantham – which simply could not survive if interest rates were too high. Every other method had been used to try to bring down inflation; reluctantly she concluded the time was finally right to give the ERM a try. There was no question of Mr Major or indeed any other senior member of the government threatening to resign.

In the end, her only objection was over the entry level. She wanted the central rate of exchange to be three Deutschmarks to the pound, but she was persuaded that the lower rate of 2.95 would be safer. As it was, the pound was locked into the system at too high a rate against the German currency. If Mrs Thatcher had got her way the eventual devaluation, and all that followed, would have occurred much sooner. Mr Major, who was being explicit about this for the first time, said, 'So those people who subsequently said she and others warned us of going in at such high rate are wrong; she wished to go in at a more punitive rate.'

Mrs Thatcher's private secretary John Whittingdale told me how she had interrupted a meeting of her advisers in the cabinet room at Number 10. The door opened and in came the prime minister, looking rather sour. 'We are about to announce that we are entering the ERM,' she said. 'But I've got a cut in interest rates.' She argued later that even the most determined leader could not stand against the cabinet, the parliamentary party, the industrial lobby and the press. But not every influential voice had joined the chorus in favour of the ERM. The party chairman Kenneth Baker told me of a meeting with her the day before the announcement in which he had pleaded with her not to join. She was not prepared to listen. 'Isn't it marvellous,' she said, trying to sound excited, 'there's going to be a reduction of one per cent in the interest rates.' Mrs Thatcher would have hated to give in to Nigel Lawson and Sir Geoffrey Howe. She had found it much easier to concede to her new favourite, John Major. It was her last significant policy decision before she was forced out of office.

9

Mrs Thatcher goes too far

BRITAIN'S ENTRY INTO the Exchange Rate Mechanism coupled with a one per cent drop in interest rates was greeted with the kind of euphoria which only comes after a period of stress. If one looks back on this sorry episode, it is hard to believe how it united opinion across the parties and produced a warm glow in the capitals of Europe. The Euro-sceptics in the Tory party, still very much in the minority, tried to dampen the mood, as did politicians from the opposition parties, who were worried that the Tories had pulled off a coup. But the great majority of commentators appeared to believe that the rather mild figure of John Major had parted the waters of the Red Sea and shown the Conservatives the way out of their difficulties. He was immediately spoken of as a possible successor to Mrs Thatcher.

In party political terms, the timing was impeccable. The announcement came on the last day of the Labour conference and just a few days before the Conservatives were due to meet in Bournemouth. For political correspondents, a lacklustre conference season had come alive. I was certainly in favour of Britain joining the ERM; I saw it as a way of providing financial discipline as well as improving our relations with the rest of Europe. In Brussels it was taken as a sign that Britain would eventually come round to the idea of a single currency. Mrs Thatcher was quick to say she had no intention of giving up the pound, but she was not averse to the suggestion that the government had set itself on a course which would reduce internal party tensions and perhaps provide some economic stability.

Political pundits have long derided party conferences as largely stage-managed affairs which tell you little about the state of British politics, but in my experience those few days by the seaside, cooped up with the enthusiasts and their often rather less confident leaders, provide a useful way of gauging a party's mood. If nothing much happens, that can be as telling as dramatic events. The Conservative conference of 1990 was as interesting as any I had attended. For a start there was Mr Major's speech, which was most unusual for a chancellor. Instead of concentrating on economic matters he went into detail about his poor background as a child and why he was a Conservative. It struck me as a clear indication that he thought a vacancy for the leadership might not be far away, and he was anxious to be considered as a possible candidate. Then there was an angry debate about the BBC, a sure sign that a party is unhappy with its image. I never minded much if politicians made general attacks on the BBC – they made us seem important – it was only when they personalized their remarks that I began to feel uncomfortable. Fortunately that was fairly rare.

If I had been able to peer into the future I would have spent more time following the activities of the two figures later to play such crucial parts in the downfall of Mrs Thatcher: Sir Geoffrey Howe and Michael Heseltine. Even though Sir Geoffrey was the deputy prime minister, he had not been consulted by Mrs Thatcher on the decision to join the ERM, not was it ever debated in cabinet. Just before the announcement a message from Number 10 had been sent to await his arrival at Balmoral, where he was due to start an official visit to the Queen. Sir Geoffrey failed to pick up the message before his first meeting and so found himself at a loss when the Queen referred to that morning's main news. As he comments dryly in his memoirs, 'She must have thought it a little odd that the only member of her cabinet who had been dealing with the subject since 1979 (apart from the prime minister) was apparently the last to hear of the government's position. It was a dramatic signal to me personally of the impossibility of securing the sort of effective working partnership with Margaret for which I had genuinely hoped when I decided to stay in the government in the previous July.'

In Bournemouth we were not, of course, privy to that extraordinary snub by Mrs Thatcher against the most senior member of her cabinet. It would have been a political sensation if the story had leaked out at the time, but Sir Geoffrey, loyal to the end, kept it to himself. He also did not comment in public on the fact that he had been excluded from the list of cabinet ministers who would make speeches in the main conference hall. He had to make do with two fringe meetings in which his dissent was so heavily coded that it did not provide a great deal of journalistic copy. At one of his meetings Sir Geoffrey applauded the decision to join the Exchange Rate Mechanism. He said the decision should be seen as all of a piece with the central thrust of the government's economic policy over the preceding ten years, and certainly not as some 'fresh surrender of British sovereignty to the dominance of the Deutschmark' but rather as 'a firm commitment to share in the management of a wider system'. Without making his disagreement with Mrs Thatcher too obvious, Sir Geoffrey gave the clear impression that Britain should join in moves towards European economic and monetary union. This is precisely what Mrs Thatcher was determined to avoid.

Michael Heseltine had spent a good deal of energy during 1990 denying that he was preparing a challenge against Mrs Thatcher. He had argued against the poll tax before he resigned from the cabinet in 1986 and had supported a backbench Tory proposal for the system to be banded in order to reflect people's ability to pay. But it was on Europe, inevitably, that the line between his approach and that of Mrs Thatcher continued to be drawn. At the Bournemouth conference he decided once again to play the loyalty card; and he could do this more easily now that the decision had been taken to join the ERM. I went round to see him in his room at the Royal Bath Hotel and he showed me the speech he would deliver at a fringe meeting. My disappointment that it was not particularly controversial was matched by his satisfaction that I could not portray it as a leadership bid. For some years now I had watched him play this part, and it was as unconvincing as ever. He obviously thought he had a chance of becoming leader, but he was not inclined to give Mrs Thatcher the ammunition she needed to shoot him down.

Fortunately for Mr Heseltine his speech was delivered at the same time as Nicholas Ridley spoke at another fringe meeting, and most of the press coverage contrasted the different approaches to Europe of these two former cabinet ministers. Mr Ridley did not repeat his inflammatory remarks about the Germans which had caused his recent resignation but he was highly critical of the ERM decision. Prophetically he warned that the decision to join the mechanism was doomed because the pound and the German mark 'will never have a stable relationship'. He predicted, rightly as it turned out, that the currencies would diverge over the next two years. But this was not what loyal Conservatives wanted to hear a week after the ERM decision had been announced. Mr Heseltine was, by contrast, keen to 'salute' John Major and express his delight at British membership of the ERM. When asked by reporters about Mr Ridley's remarks the former defence secretary was able to say, 'Mr Ridley does not agree with the British government. I happen to support the government.' The size of their audiences demonstrated a telling point.

They both attracted about five hundred people; the Conservatives were split down the middle over Europe.

By the end of the week the euphoria of the ERM announcement had disappeared as abruptly as it had arrived. The conference took on a nervous and troubled air. The last time the Conservatives had held a party conference in Bournemouth was the year before their landslide victory in 1987. Then they were bursting with confidence; this time they were beginning to look as if they were running out of steam. As often happens, much would depend on the leader's speech on Friday, and three hours before Mrs Thatcher spoke the latest inflation figures were released, providing yet further evidence that entry into the ERM was by no means the end of Britain's economic woes. Inflation over the year had risen to 10.9 per cent, the highest figure for eight years, and – horribly significant in political terms – higher than the 10.3 per cent Mrs Thatcher had inherited from Labour when she first came into office in 1979. It was more than double the European average and reinforced doubts in the financial markets of the wisdom of cutting interest rates by one per cent to 14 per cent on the back of the ERM announcement the week before. The 'Thatcher miracle' was coming back to earth.

This sense of déjà vu was reinforced by Mrs Thatcher's speech. She promised more privatization – British Rail and the major ports – a tough approach to law and order, and a determined fight against inflation. The Conservative agenda for the 1990s was beginning to look suspiciously like the Conservative agenda of the 1980s. The impression Mrs Thatcher herself gave of having passed her sell-by date is one of my abiding memories of the occasion. When I discussed the chances of Mr Major becoming leader on Radio 4's *The World at One* I could not help thinking afterwards – not that I would have been rash enough to say it – that in a year's time he could be giving the main speech. The cries of 'Ten more years' still rang out from the Tory faithful – and they gave her a nine-minute standing ovation – but even Mrs Thatcher's brave attempts at humour did little to lighten the mood.

In her last conference speech as prime minister, the most striking passage was a joke at the expense of the Liberal Democrats, who had unveiled a new yellow logo, a stylized 'bird of freedom'. Her advisers suggested a comparison with the dead parrot which had featured in one of the most famous *Monty Python* sketches on television starring John Cleese. The parrot had not merely been stunned, it had ceased to be; it had expired. How convenient it would be for the Conservatives if the bird representing the resurgent third party could be disadvantaged in the same way. Mrs Thatcher's aides were confident of a laugh as well as a cheer, but she needed some persuading. According to her political secretary John Whittingdale she had not heard of *Monty Python*, and assumed he was a character. 'Is he one of us?' she anxiously enquired. In the hall the parrot joke went down reasonably well, but looked a bit lame a week later when the Liberal Democrats overturned a big Conservative majority in the Eastbourne by-election. For Mrs Thatcher the result merely added to her deep sense of loss. Her old friend and former parliamentary private secretary Ian Gow had been the MP for Eastbourne before he was blown up at his home by the IRA.

EVERY SIX MONTHS a different member state takes over the presidency of the European Union. This system gives each country the chance to stamp its influence on the political agenda, and in the last six months of 1990 the presidency of the European Community, as it was still called, was in the hands of Italy. Not only did this mean that a European summit would be held within its borders during this period; Italy could also hold a special summit if the other member states agreed.

The fact that the treaty setting up the European Economic Community had been signed in Rome in 1957 and that Italy had been one of the six founding members, was a continuing source of national pride. Visitors to such a strikingly independent country with a vigorous individual culture were often surprised by how keen successive Italian governments were on moves towards the closer integration of Europe. In part this was due to the sheer number of successive Italian governments, many lasting only a matter of months. Italian politics was known for its lack of stability, its laxity over inflation and its tendency towards corruption. It was not only cynics who suggested that if they couldn't get proper government from Rome, they might as well throw in their lot with Brussels.

The Italians had decided to hold an extra summit with a view to speeding up decisions on 'economic and monetary union', the description invariably used to describe the path towards a single currency. No one knew the currency would be called the euro, nor indeed whether it would actually come into existence, but it had been decided that this would be a matter to be looked into over the following year by the member states in a series of meetings called the Intergovernmental Conference or IGC. The special summit in Rome was later described as an ambush on Mrs Thatcher; she was certainly poorly prepared for what happened. All the other member states were keen to demonstrate their support for economic and monetary union, but she was not. To the dismay of Sir Geoffrey Howe and other pro-European Conservatives, Mrs Thatcher made no secret of her implacable opposition. What could have been a routine summit passed into legend as the moment when Mrs Thatcher finally ran out of European allies. Chancellor Kohl and President Mitterrand, with help from the Italians, forced her into a corner; she had been completely outmanoeuvred.

During interviews she gave in Rome, the prime minister

dismissively described her European colleagues as 'on their way to cloud cuckoo land'. She insisted that Britain would veto 'the very idea' of a single currency. When news of what she had said in Rome was broadcast I was phoned at home by the political editor of the BBC, my old friend John Cole. Neither of us had gone to Rome because ironically our news editors had concluded that this was not a political story; it was therefore being covered by diplomatic staff and correspondents based in Brussels. Normally we were scrupulous when discussing news stories not to express our own political views. This time, he asked me bluntly, 'What do you think?' I was careful not to react too strongly, but I did say, 'I think she's gone too far.'

When the prime minister reported back to the Commons on the outcome of the summit, she appeared not in the least downhearted at what had happened. The final score in the match with the other member states might have been eleven to one against, but she was convinced that she had been in the right, and that was all that seemed to matter. It was on this occasion that she gave her famous reply of 'No, no, no' to a question on the possibility of increased powers for the European institutions. But it was the way she poured cold water on the British proposal for currency reform which so enraged Sir Geoffrey and indeed John Major. The new chancellor had been promoting what was called the hard Ecu, which now seems a weirdly complicated plan compared with the simplicity of the euro. The idea was that businesses would be able to avoid some of the risks of currency fluctuations by dealing in an artificial currency similar to the existing Ecu, or European Currency Unit. This was used in the budgets of the European institutions, and was based on a weighted average of all the currencies in the EC. The suggestion was that the Ecu could be traded on foreign exchange markets, and as it was less likely to fluctuate in value, would be called the hard Ecu. For British diplomats, the proposal had the great advantage of appearing to go some way towards answering the demands of the other member states for economic and monetary union, while Mr Major was originally able to sell the idea to Mrs Thatcher because the system would be entirely voluntary. It could be called a common currency, but it was certainly not a single currency. All the existing European currencies, including the pound, would still circulate in the normal way.

Mrs Thatcher, becoming increasingly intemperate as she answered questions in the Commons, made it clear she had no faith in her own government's proposal. 'In my view it would not become widely used . . . I do not believe that will happen.' Mr Major admitted years later what a blow this had been: 'I nearly fell off the bench. With this single sentence she wrecked months of work and preparation.' Other European leaders already suspected that the hard Ecu proposal was merely a device to head off a single currency; now it seemed Mrs Thatcher had confirmed their suspicions. It was as if something inside the prime minister had snapped. For Euro-sceptics it was a bravura performance, and many Tory MPs cheered her on. She accused the European Commission of striving to extinguish democracy; she railed against the danger of a federal Europe and she insisted it would be utterly wrong to abolish the pound because it was 'the greatest expression of sovereignty'. Most of her cabinet were startled, more by the stridency of her attack than by what she actually said. Her views were given all the more prominence because after years of wrangling the Commons had agreed to be televised. On the BBC six o'clock news that evening I had a feast of pictures and comment with which to tell the story. The novelty value alone gave the story tremendous impact.

Privately, I was shaken by what had happened. It seemed as if all the usual conventions of diplomacy had been thrown onto a bonfire. Mrs Thatcher had over the years provided us with an enormous range of colourful stories; during her time in office there were few working days at Westminster when at some point I had not typed her name. But on this occasion she was flouting convention to a degree which was genuinely disturbing. Often in the past she had been excused on the grounds that this was simply Mrs Thatcher being Mrs Thatcher. She was unique: she did not fit the stereotype of a senior politician. But now she seemed to have lost control; it was difficult to see how her approach could do anything but harm to Britain's position. The prime minister appeared to have taken President Mitterrand's advice about not putting a stick in someone's eye and totally reversed it. She was using the stick with a vengeance, and as a result she appeared to have angered most of Britain's key allies to no obvious purpose. Mrs Thatcher's performance in the Commons sent a shock wave through the British political establishment.

When the future of a leading politician is thrown into question, they are often asked to consider their position. On this occasion there were no calls for Sir Geoffrey Howe to resign but he hardly needed the advice of others to realize the moment had come to decide whether to continue in office. After what Mrs Thatcher had said he did not need much convincing that it was time for him to go. Two days after her flare-up in the Commons Sir Geoffrey had a formal meeting with the prime minister at Number 10. As he stood there, she read his resignation letter and concluded, 'I can see now why we shouldn't be able to change your mind. You've obviously thought a lot about it.' For the first time Sir Geoffrey could remember, they shook hands, and one of the most productive relationships in recent political history was over. His letter made clear that their key differences were over European policy. More than one form of economic and monetary union was possible. 'The important thing is not to rule in or out any one particular solution absolutely,' he wrote. It was to form the basis of British policy for many years to come, but not until Mrs Thatcher had left Downing Street. In her letter in reply, Mrs Thatcher claimed their differences over Europe were not nearly as great as Sir Geoffrey suggested. This was not simply a matter of playing down splits within her cabinet at the time; even years later in her memoirs Mrs Thatcher was oddly reluctant to concede a major rift between them: 'In his resignation letter Geoffrey had not spelt out any significant policy differences between us.' She also said it was a relief that he had gone. But that was not her mood when a fortnight after the Rome summit Sir Geoffrey made his resignation speech in the Commons with Nigel Lawson sitting next to him as a sign of support. It was the most dramatic, the most devastating attack on a sitting prime minister that anyone could remember. Much of its force stemmed from the fact that for years Sir Geoffrey had been ultra-loyal; he never usually raised his voice or displayed his temper. Now he turned on Mrs Thatcher with a cool savagery that left his colleagues literally gasping with surprise. One of them could be seen on television wincing as each blow was struck. The prime minister tried to look composed; she later admitted to being shocked. She said it was like being in the dock for a capital offence.

Sir Geoffrey began in a fairly low key, speaking of the Exchange Rate Mechanism and how it would have been preferable if the government had followed Mr Lawson's advice and gone in five years earlier – the present high inflation might have been avoided. He revealed how both of them had threatened to resign if Mrs Thatcher had not agreed to pave the way for entry at the Madrid summit. His mood hardened. He became personal, suggesting that the prime minister always complained of 'surrendering sovereignty'. She conjured up a nightmare image of a Europe 'positively teeming with ill-intentioned people, scheming, in her words to extinguish democracy, to lead us through the back door into a federal Europe'. As for the prime minister's rejection of her own government's proposal for a hard Ecu, Sir Geoffrey was scathing: 'It is rather like sending your opening batsmen to the crease only for them to find, the moment the first balls are bowled, that their bats have been broken before the game by the team captain.' The prime minister's perceived attitude towards Europe, he said, was running increasingly serious risks for the future of the country. It threatened to minimize our influence. 'If we detach ourselves completely, as a party or a nation, from the middle ground of Europe, the effects will be incalculable and very hard ever to correct.' Sir Geoffrey ended on an ominous note which many took as a call to arms. By resigning he had done what he believed to be right for his party and his country. 'The time has now come for others to consider their own response to the tragic conflict of loyalties with which I have myself wrestled for perhaps too long.'

The next day, with all eyes upon him, Michael Heseltine took the most important decision of his life. For a politician often described by his supporters as a man of destiny, there was something irresistible about his challenge. It was a monumental gamble, but when faced with difficult decisions he had often relied on instinct not rational calculation. It went against the conclusion he had reached after nearly five years out of the cabinet, that his interests would best be served waiting for her to resign, perhaps after she had lost the next election. He could see the dangers as clearly as anyone. He had not colluded with Geoffrey Howe; indeed he had had no idea Sir Geoffrey would make such a powerful speech. There was no conspiracy. The only threat Mr Heseltine faced was from those Conservative MPs who told him that if he ducked out now they could no longer support him. If there was going to be a leadership election that year, nominations had to be in by noon the next day, just two days after Sir Geoffrey's resignation speech. Mr Heseltine did not wait; he announced that day he would fight Mrs Thatcher for the leadership of the Conservative party.

10

Murder through the front door

ONE OF THE MOST SURPRISING elements in the story of Mrs Thatcher's removal from office is the ease with which she was forced into a formal contest for the leadership. It is as if the front door of the victim's home was left deliberately open on the night of the murder. As often happens in politics, it was an accident of history. The Conservative party was acting according to the rules operating at the time. These rules had been designed twenty-five years earlier to address a very different problem from the one which now faced Mrs Thatcher. In all the long years during which she had dominated the party, no one had thought it necessary to review her ability to survive a leadership challenge. Only when the rules began to pose a threat to the prime minister were the alarm bells sounded, and by then it was far too late to change the party's constitution.

In as much as anyone was personally responsible for devising these rules, this dubious honour goes to a young Conservative MP, Humphrey Berkeley, whose subsequent career hardly endeared him to the Tories. He left the Conservatives, joined Labour; left Labour and joined the Social Democratic party; and finally rejoined Labour. The journalist Alan Watkins describes him as having a scornful expression and a superior manner, and he supports this description with an alarming story of how Mr Berkeley was leaving a Chinese restaurant with the political commentator Anthony Howard. Noticing that his shoelace was undone, Mr Berkeley summoned a waiter and asked him to retie it. Mr Howard was so embarrassed that he knelt down and took over the task himself. It is not always the most deserving who make history, but at least in this case it is appropriately a footnote for which Mr Berkeley is known.

The Conservatives were slow to embrace the concept of internal party democracy. When Harold Macmillan resigned as prime minister in 1963 after a prostate operation, on the mistaken assumption that he had not long to live – he went on for another twenty-three years – there was no question of choosing his successor through formal election. Lord Home, who renounced his peerage to become plain Sir Alec Douglas Home, emerged as leader from a series of consultations carried out by senior members of the party known as the Magic Circle. Supporters of other candidates were appalled by what looked all too like a conjuring trick. The lack of any kind of proper process made it even more difficult to play down Sir Alec's aristocratic lineage. His appeal to the general public was far less than that of his rival Harold Wilson, who was skilfully promoted as an HP Sauce-loving beer drinker with an impeccable northern accent. Mr Wilson kept his enjoyment of cigars and brandy away from the public gaze, and played down the fact that he had been a senior civil servant and an Oxford academic before becoming an MP. Sir Alec was annoyed at the way Mr Wilson kept calling him the fourteenth Earl of Home and famously replied that he was the fourteenth Mr Wilson, but after Labour won the election of 1964 the Tories decided their way of choosing a leader was beyond a joke. Democracy, they agreed, should be given a chance.

Humphrey Berkeley was a keen supporter of the ablest of Sir Alec's rivals, Iain Macleod – one of the many best prime ministers we never had – and was sufficiently upset by the exclusion of his hero to mount a campaign for reform. An obsessive letter writer, he managed to win over Sir Alec to his cause and eventually produced what became known as the Berkeley Memorandum, which was accepted as the basis for the voting system. It had one strange element, which would only become crucially important in the vote which brought down Mrs Thatcher many years later. On the first ballot, and only on the first ballot, the winning candidate would have to gain not only a simple majority but an additional 15 per cent of the total votes cast. The idea was to allow for the effect caused by toadying MPs voting for their beloved leader in the first round. To get a true result, it was argued, you had to allow 15 per cent for undesirable sycophancy. By accepting this strange rule the party leadership had shown how apprehensive they were about this jump into the unknown. Oh for the Magic Circle, some of them undoubtedly thought. Then we knew what we were doing.

Sir Alec Douglas Home and his colleagues were prepared to accept the principle of an open election, but only up to a point. They were certainly not prepared to accede to the idea of voting each year for their leader. That might be too much of a good thing. 'The thought was,' Sir Alec later recalled, 'that once a party had elected a leader that was that, and it had better stay with him.' He did not need to refer to the possibility of the leader being a woman because that was generally assumed to be out of the question. When Sir Edward Heath became leader he accepted one of Mr Berkeley's original suggestions that provision should also be made for the periodic election of the party leader. In 1975 a clause was inserted into the rules allowing for an annual election. The indefatigable Mr Berkeley explained: 'You see, the point was that Ted thought he would win, so he was not worried about an annual challenge in the autumn of 1990.' Given the antipathy between Sir Edward and Mrs Thatcher, it is tempting to jump to the conclusion that he might be pleased to have introduced the rule which finished her off as leader. That is if one forgets that it was the same rule which enabled her, many years before, to dislodge him as leader. Until Mrs Thatcher was challenged by

Sir Anthony Meyer in 1989 the only other time a Conservative leader had been called to defend themselves in an annual contest was when Mrs Thatcher took on Sir Edward in 1975, and won.

The prospect of another leadership challenge in the Autumn of 1990, just a year after Sir Anthony's attempt, should have put Mrs Thatcher on her mettle. She had been warned that many more MPs than the sixty or so who had deserted her on that occasion might fail to support her this time. Her popularity in the country, and therefore her electoral chances within the party, had sharply declined over the year, mainly as a result of the poll tax and the return of high inflation. Although it was still thought unlikely that Mr Heseltine would mount a challenge – on the grounds that 'He who wields the dagger never wins the crown' – there were plenty of Westminster rumours that a candidate of some sort would let their name go forward, and it only needed two sponsoring Conservative MPs for the challenge to be allowed. It might take two to tango, but with three you had a plot. The BBC was accused of 'irresponsibility' by the founder of the SDP, David Owen, when it ran a report of mine which strongly suggested another leadership election would take place that year.

The story was broadcast a week after Sir Geoffrey Howe resigned but before his devastating resignation speech, on the day Mrs Thatcher announced the practical details of when the election would take place – if there was an election. She was not convinced there would be one that year. The details of the arrangements turned out to be highly significant because it was the prime minister herself who decided that she would be in Paris on 20 November, the day the first ballot would be held and the result known. She would be there for a grand summit, the Conference on Security and Cooperation in Europe (CSCE), together with all the main world leaders, including President Bush, President Gorbachev, Chancellor Kohl and

President Mitterrand, to celebrate the end of the Cold War. I believe she chose that setting for herself in order to play down the significance of any vote cast in London. She would be on the world stage, and people like me who concentrated on the politics of Westminster would be made to look peripheral against the background of such a momentous occasion. The leadership election could have been held up to a fortnight later. It was a classic case of hubris, of pride before the fall.

When Mrs Thatcher made the arrangements for the election she did not know that Sir Geoffrey Howe was about to make the speech of his life, nor that Mr Heseltine would feel duty bound to challenge her. All this happened within eight days, the time she had allowed between the announcement of the election details and the deadline for nominations. The political world was suddenly transformed; and Mrs Thatcher made the biggest tactical mistake of her career by not properly appreciating the enormity of that change. She had judged that allowing only eight days for her enemies to mount a challenge would cause them serious difficulties. Instead it forced them to act quickly; given more time they might have had second thoughts. She was also not sufficiently concerned that being in Paris on the eve of the poll would take her away from Westminster at a time when she might have to rally last-minute support.

Mrs Thatcher's leadership campaign hardly deserves that description. Her personal involvement was very limited. She decided to rely on her friends and advisers, as she had the year before. Given there was a threat to the position of the head of government, it may seem odd that the resources of government were not put at the prime minister's disposal. But in the British system a distinction – not always a clear one – is made between government activity and party politics. A Conservative leadership election falls definitely into the category of party politics. Civil servants, including Sir Bernard Ingham, would be expected to have nothing to do with the matter. Sir Bernard was surprised by some of the decisions taken by Mrs Thatcher's campaign team, but that was not his department. The most significant consequence of this division between party and government was that Mrs Thatcher could not employ the usual method for ensuring support, the government whips' office in the House of Commons. Mrs Thatcher's campaign was lacking the two ingredients which had served her so well in the past: her personal involvement and a dedicated, skilful team.

The prime minister was poorly served by those put in charge of her ad hoc organization. They made the classic mistake of courtiers: they told her what she wanted to hear. Many MPs lied about whether they would support her, but her campaign managers knew this was likely and they should have made greater allowance for the natural duplicity of politicians in these circumstances. 'You can count on me, old boy' was one of the phrases I overheard as I encountered the prime minister's team on their wary way round Westminster. But Promises are easy to make when the ballot is secret; I once heard the same MP give a similarly cheerful response when approached by Mr Heseltine's men as they too prowled the precincts. Lies and disinformation are the stuff of leadership elections when the electorate is made up entirely of MPs. It was an exhilarating time to be a political correspondent, with rumour fast replaced by counter-rumour, and everyone thrilled at playing a part, however small, in a moment of history.

Mrs Thatcher's parliamentary private secretary Peter Morrison behaved as if his role mattered less than it did, and afterwards he would be overcome by remorse. Much of the blame for what went wrong fell upon this tall, overweight, former public schoolboy. Often red in the face from too much drink, he seemed wrongly cast from the beginning; he was never in the top drawer of senior politicians. The great diarist Alan Clark – that funny, absurd and shocking member of the Thatcher circle – describes how he went to see Mr Morrison

1. *Right*. Welcome to the world of the photo opportunity. Mrs Thatcher fondles a new-born calf in the Suffolk constituency of John Gummer (on her left) during the election campaign of 1979. She was quick to realize that a striking picture was all that mattered, even though its meaning was obscure.

2. *Below.* Probably the best day of her life. Mrs Thatcher becomes the first woman prime minister on 4 May 1979.

3. Edward Heath addresses the Conservative party conference in 1981 while a ghostly Mrs Thatcher looks on. He regarded her as the spectre at the feast. He could never get over the fact that she had replaced him as leader.

4. With the president on the lawn of the White House, 1985. This really was a special relationship: even Ronald Reagan's dog Lucky refuses to play the role of poodle.

5. Kindred spirits: party chairman Norman Tebbit and Margaret Thatcher in 1985. Like so many of the closest relationships between senior Conservatives during this period, it did not last. But for a time even their opponents admitted that they made the 'political weather'.

6. Mrs Thatcher as political superstar visiting a monastery at Zagorsk, near Moscow, in 1987. On her left the indefatigable Chris Moncrieff of the Press Association struggles to catch every word. The author took this picture.

7. On her triumphant trip to Moscow to visit the Soviet president Mikhail Gorbachev in 1987, Mrs Thatcher delights in her role of Cold War peacemaker with the 'man she could do business with'. The phrase had been thought up by her faithful press secretary Bernard Ingham.

8. The assassin with the golden hair. Michael Heseltine after resigning from the cabinet in 1986 unofficially decides to run for prime minister. But this is London not Washington, and he ends up coining the phrase, 'He who wields the dagger never wins the crown.'

9. The Diva and the Bear: Mrs Thatcher and Sir Geoffrey Howe at a European summit in 1986. Two of the most disparate personalities formed one of the most successful partnerships in British politics – until he sparked off the revolt which brought her down.

10. In St James's Park Mrs Thatcher attempts the role of litter collector with her even less appropriately cast environment secretary Nicholas Ridley. They shared a deep suspicion of 'the Germans' but only he was forced to resign from the cabinet as a result of his nationalist views.

11. However hard Helmut Kohl tried, 'the electricity never flowed'. Mrs Thatcher's pursed lips at a press conference in 1988 only hint at her total lack of warmth for the German chancellor.

12. François Mitterrand and Mrs Thatcher, not unusually, facing different ways at a summit in Paris in 1989. The French president once famously described her as a cross between Marilyn Monroe and the Roman tyrant Caligula; but he wasn't perfect either.

13. *Above*. The author with the prime minister's private secretary Charles, later Lord, Powell at the seventy-fifth anniversary of the Gallipoli landings in Turkey in 1990. Mrs Thatcher's handbag can clearly be seen on the left of the picture. Pity the cameraman didn't seem to realize who was carrying it.

14. *Left*. 'She's behind you': the pantomime moment outside the British embassy in Paris two days before Mrs Thatcher resigned. Endlessly repeated, this became one of the most famous incidents in the short history of TV news. I did not mind. It made my name.

15. John and Norma Major pose for the media in Downing Street after the announcement that he is to become the new prime minister. He is determined to 'be his own man'.

16. But Mrs Thatcher cannot resist upstaging her protégé. This is the widely publicized picture which appears to sum up the scene: Mrs Thatcher looks down from an upstairs window. From the start of his premiership Mr Major can never entirely escape the impression he is not big enough to fill her shoes.

17. The end. Mrs Thatcher is driven away from Number 10 and the job she loved. Neither she nor the Conservative party would fully recover for many years afterwards. Mark Thatcher looks on.

in his office in the Commons the day before the vote. After his usual, fairly liquid lunch, Mr Morrison was snoring lightly in his leather armchair. 'This was the most critical day of the election,' Mr Clark wrote in his diary, describing how he woke him up and told him how worried he was about the way things were going.

A bleary Mr Morrison replied, 'Do you think I'd be like this if I wasn't entirely confident?' Pressed on the actual calculations the campaign team had made, Mrs Thatcher's parliamentary aide, whose job it was to keep her in touch with backbench opinion, was a little less sure. 'I've got Michael on 115,' he said. 'It could be 124 at the worst.' That would have enabled Mrs Thatcher to win easily on the first ballot. Mr Morrison could have done with the sort of aggressive behind-the-scenes skills of someone like the former deputy chief whip Tristan Garel-Jones, who had been on the team the year before; but Mr Garel-Jones and others skilled in Parliament's black arts were not signed up.

The Labour leader James Callaghan used to reflect ruefully on his time at Number 10, and in particular on how quickly a prime minister could lose touch. 'A few weeks?' it might be suggested. 'A few days,' he would reply with a smile. A prime minister, cocooned within the government machine, often knows little about the feelings of ordinary MPs. Members of the Number 10 staff may sometimes conclude that it is better if they do not know; and in Mrs Thatcher's time the whips did not always want their methods to be open to scrutiny from the top. When fighting to maintain support for the government line, all that mattered to them was that she should win the important votes. It is ironic that when she needed them most they were not available to help.

The methods used by the whips' office during the Thatcher years varied from the fairly ordinary to the deliberately under-hand. Canvassing support is a polite way of describing what happened; in practice it could get fairly dirty. There was often an element of subterfuge. The MP being canvassed frequently did not know his or her views were being sought; they might believe they were simply having a private conversation with someone whom they could trust. It was when that person reported to the whips' office that pressure on the potential rebel was brought to bear. Sometimes it was simply a matter of getting their constituency chairman to ring up and say how worrying it was that they appeared to be ready to join a revolt. In other cases the whips' office might have managed in the past to stifle a damaging press report; they might even have prevented a sex scandal involving the MP from getting into the press. One of the whips would simply remind the potential rebel of this favour and suggest, in the mildest possible way, that it might be difficult for the matter to be kept secret for ever. Apart from the fact that nobody is shot, it is the sort of pressure that any Mafia boss would instantly recognize.

Perhaps the most ingenious method involved a secret ally of the whips' office having an apparently innocuous conversation with the suspect and asking them whom they most admired in politics. If that turned out to be a member of the cabinet then the trap could easily be sprung. The MP would be marched in to see the person they most admired, who then told them in no uncertain terms that they must give no thought to rebellion. Such an interview, perhaps including the remark, 'I never thought you, of all people, would contemplate such a thing,' would often do the trick. The application of these methods usually fell well outside the legal definition of blackmail, but the ruthless efficiency with which they were employed left many first-time rebels vowing never to be disloyal again.

The effectiveness of such tactics cannot be disputed, but as far as I know they were not employed in Mrs Thatcher's final leadership campaign. Mr Morrison may have been too gentlemanly, and he was certainly too complacent. When he died of a heart attack five years later at the early age of fifty-one, some of his colleagues were convinced that it was his feelings of guilt as much as a growing dependence on drink which had caused his death. But making him bear all the blame is simply not fair. He had a harder task than normal because the whips' office could not be formally involved; the campaign team had to be organized on an ad hoc basis.

A succession of campaign chairmen should take some of the responsibility, including two former cabinet ministers, John Moore and George Younger, who failed to deliver; and there was the often entirely unhelpful attitude of Mrs Thatcher herself. Andrew Turnbull, her principal private secretary, believes that she simply could not accept the legitimacy of a challenge to her leadership. 'I think mentally she couldn't take these challenges seriously,' he told me. 'She thought, I am the most famous politician in the world and I have won all these elections, now what on earth is this about? That was her mindset.' I was speaking to Sir Andrew Turnbull in 2002, just before he took over as head of the civil service. He has that classic combination of affability and toughness which seems to take some people effortlessly to the top. For an hour in an office which is part of the Number 10 complex he looked back on the Thatcher years, not uncritically but with the clear understanding that she had been one of those rare political stars who will always warrant a place in the history books.

At the time of the leadership election Mr Turnbull was surprised that Mrs Thatcher did not take part in any sort of direct campaigning effort. She did not try to canvass support among those who might need some persuasion if they were to come out in her favour. All she did was talk to her close advisers. While Mr Morrison was having his afternoon nap, Mr Turnbull believes the campaign team should have been making a last-minute effort to contact perhaps twenty key doubters whom Mrs Thatcher would then see one by one in her office. 'There was none of that,' he said. 'She was talking to her supporters and expecting them to do it. It was beneath her to go round and talk to people whose support she felt she was entitled to anyway.' Sir Bernard Ingham remembers her saying to him that she had no intention of grubbing for votes in the gutter. 'If they don't know who they are voting for by now,' she complained, 'they never will.' The loyal Sir Bernard is puzzled by her performance in the leadership battle. He wonders if there is a secret explanation – perhaps she had agreed with Denis that it was time to go. 'The point is,' Sir Bernard told me, 'that she was a fighter, and she didn't fight. It was out of character.'

WHEN THE RESULT of the leadership ballot was announced, just after 6.15 p.m. on 20 November 1990, I was standing in the courtyard in front of the short flight of steps leading to the entrance to the British embassy in Paris. It had rained for much of the day and the gravel was wet underfoot. The area was lit with television lights, giving the scene the dramatic intensity of a stage set. I had earlier told viewers of an extended edition of the BBC's six o'clock news that the prime minister had been showing some signs of strain, but her camp had expressed complete confidence that she would win. I had lots of possible figures in my mind, but I knew that if Mr Heseltine won anything like 150 votes, she was in very serious trouble. The result, read out in London in a Commons committee room, was immediately followed by the comment, 'Second ballot.' It was a heart-stopping moment. She had failed to do well enough to beat off the challenge in the first round. The figures were: Thatcher 204, Heseltine 152, abstentions 16, leaving the prime minister four votes short of avoiding a second ballot. She had been caught by that weird rule requiring a majority plus 15 per cent. If only two more MPs had stayed loyal to their leader and not voted for Mr Heseltine, she would have won.

All those who had worried about her campaign were instantly vindicated. Shifting two votes should have been a relatively easy matter. The prime minister had been cruelly let down.

I thought this indecisive result, neither victory nor rejection, would delay Mrs Thatcher's public reaction. I suggested to a member of her staff that she would not be coming out of the embassy straight away, she would consult her colleagues. He emphatically agreed, and I announced to the viewers that her appearance would be delayed. I had not been informed of the closely thought out plan which then went into operation. It had been agreed by Mrs Thatcher and her advisers that if she were forced into a second ballot, she could not afford to wait for a moment. She would have to seize the initiative and immediately announce her determination to stay in the race.

She received the news of the ballot in a small upstairs room at the British embassy, sitting by a dressing table. Among the group of senior staff was Peter Morrison, who took the phone call from London. He wrote down the figures and handed the paper to the prime minister. His comment, 'It's not as good as we hoped,' said it all. Bernard Ingham told me in a recent interview that, as ever, she was icily controlled. She stood up and said, 'Well, I know what I have to do then.' She made for the lift, followed by Mr Ingham. They had to negotiate an extremely slippery marble staircase and he was concerned that she might fall over. But she didn't hesitate; she did not wait for Mr Ingham to check that all the arrangements were in place, she went straight through the front door and down the steps to where I was waiting.

Having just announced that she would not be coming out for some time, I was blissfully unaware that she had suddenly appeared. My earpiece had not conveyed to me the startled cry of the newsreader, Peter Sissons, who shouted, 'She's behind you.' I would later be able to joke that it wasn't only him – thirteen million people shouted, in pantomime style, 'She's behind you.' Only when a photographer leapt into the air did I turn round. To my great relief I saw a small group bearing down on me: Mr Ingham, Mrs Thatcher and the Number 10 official who had told me she would not be coming out. They were looking for a microphone. But it was not the one I was holding in my hand; it was the microphone which had been set up on the other side of the square to enable her to address the small corps of British correspondents. It was a wonderfully chaotic scene. 'Here is the microphone,' I protested, pushing my microphone forward. It became known as the 'handbagging incident', although it would not be accurate to say that Mrs Thatcher hit me with her handbag. Mr Ingham, though, certainly pushed me fairly roughly aside.

Having given up hope of finding the proper microphone, they decided mine would have to do, and the prime minister delivered her prepared statement: 'I am naturally very pleased that I got more than half the parliamentary party and disappointed that it's not quite enough to win on the first ballot. So I confirm that it is my intention to let my name go forward for the second ballot.' Refusing to take any questions, she swept back into the embassy. It became one of the most famous scenes in the history of television news, a brilliant BBC exclusive; and it had a curious effect on my career. Although I had made a serious mistake in front of a vast audience, I was awarded celebrity status. For Mrs Thatcher the effect could hardly have been more damaging. The misunderstanding over the microphone and the pushing and shoving gave the impression that she had lost her grip on government. The scene outside the embassy in Paris had taken on the power of a political cartoon. Many of those watching at home came to the simple, and as it turned out correct, conclusion that Margaret Thatcher had been fatally wounded by Michael Heseltine and would not be able to recover.

11

'I fight on; I fight to win'

SLEEPING ONLY FOUR HOURS a night was often cited as one of the reasons for Mrs Thatcher's success, but that night in Paris she did not sleep at all. She sat up all night talking to her devoted assistant Cynthia Crawford who, like the Queen's nanny Marion Crawford, was known to all as Crawfie. (They were not related.) One of the tasks carried out by 'Crawfie dear' – as the prime minister usually addressed her – was to help choose Mrs Thatcher's wardrobe; she also worked as a secretary. As the night wore on, the two women drank whisky and, as frequently happens with those in shock, Mrs Thatcher sought comfort in talking about familiar scenes from her past, her childhood, the success of her marriage and her children. She believed she had a lot to be grateful for but was reeling from the blow she had suffered, and her most depressing thought was that the man responsible, Michael Heseltine, might go on to take her job. Before the result of the first ballot, she had been convinced she was the best candidate to stop Mr Heseltine, but now she doubted whether she would ever recover.

When Mrs Thatcher returned from Paris later the following day, despite her public announcement that she would continue in office she had to decide whether it was really wise for her to enter the second round of the leadership contest. Outside the Paris embassy the night before, I had naively imagined that Mrs Thatcher had weighed up the situation before making her statement. Well over a hundred MPs voting against her had seemed to me such a bad result that her continuing leadership was surely unlikely. But having just received the news, she did not have to decide what to do, merely what to say. Even though the chaotic scenes in Paris led millions of viewers to doubt whether she could survive, her closest colleagues were convinced she was right to state firmly her intention to carry on.

One of her most loyal friends in politics Cecil Parkinson, who was transport secretary at the time, admitted in an interview with me in 2003 that her announcement in Paris had come over in a rather challenging, aggressive way. 'It was meant to be more thoughtful,' he told me during a long discussion in one of the vast reception rooms in the House of Lords. 'But she was under enormous pressure. She had all those grandees waiting for dinner; she was the belle of the ball and she was going to be late. So she gabbled it out. She didn't do it well, but I'm not sure it could have been done well.' Mrs Thatcher had to calculate the best way to keep her options open; the worst tactic would have been to admit to failure, because then it would have been extremely difficult for her to re-ignite the leadership campaign. When a prime minister loses the authority due to the office, it is almost impossible to get it back. Belief in one's invincibility is one of the most valuable attributes any office holder can have; and Mrs Thatcher had spent too much of her career proving that point to throw it away now.

John Wakeham, energy secretary and previously chief whip, was one of Mrs Thatcher's advisers who had planned what she should say if she failed to win on the first ballot. He had been badly injured in the Brighton bomb – his wife was killed – but he had returned to government and had remained a close and loyal colleague of the prime minister. When I interviewed him on the terrace of the House of Lords in the summer of 2003, with the dark waters of the Thames swirling beneath us, I could not help thinking of all the political advisers who had intrigued in that place. He speaks softly and quickly and has a well-deserved reputation as a behind-the-scenes fixer. Lord Wakeham is convinced her advisers gave Mrs Thatcher the right guidance. 'If she'd said, "I must go back and talk to my friends and consider the right thing to do," she would have been lost. There was a momentum against her and the only way to try to hold the line was to say, "I'm determined to go on."' Lord Wakeham accepts that Mrs Thatcher could have made a more graceful exit if she had announced her resignation in Paris. Many people have told him that is what she should have done. But he says, 'We weren't in the business of finding graceful exits; being nice and graceful about it all was a formula for defeat.'

There were signs of panic at Number 10 on the morning of Mrs Thatcher's return. When I spoke to Kenneth Clarke in his office at the House of Commons, in an interview for this book, he remembered a 'tremendous flap' in Downing Street. He was health secretary at the time. A staunch pro-European, his bluff, easy-going manner disguises a tough, unsentimental view of politics which is nevertheless coupled with an undying passion for the subject. He told me how that morning he had bluntly refused a request from Number 10 that he should become Mrs Thatcher's new campaign manager, an invitation no doubt made with the aim of winning back some of the critics of her European policy. It was an ominous moment for the inner circle when they discovered that senior ministers such as Mr Clarke, who had voted loyally in the first ballot, could not be counted on to support the prime minister in the next round.

Mrs Thatcher could not afford another rebuff in filling this key post. She decided to call on one of her colleagues whom she knew would not refuse. As energy secretary, John Wakeham was busy preparing for the final stages of the privatization of the electricity industry, but had taken a break to watch television in the hope of keeping up with the fast-moving events in Downing Street. In his interview with me he revealed that he had learnt from one of those taking part in the programme that he had just been appointed Mrs Thatcher's new campaign manager. It was hardly convenient – he was about to launch the privatization at the Cumberland Hotel at Marble Arch – but he had no doubt where his duty lay. Nor would he embarrass the prime minister by objecting to the manner of his appointment. But, as he hurried to Downing Street, he was annoyed to have been brought into the process at such a late stage. He had misgivings about whether Mrs Thatcher could survive, though immersed in the details of the new electricity share price, he did not feel in a good position to judge.

Mr Wakeham was not impressed by the mood he found at Number 10. 'The people around her were not being terribly enthusiastic or helpful.' The prime minister looked tired and anxious. He told her that there was no dishonour in being defeated, 'if you have stood up for the things you believe in'. But he warned her she would need to have the support of the majority of her MPs and her cabinet if she decided to press on. Mr Wakeham then stayed on for a lunch with 'the men in grey suits'. In the Conservative party there is a tradition that men in such attire should meet and decide the future of the leadership. It is a comforting image of eminent figures too discreet to have public profiles, who act as the real power brokers. In the past such men might have represented the landed interests or the City of London, and might have spoken for different parts of the country. In more recent times they have simply been leading members of the backbench 1922 Committee, senior MPs, often as boring as their suits, many of whom would be lucky to secure even the most junior office.

Mr Wakeham remembers an unusual feature of this particular gathering: it was the first occasion on which he was offered beer and sandwiches at Number 10. When Labour were in power union leaders were routinely served this fare, and it became a cliché to describe how major industrial disputes were settled. But beer and sandwiches did nothing to resolve the inner conflicts of the men in suits; they simply could not bring themselves to say what they really thought. They did not want to be the ones to tell Mrs Thatcher it was time to go, and a poll of opinion among government ministers which showed a lack of confidence in the prime minister's ability to win through, was not even referred to. This had been conducted by the leader of the Commons, John McGregor, but it was thought wrong for him to tell them the results because the men in grey were 'outside the inner circle'. Mrs Thatcher's courtiers had once more failed to give her a clear picture of the seriousness of her position. Denis Thatcher was far less inhibited. 'Don't go on, love,' he told her frankly when they met shortly after she arrived back in Downing Street. After lunch, as Mrs Thatcher left to go to the Commons to make a statement on the outcome of the Paris conference, she again chose to keep her options open. 'I fight on; I fight to win,' she called out to the waiting journalists, and we were in no position to contradict her.

Mrs Thatcher admitted later that she was not as confident as she seemed, and she was becoming all too aware of how humiliating it would be if she stood again and lost to Michael Heseltine. After making her statement in the Commons, Mrs Thatcher went to the MPs' tea room, accompanied by Norman Tebbit. When a prime minister drops in like this, it is usually to boost morale among their supporters, but on this occasion it was her morale which needed boosting. It seemed, briefly, to work. Cecil Parkinson found her 'rather buoyed up' when he popped in to see her in the leader's office behind the speaker's chair. She told him how Conservative MPs had given her friendly support. 'Everybody was saying, "Don't worry, we're going to be behind you."' Mrs Thatcher briefly left the Commons for an audience with the Queen, and informed her that she intended to stand in the second ballot. But privately Mrs Thatcher was beginning to question her own resolve.

On her return to the Commons she began the slow process of consulting her cabinet colleagues, following the advice of Mr Wakeham. Mrs Thatcher's decision to consult her cabinet ministers individually is still the subject of controversy. Some of her loyal supporters believe this was one of her biggest mistakes. It has become part of their deeply held conviction that Mrs Thatcher should not, and need not have been removed from office. Norman Tebbit, who revels in his image as the hard man of Conservative politics, is in no doubt that this was a tactical error. When I spoke to him in a small interview room in the House of Lords I could almost hear the swish of the bicycle chain as he laid into those who had brought down Mrs Thatcher. With great emphasis Lord Tebbit explained how she should have called them together in the cabinet room and said, 'Right, who is going to back me and who wants me to go?' The first to answer would have been the ultra-loyalists such as Cecil Parkinson. She should have left those openly prepared to vote against her, like Kenneth Clarke, right to the end. Warming to his theme, Lord Tebbit insisted, 'By the time she got to the rats, they would have been intimidated and they would have said, "Yes, Prime Minister, of course we back you." And she would have had them.' Lord Tebbit believes that silencing potential rebels within the cabinet was essential. Any cabinet ministers who demonstrated their lack of support would have had to be sacked if she continued in office. It would have been far better, Lord Tebbit argues, if they had not been asked for their views in the first place.

Other long-term supporters also believe she should have

called in the cabinet and demanded collective loyalty. Lord
Parkinson says Mrs Thatcher in her prime would have acted in
that way. He told me, 'She should have said, "You are all here
because I invited you to join me, and now I'm asking you to
do something for me." She should have raised the spectre of a
country on the verge of war, with an army on its way to the
Middle East to take on Saddam Hussein's forces in Kuwait.
This would not be the time to change the prime minister. And
what did Mrs Thatcher do?' Lord Parkinson does not wait for
an answer. 'She said, "Come and see me and tell me what you
think I ought to do." And that was totally out of character,
totally out of character.' Apart from Kenneth Clarke, Lord Parkinson believes, all the members of the cabinet would have fallen
into line.

This argument is more important than it may seem. The
manner in which Mrs Thatcher left office continued to exercise leading figures in the Conservative party for many years.
Every detail of her final hours was endlessly pored over by
those who were shocked and disappointed by what had happened. For loyalists it was not enough to say the matter was
now dead and buried. After Mrs Thatcher left Number 10
many continued to believe she should still be prime minister.
This enhanced her position later and increased her scope to
influence events. I myself am more impressed by the importance of this afterglow than I am by the view that she could
somehow have miraculously survived the first ballot debacle,
which was perhaps asking too much of the persuasive power
of a critically injured prime minister whose authority had been
severely weakened over the previous year. Mrs Thatcher was
not in her prime: the skids were under her, and she could not
count on the collective support of the cabinet.

This view is strongly backed by John Wakeham. He is in
no doubt she was right to assess the support among her cabinet, even though he knew that at least three of its members,

Kenneth Clarke, Chris Patten and Malcolm Rifkind, thought she should resign, and most of the others were convinced she would not win a second ballot. He totally dismisses the argument put forward by the ultra-loyalists that somehow she could have retrieved the situation by calling on the cabinet as a whole to come into line behind her. 'That,' he told me, 'is cloud cuckoo land.' If she had tried to continue about ten ministers would have resigned including the three from the cabinet. 'Even if we had patched it up,' he says, 'it would have gone wrong again very shortly afterwards.'

The cabinet, whose offices in the Commons stretch out along the corridors behind the speaker's chair, were given times for their interviews. This simple procedure has also been questioned. Kenneth Clarke told me it was not to her advantage as it allowed the cabinet, close together in those corridors, to come to an unofficial conclusion, beforehand, about her true position. Chatting among themselves, they reached a consensus that if she stood she would be defeated in the second ballot and therefore should resign. But would they each say this when they were asked? Mr Clarke, whose reputation for robustness is not misplaced, was in no doubt where his duty lay. He was the first to be called, and perhaps that was another mistake: everyone knew he would not mince his words.

Mr Clarke told me he and the prime minister were both 'pretty fresh and in good form'. In recent years they had built up a relationship which, he says, allowed them 'to have a good go at each other' without personal acrimony. Neither of them held back on this occasion. She accused him of being 'defeatist'. He insisted that she should accept that her cause was 'hopeless'; any attempt to go into the second ballot would be 'like the Charge of the Light Brigade'; she was 'doomed to failure' and could not recover her authority over the government. Mr Clarke did not end his assessment there. He said she should release John Major and Douglas Hurd from their undertakings to support her – they had signed her nomination papers – so they could stand for the leadership themselves. Mr Clarke admits that she was probably shaken by ten minutes of this and by the fact that he was immovable in his opinions. Mrs Thatcher later described his approach as 'brutalist'.

When Mr Clarke returned to his office he says that some of his colleagues were extremely nervous about what they should do. There were 'a whole lot of eyes looking at me' and lots of 'breathless requests' for him to reveal what he had said. He was characteristically open and helped create a mood which carried through into others' individual meetings with the prime minister. Mrs Thatcher was dismayed to find that most of the cabinet appeared to take exactly the same line; to her it looked suspiciously as if they had agreed what to say before being called in. They would support her if she entered the second round, but they were convinced she would not win. Natural allies, like the employment secretary Michael Howard, told her they had doubts about whether she could win, although he pledged to campaign vigorously on her behalf if she decided to stick it out. Even a minister outside the cabinet who outwardly professed himself one of her greatest fans, the irrepressible Alan Clark, was pessimistic about her ability to continue, but he urged her to have a try anyway. 'What a way to go!' enthused the impractical diarist. 'Unbeaten in three elections, never rejected by the people, brought down by nonentities.'

One of the most poignant descriptions of the way Mrs Thatcher responded to the views of the cabinet is provided by John Gummer, who had disagreed with her particularly on Europe. He had worked closely with her for many years, as a speech writer as well as senior minister, and was fond of her. Like most of the others, he told her she could not win. I spoke to him in 2003 in his Queen Anne's Gate office, which was being done up. It was appropriate that we were talking in a room only partly cleared of builders' mess. Everything seemed to be in the wrong place, as it had been on that turbulent day in November 1990. Mr Gummer became emotional in describing how Mrs Thatcher had responded to the reaction of her cabinet. 'She looked deflated in a way which I hadn't ever seen before,' he told me. 'I'd seen her angry and I'd seen her fed up, but never like that. There was a smallness about her. She looked different and that was quite hard to take.'

Some of those who saw her later that evening were convinced she had been crying. There is no doubt she felt betrayed, and it was a feeling that would grow as the years went on. To one cabinet minister who told her she would not win she said, rather plaintively, that she didn't expect him to take that view, as if the correct response would have been to lie about her real position. As the rumours spread that Mrs Thatcher would resign, one of her most loyal junior ministers, Michael Portillo, made a desperate attempt to persuade her to stay on; some other right-wing MPs tried to do the same. But the prime minister was beginning to accept that her cause was hopeless, and there was a slowly dawning realization that she would have to take some of the blame for what had gone wrong.

Mr Portillo told me he argued to Mrs Thatcher that she would be in a much stronger position in the second round because she would be able to talk to her MPs. 'You haven't spoken to any of them,' he remembers saying to her. 'You haven't actually campaigned at all.' She was in no mood to dispute this; she was extremely quiet and hardly said a word. Mr Portillo continues: 'She looked at me as though I had revealed a great truth to her, as though she had never thought of this. She looked shocked.' Mr Portillo believes she thought it beneath her dignity to canvass support, but he also agrees with others, such as Lord Parkinson and Sir Bernard Ingham, that there was something strange about the way she had not put up a proper fight in the first round. There was an element of mystery about her conduct.

The least likely encounter Mrs Thatcher had on the eve of the announcement of her resignation was only revealed to me while I was researching this book. Of all the people she might have talked to that evening, a Labour MP from a Merseyside constituency seems most improbable. The member for Birkenhead, the independent-minded Frank Field, had been impressed by the way she had dealt with him on a non-partisan basis over some of the problems affecting his constituency, particularly those involving the Cammell Laird shipyard, which received enormous sums in government aid. It is not difficult to see why Mrs Thatcher agreed to talk to Mr Field. A committed and high-minded Christian – as a minister under Tony Blair he was famously asked 'to think the unthinkable' about social services reform – Mr Field could be counted on to tell the truth, as he saw it. Mrs Thatcher would have been intrigued to hear his thoughts, and Mr Field would know that she would keep their meeting secret; consorting with the enemy at her time of need would not have gone down well with his Labour colleagues.

Mr Field told me he had wanted to see her as a sign of personal friendship. They had got on well in their discussions over constituency business. 'She was wonderful to deal with,' he said. 'If she agreed something should happen, it did happen; she would write a prime ministerial minute.' This curious cross-party relationship was strong enough to give Mr Field access to Mrs Thatcher at the most vulnerable moment in her career. First he had tried to see her at her office in the House of Commons, and then, in spite of the danger of being caught on camera walking up Downing Street, he had asked to see her at Number 10; and the request had been granted. News of the meeting never leaked out. The conversation they had, related to me by Mr Field, gives a remarkable insight into her thinking at this pivotal point in British politics.

Mr Field strongly advised the prime minister to resign. He says her mood was 'fragile' but she was as courteous as ever. They talked in her study. 'You can't go out on a top note, but you can go out on a high note,' he told her. Mrs Thatcher, he says, agreed with him, but implied that others were taking a different view. She kept complaining about how unfair it all was. But when Mr Field suggested 'her work might be cut out' to stop Mr Heseltine becoming the next leader, she was rather restrained. 'He's a very bad man, Frank,' she told him. Mr Field was amused by the thought that perhaps she had refrained from exposing him to stronger language. Then they moved on to discuss the vital question: who she might support in the coming leadership election. This is how Mr Field recalls their conversation.

'I said, "You should get your candidate into the ring tonight," and she said, "Who is my candidate?" I said, "It's John Major surely?" She said, "John Major . . . he's very young." And then, after a pause, she said, "Why did you say John Major, Frank?" And I said, "He was the first of the 1979 intake; he's surely your candidate?"' Mr Field was pointing out that of all the MPs who had been elected when Mrs Thatcher came to power, Mr Major had become the most prominent. Mrs Thatcher gave the impression she was not convinced Mr Major was the obvious choice, but she made no further comment. It was yet one more sign that the prime minister did not have a master plan; she could not think much beyond the awful decision she now knew she had to take. It had been a devastating day. But she was not entirely wrapped up in her own problems. She suggested to Mr Field that perhaps it would be wise if he left Number 10 by the back door.

12

One more triumph – because it's the last

WHEN MARGARET THATCHER announced her resignation at 9.33 a.m. on 22 November 1990 the whole world took notice. In the blizzard of comment which followed, from Washington to Beijing, no one doubted that she was the most famous, the strongest, and the most significant British political figure since Winston Churchill. But commentators were also quick to point out that she sharply divided the nation. Unlike most political leaders she seemed to go out of her way to create controversy and only a small minority of the population were indifferent to her arguments. One of the routine tests for insanity – Can you name the prime minister? – had to be abandoned because even the mentally ill appeared to have no difficulty recalling her name.

When the cabinet gathered that morning in Downing Street at about 9 a.m. most of its members were not sure whether she would resign. Kenneth Clarke was among those concerned that she might ignore his advice. He had told his wife that if the prime minister decided to stay he would resign that afternoon. One of Mr Clarke's colleagues remembers him letting his frustration show as they stood waiting outside the cabinet room. 'I have a very high embarrassment threshold,' he warned Mrs Thatcher's campaign manager, making it clear he would make an uncomfortable fuss if she did not resign. Mr Wakeham, anxious not to feed Mr Clarke's anxiety, told him, 'Just keep calm; things will work out, but just keep calm and see what happens.'

I was in a routine news meeting at BBC Television Centre, some miles away at White City. 'Well,' I was asked, 'will she go?' The truthful answer would have been that I had no idea. After three astonishing days I felt battered by events and, in a perfect world, would have liked some time off. But after twenty years as a BBC reporter and having risen to the post of chief political correspondent, I knew something more positive was required. 'I think she'll fight on,' I said firmly. I then fleshed out the argument with her character as a fighter, and how she would hate to be seen as a quitter. For years my professional life had been dominated by Mrs Thatcher. I had reported on her progress ever since she became Conservative leader in 1975, and had been present at most of her important speeches as prime minister. There were few sides of her character I had not directly experienced, and although this moment was entirely exceptional, I found it very difficult to accept that her time at Number 10 was about to end. It had all happened so suddenly, and it was hard to grasp the sheer brutality of the process. When I heard the ballot result in Paris I correctly calculated that her hold on office was tenuous; but that is not what I felt emotionally. Mrs Thatcher had many enemies who would like to see her forcibly removed, but for her to be cut down by her own side was not at all easy to come to terms with; my thoughts on the way the whole matter had been handled were not unlike those of the prime minister herself.

As I finished my explanation to my journalist colleagues of why she would stay, I was immediately contradicted by the loudspeaker announcement that she would go; important news is carried instantly on a system which operates in all the BBC newsrooms. Such was the impact of this particular news that my embarrassment was short-lived. It was decided that the main television channel, BBC 1, would switch to what is called a rolling news operation, presented by Nicholas Witchell; I was the first guest and for the next couple of hours I sat in the studio trying to make sense of the unfolding drama.

Inside the cabinet room the atmosphere was heavy with emotion. The prime minister found it impossible to hold back her tears. She broke down three times as she tried to read her formal statement: 'Having consulted widely among my colleagues, I have concluded that the unity of the Party and the prospects of victory in a general election would be better served if I stood down to enable Cabinet colleagues to enter the ballot for the leadership. I should like to thank all those in the Cabinet and outside who have given me such dedicated support.' The lord chancellor Lord McKay then intervened with a statement of tribute, prepared with his customary efficiency by the cabinet secretary Sir Robin Butler. On behalf of the cabinet, Lord McKay spoke of their profound sadness. 'Your place in our country's history is already assured,' he told her. 'It has been a true privilege to have served under you.' The Conservative party chairman Kenneth Baker, not one to be awed into silence, thanked her for all she had done. He claimed that Mrs Thatcher had acted selflessly. 'She had,' he said, 'put her party's interests before that of the prime minister's.'

Mrs Thatcher would dearly have liked it to have been a dignified occasion, but she was too upset and in a state of shock. She felt betrayed, stabbed in the back by a disloyal cabinet and by malign forces within the Conservative party led by the traitor Michael Heseltine, who had dared to stand against her. One of those present recorded that three cabinet ministers were also in tears. 'The rest stared down at the table – the guiltiest stared down hardest.' The only hint we received at Television Centre of her real emotions was a report, which came from Bernard Ingham, that she had told her colleagues, 'It's a funny old world.' Given her legendary lack of humour, I took this to mean she thought the whole process unfair. One of those who attended cabinet that morning told me she had not used the phrase then; she had said it several times when she had spoken to members of the cabinet the evening before. It was her concluding point following a list of reasons for staying on: she had won three general elections; retained the overwhelming support of the party; had never lost a motion of confidence and indeed had won majority support from Conservative MPs in the first round of the leadership elections. In exasperation, she had said, 'It's a funny old world,' but she did not, of course, think it was remotely funny.

During the previous week I had prepared a detailed political obituary – just in case – and this was now broadcast. It lasted for more than ten minutes and would be shown several times that day. Looking back, it is a remarkably cool appraisal. Mrs Thatcher has recovered much public esteem in the years since she left office, but at the time Labour were well ahead in the opinion polls, the economy was on the edge of recession, and the annual rate of inflation was just over 10 per cent. The triumphs of Thatcherism – the historic shift to freer markets, privatization and the curbing of union power – all seemed to have lost their shine. Since the general election landslide of 1987 she had lost two of her most important allies, Nigel Lawson and Sir Geoffrey Howe, and she had introduced the disastrous poll tax. The party split over Europe had widened, leaving her in a minority within the cabinet, while the mood among Tory MPs had become increasingly critical as they faced the prospect of defeat at the next election.

Outside the political world reaction was often extreme. A man was spotted on a London bus opening a bottle of champagne. A member of the crowd outside the gates of Downing Street started to shout, 'Maggie, Maggie, Maggie; gone, gone, gone.' A taxi driver taking a reporter from Shaftesbury Avenue to the Strand brutally summed up his feelings: 'Should have got rid of the old cow before, shouldn't they?' And the Dulwich postman who would be delivering letters to her new home was equally unsentimental. 'Good riddance,' he declared. 'I just bung letters in the box – I don't give a monkey's whose it is.' But across the country, among the many Conservative party activists who had taken no part in these dramatic events, there was a deep sense of disappointment and anger. Their feelings about the way their revered leader had been unceremoniously dumped would become a potent force in the coming years, and would have a crucial effect on British politics. But on the day their mood was perhaps best expressed by the woman who turned up at Conservative headquarters in Mrs Thatcher's Finchley constituency. She was shown on the BBC lunchtime news asking if there was a book to sign. At a time of mourning, what else would one expect but a book of condolences?

Among the comedians and satirists who had enjoyed boom years under her premiership there was a rueful recognition that, however much they had tried to undermine Mrs Thatcher, it was members of her own party who had finally succeeded in removing her from office. The editor of *Private Eye*, Ian Hislop, would concede that it demonstrated the limitations of satire. Earlier in the year the *Guardian* had run a competition for the words people would like to see on her memorial stone, and the winners were republished. 'Licensed for dancing,' was one of the more cheerfully disrespectful; a more subtle suggestion alluded to the way Mrs Thatcher had brought commercial values into public life: 'To read epitaph, insert 15p.' The playwright Alan Bennett was among those ready to celebrate. Like many people he had objected to the high-voltage politics of the Thatcher era. 'I've resented thinking about politics so much in the last ten years,' he said. 'It'll be a relief not to have to think about it any more.'

It is worth remembering the uniqueness of this event. No prime minister had ever been forced to resign as a result of doing badly in a vote of their party's MPs. No prime minister had had so little control over the timing of their resignation announcement. The procedure for the leadership contest had been settled weeks before; nominations for the second ballot were due to close at noon that day. If Mrs Thatcher was going to allow others to enter the contest, she had to announce her decision well before noon. Her original application to take part, nominated by her foreign secretary Douglas Hurd and chancellor John Major, had only been signed by them the day before.

In a glorious twist worthy of one of his own improbable plots it was a driver employed by Jeffrey Archer who had picked up the completed form at Mr Major's house in Huntingdonshire the evening before. The novelist's driver waited two hours so that a second, far more secret document could be taken to London as well. This was Mr Major's own application to take part in the leadership election, which he had also signed and sealed; if Mrs Thatcher backed out and he decided to run for the leadership he wanted to make sure that his application form would be ready. What we did not know then, of course, was that Mr Major had recently had an affair with the prominent Tory MP Edwina Currie; if that had been public knowledge he would almost certainly not have been contemplating a leadership bid. It is not the only intriguing 'What if . . .' scenario. Had we known that Mr Archer, later given a peerage by Mr Major, had perverted the course of justice in his libel case – and was to serve two years in prison – he would not have been allowed close enough to the centre of power for his driver to be entrusted with such a delicate task.

For the broadcasters this whole astonishing event was a plunge into the unknown. For many years both the BBC and ITV had practised what to do if a leading member of the royal family died, although that did not prevent a row blowing up when the newscaster Peter Sissons failed to wear a black tie when the Queen Mother's death was announced in 2002. Nevertheless the broad approach was well prepared. The sudden removal of a prime minister had never been practised. Our response to the developments that morning was totally unrehearsed and went at almost breakneck speed; we seemed to be endlessly struggling to keep up. Reaction kept flooding in. The Labour party called for a general election without believing for a moment that the request would be granted. The former prime minister Lord Callaghan, whom Mrs Thatcher had defeated in 1979, commented rather sourly on her departure, 'Those who live by the sword shall perish by the sword.' Jack Straw, Labour's education spokesman who would become home secretary and foreign secretary under Tony Blair, also showed his rougher side. 'To have got rid of that evil woman,' he said, 'after all the damage she has done to this country is simply wonderful.' We all then waited to see who would formally submit themselves for nomination in the second ballot.

The noon deadline was absolute; once that moment had passed there could be no going back. Mrs Thatcher was out; Michael Heseltine stayed in; Mr Hurd and Mr Major quickly submitted their own applications. It would be a three-horse race. The only doubt had been over the position of Mrs Thatcher's leading supporter Norman Tebbit, but he was not sure he could beat Mr Heseltine, and in any case had decided not to return to front-line politics. He wanted to continue looking after his wife Margaret, confined to a wheelchair after being badly injured by the IRA bomb in Brighton which had nearly killed Mrs Thatcher.

If anyone had planned this day they would surely have concluded that a prime ministerial resignation and three nominations for a renewed battle for the leadership was quite enough. But this was only lunchtime. There was still prime minister's questions in the Commons, as usual on a Thursday afternoon, and then a previously planned full-scale censure debate mounted by the opposition, which would also have to be answered by the prime minister. Political journalists often have to survive for days with only the merest scrap of new information and perhaps a bit of juicy gossip, but this was developing into a monumental feast. In more than twenty years reporting Parliament I have never known such an extraordinary occasion.

The Commons, with its rules and procedures, sometimes prides itself on appearing to be outside the immediate stream of events. Even at the height of some terrible row or dramatic happening the speaker, in eighteenth-century dress, silk stockings and specially made shoes, will call for 'Order' in the hope, not only of stilling the noise in the House, but also of bringing a sense of proportion to the raging debate. But on this particular afternoon the House of Commons seemed so bizarrely out of touch, it appeared to have gone mad. Trying to contain this explosive drama within the confines of a small debating chamber, with its conventions and archaic trappings, was simply not possible. The whole atmosphere was unreal. The prime minister was earnestly pretending that it was business as usual, but she had just lost a power struggle which had cost her career. Despite being so obviously divided, Conservative MPs tried to emphasize how united they were, in the face of a formal challenge from the opposition. Labour was desperate to claim some credit for removing the enemy but knew the credit lay elsewhere, and those who had carried out the deed were not keen to draw attention to their success, let alone celebrate. In the view of Thatcher loyalists such as Norman Tebbit, an enormous cloud of hypocrisy hung over the Conservative benches. In many of their smiling, comfortable faces he saw only traitors responsible for removing one of Britain's greatest prime ministers. I looked down from the press gallery and could hardly believe my good fortune at being able to witness such an event.

It was a Northern Ireland MP, Martin Smyth, who was called on to ask the routine question about the prime minister's official engagements for that day. Mrs Thatcher's eyes were moist when she stood up at the Dispatch Box, wearing a suit of the same shade of blue she had worn on her first day in Downing Street eleven years earlier. Without a glimmer of irony she replied, 'This morning I chaired a meeting of the cabinet. At 12.45 p.m. I had an audience with Her Majesty the Queen. Later this afternoon I shall lead for the government against the motion tabled in the name of the leader of the Opposition.' Mr Smyth, true to the traditions of Northern Ireland politics, could not resist adding to his expression of sympathy, a pointed remark. 'Ulster Unionists,' he said 'know what betrayal means.' She did not respond, realizing that even a detailed exposition of her government's policies towards Northern Ireland might not satisfy Mr Smyth. Instead she told him she hoped to visit the province many times in the future, 'perhaps in a slightly different capacity'. She repeated the phrase in a later answer, suggesting that she had not yet come to terms with the prospect of being an ex-prime minister. She was determined to demonstrate that she was still in charge. If war had to be declared or vital decisions made, Mrs Thatcher implied, she was ready and able to do so until the new leader was chosen; and if the Labour leader Neil Kinnock wanted to claim that her government no longer commanded the support of the House of Commons, he was merely fooling himself, as usual.

There were some emotional tributes. Her old friend from her days at Oxford, Dame Elaine Kellet Bowman, spoke of the 'love and affection of millions of people who over the years have looked to her with the greatest admiration and delight'. Winston Churchill, who shares his name with his grandfather, told her she was the greatest peacetime prime minister who had ever served this country. Neil Kinnock conceded that she was, at least, worth more than those who had turned on her in recent days. But she was dismissive of his call for a general election. 'No,' she replied firmly. 'No more than we had when Mr Wilson was replaced by Mr Callaghan.'

Mrs Thatcher's spirits began visibly to improve. What had started as a grim matter of duty did not seem quite so bad after all. Some commentators suggested this was due to a sense of relief that she would no longer have to carry the burdens of office. I concluded she knew that even her most implacable foes would find it difficult to kick her when she was so obviously down. Like the actress she was, she could not resist playing on the sympathy of her audience. What better role now than that of the dying swan, the tragic heroine who had risked all and lost? The leader of the Liberal Democrats Paddy Ashdown generously described the courage, conviction and determination that she had brought to the office of prime minister.

One of her strengths had always been her ability to concentrate on the matter in hand. Her speech had been worked on the night before, into the early hours of the morning. Those who prepared it, including Norman Tebbit, John Gummer and her political secretary John Whittingdale, knew she had decided to resign and were impressed by the way she pulled herself together and contributed to what amounted to a valedictory address. Mr Whittingdale sat among the seats in the Commons reserved for senior civil servants; he admitted to me that he had cried during Mrs Thatcher's speech. 'Our policies have brought unprecedented prosperity,' she declared. 'We have been steady and staunch in defence.' And at the end of a long list of familiar achievements: 'These are the reasons we shall win a fourth election victory.'

The most memorable moment was a brief double act with

the Labour MP Dennis Skinner, who had so often tried to get the better of her in humorous exchanges. It had been suggested that, when she left office, she would continue to fight against a single European currency run by an independent central bank. Mr Skinner interrupted: 'No, she is going to be the governor.' Amid laughter, Mrs Thatcher replied, 'What a good idea. I hadn't thought of that.' She went on to explain that if she were governor, there would not be a bank like that, nor a single currency. 'So I shall consider the proposal.' She smiled broadly. 'Now where were we? I am enjoying this.' It was a bravura performance. The House of Commons rightly decided to allow Mrs Thatcher one last triumph at the Dispatch Box. At the end of the no confidence debate the government had a majority of 120. Tory MPs took some comfort from the fact that despite all the drama they were still firmly in power. One of them was certain to be the next prime minister.

But the political world had been turned upside down. In the corridors of Whitehall the government was in turmoil. No one knew who the next leader would be. After such a long period of domination by Mrs Thatcher few doubted that the change would be dramatic, but there was considerable uncertainty about the direction of that change. Many people were concerned about the manner in which the prime minister had been removed. 'Why did it have to end like this?' was one of the most common complaints. Senior Labour figures were privately worried about the effect a change of Conservative leader would have on their electoral prospects.

The Stock Exchange had reacted favourably to the news of Mrs Thatcher's resignation, judging it would help keep the Conservatives in government, and the first opinion poll, conducted by phone, showed the Tories ahead of Labour if Mr Heseltine took over. But to loyal Thatcherites the idea that the arch-traitor should be rewarded with the post he had sought all his adult life was just too awful to contemplate.

Many Conservatives were not reconciled to the loss of the leader they had for so long admired. They were determined to avoid doing anything which would reduce Mrs Thatcher's standing and were delighted that she seemed willing to stay in the political game. If there had been a vote that day of all members of the Conservative party there is no doubt she would have won with a big majority.

Mrs Thatcher's downfall had not resolved the Conservative split over Europe; it had demonstrated the extent of the rift. Her resignation would do nothing to heal the internal divisions. The manner of her departure and the feelings it generated would not be forgotten. Conservative activists across the country would not be easily won over to the new leader, whoever it was, and there were plenty who were determined to keep alive their passion for Mrs Thatcher. Many of those representing the party in the country felt let down by their parliamentary colleagues; they would seek revenge. They would be actively helped by Mrs Thatcher herself, who had no intention of retiring from politics. The problems besetting the Conservative party were by no means over; indeed they had hardly begun.

13

Anyone but Heseltine

MICHAEL HESELTINE might have been expected to rejoice at Mrs Thatcher's decision to resign. After all, he had wielded the knife which had finished her off. But in one important respect he had been too successful. If he had not forced her resignation and instead had been able to beat her in the continuing leadership contest by obtaining a majority of the votes of Conservative MPs, the crown would have been his – a lifetime's ambition would have been realized. By removing her entirely from the contest Mr Heseltine had made himself a likely loser, and he knew it. As he put it, 'To defeat her in open combat was one thing; to be held accountable for making her quit the field was quite another.' A majority of Tory MPs were in no mood to forgive Mr Heseltine for what he had done, and he was quick to sense that his best chance of leading the Conservative party might well have passed.

The news of Mrs Thatcher's decision was relayed to Mr Heseltine as he was being driven to London Zoo to plant a tree for a children's organization. This was typical of the hundreds of engagements he had undertaken after walking out of the cabinet over the Westland Affair nearly five years earlier. For most of that time he had been conducting an unofficial campaign for the leadership of the Conservative party. In America running for president can be openly acknowledged – when the campaign starts it has to be – but Britain's parliamentary system requires a far more circumspect approach. Any direct attack on a current leader will almost certainly backfire; the Tory rank and file would not approve.

Most of Mr Heseltine's engagements were party occasions, providing opportunities for him to impress the local MP as well as his constituents; he was said to have eaten more rubber chicken on the luncheon circuit than anyone else in Britain. His audiences were left to guess why he was so keen to win them over. Once, as a joke before the start of an interview, I suggested I would be forced to switch off my tape recorder if he criticized Mrs Thatcher. It completely broke the tension and he roared with laughter. We both knew that it would be a tremendous scoop if my interview contained an attack by him on the prime minister; and we also both knew that he had absolutely no intention of making that mistake.

Like an American presidential candidate Mr Heseltine was afforded a certain status. I remember how pleased he was when a cameraman thoughtfully removed the corner of the front page of the newspaper he was reading. It had his Blackpool hotel room number scribbled on it, which if shown on television could have been a security risk for him. Underpinning his extraordinary leadership campaign was Mr Heseltine's considerable personal fortune, derived from his publishing group. He would not have been able to leave the cabinet in the way he had, he once told me, if he had not been extremely wealthy. He had no compunction, for instance, about taking his official driver with him when he resigned and buying a Jaguar which looked like the sort of car the government would provide for a cabinet minister. His wealth gave him the confidence and resources to continue to be highly active in politics – like an eighteenth-century landowner – even though he was temporarily out of favour at court. But on the morning of 22 November 1990, despite all his efforts, it looked as if the top job was moving beyond his reach.

When Mr Heseltine heard that Mrs Thatcher had decided

to resign, he knew immediately that the game was up. He had been convinced that if she had decided to take him on in a second ballot, he would win. But he was equally convinced that with other candidates entering the race, he stood far less of a chance. Mr Heseltine was relieved that his only official duty that morning was to plant a tree; he would have found it difficult to tackle anything more complicated. Trees are one of his hobbies – at his country estate in Oxfordshire he has an extensive arboretum – so he was able to carry out the task without being too distracted. It was Mr Heseltine who coined the adage, 'He who wields the knife, never wears the crown.' He knew that he would have to bear much of the blame for Mrs Thatcher's fate because he was the one person who had openly set out to remove her. Loyal Tory MPs would do almost anything to stop him becoming prime minister, and so would Mrs Thatcher.

What was particularly irritating for Mr Heseltine was that he had tried so hard to disguise his opposition. He had been welcomed at all those Conservative luncheon parties because he did not appear to be rocking the boat. His only open revolt since the Westland Affair had been over the poll tax when he backed Michael Mates, who had proposed that the tax should be banded according to ability to pay. Mr Heseltine had made suggestions which departed from party policy on a variety of issues and had continued to make pro-European speeches, but he had avoided anything which might seem destructive or personal. After the years of self-discipline his one open challenge to Mrs Thatcher ultimately failed because she withdrew from the race. Thirteen years later Michael Howard would give a textbook example of how the Conservative leadership game should be played. He remained loyal to Iain Duncan Smith until he resigned, and then was able to pick up the crown without being accused of plotting.

There is, however, one tactic which Michael Mates now

believes the Heseltine team should have considered. After the first ballot Mr Heseltine could have announced that, despite the rules operating at the time, Mrs Thatcher had won the majority of votes and therefore she should continue to lead the party. He would withdraw from the race. For this to have worked, Mrs Thatcher would still have had to be forced to resign at some point, and that might not have happened until after the next election. But Mr Mates is convinced that at the first ballot she had been mortally wounded and would soon have given up her position. Whenever that resignation came, Mr Heseltine would have been well placed in the subsequent leadership contest, and perhaps it would not have been so obvious that he had been carrying the assassin's knife. Mr Mates told me, 'I deeply regret I never thought of it. Had he done that he might have been covered in glory, having behaved like the perfect gentleman.' It is an interesting subject for speculation, but no more than that since Mr Heseltine did not even consider withdrawing after the first ballot. He was fully geared up to fight the second ballot; and when Mrs Thatcher announced she would not be standing, Mr Heseltine believed he had no choice but to fight on.

The two other candidates, John Major and Douglas Hurd, had both loyally backed Mrs Thatcher, but now were free to campaign for themselves. If Norman Tebbit had decided to stand – and some MPs urged him to do so – the right wing of the party would have had their candidate. He had come close to rejoining the government as education secretary after Nigel Lawson resigned, but in our interview for this book Lord Tebbit said he was not convinced he would have beaten Mr Heseltine: 'I don't know whether I would have beaten Michael or not; who knows which way the ball would have bounced?' But he ruled himself out, and as the Thatcherites did not believe Douglas Hurd could beat Mr Heseltine, inevitably they began to look favourably on John Major. It was significant that Norman Tebbit was one of the first to join Mr Major's campaign team.

Mr Heseltine had hopes of securing the support of Cecil Parkinson, one of Mrs Thatcher's strongest supporters. They had been on friendly terms for many years, and Mr Parkinson had often told him that he should be Mrs Thatcher's successor. But a phone call on the day of Mrs Thatcher's resignation ended those hopes. 'People are saying you have committed regicide,' Mr Parkinson told him. Mr Heseltine replied, 'Reggie who?' but he could not laugh off the accusation. Mr Parkinson voted for Mr Major. Mrs Thatcher had told the cabinet that morning that they should look for a successor from within their own ranks; the implication was clear. All the members of the cabinet went along with that decision except for David Hunt, the Welsh secretary, who was away in Tokyo at the time; he did not feel bound by the collective decision despite a personal call from Mrs Thatcher. He came out in support of Mr Heseltine and so did former cabinet ministers Nigel Lawson, Sir Geoffrey Howe and Lord Carrington. It was certainly heavyweight support, but not of the right kind. Mr Heseltine needed to gain votes from among those who had previously stayed loyal to Mrs Thatcher.

Mr Heseltine fought on in as cheerful a manner as he could muster. He remembers the campaign as quite relaxed; it would all be over in six days. After Mrs Thatcher's decision to go the mood had lifted. Mr Heseltine wrote, 'It was as if the poison had been let out of the system.' The candidates expected to serve in the cabinet whoever won. The electorate consisted of the Tory MPs, and most of the campaigning could be done behind closed doors. Mr Heseltine even tried to win over members of the Thatcherite 92 group, so named after the number of the flat in which they first met. They had become the most prominent group of Tory backbenchers, and invited the candidates to speak at one of their meetings.

Mr Heseltine told me, 'Somebody at the meeting said, "Can you give me one reason why we, the Thatcherites, the praetorian guard, the Ninety-two, should vote for you?" I smiled and said, "Yes, because if you believe in all the things Mrs Thatcher says she believes in you get people like me, self-made businessmen and all that stuff."' Mr Heseltine said, 'They had the grace to titter, but the fact is there was prejudice and bigotry about their approach, which was awful.' On policy, the only issue they really cared about was Europe, and they longed for a candidate who would echo Mrs Thatcher's 'No, no, no' to any attempt to strengthen European institutions. Mr Heseltine, even if he had not been demonized as Mrs Thatcher's assassin, could hardly provide them with such guarantees.

I PERSONALLY THOUGHT Douglas Hurd stood a good chance of winning. He was a reassuring figure, far better known than Mr Major; but he did not have the vote-winning qualities Tory MPs were desperately seeking as they peered at the opinion polls. With either Mr Heseltine or Mr Major in charge, the polls suggested, the Conservatives would go back into the lead. For many MPs this was the vital question which Mrs Thatcher had been unable to answer in the first round. She had talked about policy, mostly the familiar doctrines of Thatcherism; they wanted to know how the party could become more popular. Mr Hurd made the mistake of trying to seem relaxed by appearing on camera in a cardigan. He also tried to refute the charge that he was a toff. He explained that he had gone to Eton on a scholarship, and that his father, though a member of the House of Lords, was not an aristocrat but a tenant farmer. These subtle distinctions carried little if any weight. His attempt to be less upper class than he appeared merely invited ridicule. The way he talked, his manners and his approach to life put him in a different category from Mr

Major, and the way he tried to deal with this issue reinforced the impression that he was lacking in media skills. Mr Hurd's campaign never really took off.

From the beginning Mr Major had the advantage of having played no part at all in Mrs Thatcher's removal. Truth being often stranger than fiction, it is only fair to point out that he had a genuine dental problem which prevented him from being at Westminster during the final days of the drama. Mr Major went into hospital for an operation to deal with an abscess under a wisdom tooth three days before the result of the first ballot. He was allowed back to his Huntingdon home the next day, but did not return to London until the morning Mrs Thatcher announced her resignation so did not even attend the cabinet meeting at which she tearfully informed her colleagues of her decision. Even as his campaign for the leadership got under way he was still taking heavy doses of painkillers.

Mr Major was, of course, kept closely in touch with what was happening, not least by his friend Jeffrey Archer whose driver had made sure his nomination papers were taken to London in time. But as he told his colleagues not to canvass for support unless Mrs Thatcher bowed out, he was able to say with conviction that he had nothing to do with any attempt to jump the gun. He specifically told his aides not to organize for a possible leadership campaign. As it turned out, this was by far the best tactic. To be asked by others to lead the party is one thing, to push yourself forward is quite another; and if you are nursing a painful jaw what better place to spend the time than back at home, miles away from Westminster?

In any case, Mr Major was not convinced his time had come. Even with half an hour to go before nominations closed, he was still not sure he should enter the contest. He recalls a last-minute conversation at his office in the Treasury with Norman Lamont, who would become his campaign manager.

Mr Major suggested Mr Hurd would be the best candidate. Mr Lamont shook his head vigorously; the door burst open and a delegation of supporters poured in. They included Michael Howard, William Hague, John Gummer, David Davis and Francis Maude. Mr Major says he was astounded. 'I had heard my name was being talked about at Westminster,' he wrote. 'I had no idea that I was likely to find such strong backing so quickly.' The speed of the Major bandwagon certainly was surprising, but that he was a strong contender for the leadership was never in doubt.

Long before there was much speculation about who might succeed Mrs Thatcher I remember watching Mr Major answer his first questions in the Commons as foreign secretary. The influential political editor of the *Daily Mail*, Gordon Greig, sauntered into the press gallery and said to me, 'Well, Johnny boy, do you see him as prime minister?' I had not expected the question. 'I'm not sure about the voice,' I replied. Once there was a vacancy, though, Mr Major, who had held the two top jobs, at the Foreign Office and the Treasury, was bound to be in the running. Under the parliamentary system the pool of talent is severely restricted. In America every citizen, theoretically, can run for president. To narrow down the field, candidates have to seek the support of the parties, money has to be raised, and the battle is usually spread over two years. At Westminster, in the days before a vote of party members was required, a new Conservative leader could be chosen in not much more than a week.

Soon after his appointment as chancellor, Mr Major was invited by Peter Morrison to his house for drinks. He was told that he should stand for leader 'after she's gone'. Mr Major could not be sure whether this message was sent with Mrs Thatcher's approval but he was sure Mr Morrison would not have made the comment if he thought she would object. In her memoirs Mrs Thatcher makes clear that as soon as she knew who would be standing in the election to succeed her, she was ready to support Mr Major. She writes, 'There was one more duty I had to perform, and that was to ensure that John Major was my successor. I wanted – perhaps I needed – to believe that he was the man to secure and safeguard my legacy.' Mrs Thatcher's comments were published in 1993, when it was already obvious that on key policies, including Europe, she had fallen out with her chosen successor. It is interesting that she used the phrase, 'perhaps I needed to believe'. It was clearly an attempt to answer those of her political allies who criticized her for promoting him. She is suggesting that she might have been wrong about Mr Major, but had backed him in the fervent hope he would carry on the torch. It seems to have been a case of the wish being father to the thought, and it provides the most convincing reason why she overlooked the fact that Mr Major was quite a different kind of Conservative from herself. He had never truly been 'one of us', as would become increasingly apparent as the years went by.

Mrs Thatcher always insisted on acting with a purpose, and in her last days at Number 10 she found the Major campaign a suitable focus for her energies. She did everything she could in private discussions to make sure that her supporters went over to Mr Major. Publicly she did not say she wanted him to win, but there were no members of this tiny electorate who were not fully aware of her preference. Working on Mr Major's behalf gave Mrs Thatcher a comforting feeling that she was still at the helm; it helped to counter the fear that all her power had gone. But her involvement behind the scenes was not entirely welcomed by those running the Major campaign, who had to answer Labour jibes that Mr Major was 'son of Thatcher'. They wanted to stress that he was his own man, and Mr Major and his close supporters were annoyed when she made a tactical mistake which reinforced the impression that her departure would not lead to her retirement from front-line politics.

The day before the second leadership ballot she paid a farewell visit to Conservative Central Office, the scene of so many of her triumphs. Surrounded by loyal party workers, she gave an emotional address. She mentioned that one of the first calls she had received after making her resignation announcement was from President Bush. They discussed Saddam Hussein's occupation of Kuwait and the looming prospect of allied action to eject Iraqi forces. 'President Bush,' she declared, 'won't falter, and I shan't falter. It's just that I shan't be pulling the levers there. But I shall be a very good back-seat driver.' Attempts were made by officials to suggest that Mrs Thatcher had been misreported, but then the *Independent* revealed it had a full transcript of her remarks taken from a tape recording. Mrs Thatcher as the back-seat driver of Mr Major's new government was exactly the image her candidate was trying to avoid. However, it was seized upon by Labour, anxious to promote the idea that there would be no real change.

It was, in any case, a strange use of this metaphor. Mrs Thatcher may have been seeking to convey the idea that, although she would be out of office, she would be helpfully assisting operations from behind the scenes. This is not, though, the usual image of back-seat drivers; to have someone in the back, shouting comments about your driving is not normally regarded as particularly helpful. For Mr Major it was an ominous portent. The partial explanation, that she had not driven a car for at least eleven years and had forgotten what it was like, did not soften the blow. Mr Major feared that Mrs Thatcher, though highly useful to him at this stage, could prove in the long term a serious liability.

The prime minister was more helpful to Mr Major at one of her last official engagements in Downing Street, a large lunch with her supporters which took place after her visit to

Central Office. She made it clear that she expected them to vote for Mr Major although she was careful not to mention his name. She later claimed that most of them accepted her advice. The next day, when the result was announced, all the anxieties in the Major camp evaporated. Mr Major had won with 185 votes; Mr Heseltine was on 131; Mr Hurd trailed with 56 votes. Once again the result had its quirky aspects. Strictly speaking, under the rules of the contest, Mr Major was two votes short of an outright win, but the other candidates quickly conceded. The new leader had 19 votes less than the 204 Mrs Thatcher had won in the first round; and it was interesting that Mr Heseltine's vote was 21 votes lower than his earlier score. He had been right to sense during the campaign that his support was ebbing away. The whole process, from the first ballot to the final result, had taken only eight days.

Mr Major later described the excitement at Number 11 when the result was announced. Mrs Thatcher came through the connecting door from Number 10. 'Well done, John,' she enthused. 'Well done.' And then she went over to Mr Major's wife Norma and told her, 'It's what I have always wanted.' With other journalists, I was waiting outside to hear Mr Major's response to his victory; his campaign team could hardly restrain themselves and at least one cabinet minister was seen to wipe away a tear.

Just before the door of Number 11 was opened, Mrs Thatcher said, 'I'll come out.' Mr Lamont took her to one side and said, 'Please let him have this moment.' She stayed inside. Mr Major later claimed that he would have preferred to have gone out into Downing Street with Mrs Thatcher. But she had her own way of attracting the attention of the media. She went upstairs and, with the lights on behind her, I could see her without difficulty through the curtains. Even though it became obvious that she had drawn the interest of the cameramen, she made no attempt to draw back. In her memoirs Mrs

Thatcher says, 'This was his night, not mine.' She makes no mention of the fact that the most familiar image of that night was of her at a window, looking down on her protégé as he made his first speech as party leader. It featured prominently on all the TV news bulletins and appeared in most of the newspapers. The idea that she would indeed be a back-seat driver was strongly reinforced.

The most revealing picture of the next day also featured Mrs Thatcher – as she left Number 10 for the last time as prime minister. Her tears had started to flow when she said farewell to the staff inside, some of whom were crying too, but she managed to contain herself to make a final statement to the battery of microphones outside. 'Now is the time for a new chapter to open,' she said. 'And I wish John Major all the luck in the world. He will be splendidly served and he has the makings of a great prime minister, which I am sure he will be in a very short time.' As she got into the car with Denis she could not hold back her tears. The abiding image of that day was of a deeply distressed Mrs Thatcher being driven away from the post she loved.

14

The nice Mr Major

WHENEVER JOHN MAJOR was discussed at the time of the leadership election it was almost inevitable that he would be described as 'nice'. As I prepared a profile of him for Radio 4's *Today* programme, I tried to limit the number of times this claim was made, not because it wasn't true, but because it soon became a cliché; it also said very little about what sort of prime minister he might become. Attempts to answer that question, though, proved extremely difficult. Mr Major maintains that his platform in the leadership election was not designed to appeal to the Thatcherites. He believes that Mrs Thatcher's supporters deceived themselves if they thought that he would pursue unchanged policies. He would press for social reform, tax cuts for the less well off and improved public services. 'We must help the disadvantaged,' he wrote in the *Sun*. It was not, he comments, a clarion call to the right of the party.

But his first task was to convince his fellow MPs that he could unite the party and give them a better chance of winning the next election. He faced one of the most common problems in politics: how to promote change while giving the impression that continuity would be preserved. A good deal of vagueness on exactly where he stood was the inevitable result. 'I have always studiously avoided labels on the grounds that they are grotesquely misleading,' he said, trying to suggest this was a positive virtue. On Europe, he argued, the party should favour 'gradualism, practicalism and common sense', whatever that might mean. On the poll tax, like the other candidates, he promised a full-scale review, but would not commit himself to outright abolition. All he would say was that he was 'increasingly convinced that we cannot leave things as they are'.

Even on the question of whether he was a Thatcherite Mr Major felt he had to be careful. His advisers were concerned that if he said yes this might encourage interviewers to ask, 'If the Conservatives are interested in a Thatcherite leader, why didn't they stick with the one they had?' Fortunately for Mr Major television interviewers did not home in on this point; they seemed more interested in how he differed as a character from the other candidates. The objective for Mr Major was to get through these interviews without making any obvious mistakes and certainly not to become riled if the questions appeared hostile. On these counts he did well. His policy commitments were kept to a minimum. He did very little to frighten Thatcher loyalists, and with such strong support from the former prime minister most of them assumed he was the rightful heir. The key point for all of his supporters was that the opinion polls suggested he had a good chance of beating Neil Kinnock at the next election; there was certainly more likelihood of this than if Mrs Thatcher had remained leader.

But Mr Major did have an image problem. He seemed a rather dull fellow. He wore spectacles; his hair was grey; his face was pale; his voice was undistinguished; and his suits were boring. This was not entirely to his disadvantage. After eleven years of Mrs Thatcher there was a definite yearning for a different kind of prime minister. It is a mistake to assume that if the country has been led by a charismatic figure, another such must be found to replace them. It frequently does not work out that way, and less charismatic successors have often been highly regarded. One obvious example is the dull-seeming Clement Attlee, who followed Winston Churchill. Mr Attlee not only defeated the great war leader in the election of 1945; the achievements of his reforming Labour government, which included the founding of the NHS, established his reputation as one of Britain's most successful prime ministers.

In the United States the candidate for the presidency chooses a running mate to become vice president, and they are usually less exciting figures. But Harry Truman who took over on the death of Franklin D. Roosevelt, and Lyndon B. Johnson, who moved into the White House after John F. Kennedy's assassination, more than overcame their image problems. It seems almost a rule that immense personalities are replaced by less colourful leaders. France's great president Charles de Gaulle was succeeded by the stodgy figure of Georges Pompidou; in Britain the Conservative prime minister Harold Macmillan, otherwise known as Supermac, was followed by the diffident aristocrat Sir Alec Douglas Home. A sharp difference of character, from overwhelming to underwhelming, can work to a newcomer's advantage.

Over time, and with the relentless exposure of the modern media, people become bored with charismatic characters unable to resist the limelight; in November 1990 there was a strong sense of relief among the public at large that John Major was not remotely like Margaret Thatcher. Conservative MPs keen on the new leadership felt that the best aspects of the Thatcher period could be maintained, but without the excesses which had clouded her last period in office. It would be a far less autocratic, more consultative leadership. Other members of the cabinet would carry more weight. There would be less drama and more common sense; the government would be closer to the people. A former minister told me recently he had strongly welcomed the prospect of change. He had not been concerned that Mr Major did not have a clear philosophy for government. He had thought it would be like getting someone to clear up the mess on a building site. All the difficult design and construction work had been completed; it just needed a competent foreman to bring it up to scratch.

Mr Major's strongest card was his remarkable personal story, which read like the American dream of log cabin to White House. The new prime minister's achievement in overcoming hardship and poverty to reach the top was impressive. From a family with an invalid father living in two cramped, rented rooms in Brixton to the pinnacle of government at Number 10 was no distance in terms of miles; in practice it was an extraordinary achievement. To do this from within the Labour party would have been difficult enough, although they had senior figures proud to assert their working-class backgrounds. A Conservative party leader able to say he had left school at sixteen and apparently unaware of how many O levels he had was a source of wonder. Until fairly recently Conservative leaders had been drawn almost exclusively from the upper classes, and the obvious exceptions, Edward Heath and Margaret Thatcher, came from families who were certainly not poor and who had been able to launch them on successful academic careers at Oxford. When Mr Major talked of the need for Britain to be a classless society, it seemed to carry a great deal of conviction.

At his last conference speech before becoming prime minister in 1990 I remember being struck by his potential electoral appeal. He would never be very successful as an orator; the moment he tried to raise the volume, his voice began to sound strangled. But he could tell jokes, and there was no doubt that he related to the audience. Mrs Thatcher's biographer Hugo Young was not uncritical; he complained in the *Guardian* that Mr Major's speech extolling the virtues of capitalism was 'without the vestige of an original idea'. But Mr Young argued that Mr Major seemed to be in command of himself. 'He provides a kind of calm sanity. The thin, granite mouth speaks for well-organised resolve. This man, you sense, knows with a frightening clarity what he thinks he is doing.' While some commentators were dismissive – Andrew Rawnsley, also writing in the *Guardian*, told his readers that Mr Major had no personality – Mr Young was impressed by how well the Conservative ranks responded to this potential leadership candidate. Mrs Thatcher had always appeared to be above them, and was keen to distinguish between those who were 'one of us', and those who were not. Mr Major seemed a more inclusive figure, someone who stood closer to their own lives, to be 'one of them'. Hugo Young perceptively summed up his prospects: 'The modern Tory party relates to him with a comfort that will grow.'

Mr Major drew his strength from his family circumstances. When he was born, in 1943, his father Tom Major was already sixty-three and married for the second time, with a colourful past behind him. Major was a stage name, picked up in the early part of a career in show business that lasted for nearly thirty years. Born in Walsall but brought up in America, he was originally Tom Ball. No prime minister before had been able to claim that their father had been a trapeze artist; and that was only one of Tom Major's skills. He was also a singer, dancer and conjurer. With his first wife Kitty Drum he had formed a music hall double act, Major and Drum; he boasted that they had appeared at all the main music halls in Britain and Ireland. The marriage was childless and ended in tragedy when Kitty was badly injured during rehearsal after being struck on the head by a steel girder. Their show-business career was over and Kitty never fully recovered. She died a few years later, in 1928, after deciding Tom should marry one of her friends, a singer and dancer called Gwen Coates. This was John Major's mother.

Until the age of twelve, John, who was the couple's third child – he had a much older brother and sister – led a relatively happy and secure existence. He got on well with his loving parents; though elderly his father told marvellous stories about his career, and his mother, twenty-six years Tom Major's junior, sometimes did acrobatics in the garden. But then Tom's business collapsed. For years he had made garden ornaments, including gnomes, in a business he ran from home. But old age, infirmity and bad luck had taken their toll, and in 1955 the family were forced to rent premises in Brixton: just two rooms, with a cooker forming a makeshift kitchen on the landing outside. They shared a bathroom with the other tenants. John Major had to travel for an hour and a half to get to Rutlish Grammar School, having secured a place there the year before after passing his eleven-plus. He disliked the school and was not an academic success; with the additional problems at home, it seemed sensible to leave at sixteen, and get a job.

His first jobs were hardly inspiring; he did several years of manual work, failed to become a bus driver and eventually ended up as a clerk, first with the London Electricity Board and then with the District Bank. His first serious affair was with a much older woman. It brought his mother's disapproval; but after his father's death at the age of eighty-two, in 1962, John Major was keen to take control of his own destiny. At about the same time, though, he remained true to his father's political views by joining the Young Conservatives. His father had strongly disliked Clement Attlee's Labour government, claiming it had made life for small businesses like his very much harder.

Those who looked into Mr Major's background to try to find out why he had not become a socialist concluded that his father's influence, his preference for individual rather than collective action and his determination to get out of poverty all drew him to the Conservatives. As a young man Mr Major did not get his political ideas from books; they came directly from his practical view of the world. To him one of the great strengths of the Conservative party was that it appeared to provide a way up in class terms. It was not only an advantage to meet people in the party who might be helpful to your career; it also demonstrated to everyone else that you were the kind of person who wanted to climb the ladder. Successful people, according to this view, became members of the Conservative party – and that is what John Major wanted to be. His first attempt at office was at the age of twenty-one as the Conservative candidate in a local council election in Lambeth. His enthusiasm was undimmed by his failure; it was a safe Labour seat.

Having passed his banking exams with the international Standard Chartered Bank, he was posted to Nigeria; but once there he was badly injured in a car accident and spent most of a year recovering. He was never again able to play cricket properly. Indirectly, the accident had a marked affect on his political career. Postings abroad seemed less attractive and he set his sights increasingly on politics. He prospered at the bank and at the same time became a Lambeth councillor. He met his wife Norma through the Conservative party, although she was not keen on politics; and after failing to get elected to Westminster in the 1974 general election he finally succeeded in becoming an MP five years later. It had not been easy. He had difficulty getting selected as a candidate, and he once complained to a friend, 'People like us, with modest backgrounds and non-BBC accents, will always be at a disadvantage in selections.' But in the selection process for the safe seat of Huntingdon in Cambridgeshire he had beaten many people with more impressive CVs. The unsuccessful candidates included the future Tory leader Michael Howard, and two of the party's intellectuals, Peter Lilley and Chris Patten, all of whom would become cabinet ministers.

Much of Mr Major's success was due to his skill with people. He wanted to be liked, and he soon learned how to flatter, how to listen, how to put his arms round people without them being offended, to remember their names, and always to be extremely polite. Unlike Mr Heseltine, who was instinctively a more reserved character, Mr Major was the original 'Mr Touchy-Feely' at Westminster. He would take every opportunity to squeeze your arm or pat your hand. Much of the new prime minister's social skills and his attitude to people may have come from his mother. 'Gwen had a straightforward philosophy,' he wrote. 'Share what you have got. Be polite to others. Think of their feelings. Make allowances for them. Stand up for yourself but don't cause unnecessary offence. Don't show your own feelings.' Unfortunately, neither of Mr Major's parents lived long enough to see him become an MP, let alone prime minister.

Mr Major's rise to power at Westminster started in a solid, rather unspectacular way. He was parliamentary private secretary to Sir Patrick Mayhew and Timothy Raison, who were ministers of state at the Home Office. This was a chance to see at close quarters the legendary political skills of William Whitelaw, who was then home secretary. Mr Major then joined the whips' office, the MPs who are the military policemen of the House of Commons. It is their job to see that the government's business is enacted. When votes are counted, they make sure that the MPs who should have taken part have taken part, and if not find out why not. The whips' office – each party has one – is the engine room driving the political machine forward; it is also the place for gossip, and for promotion, the best place to start for an ambitious MP. Mr Major spent two years there; and it was as a senior whip that he had his first serious encounter with Mrs Thatcher.

It was at a dinner at Number 10 that Mr Major passed a vital test with the woman who would become his most important patron. Invited to give his views on Conservative backbench opinion, he had been devastatingly frank. 'They don't like our policies,' he told the prime minister. 'They're worried that capital expenditure is being sacrificed to current spending.' Although Mrs Thatcher made clear she did not like this message, he stuck to his guns. The temperature rose. He was shaking with anger and nearly walked out. He was, he told her, simply repeating the views of others. It was a risky line to take, but it soon became apparent that not all was lost. Denis Thatcher came up to him afterwards and said, 'She'll have enjoyed that.' The next day Mrs Thatcher had a friendly chat with him in the Commons, and a few weeks later he was given his first ministerial post, as a junior minister in the Department of Social Security. He was on his way up.

Lord Tebbit, who would eventually fall out with Mr Major, mainly over Europe, remembers being impressed by him in those early days. 'Whilst he was coming up through the ranks he was a Thatcherite,' he told me. 'And I thought he would be a considerable force in the government quite early on. I'd watched him dealing with some of those balls-achingly boring and complex issues, of pensions and things of that kind; and it struck me that he had a very good mind for understanding that stuff, which most people haven't.' Lord Tebbit also noted that Mr Major was an extraordinarily courteous person, who got on well with his officials and col-leagues. It was not only Mrs Thatcher who had taken a shine to the junior minister at the Department of Social Security.

At the same time, although this was kept secret until September 2002, Mr Major was succeeding with a far more junior woman politician, one who longed to become the second Mrs Thatcher. This was the flamboyant, ambitious Tory MP Edwina Currie, who, as she would point out, shared her birthday with the prime minister. Mrs Currie had decided that her husband was boring and insufficiently interested in what she was doing; she complained in her diaries that he spent too much time slumped snoring in front of the television.

After an unsatisfactory liaison with another man who failed to understand the importance of her career, she lighted on Mr Major. 'He was so bloody nice, and so attractive,' she wrote. 'And so quiet in public, that it was a challenge to unearth the real person, and to seduce him – easy!'

The affair went on for four years, according to Edwina Currie, and then she wrote to him saying it was all over. By this time he was a member of the cabinet, chief secretary to the Treasury. She wrote in her diaries that the relationship had changed. 'It was best,' she said, 'when he was restless, hiding himself, and lacked confidence. Recently, as he has done so well, the doubts have vanished and our conversations have become more like rehearsals for his speeches. He moves in such exalted circles that I can't match them.' The fun had gone out of the affair. Mr Major, she decided, did not need her any more. When the story became known – she revealed it on the eve of the publication of her diaries – the political world was amazed. The journalists at Westminster, particularly the tabloid reporters, resented being left in the dark. It was a brilliantly kept secret. I am frequently asked if I had any knowledge of the affair, and I reply that I am baffled to this day. Edwina Currie was so obviously pushy and attention-seeking from the day she entered Parliament, it seems extraordinary that a person of Mr Major's charm and ability would fall for her. When I say, 'But why her?' during an after-dinner speech, it usually gets a good laugh. Once, after a group of MPs had returned from a trip abroad I was having a drink with one of them. 'What was it like?' I asked. 'Well, Edwina was in the group,' my informant replied as if there was nothing else that need be said. Even Mrs Thatcher had not known of the affair at the time; apparently she was as surprised as the rest of us. Mr Major admitted it was the most shameful event of his life, but his wife Norma had known about it for many years and he said she had long forgiven him.

Unlike many of the scandals that come out at Westminster, this affair was taken seriously because it could have affected recent political history. At various stages in Mr Major's subsequent career public revelation of the relationship could have had a devastating effect. It might have prevented him from becoming chancellor or foreign secretary, and if it had leaked out while the leadership campaign was under way would have wrecked his chances of becoming prime minister. Douglas Hurd told me that if Mrs Thatcher had known at the time of the election she would 'probably not have backed him'. Mr Hurd might have become leader instead. During Mr Major's difficult period in government when he was beset by problems following his 'back to basics' speech the news would have made him a laughing stock. The speech was interpreted as a call for a return to moral values, and a number of ministerial casualties followed. If he had been accused of having an affair at that point, he might have been forced to resign.

But Edwina Currie, the talkative darling of the media circus, did not let on. Mr Major continued on what looked like his irresistible rise. Various dates have been suggested for when Mrs Thatcher decided that he might become her successor, but there is no doubt that his appointment to succeed Sir Geoffrey Howe as foreign secretary in 1989, the year before she fell, was crucial. A smiling Mrs Thatcher bestowed the surprising honour in her office at Number 10. 'Aren't there others better qualified?' Mr Major asked. She waved her hand dismissively.

Mrs Thatcher's former private secretary Lord Powell told me she had wanted Mr Major to be a leading member of the government. She did not have a clear plan and certainly did not, at that stage, expect him to move on so quickly to become chancellor of the exchequer. 'She made him foreign secretary for one reason alone,' Lord Powell said in our interview for this book. 'She thought this was the quickest way to give somebody profile, to build them up. A foreign secretary is constantly seen on television, going up and down the steps of aircraft. I don't think she ever thought he was likely to be a particularly good foreign secretary, or that he even wanted to be; and he was certainly shocked when the proposal was put to him. But she thought she was doing him a favour.'

Even as he rose to the very top, Mr Major was constantly being underestimated. It happened so often it is tempting to see this as one of the clues to his success. How was it that he triumphed while other, far cleverer politicians failed? Part of the answer must be that he did not appear threatening; those who could help him did not sense the driving ambition, the iron determination behind the smile. When people felt his hand on their backs, they did not imagine that it held a dagger. His mother had taught him: 'Stand up for yourself but don't cause unnecessary offence. Don't show your own feelings.' Well, it worked for John Major, and for a time it looked as though he might be the answer to his party's prayers.

15

Managing without Maggie

THE IDEA THAT Mrs Thatcher could have returned to government to serve as a cabinet minister under John Major never
seemed remotely likely. Such a rebound had happened in the
recent past. Sir Alec Douglas Home, defeated when the Conservatives lost the election of 1964, returned to serve as foreign
secretary under Edward Heath when Labour lost the election
of 1970. But Sir Alec had only been prime minister for just
over a year, a further six years had elapsed, and he was quite
a different character from Mrs Thatcher. He had not stamped
his personality on the office as she had, and he was not held
personally responsible for a hugely unpopular policy, as was
the case with Mrs Thatcher and the poll tax. It is a measure of
Mr Major's desire to unite his party that he even contemplated
the idea.

Mrs Thatcher's entrenched views on Europe precluded her
from becoming foreign secretary or chancellor, and anything
less would have been demeaning. There was a fleeting suggestion that she might become British ambassador to Washington,
the post she had offered her predecessor Edward Heath. But
Mr Major concluded that would look as if he was trying to
shuffle her off the stage. Within a few days of her departure,
her Labour friend Frank Field suggested to one of Mr Major's
inner circle that she should become an ambassador to Africa
for the group of seven leading industrial nations, the G7. He
thought she might be able to use her political strength to
shame some of the African leaders into doing more for their

starving populations. Mr Field asked Mrs Thatcher at an informal gathering, whether she would be prepared to take on the role. 'Of course I would do it, Frank, but they won't offer it to me.' And she was right. 'I decided,' Mr Major wrote later, 'there was no credible job to offer her.'

Mrs Thatcher was left to determine her own future, but her erstwhile rival Michael Heseltine was never in any doubt that he would be asked to join Mr Major's cabinet. To the annoyance of the Thatcherites, every effort was made to see that Mr Heseltine was given a job he wanted. Mr Heseltine was first offered the Home Office, which he declined; but then Mr Major thought of a move which a chess player would appreciate. During the leadership campaign Mr Heseltine had promised to replace the deeply unfair poll tax with a more equitable measure. Well, let him devise one; and if people thought the environment job, which included the poll tax, was less like the queen on a chess board and more like a poisoned chalice, let him try to refuse. Mr Major decided that he should be the new environment secretary, and Mr Heseltine accepted the challenge with a smile and a handshake for the cameras in Downing Street. He could not have rejected the offer, and it suited Mr Heseltine to be the head of an active department where real decisions were taken and projects undertaken. The Home Office, he was convinced, was a political graveyard. It is certainly a department where luck plays a big part – sudden breaches in security or newsworthy crime can mar the reputation of the office holder – and Mr Heseltine was no longer convinced that luck was on his side. The new home secretary was Kenneth Baker; and as it turned out, this would be his last job in government.

The easiest decision for Mr Major was to leave the third leadership candidate, Douglas Hurd, at the foreign office. He seemed born for the part. He looked and behaved like a foreign secretary, and his early career had been with the diplomatic service. To his critics he was too much the foreign office man, keen on diplomatic solutions and less ready to play the tough hand often demanded by Mrs Thatcher. But changing the foreign secretary at this stage would hardly be sensible. So much was already in train, most obviously the preparations for a possible war to eject Saddam Hussein's forces from Kuwait. Mr Major was as determined as Mrs Thatcher that the Iraqis be pushed back to their own borders if they refused to leave of their own accord. For his part, Mr Hurd was confident of having a much closer and friendlier relationship with Mr Major than he had managed with Mrs Thatcher, not least because they agreed over Europe. Mr Hurd had never been 'one of us'. With Mr Heseltine and Mr Hurd in top jobs, Kenneth Clarke appointed education secretary and Chris Patten as party chairman, the pro-Europeans had done well.

Deciding who should replace himself as chancellor of the exchequer was not so easy. The appointment of Norman Lamont, Mr Major's campaign manager, was seen by some as simply a quid pro quo for being on the winning team. There were doubts, particularly about his political skills and lack of popular appeal, and critics felt vindicated when the appointment eventually ended with his acrimonious resignation. But at the beginning of his term of office Mr Major felt the need for stability; Mr Lamont had long ministerial experience in the Treasury and he was well known to the financial markets. Given that in the end he would be remembered as the chancellor who presided over Britain's humiliating removal from the ERM, it is interesting to note his own views on the subject. He would become a committed opponent of a single currency, but he confesses to having been agnostic about the ERM when the cabinet battle was being fought on this issue. At the time, Mr Lamont wrote to Mr Lawson urging him to stay in the government; to leave over the ERM, he told him, 'was not worth it'. But if it had been his decision at the time of entry Norman Lamont says he would have said no.

Britain's membership of the ERM would be one of the crucial factors in determining the management of the economy over the next two years. The arguments over Europe, which had provided the backdrop to so much of the drama in the late Thatcher period, would now have a critical effect on living standards and the long-term prospects of John Major's government. Membership – the decision to join made by Mrs Thatcher on Mr Major's advice – gave the new chancellor far less room for manoeuvre than in the past. From now on the overriding aim would be to maintain the value of the pound within the system. There is more than a touch of irony in the fact that the chancellor responsible for this policy never had much faith in the ideas behind it.

For Mr Lamont or for any other senior member of the government to complain, even in private, about the constraints of ERM membership was not easy. It was regarded by Mr Major as his most impressive achievement in government. Mr Hurd and Mr Heseltine were fully signed up and it was in the area of European policy that Mr Major was hoping to achieve a rapid shift towards a more constructive outlook. After Mrs Thatcher's famous 'no, no, no', it would soon be Mr Major's turn to decide how to respond to the other European leaders. Newsrooms – and the BBC television newsroom is no exception – are notoriously affected by hindsight; if the first Rome summit had been a sensation, with Mrs Thatcher isolated and eventually forced to resign, then surely the second summit in Rome, held only a month later, was bound to be dramatic. I was not convinced; and when I learned that two other correspondents, the economics editor Peter Jay and the diplomatic correspondent Brian Hanrahan, would also be sent to provide television coverage I was concerned the BBC might be disappointed by the event.

I need not have worried about whether I would get a fair share of the story. Peter Jay was sceptical about the prospects for a single European currency. He was convinced it was a bad idea and took the view that before long European leaders would come to the same conclusion. Peter was happy to remain in the role of occasional commentator. Another foreign news story then came along, which took Brian away from Rome, so I was left with the bulk of the coverage. It was just as well. John Major had no intention of ruffling any feathers in his first outing on the European stage. His natural role of consensus builder fitted in with the inclination of the other leaders not to push the new British leader. It is often the case in the European Union that if the leaders combine to attack one of their colleagues – as they did with their ambush on Mrs Thatcher – on the next occasion when they meet they work hard to smooth over their differences. Mr Major's European honeymoon began in Rome, with the other heads of government genuinely relieved that, as they saw it, the obstacle to progress of Mrs Thatcher had at last been removed. The summit itself was something of an anti-climax, and Mr Major proved less able than the broadcasters had hoped to provide vivid comments. I sent him a message that I would be seeking his reaction after his first meeting with his new colleagues. Seeing him pacing up and down I assumed he was working on a suitable riposte, but when I thrust my microphone in front of him all he could manage was, 'It's been a very interesting morning.' This was hardly the sort of remark to lift a subject already burdened with a heavy yawn factor.

Back in the Commons, when he reported on the summit Mr Major's tone was markedly different from Mrs Thatcher's bristling antagonism of the month before. Whereas she had stressed the negative, he was more inclined to say maybe. He made no fresh commitments, but he did not rule out progress. I used a split-screen technique to illustrate the point on the six o'clock news: first Mrs Thatcher on one side, then fading to Mr Major on the other. The contrast was stark, and it annoyed the Labour party. The head of Mr Kinnock's office Charles Clarke, later to join Tony Blair's cabinet, was livid. We had a stand-up row. It was, he insisted, poor journalism. But I was not alone: the press generally were pointing up the way Mr Major was changing the political landscape, and if Mr Major represented change, where did that leave Neil Kinnock? Labour were desperately concerned that when the election came the electorate's traditional demand for fresh ideas and faces would already have been met, at least in part, by John Major. The election was at most only eighteen months away.

Mr Major was keen to maintain a relaxed relationship with the press. It would not last for long, but we enjoyed it while we could. In Rome the senior correspondents found themselves chatting to the prime minister on several occasions as he waited between meetings. That had been unheard of at the end of the Thatcher period, when the opportunity to put questions to her during a summit became increasingly rare: she would usually restrict herself to one news conference at the end. There had been no likelihood of a chance encounter either in London or abroad. At the beginning of his period in office Mr Major would still walk alone around the House of Commons. I remember talking to him in the members' lobby one evening about how he had changed the atmosphere with his fellow European leaders. 'I didn't think it would be difficult,' he said disarmingly. It was, in his view, a straightforward and necessary way to improve the conduct of European business. At meetings inside the cabinet there was a markedly more relaxed atmosphere. Chris Patten called it 'liberation'. Whereas Mrs Thatcher had tended to issue her opinion at the beginning and wait to see if it was challenged, Mr Major would sum up at the end of a discussion in a more traditional way. Some of this shift in mood was a necessary consequence of the weakness in Mr Major's position. He was feeling his way, not least in his relationship with Michael Heseltine. They had not known each other very well, and it would take time for trust between them to develop.

In policy terms Mr Major was in a more difficult position than those prime ministers who are appointed following a general election. Mrs Thatcher in 1979 had worked out the main changes she wanted to introduce, and indeed had spent several years in preparation. Mr Major had to get going from a standing start. The biggest problem was the poll tax, which would soon reach an average level of more than £400. The only way to lower this figure was to increase the support provided to local councils from central government. It would mean a large increase in public spending and was only a short-term solution. Mr Heseltine had to find an alternative system, preferably before the election. Although the poll tax could hardly have been more unpopular, there were still loyal Thatcherites determined that this part of her legacy, her flagship policy, should not be allowed to sink. They were obstinately wedded to the idea that it would show up wasteful councils and boost the Conservative vote.

Much depended on whether the relationship between Mr Major and Mr Heseltine could stand the strain. They had never been close, and in the leadership election they had been pitted directly against each other; now they were at least trying to be cordial. Among Mr Major's advisers there was suspicion. Having demonstrated such a burning, long-term desire to become prime minister, how could they be sure Mr Heseltine would not begin to plot against the new leader? John Wakeham, who had kept his old job as energy secretary, described to me how he acted as a go-between for Mr Major and Mr

Heseltine as they tried to thrash out an alternative to the poll tax. Instead of the two men working together on this crucially important policy, it seems they required Mr Wakeham to apply his skills behind the scenes to make sure that the final deal was acceptable to both of them.

The negotiations were eventually successful. The replacement for the Community Charge would be called the Council Tax; it would be a property tax not very different from the old rating system, and there would be a shift away from local taxation to ease the burden generally. To pay for this, VAT would go up in the next budget by 2.5 per cent. After the main details had been agreed Mr Wakeham followed Mr Heseltine out of the cabinet room and into Downing Street. 'I got up and walked out with him and I said to him, "I'm coming with you, just in case any press people see you. We don't want a message going round the world that you've walked out again."' Mr Wakeham then returned to the cabinet room, where Mr Major asked him what he had been up to. They both needed to be reassured about Mr Heseltine's activities. Mr Wakeham told me in our interview for this book that eventually they all realized that Mr Heseltine was 100 per cent loyal to Mr Major, but 'We didn't know that at the time.' That they should have had such fears is an extraordinary indication of just how jumpy Mr Major and his colleagues were.

The Thatcherites saw the position within Mr Major's cabinet in a completely different light. They were convinced that the pro-Europeans, particularly Mr Heseltine, effectively had a veto on all key decisions made by John Major. They did not regard his cabinet as balanced in the way that Mr Major did. For them it was tipped, in favour of Europe. In the light of future developments within the Conservative party it is interesting to see how at this stage it looked as though the Euro-sceptics had been defeated. The split on Europe was the one that mattered to most MPs and most activists in the constituencies. Mr Heseltine's return to the cabinet in such a prominent position caused concern and even some anger among many Conservatives; Mrs Thatcher and her close allies would never be reconciled to his political comeback.

As if the political struggle at home was not enough, Mr Major now had to contemplate the prospect of war in the Middle East. When Iraq invaded Kuwait in August 1990, the Western response was swift. The invasion was seen as a threat to oil supplies as well as an attempt to alter the balance of power in the region, and within days the first steps were made towards building a military coalition to take on Saddam Hussein. Mrs Thatcher had thrown herself into the crisis from the very beginning; she had heard the news while attending a conference with President Bush at Aspen in Colorado. For her it was an opportunity to relive some of the excitement of the Falklands campaign, and she grasped it like an old trooper. Ships were immediately deployed and plans prepared. She felt her wide experience in office and her friendship with many world leaders could be brought into play. She was totally convinced that the cause was just; at one stage she even warned President Bush not to 'go wobbly'. It does not seem likely that the US commander-in-chief would have backed down in the face of the Iraqi aggression, but she enjoyed the contrast between her complete certainty and his more doubtful approach. It is not surprising that her comment quickly surfaced in the British press.

Mr Major's task was to continue planning on the basis that hostilities would commence soon after the UN deadline of 15 January had passed unless Saddam Hussein changed his mind. There were some last-minute attempts at diplomacy. Mr Bush offered to send his secretary of state James Baker to Baghdad and invited the Iraqi foreign minister to Washington. But he phoned Mr Major before making the announcement, making it clear that this was simply to demonstrate that all possible efforts were being made to resolve the matter peacefully. He reassured Mr Major he was not going 'wobbly', making it clear that Mrs Thatcher's remark had not been forgotten, and maybe not entirely forgiven either. When Mr Major visited Mr Bush in Washington just before Christmas, he found the president easy and relaxed. President Bush had a distinguished war record; Mr Major had no military experience whatsoever. But they seemed to hit it off, and they shared a reluctance to send men into battle. Mr Major writes of how strange and unexpected it was for him to be contemplating leading his country into a full-blown land war when the high points of his career so far had been dealing with dry, technical matters in the Treasury and the Department of Social Security. 'As a non-soldier,' he says, 'I was uneasy at sending others to war, even though I had no doubt it was right to do so.'

As foreign secretary, Douglas Hurd had the invidious task of travelling the world looking for donations to support military action against Saddam Hussein. With some countries, helping financially was clearly in their interest. The ruler of Kuwait promised £600 million without any fuss. King Fahd of Saudi Arabia spoke to Mr Hurd without stopping for eighty minutes, and so grand were the circumstances – an audience chamber full of princes – that nothing as vulgar as money could be mentioned; but a satisfactory deal was sorted out later. In Europe Mr Hurd found his task easier than expected. A meeting with Helmut Kohl demonstrated the extent to which John Major's appointment as prime minister had improved relations with Germany. Mr Hurd reported that he had never seen Helmut Kohl so energetic, beaming and ebullient; he did not say he was pleased Mrs Thatcher was no longer at Number 10, but he made friendly comments about Mr Major and was generous to the cause. Having pledged DM800 million (nearly £300 million) to support military action, he asked whether that would be enough.

The coalition against Saddam Hussein held together surprisingly well, but Mr Hurd insists it would have broken down quickly if the allies had decided that removing Iraqi forces from Kuwait was merely the first objective. Within a few days of the start of the ground attack on 24 February 1991, the Iraqis had been driven out and a ceasefire was called. I interviewed Mr Major for television news and asked him more than once what he thought would happen to Saddam Hussein; he assured me that having been humiliated in battle his regime would crumble. That was certainly the assumption in both Washington and London, and pushing on to Baghdad was never seriously considered by either Mr Bush or Mr Major. The plan, which had very wide support at the UN, was simply to reverse the original Iraqi occupation of Kuwait. It would take another twelve years, and the determination of Mr Bush's son, supported by Tony Blair, before Saddam Hussein could be removed from power.

The conclusion of the Gulf War left Mrs Thatcher acutely aware of her changed circumstances. Having taken part in all the main decisions at the beginning of the crisis, it was frustrating for her subsequently to be left on the sidelines. When her memoirs were published two years later, she gave a succinct reason why this had happened: 'I was not allowed by the Conservative Party to see through the campaign to throw Saddam Hussein out of Kuwait.' How could she maximize her influence in future, and what steps could she take to make her presence felt? These were matters which increasingly weighed on her mind.

16

Finding a plumber, and a new role

WHEN MRS THATCHER left the embrace of the civil service and returned to the real world, she found life difficult in various ways. Like the rest of us she had to grapple with the mundane tasks of ordinary existence, and in particular how to find a plumber on a Sunday. Mrs Thatcher's answer to this problem was to ring her former private secretary Charles Powell, who had stayed on to work for Mr Major. Mr Powell, who previously had led her through the intricacies of world politics, thought for a moment and then came to the unsurprising conclusion that the best method would be to look in the *Yellow Pages*. He told me the story as a way of illustrating the shock to Mrs Thatcher of leaving Downing Street. Almost everything in her life had changed: not only did she have to contemplate her dramatic loss of power and responsibility at the highest level, she had to come to terms again with all the practical problems which the resident of Number 10 can blissfully ignore.

Mrs Thatcher might have found even looking through the *Yellow Pages* a strange and tedious chore, but fortunately Mr Powell was able to help. He leafed through a copy. 'So here's a number,' Mr Powell told his former boss. 'Ring this guy and I am sure he'll come round and fix the problem.' An hour or so later Mrs Thatcher phoned back to say that the job had been done; she was startled, though, at the price. Mr Powell assured her that exorbitant fees from emergency plumbers had become the norm. He might have added that this was one of the more striking changes of her period in office.

The plumbing problem occurred in the luxury flat the Thatchers had been lent in Belgravia by an admirer, the widow of the American industrialist Henry Ford. They had not met Mrs Ford before. She told Mrs Thatcher, 'I come to London for a couple of days a year. You are the greatest prime minister of Britain that there has ever been, and it would be such an honour if you stayed in my flat.' The Thatchers moved in after a few difficult weeks at the house they had bought four years earlier in Dulwich. With Denis in mind, it adjoined a golf course, but it was difficult to achieve the necessary level of security and was too far from the centre of London and the active political and social life Mrs Thatcher intended to lead. The following summer they moved to a house also in Belgravia, in Chester Square. The police security continued; ever since the Brighton bomb she had been closely guarded. I suggested to John Whittingdale, who had left Downing Street to continue working for her, that it must have been difficult for her to do any shopping. 'She didn't shop,' he replied. 'They wouldn't let her go down to Tesco. Denis had a little more freedom, but for her to go anywhere was a major undertaking, just as it had been when she was prime minister.'

One of the changes Mrs Thatcher had to get used to was the fact that the Number 10 switchboard was longer at her beck and call. This small team of highly efficient and friendly operators work hard to ensure all senior staff and other relevant contacts can be reached. As a political journalist, I was on their list. The calm announcement, 'Hello, John, it's Number Ten here,' might reach me at any time of the day or night, at home or abroad; and it was hard not to feel a twinge of excitement even if it was simply a message giving the time of the next briefing by the prime minister's press secretary. The operators could put me in touch with whoever was in that post, and a careful record was kept of our private numbers. For Mrs Thatcher it was a serious blow to be deprived of their services.

She was embarrassed to admit to one of her staff that she did not know how to reach her daughter; in the past it had been so easy to say, 'Could you get Carol for me?'

When the phone did ring in her borrowed flat, there were times when Mrs Thatcher was unable to throw off the responses which had become instinctive in Number 10. In her first television interview, recorded in the United States for an American network, she told Barbara Walters, 'The telephone goes and immediately you think, Oh goodness me, the United Nations is sitting. Then you realize that it's no longer you any more. I remember when the tanks had gone into Vilnius. I kind of leapt up and dialled the telephone. Then I realized it was no longer me.' 'No longer me' sounds as if she had left this life or was playing a childhood game where she was no longer 'it', the person who matters and takes decisions. When this interview was conducted, three months after Mrs Thatcher left office, she admitted she had not adjusted to the shock. 'Even now driving down Whitehall towards Westminster, all of a sudden my mind still thinks we'll turn into Downing Street, and then I realize we're not going to.'

When she spoke of the causes of her downfall to Barbara Walters she did not hesitate to blame Conservative MPs. 'They just ran away,' she said. 'They were frightened; you expect your party to stay with you when the going gets rough, but some of them didn't. They got scared.' She was confident that had she stayed she would have won the next election. At no point did she accept that perhaps the time had come for her to retire from politics, and she strongly defended her dominant style. 'The British people approved by returning me three times, but in my own party some of them found it difficult to take from a woman. That's small-minded.' Her failure to adjust was also apparent in the way she treated some of her former colleagues in government. Douglas Hurd would be surprised to find her on the phone behaving as if she was still prime minister. He told me, 'It was irritating. She used to ring up and sort of give me instructions really – and I didn't care for that.' I asked him whether he had had any option; did he have to take the calls from her? 'Oh yes, of course,' he replied. 'I didn't run away from her; and I'd learned how to argue with her – that's something you learn when you're one of her ministers.' He described how arguing with Mrs Thatcher was like a naval battle. 'You could not let yourself be disabled by the first broadside.' What is significant is that he should talk like this about arguments he had with Mrs Thatcher after she had ceased to have any direct power over his actions.

MRS THATCHER'S first major task was dealing with the 20,000 letters which had flooded in since her resignation. They arrived in huge sacks from the post office. Mr Whittingdale was one of the small staff who had to sort out the ones that really mattered. He said, 'In among them would be a letter from the sultan of Brunei or George Schultz [the former US secretary of state] and you had to find them; it wasn't a matter of getting a few temps in to sort it out – they wouldn't know who George Schultz was.' Mrs Thatcher was not always sensible in the way she tried to answer the letters. Mr Whittingdale remembers her coming into the office, plucking a couple of letters from the top of a pile, and settling down to write two-page replies. 'These letters,' he said, 'were from ordinary members of the public saying, "We think it's so sad; we like you so much." And she gave these lengthy responses.'

There was also a steady stream of visitors, many of them full of ideas about how she should spend her time. Memoirs would certainly be written, and they became the subject of elaborate negotiations, some involving her son Mark. A deal was eventually agreed with HarperCollins for two volumes worth an astonishing £3.5 million. With her speeches in the United States, which could bring her $50,000 a time (or

£27,000), the fees for appearances on her world tours, as well as the sums she was paid as a consultant to the tobacco giant Philip Morris, Mrs Thatcher soon became extremely wealthy. She set up the Thatcher Foundation on the American pattern to promote her political views, with headquarters in Chesham Place near Hyde Park Corner. The aim was to reinforce the impression that although she was out of office, her influence across the world was still a force to be reckoned with.

From the moment she announced her resignation Mrs Thatcher was determined that her voice would not be stilled. When she took part in her last major Commons performance that same afternoon a backbench Tory MP suggested to her that as a great former prime minister she could be extremely influential on issues of state such as Britain's future role in Europe. Mrs Thatcher tried a self-effacing joke, although no one laughed. 'It had secretly occurred to me,' she said, 'that one's voice might be listened to.' In March 1991, soon after the Gulf War ended, Mrs Thatcher made a triumphant ten-day trip to the United States.

In one of the former prime minister's many interviews she was asked what she was prevented from doing because of her new position. She declared, 'I'm not stopped from going round the world making speeches and I'm not stopped from setting up a foundation. There are a tremendous number of people coming to see me.' Asked what she would be doing in five years' time, she replied, 'Still preaching what I believe in and doing everything I can to practise it; and battling on.' For those watching closely to see if Mrs Thatcher would be at all critical of Mr Major there were some ominous signs. In one of her interviews Mrs Thatcher claimed to see 'a tendency to try to undermine what I achieved, and to go back to giving more powers to government'. Her American trip ended on a high note in one of the most right-wing communities in the United States, in California's Orange County. Dressed in imperial purple, she waved to the crowds who thronged the shopping mall of Costa Mesa. 'We thank you so much,' she intoned regally; and no one seemed to think it was inappropriate when the band played 'God Save the Queen'.

Supporters in Britain were keen to keep the flame burning. Her old friend and former cabinet minister Cecil Parkinson agreed to chair a new right-of-centre group of Tory MPs called Conservative Way Forward, with Mrs Thatcher as its president. The aim was to 'keep alive her vision' and this was coupled with an injunction to 'give positive support to John Major in carrying this vision into the future'. It did not take an expert in textual analysis to point out the veiled threat not to support Mr Major if he strayed from the path. There was also the Bruges Group, which took its name from the Belgian city in which Mrs Thatcher had made her key speech in 1988 stressing the need for Britain not to give up its sovereignty to a European super-state. At the group's second-anniversary celebrations soon after Mrs Thatcher returned from the United States nearly 300 people squeezed into the library of the Reform Club in Pall Mall. References to Mrs Thatcher were treated with reverence, mentions of John Major with a degree of suspicion and little warmth. Summing up the mood on the right of the Conservative party, *The Economist* concluded, in an elaborate marriage metaphor, 'After Mr Major's honeymoon, those right-wingers who gave away the Conservative party to meek, neat John are wondering whether the chap is after all a cad. Margaret Thatcher, self-proclaimed Mother of the Bride, has been fingering her steel-reinforced handbag.'

One reason for the growing disenchantment with Mr Major on the Tory right was his determination to abolish the poll tax. Norman Tebbit described the party as being in a febrile state since the leadership change. He called the battle to influence the prime minister 'The War of John Major's Ear'. Mr Tebbit claimed there was great unease on both left and right 'because they do not understand where John Major is coming from'. Fifty Tory MPs wrote to Mr Major asking him to think again about the poll tax. They were not only concerned about moving away from what they saw as the Thatcher legacy; they did not want to see a return to the rating system, which so many years ago she had pledged to remove. Mrs Thatcher's friend Woodrow Wyatt concluded in a newspaper column that all its possible replacements would be worse than the poll tax. Some of the potential rebels were pushing for a hybrid tax which would take into account how many people were living in a property. The lingering Tory support for the poll tax now seems almost incomprehensible, but that is to forget the emotional support the right wing wanted to give Mrs Thatcher; her policies, they felt, should not simply be overturned. To the most extreme this was a form of sacrilege. But the message from the new prime minister was uncompromising. A report in the *Independent* quoted a minister as saying, 'John Major knows that the important thing is that he should say the poll tax is dead. The right of the party can go hang.' The new Tory leader had much more vital concerns than mollifying the supporters of Mrs Thatcher: he was determined to win the next election, which increasingly looked as if it would be postponed until 1992, and the Conservatives were in far more danger of splitting on the European issue.

In the United States, Mrs Thatcher had issued a bleak warning on what for her was a familiar theme: the dominance of Germany in the new arrangements for the European Community discussed at her last summit in Rome. Mrs Thatcher made clear that moves towards a federal Europe would be increasingly opposed by her in public. She even suggested that the commitment on the European continent to democracy was in doubt; the British parliamentary tradition was so much longer. 'We are seven hundred years old,' she said, 'Germany's parliament is only forty, Spain a dozen years old, Portugal even less.' To further emphasize her point she reminded her audience of Britain's victorious role in the Second World War: 'We were the people who stood alone when the whole of the rest of Europe collapsed.'

Her comments came at a delicate time for Mr Major. Two days later he was due to make his first important foreign policy speech in the West German capital Bonn. This had been carefully prepared over the preceding weeks by among others the newly appointed head of his policy unit Sarah Hogg. Charles Powell, though still working at Number 10 as the prime minister's foreign policy expert, was not involved in the drafting. His closeness to Mrs Thatcher precluded that; he had been partly responsible for the Bruges speech, and Mr Major was determined to signal a more constructive phase in Britain's relations with Europe. I was sent to Bonn to cover the event. After the frostiness of the relationship between Mrs Thatcher and Helmut Kohl, the warmth was undeniable. The friendliness they showed to each other at their news conference was expressed in headline terms as 'The John and Helmut Show'. Both leaders made a point of referring to each other by their first names. Mrs Thatcher's renewed warning about the dangers of German dominance had clearly annoyed Chancellor Kohl, who felt obliged to say that Germany did not want to dominate anyone. And he added, 'We want the United Kingdom to play a central role in the development of the European Community.'

It was later, in his speech to the Konrad Adenauer Foundation, that Mr Major made clear his determination to change British policy on Europe. 'My aims for Britain in the Community can be simply stated: I want us to be where we belong, at the very heart of Europe, working with our partners in building the future. This is a challenge we take up with enthusiasm.' Instead of the fearful drumbeat of Mrs Thatcher's 'no, no, no' Mr Major talked of the need 'to discuss both our own ideas and the ideas of our partners openly and positively'. It was the essence of doing business in the European Community to relish the debate and the argument, and then move forward more united, not less. Some commentators drew a comparison with Mrs Thatcher's speech at Bruges three years earlier when the mood had been strikingly different. Instead of looking forward to positive agreements, she had spoken in almost apocalyptic terms of the dangers ahead. 'We have not successfully rolled back the frontiers of the state in Britain, only to see them re-imposed at a European level, with a European super-state exercising a new dominance.'

In Downing Street briefings it was confirmed that Mr Major intended his speech to repudiate Mrs Thatcher's comments at Bruges. Although she did not respond directly to Mr Major, one of her old cabinet friends Nicholas Ridley accused the new prime minister of breaking a private pledge to Mrs Thatcher that he would 'have no truck' with European unity. In the *European* newspaper, Mr Ridley wrote, 'Mrs Thatcher speaks for the majority of the Conservative party who want John Major's reassurances to be unequivocal in public, not just in private.' As the right wing of the party expressed their dismay at Mr Major's speech, Edward Heath made a point of praising the 'refreshing breeze' of the new policies both in Europe and at home. 'I am greatly encouraged,' the former prime minister said, 'that Britain once again will be at the centre of these developments, working for a united Europe from the inside, rather than insulting our partners from afar.' And to drive the point home, he added, 'At last we are beginning to shed the albatrosses that have weighed us down over the last few years.'

It was becoming increasingly clear that those who had backed Mr Major in the leadership election the previous autumn because they saw him as Mrs Thatcher's heir would have to revise their opinions. The *Observer* columnist Alan

Watkins described the mood of Tory MPs who felt they had been misled. 'What enrages the irreconcilables,' he wrote, 'is that they were made to look fools. If they were fair they would blame Mrs Thatcher rather than Mr Major for this, for it was she who urged them to vote for him.'

In just a few short weeks in March 1991 the extent of the differences between the old and the new regimes had been displayed to the public. One of Mrs Thatcher's aides said part of the problem had been the way she had answered questions in the United States; she had not appreciated how prominently they would be reported at home. But in all her eleven years as prime minister I had never found her lacking in that kind of awareness. She was always extremely careful about which questions she chose to reply to, often ignoring a subject she did not feel it was appropriate for her to speak about. Of much more relevance were Mrs Thatcher's frustration at being out of power and her determination to see that her views were still taken into account. On a rational level, she knew that in the run-up to the next election she had to support Mr Major. In her time she had suffered from the bitter criticisms levelled at her leadership by Mr Heath. It would not have amused her to learn that Tory MPs were now calling her Ted in Skirts or more alliteratively, and only in private, Ted with Tits.

At about this time the new education secretary Kenneth Clarke, who had often clashed with Mrs Thatcher in government, met her at a party, with Denis. Mr Clarke had a reputation for being frank with her – on the eve of her resignation he had informed her that she would not win the leadership election – but on this occasion she took his frankness very badly. Mr Clarke told Denis, 'Surely Margaret doesn't want to go down in history as the second Ted Heath?' The Thatchers took great offence. 'The two of them went ballistic,' Mr Clarke told me, 'absolutely ballistic.' Mrs Thatcher liked to draw a distinction between Mr Heath's antipathy to her and her principled stand for the values and policies she believed in. The former cabinet minister John Wakeham told me that her view was: I am not in the business of damaging John Major. I am in the business of continuing to make sure that the public realize I am still alive, and as an ex-prime minister I should be listened to. It's not anti-John Major, it is pro-Margaret Thatcher. But Mr Clarke was unrepentant when I spoke to him at his office in the House of Commons. 'She could have become a dignified elder stateswoman, trying to exercise occasional influence, being supportive and behaving with dignity and decorum, and facing up to the fact that her political career had come to an end. Well, she never did.'

There were no easy precedents for Mrs Thatcher to follow. When Winston Churchill was defeated in the election of 1945 he stayed on as leader of the Opposition, although it was said that for the two years that followed he was hardly seen in the House of Commons. By 1951 he was back at Number 10, and when he did eventually retire, four years later, he was eighty, fifteen years older than Mrs Thatcher when she resigned. One of the most successful ex-prime ministers was Jim Callaghan, beaten by Mrs Thatcher in the 1979 election. Lord Wakeham told me how Mrs Thatcher had once sent him to see Lord Callaghan to enquire whether he would mind if she quoted a remark he made when he was prime minister, which had turned out to be totally inaccurate. 'Or, perhaps,' Lord Wakeham suggested, 'you would like to add a comment?' Lord Callaghan replied, 'I couldn't care a bugger; what I did, I did for the best.' He paused. 'Can I rephrase that?' And then he gave a gentle smile. 'I wonder if you could convey to the prime minister my appreciation of her usual courtesy in offering me this facility, but on this occasion I won't avail myself of it.'

When he left office Lord Callaghan declared that he 'wouldn't spit on the deck'. Having served in the Royal Navy, he appreciated the remark of another former prime minister, Stanley Baldwin, who had said, 'A sailor does not spit on the deck, thereby strengthening his self-control and saving unnecessary work for someone else; nor does he speak to the man at the wheel, thereby leaving him to devote his whole mind to his task and increasing the probability of the ship arriving at or near her destination.' The flat which Mrs Thatcher had borrowed in Eaton Square was part of a house which had once been the home of Stanley Baldwin. If she had taken his advice as well it could have had a significant effect on British politics. Instead, within a few months of the change of leadership, Mrs Thatcher and Mr Major were set on a collision course which no amount of advice from their friends could alter.

17

Missing the buzz at Number 10

JOHN MAJOR PRIDES HIMSELF on the way he can read people's body language. Partly this is because, to a degree many politicians do not share, he has a genuine interest in how other people think and react. When he was in office it was sometimes a blessing, but in many ways it was a curse. He was one of the most sensitive prime ministers ever to inhabit Number 10. The sheer scale of the press interest took him aback in his early days in Downing Street, and he was never able to treat the media with the lack of interest they often deserved. Even when he was away from Number 10, perhaps in Northern Ireland, he would insist on having a press review read to him over the phone before he went to sleep. As a broadcast journalist I frequently felt that he was worrying about what I and my colleagues were privately thinking; and often the mundane truth was that we were thinking of more trivial matters than the fate of the nation or Mr Major's premiership.

Mr Major's sensitive nature was a particular disadvantage in his dealings with Mrs Thatcher. Others might have easily borne the burden of being the successor to one of the most dominant figures ever in British politics, but for Mr Major her simple presence was enough to set off thoughts about their relative strengths. To outsiders it might seem that her glory days were over; but Mr Major was extremely conscious of the extent to which the party had been cut in two, with many Conservatives convinced that it was the wrong half, the weaker half, which was now in control. Mr Major reacted badly to

Mrs Thatcher accepting with alacrity the chairmanship of the Bruges Group and the No Turning Back Group, both dedicated in their different ways to preventing any further moves towards European integration. He felt that the battle lines were being drawn, and was particularly upset that establishing friendly relations with Helmut Kohl should be looked upon as a sign of backsliding over the European issue.

Some conflict between Mr Major and Mrs Thatcher was inevitable. Most find it hard to summon up warm feelings towards someone who succeeds them in a job they have enjoyed and cherished. When you have been forcibly removed from that post it is even harder. Mrs Thatcher must have taken some comfort from the fact that Mr Major was not seen to be as talented as she was. Indeed that may have been one reason why she so strongly supported his appointment. But talent is only one of the ingredients of a successful premiership; opportunities and circumstances can be far more important. Winston Churchill's career reached its peak when he became prime minister in 1940, and he wrote that all his past life had been 'but a preparation for this hour and for this trial'. That moment, though, when the person and their position seem perfectly suited, inevitably passes – it even did with him – and Mrs Thatcher now had to try to reconcile herself to the fact that her time too had passed. As I saw her scurrying to take her place on the backbenches on one of the few occasions she went to the Commons, I could imagine her sense of humiliation and the feeling of betrayal. She was no longer the commanding and confident figure of old. She looked like the victim of a robbery, anxious to return to what she would regard as normal life.

Her change in position seriously affected her relationship with Mr Major. She was uncertain how to react to someone who held what she regarded as *her* job. As a minister in her government Mr Major had been able to exercise his considerable charm on Mrs Thatcher. They had had disagreements, but they were usually short-lived and in any case were often of the sort she rather enjoyed. A hard-fought debate would be followed by an agreement, usually but not always on her terms. But now it was essential for him to create his own style, and he knew what he wanted to do. He was hoping to forge a more compassionate image of Conservative leadership. He wanted to see 'a nation at ease with itself'. It fitted in with his personality and he believed it chimed more with the public mood, increasingly disenchanted with many of the hard-nosed assertions of the Thatcher period. He was also certain it would improve his chances of winning the next election.

But Mr Major's willingness to appear open to new ideas was easily misunderstood; his desire to conciliate was often taken as a sign of indecision or even weakness. It was a problem which would dog him throughout his premiership. People would come away from a meeting with Mr Major believing he was on their side, only to be disappointed later when his support was not forthcoming. Under Mrs Thatcher, civil servants and ministerial colleagues had become used to dealing with a highly opinionated, forceful prime minister, quite prepared to work late into the night driving the government machine. She would often become obsessed with the small print, the exact wording of a government document. Emergency meetings might be held at the eleventh hour to resolve some last-minute conflict if not between colleagues then within her own mind.

When Mr Major took over, a gap opened up inside the Whitehall machine: where Mrs Thatcher had exerted control, more often than not there was now a reluctance if not an inability to generate the same degree of influence. Downing Street was bombarded with notes from civil servants requesting an opinion from the prime minister, a 'steer to take'. Mr

Major, in the words of one of his staff, displayed a 'highly rational exasperation' at this. Often he would scribble 'Please refer' in the top right-hand corner of the note. His advisers would then know that they would be subjected to a detailed cross-examination from Mr Major before he was prepared to offer an opinion; and perhaps not even then. The truth is that on many of the complicated options facing government Mr Major did not have a view and sometimes not even a prejudice. The contrast with Mrs Thatcher could hardly have been more striking.

Mrs Thatcher's determination to initiate an argument and then master a brief before it was exposed to the public was one of her great strengths. It enabled her to dominate the government, and could leave any opposition in the Commons floundering to come to terms with a new approach or a distinctive analysis. But when she was successful in this way it was often because she had allowed herself to be argued out of her initial approach. There were many occasions, even right up to the end of her premiership, when Mrs Thatcher's initial approach had been reversed. She was forced to change her mind; the Lady was for turning.

The pro-European cabinet minister John Gummer enjoyed having arguments with her. They sometimes disagreed strongly, but she was prepared to listen 'once she knew you were loyal'. Even on Europe there were times when they formed an unlikely partnership. In his interview for this book Mr Gummer gave an illuminating example of what it was like when Mrs Thatcher grappled with the practical problems involved. In her later career she made sweeping denunciations of many of the ideas underpinning the European Union, about the single currency and the danger of federalism, but in 1989, the year before she was deposed, Mr Gummer found he could reach common ground with Mrs Thatcher – but only if he treated her in an imaginative and skilful way. The issue was hardly exciting and certainly did not make the news; it was how Europe should regulate the movement of dead meat.

Those who do not follow European Community politics may find such a subject difficult to relate to, but it is typical of the modern European agenda, mystifying to outsiders but of great importance to those directly affected. As agriculture minister Mr Gummer had to negotiate with his EU colleagues the rules covering the movement of animal carcasses. He was about to go into a final round of talks in Brussels when he realized to his dismay that the advice he had been given by British experts was simply wrong. It would not stand up to rigorous analysis. Only three weeks before, Mrs Thatcher had made a speech in which she had highlighted this issue as a classic example of Britain being right and the rest of Europe wrong. There was only one course Mr Gummer thought might work. He arranged to see Mrs Thatcher at 8 a.m., before he took the flight to Brussels. He had a set of storyboards made up, like the large cards used in Hollywood to illustrate how the plot of a film will develop. On these cards he put down the key facts which explained why the British view was mistaken. He hoped Mrs Thatcher would be so taken by the novelty of his approach that she would be prepared to listen. Mr Gummer told me, 'If you could get her to listen to the case, she was remarkably good at accepting the facts and agreeing, better than any leader I have come across.'

The agriculture minister having requested an urgent meeting, Mrs Thatcher was aware that the matter would have to be resolved quickly. Mr Gummer explained that some of the arguments were rather complicated, hence the need for visual aids. This is how the minister put his case: 'Now, Prime Minister, it's a rather complex issue. And you'll be interested in it because it's a scientific issue. But it does involve me actually explaining the details one by one. Do you mind if I do it like this?' He put up his storyboards and for five minutes held the rapt attention of the prime minister. At the end she said, to his immense relief, 'Well, John, I think you're right. I'm sorry you're right. I wish you weren't.' Mr Gummer went off to Brussels and, with as much dignity as he could muster, signalled a U-turn by the supposedly hard-line Thatcher government. Fortunately for them, political journalists like me were less interested in the movement of animal carcasses than perhaps we should have been.

What makes the story important is that it demonstrates how Mrs Thatcher could respond in government to the day-to-day problems of Britain's membership of the European Community. It highlights her attention to detail, and the way she was prepared to take on technical matters not dismiss them as issues to be left to others. Above all the story shows that over Europe she was able to be far more flexible in government than she ever seemed to manage once she had left office. In part this was due to a sharp reduction in the quality of the advice she received. No longer did she have passionate, intelligent ministers ready to argue with her at any time of the day or night. She was no longer at the centre of a vast policy-making machine. At most there were eight people working for her; and many of those who came to see her were not interested in imparting disinterested advice; they wanted to bend her ear to their own causes. More and more she was dependent on the advice of friends and allies; there was less and less chance of her receiving a non-partisan view. It was unlikely, indeed, that anyone would seek to change her mind. In office she had been brilliant at organizing the Whitehall system, maximizing her influence and even at times railing against the inconsistencies of government. But the system, too, had become adept at handling Mrs Thatcher, of making sure that her worst proposals and many of her blatant prejudices would never see the light of day. In retirement she was free to make up her own mind, and much more likely to make mistakes.

So Mrs Thatcher quickly became disillusioned with her choice of successor, while Mr Major was not being unduly sensitive when he soon began to believe he had not lived up to her expectations. He says she detected a desire to undo her achievements, which, to an extent, was true. Mr Major did not feel obliged to pursue what he considered failed policies and realized that in the coming election campaign, unless he could be presented as the candidate for change, he would be branded a failure and serve less than two years in Downing Street. As a slogan, 'Vote for Major, Thatcher's candidate' would have lost far more votes than it gained. There was no easy escape from this logic. Any idea that he could have kept her fully onside does not take into account the force of her personality and her determination to stay in politics. The difficulty for Mr Major was that he cared so much about what Mrs Thatcher thought; and this was one of the reasons why she became so influential in the years that followed.

It might have been very different if, like some of her predecessors, she had been able to retire to a country estate. But even if she had owned one, she would have found life in the country boring. Dulwich had been rejected on the grounds that it was too far from the centre of London. But despite her best efforts there was a void in her life. Apart from her relationship with Denis, her family life was not particularly close. Her son Mark lived abroad and her daughter Carol did not seem to be a frequent visitor. One of her closest friends and colleagues Lord Powell said that after she left Downing Street she never had a happy day. She lived for her work, and particularly for the work of politics. 'Home,' she once confessed, 'is what you come to when you haven't anything better to do.' Sometimes she would suggest in interviews that she was looking forward to going to the theatre or the opera when she retired, or cooking, or 'just pottering around'. But she never really believed it, and no one who knew her thought such things would be enough. One of her close friends told me how Mrs Thatcher might be watching television when she went to see her – perhaps following the tennis at Wimbledon – but it would be switched off immediately. The former prime minister would always want to talk politics. When she was abroad she would occasionally go round art galleries. The same friend remembers holidays in Venice and Barcelona when she did just that. 'Margaret,' she told me, 'would make interested comments; but I still think she hugely misses the buzz of Number 10.' And we were speaking more than thirteen years after she had left Downing Street.

Her faithful press secretary Sir Bernard Ingham, knighted in her leaving honours, would continue to visit her regularly at her office in Belgravia. He told me one of the reasons why she did not have a more successful retirement was her restricted view of life. 'She had no interest outside politics, none whatsoever. In office, she devoted twenty of the twenty-four hours to it every day, and coming off it was like somebody coming off heroin.' The routine they had established in office was maintained, though it was far less frequent in her new life. He told me how they used to meet: 'She sits down, welcomes me warmly, offers me a coffee and we are immediately down to business. No small talk, no anecdotes, no gossip. Effectively, she says, "What have you to tell me today?" Or she tells me what is troubling her. I am then set to work and I am required to make points. She takes copious notes.' It was clearly a routine both of them enjoyed, partly because it never varied. 'It's quite entertaining and very funny at times,' Sir Bernard told me. 'I am very fond of her because she is her own person and she will never change.'

But to Mr Major and his close colleagues there was nothing innocent or casual about Mrs Thatcher's reluctance to leave the political world. It posed a danger to them which increasingly they felt they could not ignore. Mr Major regards his first year or so as prime minister as his most promising period in politics, but he was soon convinced that her continuing presence had become a serious problem for his leadership. He believed that her feelings of dispossession and betrayal would not easily be dispelled; and her circle of friends and advisers would do little to bind the wounds. In his memoirs he wrote, 'Lesser men than those who had once advised her now poured poison into her ear – perhaps with the intention of cheering her up. The target was inevitably – who else could it be? – her successor.'

In October 1991 Mr Major's first party conference as leader was a nervous occasion. It set the tone for many others during his time at Number 10. The big question for the organizers was what to do about Mrs Thatcher. Her relationship with the adoring rank and file had been a source of real strength when she was prime minister. It gave her something like an electric charge to speak on the last day of the conference. The occasion seemed to banish her doubts and difficulties, and was a strange mixture of the last night at the Proms – before the BBC took some of the nationalism out of it – and a Billy Graham rally. The flag-waving standing ovation, which could go on for about ten minutes, became a ritual all of its own, essential to the true believers but rather disturbing to the rest of us. In 1991 there was no question of Mrs Thatcher deciding not to attend the conference – to her that would be accepting defeat and handing victory to her detractors – but the organizers asked her not to make a speech. A party official confessed to a journalist that this was the safest option. 'If she had been allowed to speak, it would have been difficult to stop her if she headed off in the wrong direction.'

She was escorted onto the platform by Mr Major and the

party chairman Chris Patten, and was given a standing ovation which lasted for about five minutes. There were calls for her to speak, but the woman whose recorded public comments run to more than fourteen million words kept to the agreement and said nothing. As it happens Edward Heath was also on the platform. That had not been part of the plan but did not seem to matter; the former prime minister was in a good mood, as I found out when I joined him for a journalists' dinner at the River House at Poulton-le-Fylde. The reason for Mr Heath's cheerfulness was obvious: the conference was the first one in fifteen years not being held under the leadership of Mrs Thatcher. A private lunch she gave in Blackpool was not so upbeat. Mrs Thatcher was quoted as saying that she did not want to rock the boat, but she appeared to patronize her successor by claiming that she had done the hard work when she was at Number 10 and had made it easier for him. Some senior ministers retaliated by revealing that she regularly rang them up with advice, something which was proving rather time-consuming.

It was not surprising that Mrs Thatcher did not stay on in Blackpool to hear Michael Heseltine's speech the next day. This proved a triumph. I met him later at a Jeffrey Archer party at the Imperial Hotel. The party was held in the room the Archers occupied on the third floor, but it also spilled over onto the landing outside the lift. There was the usual mix of journalists and politicians, and the customary fare: Krug champagne and shepherd's pie. I don't think this is a brilliant combination, but they – or to be more precise their staff – served it with such confidence that no one dared complain. I had known Jeffrey since he had offered to act as my agent after seeing me perform a stand-up comedy routine when I was a student at Oxford. I had declined his proposal, but since he had become deputy chairman of the Conservative party I had been keen to be invited to his parties. They always attracted the powerful, and for journalists were a happy hunting ground for news and gossip.

Mr Heseltine disapproved of Jeffrey Archer and did not normally attend his parties. On this occasion he stopped briefly on the landing only because it was on the way to his own room, which was also on the third floor of the hotel. Unlike almost all other senior Tories, Mr Heseltine simply did not trust him. It was, he admitted later, a matter of instinct rather than proof; this was long before there was any hint that Lord Archer, as he became, would be sentenced to prison for attempting to pervert the course of justice. Mr Heseltine's coolness did not deter Jeffrey, who was delighted that he had shown up. The Archers were hoping to demonstrate that, after the traumatic change of leadership the year before, they were still a force to be reckoned with; as courtiers they had managed to switch to John Major's circle without losing their place with Mrs Thatcher. The mood at the party was one of relief rather than celebration: the Tory ship was still afloat and the Archers had managed to stay on board.

I congratulated Mr Heseltine on his conference speech. He questioned whether a BBC correspondent should make such a judgement, but I quickly assured him that I was not taking sides, merely reporting a straightforward fact. He had been given a standing ovation of more than two minutes' duration. It was a barnstorming success, immediately inviting favourable comparison with his conference speeches before he resigned over the Westland Affair in 1986. The new prime minister had not watched, even on television; Mr Major's own speech was the next day and he was reluctant to be reminded of Mr Heseltine's superior skill as a speaker. After the new environment secretary's years in the wilderness, during which he had been banished to meetings outside the main hall, Mr Heseltine was once again firmly installed as conference darling. That night, on the third-floor landing of the Imperial Hotel, he told me, 'You know, a small group of protestors could have ruined my speech. All they had to do was to unfurl a banner from the balcony saying "Traitor" and I would not have been able to continue.'

In his first and not particularly impressive conference speech as leader, Mr Major tried to bring the two Tory former prime ministers together, if only as an example of the party's success. They symbolized, he said, the Conservative commitment to providing opportunity for all: the 'builder's son from Broadstairs' as well as the 'grocer's daughter from Grantham'. As the prime minister left Blackpool the assessment of the party officials was that the conference might have been worse, but on the question of how Mr Major might cope with Mrs Thatcher nothing had been resolved. The new prime minister would soon have to face what would be the most politically difficult and dangerous negotiations of his career. It was just his luck that the future of the European Community and Britain's place in it would now dominate the agenda. It was impossible for him to avoid the issue guaranteed to increase the tension between him and Mrs Thatcher.

18

'Game, set and match'

'WHEN A PARTY BECOMES obsessed by an issue, they keep picking away at it – like a scab.' The politician and writer Roy Jenkins used this striking simile to explain why the Labour party could not resist arguing about nuclear disarmament during the 1980s. It could be applied equally to the interminable debate about Europe which captivated the Conservatives throughout the 1990s. These internal debates take on a life of their own – they seem to flourish whenever a group of party members assemble – and, whatever the original issue, before long the party appears to lose touch with the public at large. As happens when a family engages in heated argument, outsiders tend to make their excuses and leave.

Any attempt to understand Mrs Thatcher's determination to pursue the European issue once she had left Downing Street has to acknowledge the obsessive nature of the debate at that time within the Conservative party. But that does not explain why someone with her breadth of interest in politics across the world should have been prepared to narrow her focus in this way. I have described how her feelings, stemming partly from her experiences as a child growing up in the Second World War, affected her view of Germany, and how she was uncomfortable with any suggestion that Britain's ambitions should be contained within the European Community. There is no doubt, too, that her negotiations with the other member states led her to become deeply suspicious of any moves towards a federal Europe. But I think another element came into play, and that stemmed from the manner of her dismissal as prime minister.

If Mrs Thatcher had been put on trial for her leadership – and she felt that what happened was not dissimilar – one of the main charges would have been that she had dealt inappropriately with the other European leaders, particularly at her last summit in Rome. This had triggered Sir Geoffrey Howe's resignation, which in turn prompted Mr Heseltine to mount his challenge. The main issue between him and Mrs Thatcher was Europe; this clearly affected the votes cast in the first ballot and also the attitude of the cabinet. Mrs Thatcher considered the way she had been treated was deeply unfair; and on Europe she had a chance of proving to everyone that they were wrong and she was right. This was a policy she could pursue without appearing to be driven by personal pride. I believe Mrs Thatcher used the European issue to get her own back.

Mrs Thatcher never publicly admitted this was part of her strategy, and some of her close friends and allies are dismissive of this explanation of why she felt so strongly about this issue. Lord Powell, in his surprisingly frank interview for this book, told me this was not part of an attempt by her to prove she was right. 'Well, let's be honest,' he said, 'she thought she was right on everything; and they were – when they disagreed with her – wrong on everything.' He painted a startling picture of how Mrs Thatcher became increasingly certain of her own judgement. 'You have,' he told me, 'a politician of such deep conviction that whatever cause she espoused she was convinced of its rightness. She didn't have the traditional British weakness of seeing both sides of the question. There was one right view and it was hers.' Lord Powell was also prepared to argue that her vision of Europe's future would be well judged by history. 'I think Margaret Thatcher foresaw, better than anyone else in the Tory party, the challenge which Europe would increasingly present to us.' Another of Mrs Thatcher's allies, Lord Tebbit, insists that Mrs Thatcher picked on Europe because it was the issue of the moment and she felt strongly that British interests were seriously threatened.

For much of 1991 Mr Major had to take into account the looming problem of the critical negotiations due to end at the Dutch town of Maastricht in December. This was the culmination of the process which had caused the flashpoint in Rome involving Mrs Thatcher. Most of the other member states were keen to let the European institutions prepare for a single currency. They were also looking for a closer, more coherent structure for the institutions. This meant further integration in a number of areas, although there would also be clearer distinction of the powers retained by the member states. From now on the European Community would be known as the European Union and every citizen would have the right to be treated as a citizen of that union.

Mr Major was acutely aware of how important it was for him to keep his party onside; the opposition parties were fully in favour of strengthening ties within the European Union. If there was going to be trouble, most of it would come from the Conservative benches. Mr Major decided to hold a two-day Commons debate to test opinion and obtain parliamentary backing before setting off for the final negotiations. On 20 November Mr Major opened the debate on a government motion which spoke of Britain's interest in being 'at the heart of Europe'. The motion fully supported the approach he had outlined in his Bonn speech earlier in the year and 'endorsed the constructive negotiating approach adopted by Her Majesty's government'. He was careful to signal where Britain would refuse to compromise, what are known as 'red lines' in the government's position. Making sure that key areas were kept in the hands of the separate states was vital if there was going to be any chance of Britain accepting the new treaty. Mr Major stressed that foreign policy, immigration and asylum matters, crime and terrorism, would all be dealt with by the governments working together, with each country able to exercise a veto.

But Mr Major was prepared to accept that on the most important issue of all – the plan for a single currency – Britain would not oppose using the European institutions to help organize what became known as the euro. Even though he made clear Britain would be able to decide at a later date whether to take part – what would become the famous 'opt-out' clause – Mr Major rejected the idea that the other countries should be forced to act outside the new treaty. For Mr Major a constructive negotiating position did not include what would be seen by the other leaders as a British attempt to block the whole idea of a single currency.

When Mrs Thatcher rose to intervene in the debate, the government thought they knew the line she would take; she had seen the foreign secretary that morning. Douglas Hurd candidly admits that he called at her office; there was no question, it seems, of the former prime minister taking it upon herself to go round and see him. In his diary Mr Hurd wrote, 'Faintly chaotic, but a good atmosphere. She is in the midst of preparing her speech and we talk entirely about the EU. She will vote for the government tomorrow, but mobilize huge forces against us after Maastricht if we sin.' Mr Hurd's use of 'sin' is significant; there was an almost religious fervour in the way the Euro-sceptics tackled this issue. In her speech Mrs Thatcher first appeared keen not to make her opposition too obvious. Having approved of Mr Major's pledge to remove unwanted proposals from the draft treaty, she said, 'In my day that would have required the occasional use of the handbag. Now it will doubtless be the cricket bat, but that is a good thing because it will be harder.'

But her best joke came later in the speech, and it was unintentional. Referring to Mr Hurd, she said, 'I was very grateful to my foreign secretary . . .' When this was greeted with a gale of laughter and cries of 'her foreign secretary' she failed to grasp the reason for the mirth. 'My right honourable friend is used to both praise and blame from me,' she responded. And then, slightly flustered, she went on, 'Agreed, excellent, good.' At one point she suggested that Mr Hurd had 'gone wobbly' – like George Bush over Iraq – in one of his recent speeches on Europe. MPs on both sides of the Commons treated her affectionately. It was like the return of a well-loved actor. She gave no impression of being reduced in her new position, and she explicitly promised to make her views known as the negotiations progressed. 'It is not my custom,' she said, 'to use coded messages.'

Mrs Thatcher went on to make clear her opposition to Mr Major's decision to allow the European institutions to take part in the management of the single currency. 'It would be better,' she insisted, 'if those who want a single currency should go to it by a separate agreement outside the Treaty of Rome.' Otherwise it would be harder for Britain to stay outside. Throughout Mr Major's premiership he would leave open the option of whether Britain would join. Mrs Thatcher was keen to slam the door shut. 'I believe passionately in this House. We should retain parliamentary supremacy. We should not make a massive transfer of power to the Community, which is not accountable to our electorate. Therefore we should not join a single currency.' She also argued that any such proposal should be subject to a referendum; it was a fundamental constitutional issue. This comment caught Mr Major by surprise. He was irritated not to have been given a warning. There was no chance now of disguising their disagreement on this issue and, for a time, it became a crucial difference between them.

Eventually, in 1995, Mr Major would agree that Britain should not join the euro without a referendum, and that would also become the position Labour adopted under Tony Blair. But at this stage the Tory leadership was not prepared to budge on this point. In the same debate – before Mrs Thatcher spoke – Mr Major had said, 'I do not favour the idea of a referendum. I do not favour referendums in a parliamentary democracy.' This had been the view of Mrs Thatcher, who used to argue that referendums were a device favoured by dictators like Mussolini. That was the line she took when she scornfully dismissed Harold Wilson's decision to confirm British membership of the Common Market with a referendum in 1975. 'It would,' she said then, 'bind and fetter parliamentary sovereignty in practice.'

What particularly annoyed Mr Major was that after the Maastricht debate Mrs Thatcher turned on him personally for ruling out a referendum on the single currency. In a television interview with ITN she accused Mr Major of arrogance. She complained that he had not answered her case for the 'voice of the people' to be heard. When it was pointed out that this went against Mr Major's stated policy, she said, 'I am aware of that, but he still has to answer the question: how will the people make their views known on whether or not they want their power taken away?'

It was a remarkably uninhibited interview, which underlined Mrs Thatcher's determination not be silenced in the interests of party unity. 'I still have a role,' she said. 'And I hope that the things I have said will influence the prime minister at Maastricht.' She also broadened the argument by suggesting that any treaty which came out of the Maastricht negotiations might not have her support. 'These changes,' she said without being specific, 'are being brought in too fast. People are against them.' Some of her supporters, including Norman Tebbit, declared that next time the issue came before the Commons they might go further than abstaining; they were contemplating voting against the government. Former chancellor Nigel Lawson also weighed in with a warning about federalist ambitions at Maastricht to give greater powers to Brussels than the US government enjoyed in Washington. Unlike his old ally Sir Geoffrey Howe, Mr Lawson was vehemently opposed to the single currency. A total of six Conservative MPs were so concerned about the approach being taken by Mr Major – even before the negotiations had started – they went into the 'No' lobby at the end of the debate. Nine others abstained.

It was not the wholehearted endorsement Mr Major might have hoped for as he prepared for his most serious political challenge since taking office. The huge government majority at the end of the debate was hardly a consolation; the landslide result of the 1987 election made it easy for Mr Major to carry the day. The government's position was also weakened by some Conservative MPs who took the view that Mr Major should go further in the cause of European integration. The former prime minister Edward Heath, diametrically opposed to Mrs Thatcher, argued strongly that Britain should not only join the single currency but also accept the Social Charter, or Social Chapter. For many Euro-enthusiasts on the continent, this was an essential part of the European project, demonstrating as it did the EU's concern for social issues as much as free market ideologies. For Mr Major it was another red line he would not cross. The government motion had spoken of the need to avoid measures in social areas such as trade union rights, which were matters for national decision. The Labour party backed the Social Chapter while declining to make a binding commitment to join the single currency. Eighteen left-wing Labour MPs refused to support Neil Kinnock's pro-European motion.

Of all those parts of Europe which might benefit from a single currency, the area around the Dutch town of Maastricht was one of the most obvious candidates. About ten miles from its centre are three obelisks which mark the Dreilandenpunt, the point where three countries meet, the Netherlands, Belgium and Germany, all in those days with their separate currencies. Some of the larger shops would accept Belgian francs and German marks as well as Dutch guilders. But it was clear that for the sake of the local economy a single European currency would be extremely useful. To illustrate my report for Radio 4 I changed twenty pounds into each of the European currencies in turn, ending up with not much more than ten pounds when all the exchange costs had been paid. With a population of less than 120,000 Maastricht was a little smaller than Swindon, but there was an international feel to the town which belied its modest size; and it was not the first time it had hosted a European summit. Ten years earlier Mrs Thatcher had attended a European council there, and a suite was named after her at the best hotel.

My overriding memory is of how cold it was in Maastricht. The radio and television studios and offices were in a large badly heated building normally used for trade fairs and exhibitions. Most of my work was for radio, which at least was inside. Television correspondents had to stand outside in the intense cold to make their pieces to camera look reasonably interesting. We had only limited access to the leading figures in the conference centre, and it was hardly exciting. The drama would take place in the private talks. For Mr Major and the other leaders, as usual at European summits, there was a mountain of documents to digest; and the small print often generated as much confusion as enlightenment.

In key discussions there was a strict limit on the number of advisers each head of government could have with them. Britain's chief expert was the chain-smoking Sir John Kerr, who would later become head of the Foreign Office. His small stature was useful; he could crouch unseen behind the table where he was briefing the prime minister when all the officials had been asked to leave. But in that position he could not pick up the simultaneous translation. At one stage, when Mr Major turned to him for advice on a particular point, Sir John hissed, 'Dutch, I don't bloody do Dutch.'

The minister for Europe was the former government whip Tristan Garel-Jones, who gave the impression he was privy to plenty of secrets, but he could seldom be relied upon to reveal them to reporters. He kept quiet about one of the most interesting moments of the two-day summit, which was when the chancellor of the exchequer Norman Lamont went missing. An anxious Mr Garel-Jones told Mr Major how officials were in despair because Mr Lamont had walked out of a meeting of finance ministers who had begun discussing what for Britain was the most important part of the negotiations, the clause which would allow the UK to opt out of the single currency. Mr Major had insisted throughout that Britain should not in any way be forced to abandon the pound. 'The rest of them are discussing our opt-out,' Mr Garel-Jones told the prime minister. '*Our* opt-out . . . and we're not there.' Mr Major agreed that Mr Lamont should be found, and some calm was restored when the chancellor arrived to join a meeting with the prime minister and other heads of government.

Mr Lamont bitterly rejects the accusation that his behaviour threatened the successful negotiation of the opt-out clause. He had no intention of even discussing it. Before the summit began, the British had drawn up a protocol in legally watertight language which would have the desired effect. It was not up for negotiation, Mr Lamont argued, because it only affected Britain. When the other finance ministers began to discuss the document, Mr Lamont walked out, leaving one of his officials to observe what happened. Mr Lamont admits to being angry. 'I tried hard to slam the door,' he writes. 'But it was a heavy thick door that only moved very slowly in a gradual creaky way. I learned later that the officials said I had gone to the loo.'

Mr Lamont says he did not hurry back and insists that the strategy worked. When he did return to the negotiating table the protocol had been accepted without amendment. 'If I had stayed there I am sure I would have been bogged down in line-by-line discussion and that would have been risky.' Mr Major is not impressed. 'It was an extraordinary way for Norman to behave,' he writes. 'He could simply have asked for a recess. Instead he just upped and went. Yet the opt-out we were seeking was part of the treaty, and every government would have to pass it in their domestic legislation.' According to Mr Major the matter was only resolved when he agreed with the other heads of government that if they left the opt-out untouched, he would help them on other matters. This still left the most difficult of the topics the summit had to deal with – how to accommodate Mr Major's insistence that Britain would not be covered by the Social Chapter, which dealt with issues involving union rights. At about 1.30 a.m. a deal was finally struck: another opt-out was agreed.

Mr Major had maintained his vital red lines. He had also managed to keep his Euro-sceptic employment secretary Michael Howard on board; messages were passed between them even as the negotiations took place in Maastricht. All that was left for the prime minister to do was not to appear triumphant. It only took a casual word from one of the press secretary's staff to prevent that happening. A comment passed on by Chris Moncrieff, the ever diligent editor of the Press Association, the news agency subscribed to by all the British media, blew the strategy apart. He wrote a piece in the early hours of the morning, which included: 'Prime Minister John Major stamped his signature on an historic deal for closer European union early today, and declared, "It is game, set and match for Britain."' This was much more exciting than the bland comment the rest of us heard later at the prime minister's Maastricht news conference. 'I am very happy at the outcome,' Mr Major told us at about 3 a.m., adding diplomatically, 'I think it is a success both for Britain and for the whole of the Community.'

The phrase 'game, set and match' would haunt Mr Major for the rest of his time at Number 10, even though he never made the comment in public. Not only did it annoy the leaders of the other member states, who objected, as they always do when one state claims victory over the others at a European summit, it also gave Mr Major's opponents, who wanted to portray his negotiations at Maastricht as a failure, a stick with which to beat him. They were able to argue that by sounding so triumphant he had shown how little he understood what had really happened: that he had failed to understand the significance of the Maastricht Treaty. But the tone of what Mr Moncrieff had written was repeated in all the coverage of the outcome of the Maastricht negotiations. When I was asked on BBC Radio 4 whether I thought the treaty, as amended by Mr Major, would placate his critics, I argued that for most of them it should allay their fears. I was convinced that Mr Major had passed the most difficult test so far of his premiership.

When Mr Major returned to the Commons to report he won the enthusiastic support of most Conservative MPs. In private Mrs Thatcher expressed her lack of enthusiasm to close friends; in public she was said to be impressed by his statement to MPs. She would study the 'small print' of the agreement before the debate. When it came to the vote at the end of the two-day debate on the Maastricht deal, Mrs Thatcher abstained. Only seven Tories voted against. Norman Tebbit was passionately critical of the deal. The Tory MP Richard

Shepherd, who would be one of the prominent rebels in the Maastricht debates after the 1992 election, declared, 'This is about the spirit and life of a nation, and I can't let this go down sinking without leastways an exclamation mark and a cry, "It's wrong."' For Mr Lamont the success of the negotiations was bittersweet. He was against any further moves towards European integration and yet he had been a significant player in a treaty which would bring a single currency to most of Europe. Sitting next to Michael Heseltine at the first cabinet meeting after the negotiations he felt it necessary to show his colours. 'I envy you,' Mr Heseltine muttered in his ear, 'because you are part of history.' Mr Lamont replied, 'It was part of history from which I would be willingly excluded.' In the end Mr Lamont declined to sign the Maastricht Treaty at the formal ceremony. He sent his deputy Francis Maude instead.

EVERYONE KNEW THAT a general election would have to be held in the first part of 1992. No parliament could last more than five years and this alone should have been enough to still divisions in the Conservative party. To a great extent it did. Mr Major was allowed to bask in his success at Maastricht. Given that Labour and the Liberal Democrats were in favour of even closer cooperation with Europe there was little chance of this becoming an important election issue. Mrs Thatcher remained largely silent. But when a private member's bill was put forward, sponsored by Richard Shepherd, calling for a referendum on the Maastricht deal, she could not resist letting it be known that she was 'thinking of supporting' it. She did not speak in the debate, but she did turn up. Political commentators correctly concluded that she agreed with the content of the bill, although again she decided to abstain. It failed to get the necessary one hundred MPs voting in favour to proceed, but a warning note had been sounded. No one knew how devastating the consequences would be of the Conservative split over Maastricht; that would have to wait until the general election was safely out of the way.

19

'Not enough oomph, enough whizz, enough steam'

I AM CONVINCED that if Mrs Thatcher had stayed on as leader the Conservatives would not have won the election of 1992. For many people this is not in any way a controversial comment, it is blindingly obvious. But where Mrs Thatcher is involved, there is always likely to be another view. According to many of those who pride themselves on being her friends and allies, if you do not believe she could have won the 1992 general election, then you can hardly call yourself a Thatcher loyalist. In order to heap the maximum blame on those who plotted against her and won, it is essential to be able to say that toppling her on electoral grounds was completely unnecessary.

But some of those who take this view consider it no more than a hard-headed assessment of the situation. Mrs Thatcher's old friend and former cabinet minister Lord Parkinson thinks she would have succeeded. 'I think she would have emerged again in the Gulf War as a commanding leader,' he told me, 'and I think she would have won more conclusively than Major did.' Another of Mrs Thatcher's allies, Lord Tebbit, is equally confident. He maintained that she would have been able to reverse the opinion polls as she had in 1983 and in the run-up to the 1987 election. 'If she had won the first round of the leadership ballot, she could have won the ninety-two election. I am quite sure of that.' He is characteristically caustic about the Labour leader Neil Kinnock. 'I don't think it was possible to lose against Kinnock. The British electorate didn't see Kinnock as a prime minister. They saw him as a Welsh boyo, a windbag.'

The two party leaders who fought each other in the general election of that year, Mr Major and Mr Kinnock, are both convinced that Mrs Thatcher would not have won. When I raised the possibility with Mr Kinnock, he quickly dismissed it. He argued that Mr Major was able to defuse the row over the poll tax, which she would not have been able to do, and was above all able to present himself as the candidate for change. After eleven years of Mrs Thatcher the country was longing for new leadership, and Mr Major was able to capitalize on that feeling. On the day that Mrs Thatcher resigned, Mr Kinnock is convinced, Labour lost its biggest electoral asset. Mr Major is equally dismissive of the suggestion that his predecessor could have produced the result he did.

But the argument that Mrs Thatcher could have won has at least one important advocate in the Labour party. In the summer of 2002 I asked him, 'Could she have won?' And he replied, 'I am one of the few people who would say unhesitatingly, yes. I personally believe she could have won, yes.' Mr Blair's view is that Labour had not carried through its internal reforms in time for the election that year. 'Come election time, everyone knew that it was a choice between this lot and that lot,' he gestured towards two imaginary piles labelled Tory and Labour, 'and we weren't in shape. Although Neil Kinnock made absolutely heroic efforts to change the Labour party in 1992, truthfully, we weren't sufficiently, fundamentally changed.'

He believes the same critical issues which allowed Mr Major to win, in particular concerns about Labour's ability to manage the economy, would have brought victory to Mrs Thatcher. Mr Major is among those who are not impressed by this argument, and he questions the motives of those who make it. Mr Blair would of course be anxious to stress the importance of the reforms he pushed through the party in the run-up to Labour's victory in 1997. If the necessary work had been carried out before then, that would cast doubt on the impact of New Labour and raise questions about Mr Blair's own record. But the fact that Mr Blair is prepared to argue this view cannot simply be brushed aside. Mrs Thatcher and her allies are unshaken in their view that her removal from Number 10 was not in any way justified, even on electoral grounds.

When the election was called in the spring of 1992 there was no general expectation that Mr Major would make it back to Downing Street. As I sat, literally, at the prime minister's feet for an impromptu press conference outside Number 10, I was convinced that he would soon be handing over to Neil Kinnock. When I asked Mr Major why he thought he would be able to hang on, I believed the die had already been cast and did not think that after thirteen years in office the Conservatives could hope to win again. The prime minister had left the election almost as late as he could, close to the five-year deadline, and the omens for the government were not good. Labour had a small but steady lead in the opinion polls. The economy was mired in recession; interest rates were just over 10 per cent. John Smith looked and spoke like a chancellor in waiting. Paddy Ashdown was considered the most impressive of the three leaders, and there appeared to be a good chance of a Lib–Lab pact if the vote was not decisive. A hung parliament, with no party holding an overall majority, looked the most likely outcome.

For Mr Major this was the most critical moment of his political career. Would he be able to win the election and therefore claim that he was his own man, the rightful occupant of Number 10? Or would he be little more than a postscript to the Thatcher era? An early sign of Mr Major's determination came on 11 March, the day he made the election announcement. He sent a spray of two dozen pink roses to Mrs Thatcher's office in Belgravia with a note telling her the election would be on 9 April. It was a peace offering to the unpredictable and still powerful queen of the Tory party. She had already received 150 invitations to speak during the campaign. Mr Major knew that how she behaved could decide whether he returned to Downing Street.

WITHIN A COUPLE OF DAYS, Mrs Thatcher was out campaigning to excited crowds in Southampton. Women shouted, 'Come back; we love you,' and one of them interviewed by a reporter gave this breathless response: 'She is marvellous; she has put this country on the right course.' The former prime minister appeared to relish her brief foray. She made little attempt to convey to her fans that it was Mr Major's re-election which they should now be fervently calling for, and that talk of her return would not help the Conservative cause. When asked to comment on the current prime minister, Mrs Thatcher struggled to find appropriate words without in some way referring to her own part in Mr Major's success. All she would say on this particular trip was, 'The policies John Major is following are, I believe, the policies I created and put into practice.' It was hardly an enthusiastic endorsement. Mrs Thatcher continued to have problems adapting to her new role.

In the following week, at the end of the parliamentary session, there was a poignant moment when she attended the Commons for the last time. She walked alone into the chamber and made for the government front bench, which was empty at the time. Mathew Parris, *The Times* parliamentary sketch writer, was fortunate to be present, and was able to describe this strangely downbeat scene. British political life is frequently decorated with theatrical moments, and those that are planned often involve trumpets and elderly people dressed up in scarlet and gold. But this moment was not costume drama, more kitchen sink; and like the best kind of theatre it was helped by being spontaneous. 'The table on which the dispatch box sits, where she had stood so many thousands of times, was littered with papers,' Mr Parris wrote. 'Mrs Thatcher walked up and tidied the mess. She put the documents together into neat little piles, glanced at her handiwork, and left.' If only, she may well have thought, I could sort out Mr Major and his ministers in the same way.

For the last part of the campaign Mrs Thatcher would be away on another lecture tour in the United States; and even when she was in London playing an active part, she was not always helpful to the prime minister. In private she complained bitterly to friends of how he had mismanaged the nation's finances. At her final meeting in her Finchley constituency she argued publicly against excessive government spending. With only three weeks to go before polling day, she spoke of the need for sound finance. 'I know full well you have no reputation overseas unless you demonstrate that you can handle the finances in your own country.' Later in the campaign she tried to soften her criticism of the government's borrowing record, but only to say, 'If this government is overspending, a Labour government would be infinitely worse.'

About fifty journalists and cameramen followed her every move. It was about half the number she had attracted in her last election as prime minister, but it showed how important she still was to the media. News editors, not the most charitable of souls, were keen to make sure their journalists were present in case she provided a big story; and the most newsworthy event would be an attack on Mr Major. Sir Bernard Ingham was no longer working for her, but he hoped that a newspaper article by him would be sufficient warning. He wrote that the media would 'want to see whether she puts her foot in it', but it seems Mrs Thatcher drew a different conclusion from the gaggle of newsmen around her: she believed they were there because of who she was not.

At Swiss Cottage in north London she spoke effusively of her hold on the public imagination. 'Many, many people come up to me and say, "Thank you for all you have done for our country; the policies were right."' Sometimes she seemed to draw comfort from demonstrators, who continued to behave as if she was still in power. Members of the Socialist Workers' Party greeted her in Swiss Cottage with banners, and chanted, 'Tory scum get off our backs; we won't pay your poll tax.' Mrs Thatcher always appeared to relish being attacked by the hard left. She knew they could be taken on with advantage, and on this occasion the protest was a demonstration that she still mattered.

Attacks from her own side she found far more disturbing – although she had plenty of experience of tart asides, as regularly dished up by Edward Heath. He still could not resist having a go at the person he felt had usurped his position as Conservative leader. It was a clash not simply of personalities; there was a strong ideological element as well. Even though this was in the middle of an election campaign, Mr Heath was devastatingly frank. He told reporters on the campaign trail that the Tories had an 'awful legacy' to live down. 'It is established that Thatcherism was an aberration,' he said. 'I want to make sure now that we carry through Conservative policies.'

There was considerable confusion about the part Mrs Thatcher was meant to play in the campaign. Whenever there was speculation that she appeared to be stepping up her role, there would be hurried denials from behind the scenes. Whatever she was doing, we were told, had been planned 'weeks before'. The campaign managers could not decide whether or not she was an electoral asset. With the main parties so close together in the opinion polls, and neither apparently able to pull ahead, her role was seen as crucial by some at Central Office. Other members of the Conservative team were determined that this should be Mr Major's campaign, and not a pale echo of the ones when she had been in charge. But the Thatcher loyalists prevailed, and it was agreed that she should make a dramatic appearance at a campaign rally with Mr Major.

When the rally took place in Central Hall, Westminster the problems of having Mrs Thatcher play a prominent part in the campaign immediately emerged. She, and not Mr Major, was generally regarded as the star of the show. She did her best by heaping praise on her successor, but he was still overshadowed. Norman Tebbit was also attempting to be helpful when he commented that no party worldwide could put such a talented duo on the platform. But he rather ruined the effect when he explained why he believed Mr Major's performance had much improved of late. 'They've stopped putting sedatives in his tea,' he said. With Conservative friends like Mrs Thatcher and Mr Tebbit, it was not surprising that there were times when Mr Major felt the odds were stacked against him. As the campaign progressed, there was a drip feed of critical comments from Mrs Thatcher. When she arrived for a brief helicopter tour in Scotland, an Edinburgh newspaper claimed that she had privately complained of her successor's 'disastrous' economic policies. Ten days into the campaign the *Sunday Times* reported that Mrs Thatcher had told friends that the Tories did not have 'enough oomph, enough whizz, enough steam'. It would have been easier for Central Office to play down the comment if it had not been so obviously true.

There was, though, one clear blessing for Mr Major as he contemplated his difficulties with Mrs Thatcher: at least Europe was not an election issue. Labour had turned strongly pro-European, and was reasonably united on this policy even though as recently as 1983 they had fought a general election, under Michael Foot, advocating withdrawal from the EEC. When he became leader, Mr Kinnock dumped that pledge and sought to project Labour as a European socialist party. Despite the strenuous efforts of left-wingers including Tony Benn, by 1992 the party was arguing strongly for the Maastricht Treaty, although Labour did not go as far as the Liberal Democrats, who were already committed to joining the single currency. Mrs Thatcher knew that whatever else she did, this was not the moment to argue about Europe. This strategy could have been successful if she had been more careful, but once again she allowed a loose comment from her to become public.

The Anti-Federalist League asked Mrs Thatcher to speak at one of its rallies, and she wrote to the chairman, Alan Sked, explaining that she could not do 'anything which would split the party at this critical time'. To make matters worse for Mr Major she promised that Conservative differences over Europe 'can be fought out after the election'. With six days to go before the election Professor Sked released details of the letter. The Anti-Federalist League chairman accused Mrs Thatcher and her allies of 'stifling the European debate to preserve Tory unity'. He added, 'They are frightened to speak out before the election. The most crucial issue of the election is not being debated.' It was hard to argue against the point made by Professor Sked because it was true.

Fortunately for Mr Major the issues dominating the campaign were the usual ones: the economy, tax and spending, public services and the suitability of the candidates for the top job. Labour had come a long way since the dismal internal battles and the ascendancy of the left in the early 1980s. Peter Mandelson and others behind the scenes had worked skilfully to make the party a much-improved electoral force, although he was now in the front line contesting his own seat in Hartlepool. All the modern arts of packaging and presentation were employed, as they had been in Mr Kinnock's first election campaign as leader in 1987. The red rose symbol had been plucked from the dressing-up box of the French socialists, and American campaigning techniques including photo opportunities and sound bites had been adopted. But Labour's strategy had been based for so long on Mrs Thatcher remaining in power they found it difficult to switch their guns on to Mr Major. They did not want to concede that he might offer a new approach, and instead tried to brand him as no more than Thatcher's heir.

Mr Major mounted a successful counter-offensive. If Labour was going to be slick and show business, he would be simple and sincere. His proudest achievement was to reintroduce the soapbox into a national campaign. A sturdy chest was provided to give Mr Major a platform for impromptu speeches at some fairly rowdy outdoor meetings. It could hardly have been less like the well-organized Thatcher campaigns of the past; and that was precisely the point. Mr Major would only win if he could demonstrate he was not Mrs Thatcher. Labour was increasingly concerned that many voters were convinced that Mr Major did provide a break with the past; and if Labour lost credibility on this issue they feared there were other parts of Mr Kinnock's programme which might not ring true.

I was sure that tax was the defining issue of the campaign and said so in broadcasts before polling day. The Tories had begun their attack on Labour's planned tax rises at the beginning of the year and mounted an extensive poster campaign highlighting Labour's 'tax bombshell' with an appropriate black bomb. John Smith's shadow budget was based on the assumption that people would be prepared to pay for improved services through increased taxes. In private conversations he accepted that this was a gamble, but he was convinced that playing straight with the public would be rewarded on election day. The Tories went through the details and estimated that the average family would be £1,250 worse off. Mr Smith himself, it was estimated, would lose nearly £1,000, and no member of the Westminster press corps would benefit from Labour's tax plans. If political reporters had a personal axe to grind, it was obvious which party would suffer.

The turning point in the campaign appeared to have been reached on 1 April, with eight more days to go, when the polls put Labour up to seven points ahead. The markets took it badly. The *FT* index of share prices plunged and interest rates hardened as the pound came under pressure. It looked like an intimation of what would follow a Labour victory. In the afternoon some building societies warned of the possibility of higher mortgage rates and a slump in house prices. That evening Labour held its disastrous rally at the Sheffield Arena, built the year before to house the World Student Games. It was a spectacular media event, with 10,000 spectators, fireworks, celebrity endorsements on video, bits of opera and rock music, as well as rousing speeches from Mr Kinnock and his deputy Roy Hattersley. But the more Labour looked confident of winning, the more the electorate took fright. The Sheffield rally turned into a famous example of what not to do.

A lot of the blame has fallen on Neil Kinnock, who arrived dramatically by helicopter. It is impressive how much responsibility he is prepared to take, and he bitterly regrets the way the Sheffield rally came over to millions of television viewers. I watched the news coverage at home with a mixture of embarrassment and irritation. It annoyed people in many different ways; for some it was Mr Kinnock, acting as MC, walking up and down, punching the air and shouting, 'We're all right.' It looked far too much like a victory rally before any vote had been cast. Afterwards the Labour leader, flushed with excitement, said, 'The only time I've experienced anything like it was in Jamaica where there was a crowd of thirteen thousand, all high on ganja and rum.' On this occasion Mr Kinnock appeared to be high on the prospect of power, and for millions of voters this was not a pleasing sight. Even members of the shadow cabinet looked uncomfortable in their role as cheerleaders. I remember Donald Dewar, the rather ascetic future secretary of state for Scotland, looking particularly ill at ease.

I think the real problem for Mr Kinnock was that the rally gave many voters an excuse not to vote Labour. The tax issue is not an easy one for opinion pollsters to get to grips with. It is difficult for many of us to tell a complete stranger that we want to keep our money, and not have it spent on the public good. Sometimes people respond to questioners with clipboards as if taking an exam: they think there must be a right answer. No one wants to look stupid by saying what they would really like, which is improved services and lower taxes. How much easier, many people thought after the Sheffield rally, simply to say, 'I don't want that lot in government.' Polls taken after the election suggested that among the crucial C2 voters, sometimes described as the lower middle class, nearly half thought they would be worse off under Labour. Without scoring well among these voters, no party can hope to win a general election.

Much to Mr Major's credit he had refused to become obviously downhearted when many of the opinion polls suggested he would lose. He insisted he would win, but the strain was enormous. His wife Norma packed their personal belongings into crates in case they had to move the day after. Election night was fraught for all the key figures; no one really knew what the outcome would be. At home in Huntingdon Mr Major became convinced of victory when the Tories held on to the key swing constituency of Basildon. But he then had to endure the sight of many old colleagues losing their seats, and the blow when his chief lieutenant, the party chairman Chris Patten, lost his seat to the Liberal Democrats in Bath.

In London Mrs Thatcher and her allies watching the results

programmes had mixed feelings as it became clear that Mr Major would win a majority in the Commons. Lord McAlpine, the former Conservative treasurer, held a party at his Westminster home attended by the Thatchers and their daughter Carol. Mrs Thatcher had arrived that day on Concorde from New York and she had been to two other election parties before the news came through, soon after 1 a.m., that Mr Patten had been defeated. A short distance away from the McAlpine party, at Central Office, there was a loud groan at the news that their chairman, who had played such a vital role in the election, had lost his seat. Several of the staff burst into tears.

But there was an astonishingly different response from the party attended by the Thatchers. Reporters had been anxious to find out how Mrs Thatcher would take the news and heard an unmistakable cheer from the McAlpine home. Mr Patten had become a bête noire for the Tory right. Pro-European and to some dangerously left wing, he had not been forgiven for telling Mrs Thatcher he could no longer support her the night before she made her resignation announcement. Some of those present at the party confirmed that Mr Patten's defeat had been applauded, but it seems that Mrs Thatcher had not joined in. For her that would have been too crude a response to the downfall of an old colleague.

At another of the parties Mrs Thatcher had attended earlier in the evening, the *Telegraph* party at the Savoy, a group of old Thatcher friends and supporters had also cheered when the news of Mr Patten's defeat came through. This was not another isolated example of bad behaviour but a reflection of the feelings of elation among many right-wing Conservatives when they heard the news from Bath. But these were meant to be private responses; accounts of what had occurred took some days to leak out. Efforts were made to stifle speculation that Mrs Thatcher had been anything but pleased with the Conservative victory. In his column in the hunting and shooting magazine *Countryweek*, which came out before the Sunday newspaper reports of the anti-Patten cheers, Lord McAlpine wrote, 'One of those who lost his seat is Christopher Patten. I am sorry for this and I echo the words of Margaret Thatcher who said, "How sad it is that a man who fought so hard for all Conservatives should lose his own seat. I hope that he will speedily be returned to Westminster."' By the time the next election was fought, in 1997, Lord McAlpine had defected to Sir James Goldsmith's Euro-sceptic Referendum Party. Mr Patten did not return to the House of Commons, though his distinguished career continued. He was the last governor of Hong Kong and then a senior member of the European Commission in Brussels, where he became responsible for external affairs.

WHEN MR MAJOR came out of Number 10 to celebrate, with his hands held high, it looked as if he had finally moved out of Mrs Thatcher's shadow. It was a remarkable personal victory. At last he had been given the chance to be his own man. But his triumph would be short lived. Mrs Thatcher's legacy had not yet passed into history; she could still cause him considerable harm. Those cheers from her supporters against one of the chief architects of Mr Major's victory – Mr Patten was behind the tax bombshell campaign – would reverberate for a long time. The following period of Conservative rule was extremely difficult and the party came close to disaster. Many Tory supporters now look back and say there is only one thing which would have been better than winning the 1992 election – and that is if the Conservatives had lost.

20

The bitter taste of victory

ANY GENERAL ELECTION tends to be called a milestone. Sometimes it marks a new departure, but it can also be highly significant even if there is no change of government. The election
of 1992 was the moment when some of the key Thatcherite
reforms of the 1980s were consolidated. Had Neil Kinnock
won he would have made a determined attempt to roll back
many of the changes she had made, particularly those which
curbed trade union power, reduced the size of the public sector
and cut back the influence of government over large parts of
the economy. By the time Tony Blair came into office – five
years later – Mr Kinnock's approach would be deemed old-
fashioned; it would certainly not be New Labour. John Major
wrote in his memoirs, 'Our victory in 1992 killed socialism in
Britain. It also made the world safe for Tony Blair. Our win
meant that between 1992 and 1997 Labour had to change.'

But for Margaret Thatcher the brutal way she had been
removed from office was still uppermost in her mind; it could
never be forgiven, or forgotten. She had once famously called
on others to rejoice when South Georgia had been recaptured
during the Falklands War; she now found the Conservative
victory of 1992 difficult to celebrate herself. After the unprecedented way the party had dealt with her not much more
than a year before, there were times when she considered the
Conservatives did not deserve to win, and she increasingly
gave the impression she did not believe that Mr Major had
earned the right to be prime minister.

Mrs Thatcher's mood had not been enhanced by her treatment during the election campaign. She disliked having to temper her remarks over policy in order to present a united front, and she was angry with Chris Patten, the party chairman, for playing down the importance of Thatcherism as part of the Tories' electoral appeal. Instead, the Conservatives had concentrated on a negative campaign – against Mr Kinnock and the danger of increased taxes. Once the election was over, the *Daily Mail* quoted Mr Patten's angry response: 'Mention any great advance of these years, the taming of the unions, the spread in home ownership and shares, the return of Britain to a senior world role, and that woman will get the credit.' Mr Patten's frustration at having to cope with a political legend – who just happened to be still alive – was obvious. He was one of the many people who had contributed to Thatcherism, and along with other former colleagues he objected to the way she attracted so much of the limelight and was not in the least shy of milking the applause. Understandably, Mrs Thatcher took a different view, resenting any attempt to diminish her role in creating the modern Conservative party. She was irritated when Mr Major, anxiously trying to establish his own position, pointed to the Conservative election manifesto and said, 'This is all mine.'

Two weeks after polling day she let fly in an article for the American magazine *Newsweek*. The uncompromising headline was aimed directly at the prime minister: DO NOT UNDO MY WORK. She criticized the rise in public spending and the appointment of Michael Heseltine as trade and industry secretary, and she made clear her disillusionment with Mr Major's overall approach. There was even a personal jibe at her successor, suggesting that he would never count for as much in the world as she did. 'There isn't such a thing as Majorism,' she declared, ignoring the fact that Mr Major had made no claim to an –ism. As the *Sunday Times* commented,

'The *Newsweek* piece comprised a long toot on her own trumpet, glorying in the "-ism" that has attached itself to her name; in contrast, she haughtily deprived her successor of any such eponymous glory.' Mrs Thatcher seemed to have little regard for the skills and talent Mr Major had brought to Number 10, preferring to stress how much he had gained simply from following her. 'I don't accept the idea that all of a sudden Major is his own man,' she said. 'He has been prime minister for seventeen months and he inherited all these great achievements of the past eleven and a half years which have fundamentally changed Britain.' She was also sharply critical of what was generally considered one of Mr Major's strengths: his ability to reach consensus on difficult issues. She described consensus as 'the absence of principle and the presence of expediency'.

Even her loyal former press secretary Sir Bernard Ingham publicly reacted badly to the article, complaining in the *Daily Express* of the way she had used such 'petulant terms'. She should remember the 'public contempt' Edward Heath had earned for 'the longest sulk in history'. Sir Bernard concluded that reticence becomes former prime ministers rather than 'chattering to the chattering classes'. But there is no doubt Mrs Thatcher was expressing the thoughts of many of her loyal followers. They were annoyed at how Mr Major had bolstered his own position with his appointments to the new cabinet; on Europe and other issues it would reflect a more centre-left approach. Mr Heseltine had chosen to revive the job title President of the Board of Trade, and I congratulated him, in private, by calling him 'Mister President'. His influence in the cabinet pleased the pro-Europeans, as did the continuing presence of Mr Hurd at the Foreign Office and the appointment of Kenneth Clarke as home secretary. The latter replaced Kenneth Baker, who retired from the cabinet after turning down an obvious demotion to Welsh secretary. There were some concessions to the right of the party, with Peter Lilley installed at social security, Michael Howard at environment and Michael Portillo, then seen as an ultra-loyal Thatcherite, joining the cabinet as Treasury secretary.

In the immediate aftermath of the election not a great deal of attention was paid to Mr Major's majority, just twenty-one, in the House of Commons. It was such a long time since the Conservatives had had to worry about knife-edge votes that this majority seemed quite adequate for a full term. Little if anything was made of the fact that if the opposition parties united and only eleven Tories decided to vote with them, it would be enough to defeat the government. Only later would it become clear that Mr Major's small majority was one of the critical factors which undermined his premiership.

There was little comment either about the composition of the new House of Commons, and in particular how the outlook and political views of the new intake of Tory MPs differed from those of its predecessors. It always takes a long time for a leader to have the MPs they would like; Members of Parliament have to be selected and win a seat and then begin the slow progress up the Westminster ladder. However determined a leader is to have colleagues of their own sort, it is bound to be many years before they can look round the House of Commons with much feeling of parental pride.

One of the great ironies of this story is that Mrs Thatcher became more popular among Tory MPs after she had been forced out. It was only when she had gone that Thatcher's children arrived in force on the green benches, but by then it was too late to be of any use to her as prime minister. This was one of the effects of her long period in office: selection committees in constituencies spread across the country had been faithfully reflecting her leadership, but it had taken until now for there to be a significant shift in the balance of power among the Tories at Westminster. The old guard, which included some who had served in the Second World War, had given way to a less upper-class, less snobbish kind of Tory who tended to be more Euro-sceptic and more ideological.

Before Mrs Thatcher became Conservative leader in 1975 there were cliques and factions, as there are bound to be in all major parties, but Tory MPs were far less likely to divide on political grounds. The Labour party, traditionally split between left and right, was a living example of the dangers of that tendency. Under the British system, to have much chance of forming a government a party has to embrace a wide range of views, and often the parties are more like coalitions than single political groups. Under a different system, such as proportional representation, parties can take a narrower view, but with single member constituencies decided on the basis of first past the post it is crucial for differences to be settled internally, before a party reaches out to the electorate. The Conservatives used to pride themselves on doing this without too much fuss. They stressed loyalty as much as winning; and the two were, of course, related. They would boast that, unlike the ideological Labour party, they were the natural party of government, able to change and adapt to the times. They did not take their politics too seriously.

This changed under Mrs Thatcher and was just one of the ways in which her legacy proved highly damaging. She took her politics very seriously indeed. As she tried to put her stamp on the party at the beginning of her leadership and then take a grip on government, it became clear this could not be done without a struggle. She had to be careful at first: the Tory establishment found it hard enough coping with a woman leader without her radical instincts being flaunted as well. It was only in time that ambitious Tory MPs realized that they could only advance quickly if they could prove to Mrs Thatcher that they were loyal. As we have seen, this ideological rift became known as the battle between the wets and the dries. The terms arose from one of Mrs Thatcher's favourite remarks, used to dismiss those on the centre left of the party, such as Sir Ian Gilmour, whom she accused of 'being so wet'. They adopted the label as a badge of honour, and the Thatcherites became known as the dries.

In the Labour party the split between left and right was largely determined by the extent to which those involved were prepared to move towards socialism, although other issues such as nuclear disarmament played their part. In the Conservative party of the 1980s it was a matter of how far MPs were prepared to go in advocating the right-wing views associated with Thatcherism. Internal elections for backbench committees dealing with the full range of party policy were increasingly fought along these lines. Michael Heseltine remembers returning to the backbenches when he resigned after the Westland Affair and being puzzled at how these differences had begun to matter. For the first time, it seemed, the right of the party was happy to be called that; the left still regarded itself as being in the centre.

By the time Mr Major won the 1992 election many new Tory MPs had been chosen by a selection process which heavily favoured Thatcher loyalists. The relevant test now was not so much being 'one of us' or even 'dry'; what those who made the selection most wanted to know was a candidate's views on Europe. Although the cabinet was still firmly in the hands of the pro-Europeans they found less support on this issue among their own backbenchers. As Mr Major prepared for the first session of Parliament after the general election, this change could hardly have been more significant. Europe was the issue from which he could not escape; and it was precisely the question on which he would find himself most at odds with members of his own party.

The focus of attention was the Maastricht Treaty. Unlike Congress in the United States, there is no simple way for the

British Parliament to ratify a treaty. The US Senate has to vote before a treaty, signed by the president, can come into effect. In Britain Parliament has to pass any laws which are necessary for a treaty to be implemented; the treaty itself cannot be amended. Exactly how debates should be conducted and which motions should be accepted by the speaker of the House of Commons are matters open to argument. It is a legal minefield. There are students of current affairs who at the very mention of Maastricht start glancing at their watches and looking out of the window. The BBC became concerned about the way young people during this period became distinctly less interested in politics. It was discovered that for many of them politics meant Maastricht, and it was a subject which even the brighter ones found irresistibly boring.

This was unfortunate because many of the details were not all that difficult to understand. Essentially it set the European Union on a new course which would lead to the adoption of the single currency by most of its members. Because of the treaty's ambitions for a more coherent, more integrated system of government within the EU it was anathema to those Conservatives who wanted nothing to do with a federal Europe, but each item of the treaty, as negotiated by Mr Major, was nothing like as controversial as its apparent overall effect. There is no disguising the fact that other European leaders were keen to see the EU emerge with some kind of federal structure, and this is not what either Labour or the Conservatives wanted, but what annoyed Mr Major and his colleagues was that in practice, they believed, the changes would not be anything like as dramatic as the Euro-sceptics or their opponents the Euro-enthusiasts expected. When I spoke to Douglas Hurd in the summer of 2003 he pointed out that even though the Maastricht Treaty had been in force for many years, the Queen was still on the throne and Tony Blair had been able to commit British forces to the invasion of Iraq despite the opposition of France and Germany.

For Mr Major there was a straightforward way of looking at the treaty: by negotiating opt-out clauses covering the European Social Chapter and the single currency, he believed he had fully answered the concerns of those such as Mrs Thatcher who wanted Britain to stay out of any further moves towards European integration. He was particularly anxious, once these concessions had been secured, that Britain should not be seen as the wrecker of the Maastricht agreement. If other countries wanted to proceed faster along the path of 'ever closer union' as laid down in the original Treaty of Rome, they should be allowed to do so. If Britain refused to implement the treaty, it would mean that Mr Major and his government could be accused of having negotiated in bad faith. They had given their word. They had agreed terms at Maastricht; and it was now inconceivable for Parliament to turn round and reject the deal. It would make a mockery of Mr Major's desire to be 'at the heart of Europe'.

The government decided to press ahead with the necessary legislation as soon as possible after the general election. With support from the Liberal Democrats and with Labour now firmly pro-European, getting the bill through Parliament did not seem to present serious problems. There was even a slight hint that Mrs Thatcher might decide to be more accommodating. In a speech in Holland she complimented Mr Major on his negotiating position at Maastricht. She said he deserved high praise for ensuring that Britain would not have either the single currency or 'the absurd provisions of the Social Chapter' forced upon it. But the tone of the rest of her speech – a blistering attack on the powers of the European Commission and yet another warning of the dangers of German dominance – gave heart to those Conservative MPs preparing to defy the government over Maastricht. Her remarks were in stark contrast to those made in the same week by the Queen, who for the first time addressed the European Parliament in Strasbourg. She had been prevented from doing so as a matter of government policy while Mrs Thatcher was at Number 10. On this occasion, with a large part of her speech in French, the Queen gave open support to Mr Major's desire to appear more constructive in European affairs.

When the first of the important votes on the Maastricht legislation came on 21 May, at the end of a two-day debate, twenty-two Tory MPs went into the 'No' lobby against the government, just one more than Mr Major's overall majority. Three times that number of Labour MPs voted against Maastricht, but it was the Tory rebellion which would prove far more significant. On the surface ministers took the result calmly, but in the whips' office the warning was understood. It was decided to move quickly on the bill, allowing the Tory rebels as little time as possible to build up their support. But just over a week later came the first of the hammer blows from abroad: by a close margin Denmark rejected the Maastricht Treaty in a referendum. For the agreement to come into force all the member states had to ratify it, in their own way. It now looked as if the treaty might have to be abandoned.

The Danish result sent a tremor through Whitehall. Ministers were forced to accept they would have to rethink their European strategy. Tory rebels were jubilant, believing the treaty was now dead. Norman Tebbit declared, 'It saves the EEC from a disaster.' One of the Conservative MPs who had voted against the Maastricht bill, Nicholas Winterton, said, 'I am only sad that it is the Danes and not the British who are taking this decision. I think the British people would have turned it down flat if they had been given the opportunity.' The chancellor Norman Lamont, who became openly far more Euro-sceptic when he left office, heard the news as he was getting into his official car after a dinner with the chairman of the Reuters news agency in Fleet Street. 'I leapt into the air, punching it with my fist,' he wrote in his memoirs. 'I could not believe it. Could this, I wondered, be the end of the single currency?' When he phoned the prime minister early the next day, Mr Major said, 'I don't know whether to laugh or cry.' Mr Lamont told him it was quite clear what he should do, although the idea that Mr Major would have laughed at a moment like this seems rather far-fetched.

The prime minister was torn. Letting the Maastricht Treaty fail would have rid him of a problem of internal party management, but would also have destroyed his foreign policy. For the Tory Euro-sceptics, there was no such dilemma: they were convinced that at this point Mr Major should have ruled out any attempt to revive the treaty. Unknown to Mr Lamont a decision had already been taken. As he was talking to Mr Major the foreign secretary was making clear on the Radio 4 *Today* programme that Britain would proceed to implement the treaty. Douglas Hurd revealed that attempts to keep Maastricht alive would be backed by Britain. The Euro-sceptics were furious. Within twenty-four hours of the Danish result seventy Conservative MPs had signed a motion calling for a fresh start on European policy.

It was reported that two members of the cabinet, Peter Lilley and Michael Portillo, had joined other Euro-sceptic ministers in urging the prime minister to ditch the treaty. The former home secretary Kenneth Baker joined those calling for a change of tack; this particularly annoyed Mr Major and his allies, who remembered Mr Baker warmly praising Mr Major for his negotiating skills at Maastricht. Many of the new Conservative MPs who had been persuaded to vote with the government only a fortnight before paraded their Euro-sceptic views for the first time by signing the 'fresh start' motion, which later gave its name to yet another Euro-sceptic faction.

The Conservative MP Sir Rhodes Boyson likened his fellow MPs to a reluctant coach party: 'They had not wanted to desert the driver; now the door had been opened and they could get out.'

Mrs Thatcher let it be known that she thought the treaty should be abandoned. Denmark, she said, had 'done a great service for democracy against bureaucracy'. But it would have been very difficult for Mr Major to go back on the government's initial response, although in what looked like a sign of panic, ministers were forced to stop proceedings on the Maastricht bill, at least for the time being. Mr Major repeated his commitment to the treaty and hoped the Danes would be able to join 'in due course'. He also ruled out the possibility of Britain holding a referendum on Maastricht. In this ungainly fashion, the battle lines were thus drawn between Mr Major and a large section of his own party which included a formidable former prime minister. It was less than two months after his remarkable election victory.

Mrs Thatcher prepared for the fight. She was anxious to take her seat in the House of Lords so that along with her fellow Euro-sceptic new peers, who included Norman Tebbit, Nicholas Ridley and Cecil Parkinson, she could play her part in trying to block the Maastricht bill when it resumed its passage through Parliament. Within a few days it became known that Britain, which was due to take over the rotating European presidency in July, would back an additional protocol to the treaty in the hope that this would allay Danish concerns. But that was a long-term strategy which did nothing to solve Mr Major's immediate problems. The delay to the Maastricht bill would give time for the Euro-sceptics to marshal their forces, and it was now impossible to disguise the seriousness of the Tory split.

After a referendum in Ireland in June had supported the treaty, the prime minister insisted there would be no retreat over Maastricht. 'If Britain broke its word,' he declared, 'it would not be trusted again.' He privately told colleagues he would resign if rebel Tory MPs defeated the bill. It was a matter of personal as well as national honour. Baroness Thatcher, as she had become, within days repudiated her successor. 'Britain,' she declared in a television interview, 'should forget Maastricht.' Asked if she would vote against the ratification bill in the Lords she replied, 'Most certainly. I didn't vote for the Treaty of Maastricht.' And she went on, 'Maastricht is a treaty too far. I most earnestly hope it will not be ratified. It takes so many powers from ours, the oldest parliament, which has been the example and inspiration to others.' In her maiden speech in the Lords she repeated her call for a British referendum on the treaty and accused the leaders who had negotiated the deal of being out of touch with the people of Europe.

As if Mr Major did not have troubles enough, the summer of 1992 brought serious economic problems. Britain was still caught in the tail end of a recession; business longed for lower interest rates to stimulate demand but that was not possible while the pound was within the ERM. If interest rates fell, the pound would have to fall. Mr Major and Mr Lamont could not offer any immediate solution. They argued that recovery would take time – people would have to be patient – but this advice carried less weight than usual because at the Conservative party conference less than a year before Mr Lamont had famously declared that 'the green shoots of economic spring are appearing once again'. Doubts about the government's economic credibility were growing. But all this was nothing compared with what was just around the corner. Mr Major was about to become the unlucky prime minister. The government would be hit by a second hammer blow from abroad, and it would be much worse than the first one.

21

The unlucky prime minister

FOR EVERY JOURNALIST there is pride in being in the right place at the right time. It was very satisfying for me to greet Mrs Thatcher outside the Paris embassy when the leadership ballot suggested she might well have to resign. But, given the vagaries of the news business, being there when it really matters cannot be guaranteed. I was in Leeds, reporting on a by-election, when Sir Geoffrey Howe resigned; and I was in Harrogate on 16 September 1992, the day the pound fell out of the ERM. I was there to follow events at the annual conference of the Liberal Democrats, but when it emerged that a major crisis was sweeping the foreign exchanges, I became acutely aware that I was in the wrong place at the wrong time. It turned out to be the most significant moment in Mr Major's period in office.

As I sped south to London by train, I clutched a radio to my ear to follow the pound being savaged by dealers in all the main financial centres. Most of the senior political reporters assigned to the Liberal Democrats were now leaving Harrogate as fast as possible. At the same time cabinet ministers in Whitehall were searching for radios or televisions, just to keep up with the news. The markets were giving their judgement, minute by minute, on the strength of sterling, and ministers had to come to terms with the fact that there was little they could do to stop the avalanche. Even those meant to be controlling events felt they were not in the right place; and they undoubtedly wished they could somehow have avoided the disaster which they now faced.

Like many of the issues I have discussed, the problem had a German connection. It stemmed from the political generosity of Chancellor Kohl, who was determined to unite Germany by treating the two parts of the country as if they were equal. The communist East German economy – often referred to as a 'basket case' – was no match for the mighty West German economic system with its immensely strong currency, the Deutschmark. But Chancellor Kohl had decided, purely on political grounds, that the East Germans should be allowed to exchange their weak currency, the Ostmark, for exactly the same number of D-marks. Effectively the East Germans had been given a great mountain of cash, but in order to stop prices rising and the benefits of Chancellor Kohl's generosity simply being frittered away, interest rates had to go up, to keep a lid on demand. For many years – much longer than expected – the German economy was saddled with high interest rates as they desperately tried to limit the problems of absorbing the backward East German economy. It has been estimated that the equivalent in Britain would be for the country to take on nearly twenty more depressed areas like Merseyside. Chancellor Kohl wanted to be known to history as the man who united Germany; he achieved this, but at considerable cost to those living in West Germany at the time. His policies also had a knock-on effect in Britain, which was still suffering from recession.

High interest rates in Germany made the Deutschmark more than usually attractive to holders of foreign currencies: they could get a better return on their investment. But the more the D-mark strengthened, the more the pound weakened. Sterling had been under pressure for months before what became known as Black Wednesday. Tied into the ERM, there was little the British authorities could do. They were reluctant to raise interest rates simply to strengthen the pound against the D-mark. They were already cripplingly high at

10 per cent, where they had been for the past year. Like vultures – although many of them may have been perfectly decent people – the foreign exchange dealers began to circle. They became convinced that, even if the system survived, the weaker fry, including the pound, would not be able to continue to trade at their present rates. Currencies would have to be devalued; and if the dealers judged it right, a lot of money could be made. It was calculated that by betting against the pound the financier George Soros made the equivalent of £1,000 million.

IN THE EARLY DAYS of the ERM the system had a good deal of flexibility: currencies had been able to move about with a certain amount of freedom as their economies adjusted to the new discipline. But by the time Britain joined in 1990 the ERM had become more rigid. Indeed that was part of its attraction to Mrs Thatcher and Mr Major; they saw it as a vital part of their strategy to get on top of inflation, other methods having failed. They wanted to send a clear signal to the markets that the British authorities were taking a firm grip on the situation and not preparing to devalue. One of the tactics governments have to use to combat currency dealers is a game of expectations. If the British government can convince the dealers that the pound's value will be maintained, then some of the pressure on the currency can be eased. In the weeks leading up to the crisis Mr Major and Norman Lamont did all they could to talk up sterling.

For Mr Major the nightmare scenario was that economic problems would in some way collide with his faltering European policy. Keeping the two apart would have made matters much easier to deal with, but such was his luck, separation proved impossible. As if caught by some awful curse, whichever way he turned the European issue fell across his path, and as so often happened during his premiership, it was not the official Opposition who caused him problems. One evening I had drinks on the terrace of the House of Commons with the shadow chancellor Gordon Brown. He had been appointed by John Smith, who had replaced Mr Kinnock as Labour leader. We had in the past talked over economic issues with a fair degree of frankness, but on this issue Mr Brown was immovable. I tried my 'But surely . . .' mode, suggesting the pound was overvalued; he replied with his friendly but no comment posture, which would serve him well when he eventually became chancellor. There is a tradition that the Opposition does not talk down the value of the pound; it is regarded as unpatriotic as well as damaging to the economy.

Conservative Euro-sceptics appeared to have no such inhibitions. They were buoyed up by having the Maastricht bill suspended and were keen to stay in the public eye. If Maastricht was temporarily off the boil, they were happy to turn their attention to the indirectly related issue of the pound within the ERM. It was, after all, part of the system designed to move towards European economic and monetary union which they were totally against. One of the requirements of any country hoping to join the single currency was membership of the ERM for at least two years. The Euro-sceptics wanted Britain's membership to end, and they openly called for the pound to be devalued.

One of the problems of a fixed exchange rate, or membership of a system like the ERM which makes devaluation difficult, is that governments may have to lie if their currency comes under pressure. If sterling looks weak and the market believes it will get weaker, the pound is bound to go on falling. Governments can only stop this happening by putting up interest rates, so that holding pounds becomes more attractive, or by making clear they will intervene in the markets by buying pounds to prevent sterling falling any further. Throughout the summer of 1992, when the pound was under pressure, ministers gave every impression they would not allow sterling to be devalued. A large international loan was negotiated to allow for foreign exchange reserves to be built up in case intervention was necessary. Three weeks before Black Wednesday Mr Lamont announced, in a dramatic statement before the foreign exchange markets opened at eight o'clock one morning, that Britain would neither leave the ERM nor devalue. He had made the statement, he said, 'just in case there is a scintilla of doubt'. Only five days before the crisis broke, Mr Major was still insisting the government would not change course.

I went to Glasgow to report a speech the prime minister was making to the Scottish CBI. Now I am no longer involved in politics day by day I am often called upon to make after-dinner speeches at gatherings such as this. I tend to speak off the cuff using jokes hopefully not familiar to the audience but well known to me. Despite being nerve-racking, it can be fun. But when Mr Major faced that audience in Glasgow his task could hardly have been more different. There would no light-hearted moments for him that evening, as he faced one of his most difficult and serious tasks since becoming prime minister. He had to sound convincing about the strength of sterling even though we all knew that if the pound was strong he would never have needed to make such a speech. In a modern hotel ballroom with a low ceiling and in a fairly downbeat atmosphere we set up our camera at the back. Only a small part of what he had to say suited my report for the BBC nine o'clock news.

Mr Major went further than ever before in closing off the devaluation option. 'All my adult life,' he said, 'I have seen British governments driven off their virtuous pursuit of low inflation by market problems or political pressures. I was under no illusions when I took Britain into the ERM. I said at the time that membership was no soft option. The soft option, the devaluer's option, the inflationary option, would be a betrayal of our future.' I remember thinking what a risk he was taking by using such forceful words. I wondered how he could be so sure; but he gave no hint of any doubt. To underline his point, he said, 'There is going to be no devaluation, no realignment.'

In his memoirs, Mr Major admits that he was not telling the truth. 'Events,' he says, 'were making a dissembler of me.' In private, ministers and officials had seriously considered devaluing the pound but this option had been rejected. The Treasury had argued that this could lead to interest rates having to go up to counter speculation of a further devaluation. They wanted the Germans to reduce their interest rates in order to allow rates across Europe to be lowered. At a bad-tempered meeting with other European finance ministers in Bath Mr Lamont repeatedly pressed the Germans to do this, but they resented the suggestion that their independent central bank, the renowned Bundesbank, duty bound to fight inflation, could be forced to bow to political pressures. Mr Major was left with what seemed like the only option, to wait and see.

Lack of confidence in the foreign exchange markets spread across Europe. Sweden and Finland were the first countries forced to devalue, followed soon after by Italy. In a German newspaper Dr Helmut Schlesinger, the head of the Bundesbank, was quoted as saying, 'The tensions of the ERM are not over . . . further devaluations are not excluded.' Mr Major cancelled a visit to Spain, citing 'pressure of work' as the official reason why he had to stay in London. The idea that exchange rates within the ERM were unlikely to be maintained was given further impetus by an opinion poll which suggested that a majority of French voters would reject the Maastricht Treaty. It looked like moves towards a single currency had stalled, and therefore holding firm to the ERM was now less important.

Sterling plunged from the moment trading started in London on 16 September. Before I left Harrogate that morning – by 8.30 a.m. – the Bank of England had spent more than £1billion in foreign exchange buying pounds from traders who wanted to sell sterling, this being one of the rules of ERM membership. At 11 a.m. the government decided to put up interest rates by 2 per cent, but it was too little, too late; the move had no effect on the pressure against sterling. The chancellor sensed the game was up. Norman Lamont described it as being like a scene in a medical drama: the heart monitor stops bleeping and all the nursing staff can do is to switch off the machine.

There then came, at the end of the morning, one of those bizarre moments which have bedevilled the relationship between Mr Lamont and Mr Major. The chancellor needed to get permission from the prime minister to take Britain out of the ERM and allow sterling to find its own level; as every minute passed, further vast sums were haemorrhaging from the foreign reserves. But Mr Major was tied up in a meeting with backbenchers which had been arranged some time before. He emerged after nearly half an hour, looking relaxed and smiling. The head of the Treasury, the governor of the Bank of England and Mr Lamont were waiting outside the meeting. The former chancellor is not convinced by suggestions that Mr Major may have had some kind of nervous breakdown on Black Wednesday. Mr Lamont's complaint is that the prime minister should have been far more agitated than he was; he describes the discussion he had with Mr Major as having little sense of urgency. Mr Lamont wrote in his memoirs, 'He seemed unwilling to face up to the issue.'

Other cabinet ministers were brought into the discussion including Michael Heseltine, Douglas Hurd and Kenneth Clarke, the most powerful pro-Europeans in the government. Every possibility was discussed as the minutes passed and the foreign reserves continued to decline. Mr Lamont says, 'We were bleeding to death, and all we were doing was talking. We had clearly lost the battle but the generals refused to recognize it.' It was an hour and half after the meeting had started before a conclusion was reached. Mr Major decided that interest rates should go up a further 3 per cent to a staggering 15 per cent. Mr Lamont did not believe this would work and he was proved right: once again the government move had no effect on market sentiment. By the time the markets closed at 4 p.m. the government had spent more than £14 billion from the foreign reserves, roughly half the total held by the Bank of England. At 7.30 p.m., after consultations with other member states, the chancellor announced before television cameras set up in the Treasury courtyard that Britain's membership of the ERM would be suspended. 'Today,' he said, 'has been an extremely difficult and turbulent day.' This scene, with Mr Lamont brushing back his hair with a hand and looking like a public schoolboy called before the headmaster for a beating, became one of the enduring images of the Major period.

It is not surprising that Mr Major seemed slow to take emergency decisions that day. Part of his style – unlike that of Mrs Thatcher – was to involve colleagues as much as possible; it was also part of his natural defences. The more others were involved, the less blame might be attached to himself. He was anxious to ensure that every possible move had been considered before defeat was acknowledged. The blow to his own prestige was enormous, and he was in no doubt about the seriousness of the setback. As chancellor he had obtained the backing of Mrs Thatcher two years before to take Britain into the ERM; now he was the prime minister who had presided over the ignominy of sterling being ejected from the mechanism. He was also annoyed by the role of the Germans after all his efforts to form an alliance with Helmut Kohl. His determination to put Britain 'at the very heart of Europe' was open to ridicule. The Tory Euro-sceptics, he knew, would have a field day. His plan to see off those Conservative MPs trying to prevent Britain ratifying the Maastricht Treaty seemed even more likely to end in disaster.

Mr Major was quick to let his colleagues know that resignations might have to follow. At one of his meetings with the chancellor on Black Wednesday Mr Major confessed to feeling humiliated by the withdrawal from the ERM. As Mr Lamont recalls, 'He said that there would be demands for my resignation, adding "and my own as well".' After a break their discussions resumed and Mr Major slipped Mr Lamont a note: 'I am not going to resign and you must not consider it either.' But that evening, according to Mr Major's memoirs, he debated stepping down as prime minister. He even discussed it with some of his senior officials. 'I went to bed,' Mr Major wrote, 'half convinced my days as prime minister were drawing to a close. I was not sure whether Norman and I could reconstruct economic policy. After such a setback, was it even possible (or proper) for me to stay in office? My own instinct was clear: I should resign. I was not sure I could ever recover politically from the devaluation of the currency. The collapse of sterling was a catastrophic defeat, and one which I felt profoundly.' Other thoughts, mainly the effects of leaving his colleagues in the lurch and precipitating a leadership crisis, began to intrude, but the next day Mr Major says he continued to contemplate leaving Number 10 and even got as far as drafting a resignation speech. He still believes that might have been the right course, although cabinet ministers and members of his family urged him to stay.

At the time none of these doubts surfaced in public, and there was no suggestion of an immediate change in policy. The pro-Europeans in the cabinet were insistent that there should be no U-turn on either the ERM or European policy in general. It was left to outside commentators, notably *The*

Times columnist Anatole Kaletsky, to proclaim that Black Wednesday was not black after all. In the article he wrote that day, he said, 'With one bound we are free. After two years of pointless self-destruction, common sense has finally prevailed. Britain is free to fashion its economic destiny.' Kaletsky went on to rail against what he saw as the completely unnecessary constraints of the ERM; the policy had been an 'utter failure'. Within a few days a senior cabinet minister was reported as saying that Mr Major would take Britain back into the ERM only over the dead bodies of half the cabinet. At the weekend in his first public comment, Mr Major said that Britain would not resume membership of the ERM until it was run 'in the interests of all the countries of Europe'.

In Washington Lady Thatcher, on yet another American tour, could not resist sounding a triumphant note in her first comment on the crisis. She repeated the remark she had used to dismiss Nigel Lawson's attempt to shadow the Deutschmark, 'If you try to buck the market, the market will buck you.' The lesson was obvious: 'If the divergence between different European economies is so great that even the ERM cannot contain them, how would they react to a single currency?' She warned Mr Major that the crisis over sterling would pale into insignificance if he pressed ahead with the Maastricht Treaty. 'It is high time to make as complete a reversal of policy on Maastricht as has been done on the ERM.' Lady Thatcher was convinced that the economic outlook now looked more promising. Having left the ERM, interest rates should be cut and Britain allowed to pull out of the recession. 'The histrionics of the time will soon be forgotten,' she said. 'The benefits will increasingly be appreciated. Dire warnings of what will happen when the economic straitjacket is removed will quickly prove false.'

The fact that Lady Thatcher as prime minister, after years considering the matter, had decided with Mr Major that Britain should join the ERM did not seem to give her any cause for embarrassment. Thatcher loyalists, including the Conservative MP John Carlisle, were full of praise for her comments: 'My feelings are that they will bring great delight to many thousands of people,' he said. 'They were probably the first sensible words we have heard from a senior politician.' Just six days after Black Wednesday it looked as if some of the benefits outlined by Mrs Thatcher were starting to come through: interest rates were reduced by one per cent. Mr Major and Mr Lamont had difficulty welcoming the news. Having predicted severe consequences if Britain left the ERM, they could hardly extol the advantages of a floating pound. The most serious political consequence for the government was their loss of credibility; the crisis had destroyed one of the Conservatives' most powerful electoral assets – their reputation for economic competence. In a Commons debate the Labour leader John Smith made the most of it, describing Mr Major as 'the devalued prime minister of a devalued government'.

But the glum faces of MPs on his own side were more important to Mr Major than the jibes of the Opposition, and it was not only the collapse of their economic policy which was exercising the minds of Conservative members. Sorting out how the Tory party could find its way through the European minefield now looked harder than ever. There had been a glimmer of hope that the French might reject Maastricht in their referendum, but in the event France decided by a very small margin to accept the treaty. The issue would not go away. As a sign of the growing confidence of the Eurosceptics, more than seventy Tory MPs signed a motion calling on the government to turn its back on the ERM.

Open warfare over Europe was one of the main features of the Conservative party conference in the autumn. The euphoria over their election victory earlier that year had long since disappeared, with the opinion polls now giving them the lowest ratings since the poll tax was introduced in 1990. Mr Major had never been more unpopular. On the first day Lord Tebbit mounted a passionate attack on the government's European policy. With Mr Major looking on stony-faced, Lord Tebbit offered him support only if he pursued policies 'to preserve the rights of these islands to manage our affairs for ourselves in our own interests'. Referring to suggestions that Mr Lamont should resign, he said, 'I hope, Prime Minister, you will stand by your chancellor; after all, it was not Norman Lamont's decision to enter the ERM.' After a noisy debate and frequent attacks on Maastricht at fringe meetings Douglas Hurd warned that the party could break itself apart over Europe.

The former home secretary Kenneth Baker announced that he would vote against the Maastricht bill, and Lady Thatcher gave a Euro-sceptic interview to the *European* newspaper. She said, 'Once we realized that the ERM lacked the flexibility we expected and required we should have left.' With the former prime minister's support, rebellion became almost respectable. Tory right wingers opened fire on Mr Major in public and private in a way that would have been inconceivable a few months earlier. Lady Thatcher's former deputy Lord Whitelaw made a passionate appeal for her to show loyalty to Mr Major: 'I can only hope that before it is too late, Lady Thatcher, who did so much good for our country and for the world as Britain's prime minister, will not appear to be undermining her successor.' But it *was* too late; and the battle for Maastricht had only just begun.

22

The end of the beginning

JOURNALISTS OFTEN EXPERIENCE EVENTS in a quite different – sometimes diametrically opposed – way to those directly concerned. The worse the episode for those involved, the more dramatic and exciting it can be for the journalist to report: what for us is a good story is often inextricably linked to a bad time for those forced to take part. But political journalism is not the same as covering the tragic happenings which fall to the lot of the general reporter. Politicians are in the business of dealing with events; they are judged by how they cope under pressure; they have not been forced into the front line. And political journalists should not get too involved. But I still felt a mixture of confusion, anger and a good deal of concern over the mess which Mr Major presided over in his first year after winning the election of 1992.

Like many people I believed that at the very least Norman Lamont should resign as chancellor. Someone should take the blame for the collapse of the government's economic policy and the cost of Black Wednesday. The net loss to government funds as a result of the frantic trading on that day was unofficially estimated to have been £1.8 billion, which could have been far more usefully spent on hospitals and schools. Interviewed on the *Today* programme, I pointed out that when the pound had last been formally devalued, in 1967, the Labour chancellor James Callaghan had been shifted to the Home Office. He too had talked up the pound, for the same reason as Mr Lamont – to try to maintain confidence in sterling. But this policy having failed, Mr Callaghan and the prime minister Harold Wilson agreed that it would no longer be appropriate for him to stay at the Treasury. In the long run it did not unduly harm Mr Callaghan's career: when Labour were back in office and Mr Wilson resigned, he took over as prime minister. In sharp contrast to those events twenty-five years earlier, Mr Major decided to make no changes to the cabinet. I still believe this was a mistake.

Mr Major wrestled in private with this question, taking advice from members of his own family and political colleagues. He felt that Mr Lamont had loyally carried out the government's policy; if anyone should resign, it should be himself. But those outside his inner circle knew nothing of Mr Major's personal anguish. The prime minister seemed to breeze on regardless, even though subsequent events appeared to mock the way he and his chancellor had stuck with the ERM. The first fall of one per cent in interest rates was quickly followed by another the same, and Britain began to enjoy a prolonged period of growth which would continue throughout the rest of Mr Major's period in office. It looked as if the economy did well as long as the government were not too closely involved. Mrs Thatcher had been right.

It seems to me that one of the reasons Mr Major decided to hold on to Mr Lamont was that it would take some of the pressure off himself. Sacking a member of the cabinet in such circumstances amounts to a frank admission of serious failure in the way government has conducted business and may not be enough to satisfy public opinion. Once the scapegoat has been removed, the prime minister may attract much of the blame. When a political storm is raging, an unpopular cabinet minister can be an extremely useful lightning conductor. All the energy of the government's critics is aimed in their direction, while the prime minister may manage to survive relatively unscathed. That could certainly help to explain the surprisingly buoyant mood Mr Major was in when I joined a group of journalists accompanying him to Egypt in October 1992.

Despite all the problems of the summer and the manifest difficulties of the recent party conference, he gave no sign of undue stress. He was encouraged by the nature of the visit. I have described how Mrs Thatcher was unusually relaxed on a trip to commemorate the seventy-fifth anniversary of the Gallipoli campaign in the months leading up to her resignation. Now it was Mr Major's turn to find solace in a significant episode in the life of Winston Churchill. His visit was to celebrate the fiftieth anniversary of one of the turning points of the Second World War, the Battle of El Alamein. This was the battle Churchill had summed up with memorable restraint: 'Now this is not the end. It is not even the beginning of the end. But it is, perhaps, the end of the beginning.' Mr Major's spirits seemed to lift at the prospect of seeing where the victory had taken place. But first he had talks with the Egyptian government in Cairo.

Mr Major had grown suspicious of the media, and in talking to us was not always helped by members of his press office. Before we left Cairo they proposed an interview with him in the grounds of the British embassy. I suggested it would look better if the prime minister stood in front of the impressive palm trees flanking the embassy entrance. This move was resisted until I said, acidly, that I did not think we had travelled all this way to make the prime minister look as if he was in a car park. It was strange how long it took many Whitehall press office staff to develop even a basic grasp of television techniques. Radio was easier, and inside the embassy Mr Major gave me a long interview for Radio 4's *World this Weekend*. The subject was inevitably Europe, even though it seemed out of place in the heat and bustle of the Egyptian capital. Mr Major was keen to make clear that he had no intention of giving up on the Maastricht Treaty. Unfortunately I had not heard the speculation which would dominate the rest of the trip – that he would call a general election if the government failed to get the necessary legislation through Parliament. This was a trial balloon, given to only one or two journalists on the clear understanding that it could be denied if necessary. Efforts were made by the press office to play down the speculation, but they were happy to reinforce the simple message: Mr Major was going to throw everything into the battle for Maastricht. As it happens, it was the tactic General Montgomery had used fifty years earlier.

The prime minister was now keen to press on to El Alamein as his talks had finished earlier than expected. His schedule was brought forward, and his chartered plane took off for Alexandria. Unfortunately, that left me stranded at Cairo airport. I had been at a radio station arranging for my interview with him to be sent to London and I was racing towards the plane in a taxi when it took off. I wandered pathetically along the tarmac, waving at the departing aircraft, and then had to spend four hours in a car on the desert road to Alexandria in order to catch up with the rest of the party. But the ceremony the next day, with spirited veterans and an impressive contingent of British forces, made up for my discomfort. It was a very moving and emotional occasion, and it was a thrill to sign off my radio report with the words, 'John Sergeant, BBC, El Alamein.'

On the plane home I had the chance to find out what Mr Major thought about the problems ahead when he came down to talk to us for about half an hour. But it was difficult to know what he was really thinking. He mounted a strong defence of the need to get the Maastricht Treaty approved by Parliament, based on the familiar argument that he had negotiated in good faith and Britain had given its word. I said it was surprising that anyone thought of him as being anything but pro-Europe. He turned on me with mock disapproval and said, 'But John, I am the biggest Euro-sceptic in the cabinet.' He would use this phrase later with his backbench MPs as he tried to convince the rebels that he was as sceptical as they were when it came to defending British interests; but they were not impressed.

There was no formal reason why there should be another vote on the principle of the Maastricht bill, but a promise had been made to the Opposition, and the decision to hold a vote on 4 November had been taken on the very day the pound fell out of the ERM. Labour considered this too good a chance to miss, even though they were in favour of the treaty. They decided – along with about thirty Tory rebels – to vote against the government. It looked as if Mr Major would suffer a serious defeat. The prime minister and other members of the cabinet made strenuous efforts to quell the revolt, but to their intense annoyance found themselves up against an implacable force originating from the House of Lords. As Tory MPs trooped in to see the prime minister in his office at the Commons, Lady Thatcher was preparing to see some of the same MPs in her office at the other end of the building. When an extraordinary event such as this takes place, it is not surprising that Parliament still keeps such a tight grip on the use of cameras at Westminster. If we had been able to film the MPs filing in to hear mutually contradictory advice from their past and present leaders, it would have been sensational.

The tension within Conservative ranks was obvious. Mrs Thatcher's allies insisted that she intended to remain loyal to Mr Major. A minister reacted sharply: 'She doesn't know the meaning of the word loyal.' The home secretary Kenneth Clarke, in a BBC interview, said the Tory rebels had a 'kind of theological attachment to the days of our former leader'. He described her as 'the lady over the water'. Sir Edward Heath,

18. The author with Mr Major in his flat overlooking the Thames in 2003. For the first time he reveals in public the extent of his disagreements with Lady Thatcher. He says she had the same gift 'that Elizabeth I had, of shifting the blame for unpopular things onto other shoulders'.

19. In 1992, Norman Lamont, chancellor of the exchequer, announces that the pound is leaving the Exchange Rate Mechanism. Mr Major's government never recovers its reputation for economic competence.

20. Mrs Thatcher sizes up a potential successor at the Tory party conference in 1977. At sixteen, William Hague is no threat.

21. Twenty years later when she endorses him for leader, it's because she wants to stop Kenneth Clarke, whom she partly blames for her own downfall.

22. Iain Duncan Smith benefits from Margaret Thatcher's implacable policy of ABC. She will support Anyone But Clarke, as long as they have a chance of winning.

23. 1999, two years into Tony Blair's premiership, at a memorial service for King Hussein of Jordan. Mrs Thatcher now seems to accept that Mr Blair has been the main beneficiary of her legacy. And he is prepared to acknowledge his debt.

24. The retired couple in November 2000, ten years after she left office. Denis has been retired for years, but she finds it almost impossible to remove herself from the business of politics. It is her only interest.

25. 'The Mummy Returns': at a campaign rally in 2001 in Plymouth, she approvingly quotes the title of a film showing locally. But the joke backfires. Many Conservative supporters dearly wished to see her return to power.

26. *Left*. The formal end of Lady Thatcher's career. In March 2002, her office announces that she will no longer be giving public speeches.

27. *Below*. A trio of prime ministers at the Queen Mother's funeral in April 2002. Sometimes they tried to disguise their differences, sometimes they hardly bothered. They were solo players, who between them dominated British politics for twenty-two years, with three very different views about the true nature of the Conservative party.

28. *Right.* Baroness Thatcher in splendid isolation in the House of Lords in 2003. She believed that her move from the Commons would give her more freedom to attack Mr Major's policy on Europe.

29. *Below.* Lady Thatcher lays her hand on Ronald Reagan's casket in Washington, June 2004. In her eulogy, she says, 'I have lost a dear friend.'

30. In the Downing Street garden with Tony Blair in 2002. For half an hour we talked about Mrs Thatcher's achievements. He revealed how much she helped him in the first part of his premiership, and argued that if she had not been ousted she would have won the election of 1992 against Neil Kinnock.

31. Lady Thatcher poses in May 2004 with Michael Howard, six months after he became leader. He is the first of her successors who no longer has to worry about the 'back-seat driver' she promised to become when Mr Major took over in 1990.

who was still an MP, believed the threat of rebellion was unprecedented in his forty-year career as a politician. 'I cannot recall any episode in which those with a different view were prepared to endanger the life of their government.'

The rebels were not united. Some were having second thoughts about a vote which was increasingly seen as a direct threat to the prime minister. They did not want to vote against Maastricht if this meant the end for Mr Major. There is some dispute about Lady Thatcher's intentions – whether her aim was really to force him out of office. I sought the views of her former political secretary John Whittingdale, who had become a Conservative MP by the time of the Maastricht vote. In 2003, in one of the restaurants at Westminster, he described a more innocent motive for those meetings Lady Thatcher had had with MPs. She was by far the biggest political star of her time, and even those who did not agree with her views on Europe were anxious to meet her. Mr Whittingdale was seen as the vital go-between, but he strongly disputes the charge that he actively buttonholed MPs and then sent them in for a pep talk by Lady Thatcher on the evils of Maastricht. Mr Whittingdale told me that a large number of the new intake would say to him, 'Oh, she's wonderful; that's why we came into politics. She is our inspiration. How is she? I've never met her. I would love to meet her.' Mr Whittingdale would then arrange for groups of them to see the former prime minister. No one ever refused one of these invitations. He told me what happened: 'They all sat round, with her like a teacher in the middle, and they had a political discussion, which within a minute was on Europe.' It was not her intention, he says, to undermine Mr Major but because of her legendary lack of small talk she could not resist giving her views 'in pretty robust form' on this burning topic. He admits this was an inevitable outcome. 'She's never,' he said, 'been exactly good at, "Where do you live and what does your wife do?" The discussions turned to Europe and politics instantly, but it was not a deliberate, calculated act at all.'

Lady Thatcher was in a cleft stick. If she presented her own views too forcefully, she was accused of attacking Mr Major. But that is politics, and she could not deny that her meetings were a great comfort to those who were planning to rebel; she knew they would be taken as a clear sign of her support. One of those who went to see her was a new Conservative MP, a former army officer who had taken over from Norman Tebbit in the Chingford constituency. He was unknown to the general public and sad that in his first significant vote in the House of Commons he would defy the prime minister and the entire cabinet. This was the unlikely beginning of the parliamentary career of the next Conservative leader but one, Iain Duncan Smith.

When I spoke to him about his time as a Maastricht rebel it was in the autumn of 2003, some weeks before his fellow MPs decided that he should no longer be their leader. Mr Duncan Smith was anxious, just like John Major and later William Hague, not to appear to have been unduly influenced by Margaret Thatcher. Coping with the Thatcher legacy was never easy, or simple, for her successors. But that did not prevent him saying to me that he would bow before nobody in his admiration for Lady Thatcher. 'This party should be immensely proud of her time as prime minister, and I think we always will be.' He told me what it had been like to accept one of those invitations to see her before the Maastricht vote. 'Oh, of course it was exciting to see somebody who had only just ceased being prime minister, who was one of the reasons why you came into politics,' he told me. 'I make no bones about that.' But although she was supportive of his views on Europe, he did not consider she changed his thinking on the issue. 'I believed,' he said, 'that the Maastricht Treaty was just full of holes and that it could and would be used to change dramatically the relationship between Britain and Europe, even if that was not John Major's intention.'

Mr Duncan Smith told me that he had been very uncomfortable about being a rebel. 'I used to go home at night, hating the whole process of being in Parliament at that stage.' Apart from Lady Thatcher there was little comfort to be had from his own side; he discovered greater sympathy among Labour MPs. After listening to one of Tony Benn's anti-Maastricht speeches, the new Conservative MP found himself alongside Mr Benn in the loo. 'I have just listened to your speech,' he told him, 'and I have to say it is probably the finest speech I have heard in the House, and probably the finest I am likely to hear.' Mr Benn thanked him in his customarily polite way and said, 'You know, I have often thought watching you, that this must be a terrible time for you. It must be awful for you to come into the House and to find yourself at odds with the government that you support. But you must do what you think is right. This is a terrible, terrible time for you.' Mr Duncan Smith was taken aback. He told me it was possibly the nicest comment made to him at that time. 'And,' he added wistfully, 'it wasn't said by anyone on my own side.'

Not all the potential rebels were as steadfast as the former army officer. Mr Whittingdale, who had worked so loyally for Lady Thatcher, was forced to compromise. When I spoke to him in 2003 he was a member of the shadow cabinet and still had the air of the clever public schoolboy he once was at Winchester. Although anxious to tell the truth, he does not want to let his friends down. Lady Thatcher gave him a hard time over the Maastricht vote. 'She wanted to defeat the government on Maastricht,' he told me. 'I didn't know what to do.' He faced a classic political dilemma: he was strongly against both the likely outcomes – the survival of the Maastricht Treaty and the end of Mr Major's government. With another young MP, the like-minded Bernard Jenkin, he decided to abstain but felt that because of his long and close personal relationship with Lady Thatcher he should tell her in person what he intended to do. 'She expressed herself very forcefully and made it clear she felt I should vote against,' he said. 'It was not a pleasant conversation.' Lady Thatcher was reported to have told Mr Whittingdale, 'The trouble with you, John, is that your spine does not reach your brain.' He is not sure to what extent Lady Thatcher believed a defeat would damage Mr Major's political career. I asked him directly, 'What if you had said to her that there might have to be a general election, that Mr Major might resign?' Mr Whittingdale replied, 'She believed that the Maastricht Treaty represented a greater threat to the country; it was an issue bigger than the party.'

After the ERM debacle, and with Labour strongly ahead in the opinion polls, a general election would almost certainly have resulted in a victory for John Smith. What was far more likely, though, was Mr Major calling and winning a vote of confidence in the House of Commons and, though badly wounded, continuing as prime minister. The obvious candidates to succeed him, Michael Heseltine, Douglas Hurd and Kenneth Clarke, would have had no greater appeal to the Euro-sceptics. Although Mr Major often took the attacks on Maastricht personally, it was the issue itself which was the spur for the rebellion. If the vote was lost, it would cast serious doubt on whether Britain would be able to ratify the Maastricht Treaty. But even taking all these matters into consideration, it is very surprising how far Lady Thatcher was prepared to go in giving comfort to the rebels.

Throughout this period she was given extravagant support by commentators who now had it in for Mr Major. One of the most extreme of her cheerleaders was Paul Johnson. As a young man he had been editor of the Labour-supporting *New*

Statesman; now he had turned into a tribune of the Tory right. He argued that Mr Major had forfeited his authority after the devaluation of the pound and lacked democratic principles, as shown by his refusal of a referendum on Maastricht; he should go. The article promoting this view was published in *The Times* after it was turned down by the still-loyal *Daily Telegraph*. Mr Johnson said of Mr Major, 'The longer he stays, the more the Tory crisis will deepen, and the more likely it will be that, in desperation, they will have to turn to Margaret Thatcher, as they turned to Churchill in 1940. That is certainly what I desire and foresee.'

A few days earlier there had been a report in the *Sunday Times* suggesting that close friends of Lady Thatcher were investigating the possibility of a return to power. 'If John Major quits or is removed, she is ready to re-enter Number 10,' one of her friends was quoted as saying. There was even speculation about how this might be done, possibly involving Lady Thatcher renouncing her peerage, but she would still have had to be elected by Conservative MPs, and at this point the idea bordered on the absurd. In such circumstances a party would seek a leader to unite them; Lady Thatcher could not possibly have done that. But the fact that there was even the merest hint of a Thatcher comeback shows how febrile the atmosphere within the Tory party had become. On the morning of the debate on 4 November, I had no idea how the vote would go.

Mr Major says that at this stage he believed he would have to resign if the vote was lost; he had decided it was not the moment to call an election. When he opened the debate he said the essential issue was quite simple: 'In this country are we or are we not to play a central role in Europe's future development?' This question was fundamental to our future well-being, both economic and political. 'I have no doubt,' he concluded, 'the answer will be yes.' Mr Major did not criticize the Conservative rebels directly; he simply pointed out that by rejecting the Maastricht Treaty the UK would encourage moves towards a 'centralized, federal Europe'. This was more likely to occur if Britain 'scowls in frustration on the fringes'. It was a cool, authoritative speech, devoid of any petulance or anger.

Most of the hard-core Tory rebels did not speak; the excitement was behind the scenes. But when the obscure Conservative MP for Great Yarmouth Michael Cartiss announced in the chamber that he would be voting against the government, the chief whip Richard Ryder was convinced that defeat was certain. John Major and Michael Heseltine went to his office to be told that it seemed the government would lose by one or two votes. It was about 8.30 p.m. One of the committed rebels, John Wilkinson, was on his feet in the Commons, praising Mr Cartiss for his speech, but at that very moment it was being agreed that Mr Heseltine should offer Mr Cartiss an olive branch. Secretly the same message had also been carried to a few other potential rebels. The deal was simple. If they agreed to vote with the government the final stages of the Maastricht bill would not be considered by the Commons until after the second Danish referendum. This was expected the following spring, and the treaty would die if the Danes said no a second time.

Back in the Commons, Mr Heseltine tried to tell the foreign secretary about the deal but Mr Hurd was listening to the debate and he brushed Mr Heseltine aside. Fortunately in his final speech Mr Hurd did not refer to the timing of future debates, but when he realized he had been left out of the loop there was a frosty conversation between the two men, and Mr Hurd admits to being cross 'for a couple of days'. But the drama was now on the floor of the House. As the voting started at 10 p.m. I could see Mr Heseltine speaking earnestly to Mr Cartiss. Finally Mr Major came up, put his arms around the MP's shoulders, and steered him firmly into the lobby to vote for the government.

The vote was 319 to 316; the government had won by just three votes. The secret deal had worked. Mr Cartiss said later, 'I could not bring myself to do something which would destroy John Major. I believed it would be the end of him, and he is the best prime minister for this country.' The vote of 4 November had done little to resolve the fundamental problems over Maastricht within the Conservative party, but it had given Mr Major a vital breathing space. This was not the end. It was not even the beginning of the end. But, perhaps, it was the end of the beginning.

23

Maggie backs unity – but not for long

IF LADY THATCHER had been in the habit of making New Year resolutions, somewhere in the list for the beginning of 1993 would be the simple instruction to herself: 'Don't rock the boat.' There is no doubt she fully realized as an ex-prime minister, particularly one as eminent as herself, that she should bite her tongue and not appear to go out of her way to be critical of John Major. The problem was that there were other items on this imaginary list which she found equally if not more compelling. She was determined to express her views on the most important topics of the day, and the most important topic to her at that time was the government's totally misguided attempt to implement the deal made at Maastricht. She tried, where possible, to limit the damage, by speaking to meetings abroad where journalists were specifically barred or by restricting herself to private gatherings to which reporters were not invited, but politics remained her chief interest – she could not live without talking politics – and there appeared to be an insatiable demand from press and public to hear what she had to say, particularly if it was critical of Mr Major.

At the end of January 1993 Lady Thatcher was quoted as saying – in a speech to a private meeting of Conservatives in London – that Mr Major should not be so bothered by criticism in newspapers. Her audience laughed heartily when she said, 'I didn't read the papers. I just got on with the job.' One of her other comments was even more barbed; it was taken to be an attack on his more consensual approach. 'You need,' she declared, 'to have fixed stars and a compass to steer by, otherwise you find yourself following shooting stars, the shooting stars of compromise and consensus.' On government borrowing, she was openly critical: 'It is when you abandon financial orthodoxy that you get into trouble.' Independent analysts supported her view. In that year public borrowing rose to 7.8 per cent of national output, and the following year was over £50 billion. Such levels could not be sustained.

John Whittingdale, who was still working with her, admits that whatever her good intentions she would regularly undermine her generally constructive approach with off-the-cuff remarks. I asked him what her reaction was when the criticisms she made of Mr Major appeared in the newspapers. 'Well, embarrassment, actually,' he replied. 'She wouldn't talk about it, and we would say, "This is really very unhelpful," and she would look very embarrassed and also would look a bit guilty.' She was very sensitive to the charge that she was not supporting her successor and particularly disliked any suggestion that she was behaving in the same way Edward Heath had when she was prime minister. 'She didn't like even to accept that she had been unhelpful,' Mr Whittingdale said. But the effect of what she was doing was obvious. There would be regular stories in the newspapers detailing what she thought about Mr Major and she had every opportunity to change her behaviour. Mr Whittingdale shook his head, almost in disbelief, as he recalled those times. 'There were good friends who would come in and say "Come on, you can't behave like this." It wasn't as if she wasn't told.'

Edward Heath was one of the few leading Conservatives ready to attack Lady Thatcher in turn, accusing her of simply being anti-European and in particular anti-German. The feud between the former prime ministers was a gift for the media. Sir Edward did not hesitate when asked on television whether she was inciting the rebels. 'There is no doubt about it,' he said, and he gave Mr Major some firm advice on what to do. He should not be 'quite so nice' in dealing with them. 'You can never appease the right wing, never,' he declared. Sir Edward also developed a standard withering response if he was asked why Lady Thatcher had made a particular critical comment. He would reply, 'I don't know; I'm not a doctor.'

Lady Thatcher's good friend and closest adviser Lord Powell accepts that there was no thought-out logic to her behaviour; it was a question of her character and the freedom she gained once she had left office. 'I think the great thing about Margaret,' he told me, 'was this huge energy which bubbled the whole time, on many different issues. When she was in government, that energy was channelled by the discipline of meetings and conclusions written by people like me, so it was directed and extremely potent and authoritative. Out of office, it all spilled out rather at random, like water overflowing a basin, sort of out of control.'

Lord Powell was one of those who tried at times to be a restraining influence on Lady Thatcher. When warnings were given to her, he says, 'She would, to a degree, take it to heart, but not for long.' Her underlying resentment at the way she had been removed from office and the policy differences with Mr Major 'just came out'. The contrast with her time in government was striking. 'There is a huge difference,' Lord Powell told me, 'between being a prime minister who is surrounded by people dedicated to trying to keep her on message – *her* message of course – and being suddenly taken out of office with no political staff and no civil service staff.' She was 'much more vulnerable' in the outside world, where there was no one to advise her of the political consequences of her meetings and comments. As the year progressed and the vital argument over the Maastricht Treaty continued, Lady Thatcher's 'vulnerability' became all too obvious.

The Major loyalists, of course, saw her behaviour in quite

different terms: they regarded it as a wilful disregard for party discipline, unacceptable from someone who had depended on such restraint when she was at Number 10. Looking back, Douglas Hurd believes that Lady Thatcher, then sixty-seven years old, was beginning to show her age. One of the characteristics of growing old is that people's views tend to narrow; they get 'fierce on small things', he told me in an interview in 2003. 'Most of us have a brake which operates between what we think and what we say; but that brake wears out, and it wore out with her. So she was saying things that were on her mind, but there was no sort of sieve or filter.'

Part of the reason for Lady Thatcher's behaviour was a natural desire for her voice to be heeded and for the government to accept that she was still a force to be reckoned with. Other leading politicians leave the public stage and there is no clamour for them to return. Lady Thatcher could not walk down a street without being mobbed, and had to go everywhere with a police escort. It was easy for her to think she was too important to the nation's political life simply to disappear. The Friargate Waxwork Museum in York appeared to agree. Soon after Mrs Thatcher had ceased to be prime minister, the museum had put its wax model of her into storage; it was now put back on display. The director said they were responding to demand. 'We have had an upsurge of people asking where she is, so we redid her hair and pushed John Major to the side; no one is interested in John Major.'

Lady Thatcher threw herself into the national campaign for a referendum on the Maastricht Treaty even though she must have thought there was little chance of Mr Major agreeing to a vote he was likely to lose. She became a patron of the main referendum group, and in January 1993 about eight hundred people from all political parties took part in a march they sponsored in London. At a rally in Trafalgar Square words of support from Lady Thatcher were read out to roars of approval.

Of the platform speakers only the Labour veteran Tony Benn failed to applaud. He puffed firmly on his pipe, his eyes fixed firmly on the ground, as the comments from one of his staunchest political opponents delighted the crowd. 'I believe the people do not want the treaty,' she was quoted as saying. 'There is an easy way to find out. Hold a referendum.' The next month Lady Thatcher, in person, launched a telephone poll on the referendum question. It attracted more than 90,000 calls and, as often happens with a campaigning exercise of this sort, about 90 per cent of those who took part backed the views of the organizers.

When Lady Thatcher visited Denmark, where a second referendum on Maastricht was due to be held in May, the trip was described in newspapers as a private visit as if she might have decided to make it official. This was yet another example of the way journalists found it easy to accord her the trappings of power. Strictly speaking, her only official position was her membership of the House of Lords. She talked to leading figures in the Danish 'No' campaign and gave a public endorsement to the opponents of Maastricht a month before the vote. They received a message from her office which read, 'Lady Thatcher very much believes that Denmark's referendum is Britain's referendum and wishes you every success.' Lady Thatcher's office also sent the Danish group the text of one of her 'private' speeches in which she dismissed the deal negotiated by Mr Major at the Edinburgh European summit before Christmas. This had given the Danes opt-out clauses from the Maastricht Treaty on the same lines as those Britain had obtained. But Lady Thatcher argued that the Danes were no better off as a result.

Mr Major found it difficult to criticize Lady Thatcher directly without giving their differences greater publicity. He was irritated by reports that Lady Thatcher had met two prominent right-wing members of his cabinet, Peter Lilley and

Michael Portillo, at a lunch at her office which was also attended by Lord Tebbit. There were even hints that Mr Lilley and Mr Portillo might suffer in the next cabinet reshuffle. But Downing Street backtracked, denying that Mr Major was 'extremely irritated'. It was pointed out to lobby journalists that the prime minister needed to have members of his cabinet from the right of the party; and in fact Mr Lilley and Mr Portillo did stay until the end, in 1997. An open attack on them came from a prominent pro-European backbencher, Hugh Dykes, who said that he found it 'astonishing' that two members of the cabinet were prepared to have lunch with Lady Thatcher. It was, he said, 'most unwise'. Mr Major was said to be more concerned by the fact that nearly fifty Conservative MPs, nearly twice the number who had opposed him in the autumn, were refusing to support the government as they struggled to get the Maastricht bill through Parliament.

Lady Thatcher's opposition to Maastricht strengthened the hand of the growing number of Tory MPs prepared to vote against the government. As the whips tried to devise ways of putting pressure on the rebels, it became increasingly obvious that many of them also had the support of their constituency associations. Many grass-roots Tories and their association chairmen, as was shown by a number of surveys, were fully behind Lady Thatcher. An opinion poll of Conservative voters suggested that if Mr Major were to leave office the most popular replacement as leader was Lady Thatcher. This is partly because she was the most prominent Euro-sceptic; all the likely leadership candidates were pro-Europe. When the whips appealed to party chairmen to see that their MPs came into line over Maastricht, they were often disappointed. John Whittingdale believes Lady Thatcher's support gave many potential rebels the political protection they needed. 'The fact that Margaret Thatcher was seen to be giving them endorsement was a fantastic cover,' he told me. 'The associations still thought she was wonderful; nobody in the voluntary party had wanted her to leave Number Ten – they still wanted her to be in office.'

Mr Major let it be known that he was determined to take a tougher line with Tories holding 'extreme views' on the treaty. He was reported to have told colleagues that those who thought they could push him around were wasting their time. But the reality was rather different. As was confirmed by much later events, the Conservative party was warming strongly to the Euro-sceptic cause; Lady Thatcher and her colleagues were by no means out of the mainstream of party thinking. Significantly, one of the other Euro-sceptics in the cabinet, Michael Howard, who ten years later would become party leader, declined to condemn the rebels. He merely argued that while the treaty was not ideal, it was an acceptable price to pay for Britain to continue to have a voice within Europe. John Whittingdale gave me a bald assessment of Mr Major's position at this time: 'He either simply did not understand the strength of feeling in the party on Europe, or he was at odds with the majority of the party on Europe; either way the result was a disaster.'

The problem for the Maastricht rebels was that to defeat the government they needed to rely on the support of Labour MPs who were broadly in favour of the treaty. It is usually very difficult for MPs in the government party to support an amendment put down by the Opposition, but on 8 March the rebels inflicted their first defeat on Mr Major by doing just that. Forty-four Conservative MPs ignored repeated demands for party unity and either abstained or voted with Labour. The government lost by twenty-two votes. The issue was not very important – Labour proposed a new committee of the European regions be made up entirely of elected councillors – but it showed how far the rebels would go. It meant that taking the Maastricht bill through Parliament would take even longer.

Major loyalists were extremely angry; they were quoted as describing the rebels as 'unprincipled bastards' and 'robots out of control'. Mr Hurd described the effect of the vote as 'a delay for delay's sake, and a perverse delay at that'.

One of the leading rebels was Bill Cash, a tall, obsessive lawyer, who it was often said could 'bore for England' on the subject of Europe. Journalists, whose interest in arcane aspects of the European Communities (Amendment) Bill was strictly limited, had to get to know Mr Cash in order to remain well informed. Ignoring him was far too dangerous; as the bill continued its tortuous way through Parliament, any one of the 240 amendments he personally drafted could have been a dagger aimed at Mr Major's heart. Many was the time I listened to Mr Cash pouring out a flood of details, hoping that one of them at least might turn out to be newsworthy.

The only consolation was that everyone following the subject had the same problem: for months, it seemed, if you yearned to be a political heavyweight, you had to live off the Maastricht diet. When I interviewed Mr Cash in the autumn of 2003 he was keen to explain that the Commons rebels had not been part of any general Euro-sceptic plot. 'We weren't taking instructions from anybody,' he told me. 'We were doing this on our own terms.' He admits though that Lady Thatcher's role was very significant. 'It was immensely important to keep her in touch, and to know that she was on our side, which she was – completely.' Although there were only about twenty hard-core rebels, more than fifty Conservative MPs failed to support the government at some stage as the bill went through Parliament. It was one of the most persistent and well-organized rebellions of modern times.

The sheer ruthlessness of the rebels came as a surprise, and I found it difficult to keep my head straight as more and more bizarre tactics were employed. Take just one awful example of what we had to try to explain to the five million people who normally watched BBC television news programmes. In order not to be defeated, the government accepted a rebel amendment allowing for a separate vote on the Social Chapter once the rest of the bill had been considered by the Commons. This was merely postponing a likely defeat for the government, because the rebels announced that when the vote eventually came they would side with Labour. But – I hope you are still with me – the rebels were totally against the Social Chapter and Labour were strongly in favour. It was all about trying to defeat the government. I won't go on except to say that this amendment was known as the 'ticking time bomb', and Lady Thatcher signalled her support for the use of this device.

In April detailed discussion of the bill in the Commons was over – to almost everyone's relief, except of course the indefatigable Bill Cash. The committee stage had involved 163 hours of debate, the longest anyone could remember. Mr Major took the opportunity to make his most positive speech on the EU for two years. He repeated his desire to have Britain at the heart of Europe, and he accused the Euro-sceptics of being narrow-minded. 'Many who oppose Europe,' he said, 'are like the fat boy in *Pickwick*. They want to make your flesh creep. They think we are always going to lose the argument in Europe. That is defeatist and wrong.' The speech is remembered for Mr Major's final, lyrical passage about how Britain in fifty years' time would still be the land of 'warm beer' and 'old maids bicycling to Holy Communion through the morning mist'. It was often quoted, to Mr Major's annoyance, by those looking for an easy way to sum up his political outlook: he was accused of having a fuzzy, sentimental view of the future.

At the beginning of May poor local election results and a humiliating by-election victory for the Liberal Democrats in the supposedly safe Conservative seat of Newbury added to the impression that the government was on the run. Much now depended on the second referendum in Denmark. As a result of the deal which had averted a government defeat the previous year, no more progress could be made on the Maastricht bill until the people of Denmark had spoken (again). Although Lady Thatcher and others believed that the deal giving Denmark essentially the same opt-out clauses as Britain had made little difference, there had been a shift of opinion. When the result was announced on 18 May, it was greeted by European leaders with unrestrained relief: on a turnout of well over 80 per cent, the voters had backed the treaty by 57 to 43 per cent. Of all the member states, only Britain had failed to implement Maastricht. It was a blow to the Euro-sceptics, but they were determined to fight on.

There was not much relief for John Major, though, as he at last tried to tackle the problem of the government's lack of credibility in the economic field. During the Newbury by-election campaign Mr Lamont had notoriously declared, in the words of Edith Piaf, 'Je ne regrette rien.' This was treated by Mr Major as the last straw. Having resisted calls for the chancellor to be removed after Black Wednesday, the prime minister belatedly took action. He sacked Mr Lamont and replaced him with the pro-European Kenneth Clarke. Mr Major told me the next day, in a private chat during an Anglo-French summit in Paris, that nobody now believed Mr Lamont. 'If he says it's Wednesday, people think it's Thursday,' he said. I was amazed at the prime minister's frankness. As it turned out, there were plenty of people ready to believe Mr Lamont when he mounted a bitter attack on Mr Major in a resignation speech in the Commons reminiscent of the one Sir Geoffrey Howe had made. In what became a well-known phrase, Mr Lamont accused the government of appearing to be 'in office, but not in power'.

In the short term, sacking the chancellor did little to improve confidence in the government. It led to speculation about the prime minister's position, just as Mr Major had feared after Black Wednesday, and Mr Lamont's successor Kenneth Clarke was soon being talked about as a possible leader. Lady Thatcher was so concerned that the party might be plunged into another leadership crisis that she appealed to her colleagues to throw their weight behind Mr Major. 'We must all get behind John,' she said. But this gesture was more likely to have arisen from her fear that the new leader might be Mr Clarke, whom she disliked and mistrusted, rather than any real change of heart over Mr Major, and it certainly did not prevent her from continuing with her anti-Maastricht campaign.

Lady Thatcher next intervened when the House of Lords began considering the Maastricht bill in June. She told a packed chamber that a voluntary alliance of nations was being turned into a European super-state without people realizing the consequences. She repeated her demand for a referendum. 'No elector in this country has been able to vote against Maastricht, none. It has been impossible to do so. It is disgraceful if we deny them that opportunity.' Her former colleague Lord Parkinson condemned the treaty as a 'major preparation for trade wars and protectionism'.

Euro-sceptic peers proposed five hundred amendments to the bill, but its passage through the Lords was relatively uneventful. The referendum proposal was easily defeated, although Lady Thatcher voted in favour; it was the first time in her political career that she had refused to accept the party's three-line whip instructing her to vote with the government. For most MPs or peers such a step would have been significant, but after all Lady Thatcher had said and done, it did not give rise to much comment. In July the Maastricht bill was finally passed by Parliament. But then all those journalistic attempts at explaining rebel tactics had to be repeated: the 'ticking time

bomb' was set to go off. The promised vote on the Social
Chapter now had to come before the Commons.

Mr Major reflected bitterly on how far the rebels were
prepared to go. They would even support the hated (by them)
Social Chapter if this meant they could inflict a defeat on
the government. It was agreed behind the scenes that if the
government lost ministers would immediately call for a vote of
confidence, which would make it difficult for the rebels not to
vote with them. The motion would include a reference to the
Social Chapter to enable the vote to be treated as final
implementation of the Maastricht Treaty. (I am sorry but we
are back to advanced parliamentary tactics – not a subject for
the faint-hearted.) This time the idea was that nothing mattered except making sure the government won and the Maastricht Treaty was agreed. It was a risky strategy, but it worked.
The government were defeated in the crucial division by eight
votes and there was uproar in the Commons, but the next
morning the rebels had a stark choice: if they failed to support
the government in the debate on the confidence motion that
day, there would be a general election. This time Mr Major
made that threat explicit. When the vote was taken the
government had a majority of thirty-eight.

The threat of a general election was all the more potent
this time because the opinion polls suggested that Labour
would easily win, and some of the hard-core rebels knew
they would lose their seats. But then a pleased but exhausted
Mr Major made a serious mistake as he was giving interviews
to celebrate the end of the long parliamentary struggle over
Maastricht. It came during what was meant to be a private
conversation with the political editor of ITN, Michael Brunson, which was recorded by technicians and subsequently
leaked. The prime minister was asked about the suggestion
that three Euro-sceptic members of the cabinet had threatened

to resign over Maastricht. Why hadn't he accepted their resignations? Mr Major described graphically how he saw the festering problem among his own MPs: 'Where do you think most of this poison is coming from? From the dispossessed and the never-possessed. You can think of ex-ministers who are going around causing all sorts of trouble.' And then he delivered a comment which would come to haunt him, to explain why he didn't sack the Euro-sceptics: 'We don't want another three more of the bastards out there.' Just as the wets had done years before, many of the Euro-sceptics adopted the term 'bastard' as a badge of honour. The incident would add more fuel to the fire between the rebels and Mr Major; but even before this remark produced sensational headlines, he had failed to draw a line under the battle over Maastricht in the way he had hoped. Mr Major took the unusual move of speaking to Bill Cash immediately after the final vote. He asked him, 'It's all over now, isn't it?' Mr Cash told me he did not hesitate. 'No, it's not,' he replied firmly.

24

In the foothills, with Mr Major

JOHN MAJOR'S LOSS of authority was permanent. After the ERM debacle in 1992 his government never regained the position they had held in the opinion polls and his premiership was dogged by speculation over a possible change in leader. The Conservative 'civil war' over Europe, as it was often described, had left scars which could not be healed; Mr Major would never be forgiven by Tory Euro-sceptics who felt he had missed an historic opportunity to pull out of the Maastricht Treaty once the Danes had voted no in their first referendum. To the wider public Mr Major had demonstrated a disturbing lack of competence over economic policy; this was far more important to them than complicated arguments over a treaty which even experts found impossible to resolve. All this boiled down to a simple point: Mr Major had lost the trust of the electorate. He could have coped better with this problem if he had not also been weighed down by the Thatcher legacy.

This burden on Mr Major came in different forms. Some of it was directly attributable to the continuing, active presence of the former prime minister; some of it was simply the result of her domination of British politics for more than a decade. She had so altered the way a prime minister was perceived that few discussions about Mr Major's performance could take place without some damaging comparison being drawn with how Mrs Thatcher had done the job. It was a paradox that Mr Major could only have won the election of 1992 by convincing the electorate that he was not Margaret

Thatcher; and yet in the years that followed he endlessly suffered from the complaint that he was not as much like her as he should have been. There is no doubt that an objective assessment of their abilities would put Lady Thatcher well ahead. She was a conviction politician of unusual quality; he was a far more cautious, less inspired leader who lacked her inner confidence. But some of his most serious difficulties arose because the political circumstances had altered.

At the height of her powers Mrs Thatcher had been able to push through significant reforms which would stand the test of time. This had been both a challenge and an opportunity for an extremely determined political leader. Most of those reforms having been completed – particularly the reduction in the power of the unions and the increased scope for the private sector – there was a limit to how much any successor could hope to keep up the Thatcher crusade. But Mr Major was also disadvantaged by the fact that unlike Mrs Thatcher he led a government with a small parliamentary majority, and a party which had been so long in power that it was inevitably running out of steam.

Mr Major – in his famous 'bastards' conversation – complained that some Conservatives spoke of a golden age, 'a golden age that never was', in his opinion. He remembered Margaret Thatcher's lack of consistency over Europe, how instead of being an ideologically driven Euro-sceptic she had often been pragmatic and ready to compromise. She had ensured the passing of the Single European Act. But those Tory MPs disappointed in the Major government were surely right to sense they were coming down from a political peak. Mrs Thatcher had been an exciting and powerful leader, and now to their frustration and annoyance they seemed to be wandering aimlessly around in the foothills with Mr Major. This was a general feeling, and it goes some way towards explaining how his loss of authority expressed itself in the daily interaction between the prime minister and the media. More-over, this was the precise moment when the achievements of his predecessor were about to be given a carefully calculated boost with the publication of her memoirs, which would quickly become a best-seller on both sides of the Atlantic.

It was on a trip to Japan in the autumn of 1993 that all of these elements came together to give Mr Major one of the worst weeks of his premiership. Lady Thatcher had a large fol-lowing in Japan. When she visited Tokyo later that year she would entrance an audience of nearly a thousand Japanese businessmen. According to a reporter who was present, she was by turns hectoring and then full of praise, telling them how clever they were. One of the businessmen said, 'She's like a queen, so beautiful, so stately. The world would rejoice if she were re-elected prime minister.' In September, when I travelled to Japan with Mr Major and a group of about twenty journalists, his reception was quite different. There had been yet more speculation of a possible change in the leadership, which had been given added impetus by Mr Major himself who had said he would resign 'when people least expect it and on my own terms'.

Because he knew he would be questioned further about his position, it was only right at the end of the fifteen-hour flight that Mr Major was prepared to come down the plane to talk to the press. He managed to sound fairly upbeat. 'I think,' he told us, 'you can expect to be having conversations like this with me for quite a long time ahead. I look forward to them very much.'

To my annoyance this briefing was off camera. I was due to deliver a television report shortly after we arrived, and there was a danger I could not cover the burning political topic of the day: how Mr Major was responding to calls from some Euro-sceptics that he should step down. It was finally agreed that I would be given an interview outside the British embassy soon after we landed in Tokyo. But a message, relayed to me by a junior member of his staff, said that that I should not ask about the leadership speculation. Mr Major wanted television news to concentrate on the formal aspects of his visit to Japan, including yet another attempt to win compensation for British servicemen captured during the Second World War.

When Mr Major arrived at the embassy, I asked him three short questions about the demands for his resignation from some of his backbenchers. After our brief encounter, during which he tried to shrug off these attacks, Mr Major stormed off into the embassy. His press secretary Gus O'Donnell was highly civilized and intelligent, and would later, under Tony Blair, become head of the Treasury, but on this occasion he came back out of the embassy to express Mr Major's anger, and hissed, 'You jerk.' He was quick to apologize in front of the other journalists, and this was widely publicized, but I could never look on Mr Major in quite the same way. His reputation for niceness was not always deserved. Some of those who worked with him at Number 10 look back with bitterness on his temper tantrums, which were often provoked by circumstances over which they had no control.

Having realized he could not avoid questions about his leadership, the next day the prime minister publicly admitted that the speculation was sapping the authority of the govern-ment. 'It is time,' he said, 'to cut out this stupid internecine squabbling and get on with the job that the country elected us to do.' He attacked former ministers trying to undermine him as 'a few mavericks' and 'devils on the fringe, living out past glories'. There was then a strange news conference at the Tokyo Press Club, which turned into a clash of cultures. The two hundred Japanese journalists stood and clapped when Mr Major entered; the twenty British reporters retained their usual demeanour and stayed silently in their seats. The Japanese would not dream of asking their prime minister, in similar circumstances, about his leadership; the British could not wait to raise the issue. Mr Major tried to calm down the increasingly excitable questions from the British contingent by saying there was no vacancy and nor would there be. But not for the first time it was off-camera discussions with TV correspondents after the news conference which proved his undoing.

Two newspaper journalists had been allowed to leave their tape recorders on the table where Mr Major was conducting broadcast interviews, and his unguarded comments between these filmed sequences were published. At one point Mr Major said he could identify eight backbench Tory MPs who were 'barmy' or 'semi-loopy', and when he heard the name of one of them he could hear the sound of 'flapping white coats'. Sir Richard Body and Teresa Gorman were identified as being on Mr Major's list. What was meant to be a high-profile trip abroad, demonstrating the prime minister's grasp of international affairs, turned into a defensive squabble about Mr Major's enemies and the chance of a leadership challenge. Among Conservatives at home the lesson was obvious: this would not have happened when Mrs Thatcher was in charge.

It was not only Mr Major's loss of authority which was causing unease. Increasingly there were complaints about his failure to provide an 'overview'. Many Conservatives looked back longingly to the Thatcher period, when they had felt they knew where they were, and where they were going. Even the daughter of the former prime minister was prepared to make this point. Carol Thatcher, now working as a journalist, told the *People* that the Conservatives would lose the next election because they did not seem to have a vision, and that by the next election people would want a change. It was partly to counter the charge that he did not have a long-term strategy that Mr Major submitted an essay to *The Economist* presenting his views on the future of Europe. Journalists accompanying Mr Major were presented with copies of the magazine just as our plane was touching down at Heathrow on the flight back from the Far East.

I was very surprised that Mr Major seemed to write off the prospect of a single currency. He appeared to have reached an entirely different conclusion from those on the continent who had worked so hard to see through the Maastricht Treaty. Mr Major argued that the single currency plan was part of an old and stale policy agenda. Writing about the prospects for the next European summit, he said, 'I hope my fellow heads of government will resist the temptation to recite the mantra of full economic and monetary union as if nothing had changed. If they do recite it, it will have all the quaintness of a rain dance and about the same potency.' He suggested that a single currency would not be established by the end of the decade, as laid down in the official timetable, and that this had become 'glaringly apparent to many across Europe'. Mr Major declined to be interviewed by me on his vision of Europe's future; perhaps he was still annoyed over the incident at the Tokyo embassy. When the summit took place a month later, the German chancellor Helmut Kohl announced that the single currency was 'unstoppable'. Mr Major was fighting a hopeless rearguard action. His policy of being at the very heart of Europe seemed long gone. The euro was established within six years, on 1 January 1999.

Lady Thatcher had decided that her memoirs, *The Downing Street Years*, should be published immediately after the Conservative party conference in Blackpool. She knew that her observations on recent events and on her closest colleagues would not be welcomed by many of those still involved in Conservative politics, and she did not want to be accused of hijacking the conference. But the *Mirror* rushed out a partial and in parts inaccurate report on the memoirs the day the conference started. Most damaging to Mr Major was the allegation that Lady Thatcher had called him 'small-minded, politically naive and an intellectual lightweight'. Without being able to say in detail what she had said about the prime minister until the week after, when the book would be published, she was forced to issue a statement of support for Mr Major; not surprisingly it simply ensured maximum publicity for the original damning comment.

Inevitably, Lady Thatcher became the main talking point of the conference and the focus of most television coverage. The weekend before the conference opened she gave a long interview to the *Sunday Times*, which had bought the serialization rights to her memoirs. Although she refused to take questions on domestic policies in order not to embarrass the prime minister, this did not prevent her mounting a bitter attack on British policy in the former Yugoslavia. For the previous six months she had been calling publicly for the Bosnian Muslims to be given arms by the West and for the Serbs to be attacked with air strikes. In her newspaper interview she argued that attempts to get a European consensus had produced a negation of leadership. 'It's terrible what has happened in Bosnia,' she said. 'What kind of idealism is it that thinks it is enough to send in food and medicine and not to *do* anything while people are shot and murdered?' She repeatedly invited comparisons with her time in office. 'I didn't ring up the EC when I was with George Bush when the Iraqis went into Kuwait. What has happened that people have to have someone else holding their hand before they will take a courageous decision?' She gave a stark warning of her determination to continue attacking Britain's position within Europe and complained about the loss of parliamentary sovereignty and the subordination of the legal system which meant that 'much of the country's traditions have been lost'. For some it was pure, vintage Thatcher, greatly to be welcomed; to the Conservative party hierarchy it was yet another sign that the coming party conference could be as difficult as the disastrous event of the year before. Their mood was not helped by a survey of votes cast in recent local elections which put the Conservatives trailing in third place, behind Labour and the Liberal Democrats.

One of the main problems for party officials was how to organize Lady Thatcher's visit in order to minimize the potential damage. Such things may seem petty, but the arrangements at the party conference seem to have been as tightly fought over as the seating plans for nuclear disarmament talks. Both Lady Thatcher and Mr Major had to be satisfied they were being treated in an appropriate way. On this occasion it was decided by the party chairman to promote Lady Thatcher's appearance as a sign of party unity. It was argued that if things went wrong and the former prime minister produced more divisive headlines, then Lady Thatcher, and not the party leadership, would be held responsible. In line with this plan, the chairman Sir Norman Fowler announced, 'For years I was called a Thatcherite. Now I am called a Majorite. And let me say I wear both those labels with pride.' I could not recall Sir Norman being given either label – under both prime ministers he was usually described as 'loyal'. The chairman was suggesting that the Conservative party was big enough for both of them, but this was a proposition which would continue to be tested as long as Mr Major remained in Downing Street.

A media scrum of cameras and reporters attended Lady Thatcher's arrival on the second day – bigger than the one she had been used to as party leader. The official plan then went smoothly into action: she appeared on the platform for thirty seconds with Mr Major in a public display of reconciliation. The ovation for her was slightly longer than the one given to Mr Major, but his was unanimous; she had to put up with some of the representatives refusing to clap, to show their disapproval of her criticisms of the prime minister. 'Was that all right; did it go all right?' she asked officials as she left the platform. The former prime minister was pleased with her reception. She even managed to be friendly to Michael Heseltine when she saw him having lunch in the restaurant of the Imperial Hotel. He had recently had a heart attack, and an MP who saw Lady Thatcher greet Mr Heseltine said, 'It is a pity it took a heart attack for that to happen.'

In Mr Major's speech, after she had left, he was able to make light of the looming problem of her memoirs. 'I am not about to write my memoirs,' he said, 'not for a long time.' In fact it would only be six years before *John Major, The Autobiography* was published. The conference as a whole went quite well – Mr Major was given an eleven-minute standing ovation – but his speech became famous for the wrong reason. It would be remembered not so much for what he said, but for how it had been portrayed by one of his media advisers. There is always something of a battle behind the scenes when it comes to interpreting the leader's speech. The party cares desperately about the line journalists will take, and to encourage the press to support the official view there are usually briefings at which the main points of the speech are read out beforehand.

On this occasion we were told by Tim Collins, who would later become an MP and a member of the shadow cabinet, that Mr Major would call for a 'return to the old core values' of the Conservative party. I did not think this meant the values of the 1960s generation were being called into question, but one of my colleagues suggested that this call contained a moral as well as a practical message, and that interpretation was given official approval. So when Mr Major spoke of a move 'back to basics' this was widely reported – but not by me on the six o'clock news – as a return to moral rectitude, a reversal of the liberalism which had swept the country since the 1960s. After the headlines had been published and the address dubbed the 'back to basics speech', the trouble started. Whenever a government minister or even a backbench Conservative MP was involved in a sex scandal – and there were plenty of those in the Major years – the prime minister himself was put on the rack. The speech became a spectacular own goal.

When Lady Thatcher's memoirs came out the following week, it was as if all Mr Major's pleas for unity in Blackpool – differences, he insisted, should be aired behind closed doors – had been ignored. The prime minister was not described as the *Mirror* had suggested, as 'small-minded, politically naïve and an intellectual lightweight' but he hardly came out well from the memoirs and in comparison with her seemed puny indeed. Lady Thatcher was clearly determined to shift as much of the responsibility for the ERM fiasco onto Mr Major personally. She wrote that his 'tendency to accept the conventional wisdom' had shown up particularly in his support for the 'fashionable consensus' in favour of joining the ERM. He had been 'intellectually drifting with the tide', whereas she had strongly opposed the move. It was the absence of any obvious successor which, she said, influenced her determination to stay at Number 10. Her thinking was that, 'given time, John might grow in stature, or someone else might emerge'.

Lady Thatcher damned Mr Major with faint praise. He was not her first choice as chancellor – she would have preferred Nicholas Ridley – but he had been an 'effective and competent' chief secretary. She described his only budget as 'a modest success'. When he succeeded Nigel Lawson she had been disappointed with his style. 'I was increasingly conscious of dealing with a very different sort of chancellor than Nigel,' she wrote. 'John Major, perhaps because he had made his name as a whip, or perhaps because he is unexcited by the sort of concepts which people like Nigel and I saw as central to politics, had one great objective: this was to keep the party together.' Lady Thatcher was drawing a harsh distinction between those in politics who think up the ideas and those who simply put them into practice. Her reference to Mr Major having been a whip was not flattering; it suggested his forte was getting people to toe the line. The observation that Mr Major reached his peak as a competent chief whip is still made today.

In Lady Thatcher's memoirs even Mr Major's loyalty to her at the time of her fall from office was called into question. She described how he had stayed silent and kept his distance at her time of maximum need. She did not appear to accept his explanation – that he had been at home recovering from a dental operation. 'I asked John to second my nomination,' she recalled. 'The hesitation was palpable. When urging my supporters to vote for John for the leadership, I made play of the fact that he did not hesitate. But both of us knew otherwise.' It was only a slight consolation to Mr Major that she was even more dismissive of some of the others who had served in her cabinets. She accused Sir Geoffrey Howe of 'bile and treachery', and spoke of Nigel Lawson's 'folly' in trying to manage the exchange rate. They protested, but Mr Major refused to be drawn in public. It would only have made the rift look even more serious than it was. Michael Heseltine confined himself to general criticism of former ministers rushing into print with 'self-serving, pseudo-history'. Surprisingly, the politician and diarist Alan Clark, who had doted on her when she was prime minister, complained that Lady Thatcher had 'not behaved in a responsible way' since leaving office. But there was plenty of praise. Her former party chairman Lord Baker – no fan of Mr Major – summed up the arguments in favour of publishing her views so soon after leaving office. 'Yes,' he wrote emphatically. 'Hers was a great and important premiership. It was a golden decade and I can see no harm in her explaining and justifying her role.'

In publishing terms, there was never any doubt that the book would be a phenomenon. More than 250,000 copies were sold in hardback in Britain (and, as it happens, the cost of the extra police she required for her protection while promoting the book was estimated at £250,000). *The Downing Street Years* was translated into many languages, including Japanese. In America her memoirs provided the perfect excuse for another barnstorming tour. In two weeks her book sales in the United States reached 175,000 copies. The *Wall Street Journal,* normally fairly sober about such matters, described the effect she produced as 'Thatchermania'. People waited for six hours for a book-signing session in one of the Washington suburbs. When Lady Thatcher arrived, the queue stretched round the bookshop, round the shopping mall outside and down a side road. On the *Larry King Live* television show Lady Thatcher was given yet another chance to explain how she had lost power: her fellow MPs and ministers 'just lost their nerve'. In a BBC television series her career as prime minister was reviewed, on the whole sympathetically. Interviewed at length, Lady Thatcher was given ample opportunity to give her side of the story.

The strategy agreed by the Tory leadership and discussed behind closed doors at Blackpool had failed. The idea that if her memoirs were critical of Mr Major she would be blamed for 'rocking the boat' stood little chance once the more powerful force of Thatchermania had taken hold. The success of her book appeared to justify her continuing presence on the political scene. Much like any veteran show-business star she could always justify one more 'final tour' on the grounds that her public demanded no less. There was a natural thirst to know how she saw the extraordinary events of the 1980s: the Falklands War, her fight with the unions, the battle with the miners, the Brighton bomb, the collapse of the Soviet Union, the unification of Germany, the end of the Cold War, and finally her dramatic fall.

Extensive studies have been made, particularly in the

United States, of how politicians make an impact. The explanation can often be found in the answers to a couple of simple questions. Can they tell a story about the country and themselves? If so, can they make sure the story encourages people to support them? This story provides a 'narrative' for the voter. In Britain it turns a complicated series of events into another chapter in 'our island story', and if the politician is extremely successful, it can have the narrative power of legend. Many people who knew little of politics generally became completely familiar with the Thatcher story, and much of the picture which emerged from the great events of her career was painted by Lady Thatcher herself. In creating and where possible touching up her image, she had an advantage over all her predecessors: no prime minister before her could rely on colour television pictures to tell her story.

From almost the exact moment she was elected Conservative leader in 1975, television news was in colour. This greatly increased the impact and therefore the apparent relevance of all the documentaries made about the Thatcher years. No longer was the story of a former prime minister told in black and white film, or even grainy stills. For Mr Major, trying to establish his own narrative with the voters, none of this was helpful. His far less charismatic image – cartoonists sometimes dipped him in grey paint – could hardly compete with her colourful outfits. She could look striking even at a formal meeting of other world leaders; driven at speed on the top of a tank and wearing goggles, she became a superstar. By publishing her memoirs and encouraging the enormous publicity they brought, Lady Thatcher had dealt Mr Major a severe blow; her legacy had become even more difficult for him to bear.

25

Enter Mr Blair

WHEN I WAS GROWING UP – in the 1950s and 1960s – politics was much more of a tribal affair. There were two big tribes, Labour and the Conservatives, and the main job of the party organizations at election time was 'getting the vote out'. As a student I did my fair share of this for the Labour party. If you were interested in how someone voted and were too shy to ask, you might slip in a question about who their parents supported. In the great majority of cases that would provide the answer. People tended to vote for their tribe. For a whole variety of reasons – not least that in an affluent society young people could more easily go their own way – this changed over the last half of the twentieth century. By the 1990s politicians had to work hard to capture the attention of the public and could no longer rely on simply getting the vote out at election time. There was far less class loyalty, and of course far less deference.

Winning the battle for the political agenda, in other words making sure your chosen issues rather than those of your opponents are discussed, became crucial. From now on neither of the two main parties could depend on their traditional supporters – there aren't enough of them – nor could they expect the 'swing of the pendulum' automatically to put the opposition into government when voters were bored with those in power. Modern political parties increasingly have to find ways to be noticed, to be different and best of all to look new; a change of leader is often regarded as the easiest method.

At the beginning of 1994 there were many Conservatives anxious to see such a change. They came mainly from the centre right of the party, in particular the Euro-sceptics. Fortunately for Mr Major, all the obvious candidates for the leadership were on the centre left, including the most obvious of all, the pro-European chancellor Kenneth Clarke. It looked as if the leadership issue might have nowhere to go.

Then, in May 1994, the party's opponents were thrust into the limelight for the saddest of reasons: the Labour leader died. Some Labour MPs cried openly when the news spread. I saw them embracing each other in grief in the corners and corridors of Westminster. John Smith was only fifty-five, in his prime as a politician, and there was a palpable feeling of shock among MPs of all parties that morning at Westminster. A member of the cabinet told me a few days later how senior ministers had received the news at Number 10. It was more than an intimation of their own mortality; many of them were older than Mr Smith and were visibly shaken. Parliament was suspended; the nation went into mourning. There was an astonishing and profound sense of loss across the country. Conservative-supporting newspapers were among those promoting the view that Labour had lost an exceptional leader who might well have become prime minister. In the Commons Mr Major led the parliamentary tributes, describing Mr Smith as 'one of the outstanding parliamentarians of modern politics'.

I was shocked by Mr Smith's death. For many voters his solid, middle-class virtues coupled with a marked social conscience were the perfect antidote to Mrs Thatcher's emphasis on the importance of individual advancement and the needs of business. I had known Mr Smith reasonably well since we had made a documentary together when he was the youngest member of Mr Callaghan's Labour cabinet. He was a strong family man with a clear commitment to his local community.

On a cold winter night I had gone with him to a small snow-covered church where he was to be filmed singing hymns in a male-voice choir. He was a highly paid lawyer and very much an establishment figure; only in Scotland perhaps would it seem so natural that he should be a lifelong member of the Labour party.

I was intrigued to hear how far Mr Major would go in applauding the man who had worked so hard to bring him down. The prime minister explained his feelings about Mr Smith in this way: 'He carried his fight fairly, without malice, without nastiness.' And Mr Major revealed how much he had enjoyed meeting Mr Smith unofficially. He was 'courteous, fair-minded and constructive, but also tough'. The funeral in Edinburgh, at Mr Smith's small parish church, was attended by so many dignitaries it seemed like a state occasion. The official guests – among them John and Norma Major – came from across the political spectrum. The BBC broadcast the proceedings live. I was one of the radio commentators during the service, which overflowed with emotion. There was a eulogy from Mr Smith's old friend Donald Dewar and a haunting lament sung in Gaelic.

The reaction to Mr Smith's death took many people by surprise, including a letter writer to *The Times*, who pointed out ironically that during Mr Smith's lifetime the news media had never mentioned the fact that he would be 'a great, great prime minister'. Part of the reason for the grief was that a long time had elapsed since a party leader had died suddenly in office; the death of the Labour leader Hugh Gaitskell had occurred thirty-one years earlier. Mr Smith, like Mrs Thatcher, had been a beneficiary of the new age of television. His clashes with Mr Major at prime minister's questions were given enormous coverage. With his trusting, bank-manager image, he was extremely popular; under his leadership Labour had reduced the fear factor among floating voters. The party appeared to have the best chance of gaining power since its defeat by Mrs Thatcher fifteen years before. Mr Smith's death also resulted in an alteration in the political landscape. Instead of the media concentrating solely on the internal arguments of the Conservative party, much of the interest switched to Labour; it would stay there until the general election. For the first time in many years Labour had an opportunity to capture the attention of the public.

The change in focus began almost immediately at Westminster, with grief for the departed quickly giving way to speculation about the new leader. There were two obvious front-runners, Tony Blair and Gordon Brown. Until recently it had been assumed that of the two Mr Brown was the more likely choice. But Mr Blair had the advantage, in the words of a famous lager advertisement of the time, of reaching parts of the electorate that Mr Brown could not. Tory disunity over Europe was a stark illustration of the consequences of a split; and that is what would have occurred if both of them had stood for the leadership. All those frustrating years in opposition had strengthened their determination to see Labour form a government, and they did not let personal rivalry get in the way. The two men, then the closest of friends, agreed not to stand against each other, and Mr Brown did not contest the leadership.

The simple fact was that Mr Blair, without such deep roots in the party as Mr Brown, stood a much better chance of winning over doubters, particularly in the south of the country. He was also better able to break away from the assumption – actively promoted by Mr Smith in his shadow budget at the previous election – that in government Labour would 'tax and spend'. As a former cabinet minister, Mr Smith was directly linked to the administration which had presided over the notorious winter of discontent. Television pictures of how militant trade unionists in the winter of 1978 had refused to collect rubbish or even bury the dead had been turned by Mrs Thatcher into perfect anti-Labour propaganda. Under a new leader not tainted by these images – Mr Blair had only entered Parliament in 1983 – fresh opportunities beckoned. The *Sunday Times*, in a leader column on 15 May, came out firmly in favour of Tony Blair. 'Those in the Labour party,' the paper said, 'who baulk at being led by a youthful, public school-educated moderate who rarely uses the language of traditional socialism would do well to realise that such a prospect is now the Tories' worst nightmare.' The *Financial Times* was also surprisingly supportive of Mr Blair. Their columnist Joe Rogaly wrote, 'This is getting dangerous. If Tony Blair is chosen to succeed John Smith, we shall have to consider voting Labour.' Other newspapers swung behind the shadow home secretary, with the *Sun* declaring, 'If there were an acceptable face of socialism, it would be that of Anthony Charles Lynton Blair.' With Mr Brown out of the race and the only other candidates John Prescott and Margaret Beckett, Mr Blair romped home.

The leadership contest ended with an event at a conference hall in London, and so little doubt attended the outcome that it was referred to, almost without irony, as Mr Blair's coronation. There was indeed something regal in the way he picked up the Labour crown, as if to the manner born, and the language he used was different from ordinary speech, as one might expect from a young monarch. He did not speak of his programme for government, he spoke of his 'mission'. The Labour rose, projected behind him, turned from white to red as his speech continued. It was the first time many voters had had the chance to appreciate his performance skills and to be impressed by his ability as a political actor. There were few detailed points in his address, but plenty of heady passion. His voice nearly breaking with emotion, he talked of right and wrong, of national renewal, of hope and change.

Later it was a style that many people came to distrust, but at the time it perfectly caught the mood of those anxious for a break with the past. The most memorable moment came when Mr Prescott showed how pleased he was to have been elected deputy leader. To many voters, Mr Prescott represented the true face of Labour. 'This man,' he declared, pointing at Mr Blair, 'has got what it takes. He commands moral authority and political respect. He has the energy and the vitality to win people over to Labour. And he scares the life out of the Tories . . .' He then added in a stage whisper, 'And me.'

This event took place in the Logan Hall, part of London University, and as we streamed out into the sunshine I remember thinking I would have to be careful not to show any personal enthusiasm for the new Labour leader. My usual determination to avoid any political bias would have to be maintained. Mr Blair was a far stronger contender for the post of prime minister than John Smith had been, and it would soon become commonplace to regard him as a natural successor to Lady Thatcher. The former prime minister did not rush to comment at this stage, but she certainly appreciated the importance of his appointment. She also took pleasure from the fact that even Labour supporters acknowledged that it was because of her that Mr Blair was able to become leader of the Labour party.

Without her determination to curb the power of the unions, her insistence on strike ballots and her success in weaning the country off traditional forms of socialism Mr Blair would have stood little chance. Labour had been forced to change, and by 1994 had changed enough to elect a leader with none of the political baggage which had weighed down his immediate predecessors. The ferocious battles between left and right which had dominated so much of the 1980s were over, and there was a resolve to do whatever was necessary to win the next election. Mr Blair was not only prepared to appeal to Conservative voters; he set out from the beginning to win the greatest possible support from every region and from every class. He behaved more like the candidate of one of the main parties in an American presidential election than a home-grown Labour leader. He took a leaf out of Bill Clinton's book by quickly renaming his party New Labour, in the same way that the Democrats had become New Democrats.

Even before Mr Blair took over, he was prepared to go further than his colleagues in acknowledging Lady Thatcher's importance. In a review of her memoirs published the year before in the *Sunday Times*, Mr Blair produced a balanced assessment. Praise for her as a politician of 'extraordinary abilities' was matched by criticism of her for having 'extraordinary prejudices'. He pointed out that she had come to power in 1979, 'helped enormously by sections of the Labour party'. He described the 'vibrancy' of her personality, 'the uncluttered quality of her intellect' and 'the sense she conveyed, whether correct or not, of shaping events rather than being led by them'. And he concluded by saying, 'She was not wrong to stress the importance of individuals and families, but wrong to ignore the importance of building a strong society in which they could develop to the full.' In this brief review it is surprising how many clues there are to the future policies of New Labour. Mrs Thatcher's skills were highly relevant to Mr Blair because she was the last British leader to beat an occupant of Number 10 in a general election. In his own leadership campaign he had consciously followed her example. He admired her ability to develop a 'clear sense of an identifiable project'. Thus New Labour's project was born. It was not only her tactical skill he learnt from; he also adopted some of her ideas of party management. This political cross-dressing was to Mr Blair's advantage. Voters were not put off. It was more than just a joke when it was pointed out that it might make more sense if the grammar-school-educated Mr Major were to

lead the Labour party, and the handsome, well-scrubbed former public schoolboy Mr Blair should take charge of the
Tories. It helped Mr Blair's cause.

Mr Blair appeared quite unabashed by suggestions that he
was a natural Conservative, and when he spoke of the need for
'a dynamic market economy' the full potency of the Blair
effect on Tory voters began to be noticed. In a Mori opinion
poll published a month after Mr Blair became leader, his party
recorded an amazing 33 per cent lead over the Tories. Of
those interviewed, 56 per cent said they would vote Labour.
This poll was in line with other opinion surveys, and it showed
that Labour was winning over many of the bedrock voters
who had kept the Conservatives in power for more than
fifteen years. While Tony Blair appeared to benefit from
comparisons made between him and Mrs Thatcher, Mr Major
continued to be lumbered with her legacy. He had failed to
win back the trust of Conservative voters disillusioned with his
premiership.

On overseas tours, particularly, there always seemed to
be a Thatcher factor. When Mr Major went to Poland in
August 1994 many of the ordinary people seemed to believe
Lady Thatcher was still in charge in Britain, and he was her
underling. In a popularity poll in Poland she had come second
only to Bill Clinton among 'world leaders'; Mr Major was at
the bottom of the scale. Asked about Lady Thatcher, Mr Major
could only respond, rather limply, 'Ah well, she's shorter than
me, and blonde.' In September Mr Major took a trade mission
to South Africa, while Lady Thatcher was in Bombay. She
told Indian businessmen that investing in South Africa was
risky because of violence and fears of unrest. Speaking in
Johannesburg, Mr Major was clearly irritated and said that her
views did not accord with what he had seen. The statement
which she issued within a few hours, pledging full support
for the 'new democratic government of South Africa' and

expressing her confidence that 'the country will attract the inward investment it so much needs', came too late to dispel the impression that Mr Major was once more at odds with his predecessor.

At the party conference in October Lady Thatcher attempted not to draw attention away from Mr Major, but once again failed. Before the conference started the Conservative Way Forward group, sponsored by the former prime minister, demanded a bold reduction of two pence off the twenty-five-pence basic rate of income tax. 'The Tory party,' they said, 'is not bruised; it's bleeding.' They questioned whether Mr Major could ever again have 'street credibility'. On the eve of the conference the newspapers were full of claims that Lady Thatcher's son Mark had made £12 million from an arms deal with Saudi Arabia. This came after a succession of Tories had been accused of 'sleaze'. She insisted that she was 'absolutely satisfied' that the al-Yamamah deal had been properly negotiated, and was 'totally heartbroken', according to a member of her staff. 'She feels any attack on any member of her family very deeply.' In 2004, when Mark Thatcher was arrested in South Africa over his alleged involvement in an attempted coup, it was therefore all the more poignant that his mother issued no statement at all.

Her appearance in the conference hall was a more muted affair than the year before. She had lost a stone in weight, and had recently endured a four-hour dental operation. She did not look well, and within a few days it would be her sixty-ninth birthday. But her star quality had not disappeared. After the battering he had received in her memoirs Mr Major had to try to look pleased to see her, but he seemed to shrink when the party faithful stood up to cheer her arrival. He led the clapping and managed to put on his usual headlamp smile, but behind the glasses his eyes were cold. One of his staff told a reporter that 'he was fuming inside'. Even their clothes were critically compared. She had arrived in a purple suit, and changed to blue for her conference appearance. He was in one of his greyest suits. A woman journalist wrote dismissively, 'He won't take advice.'

When Parliament resumed, Mr Major had to deal with questions which again provoked comparisons with her time in government. To the annoyance of right-wing Conservatives, it was announced that ministers would not after all be proceeding with the privatization of the Post Office. Thatcher loyalists protested about the change of tack; it was not the way *she* had conducted herself in government. It did not seem to matter to the critics that as prime minister Mrs Thatcher had decided not to privatize the Royal Mail, partly because of its royal connection, but also because it was seen as too radical a step. Mr Major had decided he might not be able to get the bill through Parliament.

Then there came another dispute over Europe, with eight former Maastricht rebels refusing to support Mr Major over the budget deal he had negotiated at the Edinburgh summit. This had been deemed a confidence motion, with Mr Major threatening a general election if he lost, but this had not stopped the revolt. He won quite easily, but in retaliation removed the Conservative whip from the rebels; technically they were no longer Conservatives. It was a serious mistake. The rebels were not cowed, and it was Mr Major who had to back down. The government only had an overall majority of fourteen, and the rebels eventually had to be brought back into the fold without firm guarantees from them of good behaviour. In the meantime they helped defeat the government on a budget measure, a plan to increase VAT on fuel. It was a humiliating blow to Mr Major, suggesting that he was no longer able to control the political agenda.

By the end of 1994 criticism of the prime minister from supposedly friendly sources had become routine, with widespread complaints of drift and lack of vision. Lady Thatcher continued to voice dissent behind the scenes. She was quoted as saying that Mr Major had been 'wimpish' when he did not personally mount the Commons defence of the government in the European budget debate; he had given that task to the chancellor Kenneth Clarke. Privately, Lady Thatcher expressed how disappointed she was with Mr Major. She told friends how she had always led from the front when there was a crisis affecting her premiership, and she also continued to press the government to take military action in Bosnia to counter Serbian aggression. This almost constant stream of comments from Lady Thatcher took its toll on her successor.

Since the beginning of 1994 Mr Major had had a new press secretary, the Foreign Office high-flyer Christopher Meyer, who would go on to become British ambassador in Bonn and later Washington. After he had left government and collected his knighthood, he became chairman of the Press Complaints Commission. He has a brisk, stylish manner, a quick mind, and was thoroughly on top of every aspect of the Whitehall machine. Among his tasks was to avoid the mistakes which had occurred on the trip to Japan. On a brief secondment to Harvard University he had written an influential paper on the relationship between journalists and government press officers. He made no bones about joining the battle over which issues should have prominence in the media, fighting for the best possible coverage for Mr Major. But he did not lie, and he did return your calls. I liked him a lot. When he left, after two years, I attended his farewell lunch at Number 10. Mr Major gave a defensive speech from behind a lectern; Mr Meyer strolled nonchalantly up and down, speaking off the cuff, apparently without a care in the world. From simply observing the two speeches one might have concluded that Mr Meyer was in charge and Mr Major was his less confident press secretary. By this time the prime minister's relations with the media had reached such a low point that any occasion of this sort was uncomfortable for both sides. The messengers who carried the bad news were assembled, but Mr Major would dearly like to have seen the back of us.

When I interviewed Sir Christopher Meyer for this book, in 2003, he confirmed that by the time he arrived a 'bunker mentality' had set in at Number 10. He paints a grim picture of how Lady Thatcher had cast a pall over Mr Major's premiership. 'He would have been a happier man had she not existed,' Sir Christopher told me. 'She became more and more like a dark shadow in the background. It was not just the Euro thing, it was the leadership thing. People who decided they were going to conspire against John Major – most of whom are now to be found in the leadership of the Conservative party – had a problem with John Major over Europe. They also had a problem with John Major as leader of the party. And the impression I had progressively, through 1994 and 1995, is that John Major could see that his every move was being measured and judged by Margaret Thatcher. Where she disapproved, this became rapidly known to those who still regarded her as a talismanic figure.'

News of Lady Thatcher's disapproval could come from a variety of sources: from a newspaper or direct from a journalist, from the whips' office or from a cabinet minister who had been talking to someone who had been with her. 'Jeffrey Archer always had something to tell us, and sometimes he picked up something Margaret had said. And then there was the Conservative journalist Woodrow Wyatt. He was one of those people who kept in touch with Downing Street.' Lady Thatcher was critical of many aspects of the work of her successor but, Sir Christopher said, 'In the end it crystallized around Europe; and was he a tough enough leader of the Conservative party?' The desperate position in the opinion polls and the small government majority were constant concerns and made the prime minister look 'endemically weak'.

Then the collapse of the back to basics strategy and a resurgent Opposition meant Mr Major's opponents had 'a strong smell of blood in their nostrils'. There were 'all these guys behind him putting knives into his back'. In retrospect, Sir Christopher does not see how Mr Major could have mollified Lady Thatcher or placated her. It was, he said, 'intrinsically imposs-ible'. Part of the problem was that Mr Major was far too interested in what other people, including Lady Thatcher, were saying. 'It wasn't as if she was always attacking him,' Sir Christopher told me. 'These things came and went, but he was always aware that there was this brooding presence out there.'

Sir Christopher looks back on his time in Downing Street as a period of constant defensive action. 'There were occasional moments when he seemed to have pulled himself out of the bog and was at last starting to get some momentum, but no sooner did that start than something else came and wiped him back down again. It was two years of siege warfare.' But not everything went wrong. Although the government, in Sir Christopher's view, was politically exhausted, ministers were technically competent because they had been in power for so long. And he was personally impressed by Mr Major's 'great natural charm' and 'huge courtesy'.

Unfortunately for the prime minister, he would need much more than those qualities to see him through.

26

'No change, no chance'

IN THE ELEGANT OFFICES of the Thatcher Foundation in Chesham Place, Belgravia it was easy for visitors to imagine that Lady Thatcher was still in power. Police guarded her night and day in London, and on her frequent trips abroad. On a typical day she might be found dressed immaculately in a royal-blue suit, with a lavish diamond brooch and handmade shoes; her talk would almost invariably be about politics. The few media interviewers she met were not allowed to suggest for a moment that she had opted for a comfortable retirement. An earnest approach to public affairs and the need for hard work were stressed, as they had been when she was in office, and the first-floor room where she received visitors had, as one of them put it, 'a serious ministerial air'. There were two flattering portraits of her, maps of the south Atlantic, and oil paintings of soldiers by war artists. It was like a film producer's inaccurate but believable version of the inside of Number 10. Lesley White of the *Sunday Times* described how, like a queen served by loyal retainers, she waited in exile. But she was not waiting to be called back into government; she simply wanted to go on expressing her views.

Lady Thatcher was a politician who had become famous for knowing where she wanted to go, for having an 'identifiable project', and Mr Major and his allies were puzzled, at times bewildered, by what seemed her loss of tactical sense. It was as if she no longer really cared. Much of her criticism the prime minister found unnecessarily damaging, not just to himself but to the Conservative party for which she had striven so mightily over the years. In May 1995, in her interview with Lesley White, she was quite prepared to praise the new Labour leader. It was put to her that Tony Blair had declared himself an admirer, and she was quick to return the compliment. He was, she said, 'probably the most formidable' Labour leader since Hugh Gaitskell, which ranked him higher in her eyes than Harold Wilson, James Callaghan, Michael Foot, Neil Kinnock or John Smith. Lady Thatcher went on, 'I see a lot of socialism behind their front bench, but not in Tony Blair. I think he genuinely has moved.'

It was then suggested she might agree with her former treasurer and close friend Lord McAlpine that the Conservatives could do with a spell in opposition to recoup their strength and iron out their differences. Lesley White recalled, 'She looked at me as if I were quite mad.' Lady Thatcher had switched back to her more customary role of the dedicated party warrior. She responded as if she had always committed herself to the objective of keeping the Conservatives in government. 'Never, never give up power,' she insisted, and then added with greater significance than she could ever have imagined, 'If you give it up, you never know when you will get it back.' For the Conservatives, who were soon to begin many years in opposition, it amounted to an awful warning. But the underlying question remains: if Lady Thatcher was so keen for the Conservatives to retain power, why was she ready to praise the man who was poised to take it from them?

Lady Thatcher made an attempt to explain the rationale behind her public comments in the second volume of her memoirs, which came out at this time. *The Path to Power* was largely devoted to her career before she reached Number 10, but this did not prevent her from commenting on recent events – and criticizing Mr Major. She had been dismayed at the speed with which her European policies had been 'entirely reversed'. In a revealing passage she described how she left the Commons in order to be able to speak out more freely. 'My every word,' she wrote, 'would be judged in terms of support for or opposition to John Major. I would inhibit him just by my presence, and that in turn would inhibit me.' That was why she had accepted a peerage.

'I felt,' she said, 'newly liberated to continue the argument about Europe's future.' She refused to accept responsibility for seriously weakening Mr Major's position. Referring to his first year in office, she wrote, 'I wanted to avoid appearing to undermine my successor. I knew that his position was still fragile and I wanted him to succeed. I had faced sufficient difficulties from Ted Heath not to wish to inflict similar ones. But I could not in good conscience stay silent when the whole future direction of Britain, even its status as a sovereign state, was at issue.' One of those who worked closely with her explained to me that she felt her views had 'quite as much legitimacy as those of the prime minister'.

The Path to Power generated another wave of publicity, with radio and television interviewers unable to resist the temptation to goad Lady Thatcher into more criticisms of the prime minister. From Europe she moved on to attack the government's spending record, its failure to promote home ownership, and tax increases. The effect was soon felt in the fevered atmosphere at Westminster, where hardly a day seemed to pass without some kind of government crisis. Conservative MPs were aware that their days could be numbered. With the continuing bad news from the opinion polls, many of them were already planning what to do if they were thrown out at the next election; they were increasingly desperate to find some way of escape.

A group of about fifty Euro-sceptic Tory MPs pressed Mr Major to rule out any possibility of Britain joining the single currency, a move long advocated by Lady Thatcher. When they came out of a meeting with the prime minister one of them said, 'This was his chance to put things right, but he tossed away his lifeline.' He would not change his 'wait and see' policy. There was renewed talk of a leadership challenge. Under the party rules this would have to wait for the autumn, but Mr Major – shocked and saddened by the intemperate meeting with his critics – decided to seize the initiative. In a dramatic statement in the garden of Number 10 he announced that there would be a leadership election in two weeks, and he challenged those who were against him to declare their hands. His message was, 'Put up or shut up.' There was speculation that Norman Lamont would throw his hat into the ring, and it was noted that John Redwood, the Welsh secretary, was refusing to say publicly that he would support the prime minister. The rest of the cabinet loyally backed Mr Major.

That weekend in late June I set off for the south of France. It was not a holiday, just another example of how controversies surrounding Mr Major frequently extended overseas. He was attending a European summit in Cannes, and instead of immersing myself in the usual tedious details of summit politics I could follow a Conservative leadership campaign under a bright sun and within sight of some of the best beaches in Europe. We managed to film the foreign secretary Douglas Hurd taking a dip in the Mediterranean. On Monday morning I was in a makeshift radio studio, in a building just set back from the front, interviewing the chancellor Kenneth Clarke live on the Radio 4 *Today* programme. The editor Roger Mosey, who was in London, told me through my headphones, 'John Redwood has announced he's standing.' A typically unabashed Mr Clarke reacted calmly when I broke the news to him and to our millions of listeners. But the challenge was dramatic: Mr Major would face a serious threat from one of Lady Thatcher's strongest supporters.

If Mr Major had been attempting a bluff, his bluff had been

called. The prime minister's strategy was without precedent in British politics. He was asking for a vote of confidence from his own MPs, but there was a strong possibility that even if he won, he would be badly wounded. A general election had to be held within two years. With stakes as high as this, Mr Major hoped that his colleagues would, in a phrase which was soon in danger of being overused at Westminster, look into the abyss and pull back. But Mr Redwood, highly ambitious and with a strange intensity of manner, was not in the mood to compromise. His slogan was, 'No change, no chance.' If MPs did not remove Mr Major, he declared, there was no chance they would win the next general election.

Some – but not many – Conservative commentators came out in favour of Mr Redwood, and so, in her fashion, did Lady Thatcher. She was in Washington promoting her memoirs, when she was asked whom she supported. 'We must,' she replied, 'have the true Conservative policies that I pursued: policies of lower taxes, keeping our national parliamentary sovereignty, and the independence of the pound sterling.' She described Mr Redwood as very able, very articulate and one of her party's rising stars. She made no mention of Mr Major. A reporter persisted: was she endorsing Mr Redwood? She demurred: 'Both candidates are sound Conservatives; next question.' Lady Thatcher would have come under greater pressure to show her hand if her real favourite at the time, Michael Portillo, had decided to run. As part of a rather clumsy plan, a battery of telephone lines was installed in his proposed campaign headquarters, but he 'looked into the abyss, and pulled back'. Unfortunately for Mr Portillo television cameras had filmed the lines being put in, and his moment of indecision tarnished his image as a man of destiny.

Fortunately for Mr Major, Michael Heseltine and most of his supporters stayed loyal – he said later he had no differences with Number 10 – but the result was far from overwhelming for the prime minister. Mr Major had 218 votes, Mr Redwood 89. Including abstentions, more than a hundred Tory MPs had failed to support their leader. Mr Major admitted privately that he had set himself a target of 215 votes; if he had won just three votes less he would have considered resigning. Other candidates would then have had a chance of entering the race in the second ballot. Mr Portillo might well have been among them.

In the cabinet reshuffle which followed, the Euro-sceptics were furious to see Mr Heseltine promoted to deputy prime minister with a wide range of extra responsibilities. He denied accusations that this was part of a bargain struck with Mr Major prior to the leadership election. Before he announced the election Mr Major had mentioned to Mr Heseltine that he might be given the post of deputy prime minister, but both of them maintained that no deal had been reached. What seemed incontrovertible was that, following his recent heart attack, Mr Heseltine had finally decided that he could not hope to fulfil his lifelong ambition to be prime minister. I was personally pleased with his appointment as Mr Major's deputy. We had a long-running private joke, going back to the time he was out of office, which involved Mr Heseltine telling me there had been 'another triumph' when things had gone badly. Other correspondents would be puzzled to see him mouthing these words to me across Downing Street. It was of no great importance, but in the stress of daily reporting I was grateful for the joke: it made our professional lives more enjoyable.

For a time Mr Major's strategy appeared to have worked, Tory right wingers retired to lick their wounds. It was now widely assumed that Mr Major would lead the Conservatives into the next election. But the official Opposition continued to strengthen its position. Tony Blair kept up the momentum behind Labour's 'modernization' by successfully removing Clause 4 which called for widespread nationalization, from the party's constitution. Mr Blair was also able to argue that the Tories' leadership election demonstrated their divisions. Mr Redwood's slogan 'No change, no chance' was a gift to Labour MPs, who were happy to endorse his analysis.

Mr Major tried hard to unite his party, and briefly it looked as if Lady Thatcher might help. In late September the prime minister hosted a party at Number 10 to celebrate her seventieth birthday. At her official party at Claridge's – attended by the Queen – the guest list contained the names of many of those who had caused him trouble. John Redwood was there; Michael Portillo appeared very much the favoured son; and Sir James Goldsmith was also invited. Within a few weeks the billionaire Euro-sceptic would announce that he would stand at the next election as a candidate for his Referendum Party, with hints of at least some support from Lady Thatcher. At yet another birthday party, at Union Station in Washington, there was a distinctly right-wing flavour, with the speaker of the House of Representatives Newt Gingrich placed next to Lady Thatcher. The tickets cost £625 each, and a staggering £1.5 million was raised for the Thatcher Foundation. No one could be in any doubt where Lady Thatcher's heart lay.

At the Conservative party conference in Blackpool her brief visit was better managed than usual. This was the result of elaborate negotiations carried out by the new party chairman, Sir Brian Mawhinney. In an interview for this book in the summer of 2004 he told me how they agreed several weeks before the conference what should happen. As chairman he would accompany her onto the platform, where she would be applauded; he would then go and collect the prime minister. Mr Major and the chairman would return to the stage, where they would each kiss Lady Thatcher once on the cheek, in the British fashion. The three of them would then be given a standing ovation. Everything went according to plan except that the effect was somewhat marred by television pictures, which I used, of some very slow handclapping from Michael Heseltine and the European commissioner Sir Leon Brittan.

Lady Thatcher returned to London before Mr Major's speech, the usual practice for a former leader; she told reporters that she had only caught a little of it on the car radio, but she said, 'I am sure it was terrific.' Mr Major had been given an easy ride. 'Today,' he declared, 'we meet united, healed, renewed and thirsting for the real fight with Labour.' For a few months the impression lasted that perhaps the Conservatives had collectively looked into the abyss and pulled back, but Lady Thatcher had her own agenda, which ran counter to that favoured by the party leadership. Sir Brian Mawhinney had been hoping to build on the public reconciliation achieved at the party conference. He regularly held talks with Lady Thatcher to try to improve relations between her and Number 10, but there were limits to what he could do. The gulf was never really bridged.

One of the problems was that the former prime minister was restless, even bored. After an hour and a half talking politics she was likely to say to a busy visitor, 'Can't you stay for a bit longer?' One of her favourite sayings was, 'The devil makes work for idle hands,' but it was in precisely this situation that she now found herself. She hated not being busy. At the end of 1995 Lady Thatcher began planning a lecture in the City of London, to be given in memory of her colleague and mentor the late Sir Keith Joseph. It would be her first formal speech on domestic politics since her resignation from government more than five years before, and when it was delivered, in January 1996, it caused a sensation. Lady Thatcher made some attempt to soften the blow – she did not attack Mr Major directly and said the electorate would be 'ill-judged' to throw the Conservatives out – but her message was still devastatingly clear. It was a frontal assault on the prime minister's stewardship of the Conservative party, and seemed based on the assumption that the next election had already been lost.

'Our policies and performance have not lived up to our analysis and principles,' she declared. 'We are unpopular, above all, because the middle classes – and all who aspire to join the middle classes – feel they no longer have the incentives and opportunities they expect from a Conservative government.' She dismissed as 'baloney' the claim that the government was in trouble because it had moved to the right; she warned against any move towards the centre ground, which was 'as slippery as the spin doctors who have colonized it'. To the intense irritation of centre-left Conservatives, who saw themselves as part of a long tradition stretching back to Disraeli, she ridiculed those who wanted to return to 'something called One Nation Conservatism'. Using a phrase which would be bitterly resented by many Tories, she said, 'As far as I can tell from their views on European federalism, such people's creed would be better described as No Nation Conservatism.'

Acknowledging that her relations with the prime minister were problematic, Lady Thatcher said, 'It is no secret that between John Major and me there have been differences on occasion, but these have always been differences about how to achieve objectives, rather than what those objectives should be.' She did not say what had now become obvious to those in the know, that relations between them had almost completely broken down. Until they met at the party conference there had been an ice-cool stand-off which had lasted for many months. Perhaps she hinted as much when she said, 'Avoiding debate about the large issues of government and politics leads to directionless failure.' And Lady Thatcher continued: 'Splits and disagreements over important issues never did a party so much harm as the absence of honest principled debate.'

She seemed oblivious to the damage her comments might

cause to Conservative chances at the next election but nevertheless invited people to conclude that the government had not lived up to its principles. 'The test is simple,' she said. 'Just ask yourself, Is it because the government has not spent, borrowed and taxed enough that people are discontented? Or is it that we have gone too far towards increasing government spending, borrowing and taxation?' The party should still be following the policies she pursued in the 1980s: 'small government, a property-owning democracy, tax cuts, deregulation and national sovereignty'. Only a small part of her speech was devoted to attacking Labour – for wanting to spend too much and to control too much. Right-wing Conservatives reacted predictably. John Redwood hailed it as a 'knockout performance – star quality'. Peter Luff, an MP from the centre left, was dismayed. 'She never tolerated open debate when she was leader,' he said. 'I think she has forgotten about the realities of politics.'

Lady Thatcher appeared pleased with the effect of her speech. Friends were quoted as saying she had known perfectly well it would 'explode in Westminster with the force of a neutron bomb'. Some of her supporters tried to play down the anti-Major comments. One of her most extreme fans, the journalist Paul Johnson, wrote in the *Daily Mail*, 'Margaret Thatcher strove mightily to avoid anything which might cause Major embarrassment. But, being an honest woman, she simply could not bring herself to give him a ringing endorsement. In the context of her battle for the Conservative soul, she made Major seem like a temporary irrelevance.' It is difficult to see how the two halves of Johnson's argument add up: surely it would have been less embarrassing for Mr Major if Lady Thatcher had not hinted that he was irrelevant?

The Thatcher fan club had difficulty keeping their feet on the ground. Mr Johnson wrote of his emotional response, which 'virtually everyone' in the packed lecture hall had shared: 'What we felt was this. Why is it that this astonishing woman – who speaks so splendidly, who leads so clearly, who grasps so firmly what the principles of Conservative government are about – why is she addressing us as a retired elder stateswoman and not as our actual Prime Minister? Why were we such fools as to let her go?' The defence secretary Michael Portillo, the Scottish secretary Michael Forsyth and the two former cabinet ministers Lord Parkinson and Lord Baker were among those who joined the standing ovation afterwards.

Mr Major tried not to give the impression he was upset, but a few days later, during a visit to his Huntingdon constituency, the prime minister was forced to respond in public. 'We have been a One Nation Conservative Party since the beginning of time and we are now,' he said. 'I have set out what I believe to be right and I shall fight for what I believe to be right.' Although the backbench 1922 Committee would soon announce that no further leadership contest could be held before the next election, rumours about a possible change in the leadership persisted. The Euro-sceptics continued to press their case. A private member's bill to curb the powers of the European Court of Justice, proposed by Iain Duncan Smith, was supported by sixty-six Tory MPs. Mr Major made sure that proposal went no further, but he finally got cabinet agreement – despite opposition from Michael Heseltine and Kenneth Clarke – to a referendum if the government were ever to propose joining the single currency. It was his last policy concession to the Euro-sceptics. In June, following the announcement that Lady Thatcher would be donating money to the anti-federalist European Foundation set up by the Maastricht rebel Bill Cash, Mr Major said he 'had had a bellyful' of Conservative infighting over Europe. This was after Mr Major had told Mr Cash not to accept any more money

from Sir James Goldsmith. The prime minister was so annoyed
at Lady Thatcher's donation that he avoided her at a party to
mark Lord Archer's thirtieth wedding anniversary.

But the Conservative chairman Brian Mawhinney was
still working to maintain the semblance of unity between
Mr Major and his predecessor. In October 1996, at the party
conference, Lady Thatcher came onto the platform to applause,
and then Mr Major appeared to more applause. She beamed at
him, and, as before, the prime minister kissed her on the
cheek. She invited him to sit next to her, patting the seat
beside her to make the point, and he accepted the offer with
as much grace as he could muster. She even smiled at a less-
than-enthusiastic Michael Heseltine. At last it seemed as if the
Conservative party appreciated the value of unity. It was their
final party conference before they would have to face the
electorate. The rank and file even managed to applaud speeches
in the hall by pro-European cabinet ministers including Mr
Heseltine; but at fringe meetings in the evenings they cheered
to the rafters their real heroes, Euro-sceptics such as Lord
Tebbit.

Labour remained firmly in the lead in the opinion polls,
but although it looked as though Mr Blair would win the
coming election, the Tories knew that whatever happened
they had to put up the best fight they could. Candidates and
party activists wanted to limit the damage but could not wipe
from the public mind their intense internal battles of recent
years. The party looked divided and, after eighteen years in
office, politically worn out. The general election was called for
1 May 1997. Mr Major left it almost to the last possible date;
it was just over five years since the previous election.

When Lady Thatcher went on the campaign trail in Hamp-
shire, wearing her customary uniform of electric-blue suit,
black handbag and pearls, she gave the impression of enjoying
herself. 'Marvellous,' she replied when asked how she felt. An

American reporter who had the temerity to suggest that Tony Blair was the new Margaret Thatcher was given short shrift. 'They have got the sex wrong, they have got the willpower wrong, the reasoning wrong, and the strength wrong,' she thundered. But she refused to deny a report that privately she had said that if Mr Blair became prime minister, he would 'not let Britain down'. She tried to avoid the subject of Europe, but that was far from easy.

A wealthy Euro-sceptic, Paul Sykes, had offered campaign support of up to £3,000 to each Tory candidate who would rule out joining a single currency. Although such a commitment was against the party policy of keeping the option open, most Tory MPs accepted the money; only members of the government, who were bound to support the official policy, and about twenty-five pro-European MPs refused. Conservative Central Office was annoyed at the way this added to the impression of a divided party; and with the Referendum Party standing in seats across the country, the leadership believed the whole issue should be avoided if possible. For the last time while Mr Major was prime minister, Lady Thatcher publicly disagreed with party policy. During another day of campaigning, in Essex, she was asked whether Britain should join a single European currency. 'Good heavens, no,' she answered without hesitation. 'I was the one who invented the answer, "No, no, no."' At a Tesco supermarket in Maldon a woman asked her nervously, 'You are going to support Mr Major, aren't you, Lady Thatcher?' She replied briskly, 'Of course, dear.'

27

'Were you up for Portillo?'

ELECTION NIGHT 1997 was remarkable in many ways. (Forgive me if I go into political anorak mode.) It produced the worst Conservative result in more than 150 years – their 31 per cent share of the vote was their lowest since 1823. It was the most extraordinary turnaround in political fortunes since Churchill was rejected in 1945 – from opposition, Labour secured a landslide majority of 179, bigger than any of the majorities won by Mrs Thatcher. There were 419 Labour MPs, while the number of Tories, 165, was their lowest total since 1906. Half of all Conservative MPs lost their seats, including a third of the cabinet. The Tories had hardly any MPs in the major cities outside London, and in Scotland and Wales they had no seats at all.

For many people the night was summed up in a simple comment: 'Did you see the look on Portillo's face?' At about 3 a.m., in the supposedly safe Tory seat of Enfield Southgate in London, a young and nervous Labour candidate, Stephen Twigg, defeated the standard-bearer of the Tory right, Michael Portillo, who was widely expected to become the next leader of the Conservative party. The Labour majority was 1,433. In the previous election the Tories had had more than twice the Labour vote. The swing to Labour in Enfield was an astonishing 17.4 per cent, nearly twice the average across the country. When the result was announced it looked as if the blood had drained out of Mr Portillo's face; he only just managed to control his emotions. Looking grim and deflated, he said,

'I am weeping for the Conservative party; it's been a terrible evening for us.'

Mr Portillo's shock – and the way it highlighted the extent of the Labour victory – became the most enduring image of the night. When anyone discussed the election, they would invariably ask, 'Were you up for Portillo?' I was watching at home in Ealing; and it was obvious that Mr Portillo's leadership ambitions had been dramatically thwarted. It was not at all clear who the front-runner might be. I went to bed about an hour later – at around 4 a.m. – because I was all too aware that a hard day's work was about to dawn. But it was difficult to sleep. I was in Downing Street later that morning to hear Mr Major announce that he would be standing down as party leader as well as prime minister. Outside Number 10 he used words which would have appealed to his show-business father: 'When the curtain falls, it is time to get off the stage.' Typically, he showed little emotion. Mr Major had known he could not win but he had not expected such a devastating result. Within the hour I was surrounded in Downing Street by Labour party aides frantically waving miniature Union Jacks provided by their ever-efficient campaign organizers. Tony Blair and his family stood on the steps of Number 10 basking in their moment of glory. 'This is not a mandate for doctrine or dogma,' he declared. It was the appropriate and inevitable conclusion of five years of Tory infighting.

Lady Thatcher was quick to congratulate Tony Blair on becoming prime minister. But she hinted that her ambitions for the Conservative party were still very much alive, and indeed she suggested that defeat could bring about useful change. 'Over the last eighteen years it was the Conservative party that rebuilt Britain,' she said. 'Now perhaps it is time for us to rebuild ourselves to face the future. It is a new beginning; life is full of new beginnings.'

Polling experts pored over the results to discover why the

Conservatives had done so badly – apart from the obvious reason that Labour under Mr Blair had done exceptionally well. The collapse of back to basics and the series of scandals collectively known as sleaze had clearly had an effect: one of those accused of misconduct, the former minister Neil Hamilton, was soundly beaten in Tatton, Cheshire by the anti-sleaze candidate Martin Bell, the former BBC war correspondent. Many other issues had played their part, including the long-drawn-out controversy over government involvement in the supply of arms to Saddam Hussein in Iraq and the setbacks in the fight against BSE, or mad cow disease. There were also those who criticized Mr Major for being prepared to negotiate with Gerry Adams and Provisional Sinn Fein in an attempt to produce a settlement in Northern Ireland. But the key problem facing Mr Major had been the party's civil war over Europe. On election night Mr Portillo had said, before his own result was announced, 'We had a disagreement on the single currency and that made it more difficult for us to be a credible party, presenting ourselves to the public. I think what the party needs to reflect upon is that it's done itself no good by showing its divisions.'

It seems that a large number of Conservative supporters decided not to vote at all; they were so disillusioned with their party that they simply abstained. Voters did not seem to have been particularly swayed by a candidate's stance on Europe. Being Euro-sceptic did not save Mr Portillo, or Norman Lamont, who also lost his seat. The main problems for the Conservatives were their image as a divided party and lack of confidence in Mr Major to manage the economy. The Tories had never fully recovered in the polls after the ERM debacle, and there was evidence that some voters in Enfield and other constituencies had voted tactically to ensure a Tory defeat. In Enfield Liberal Democrat support had gone down when it became clear from newspaper coverage of an opinion poll that Labour had a chance of defeating Mr Portillo.

The pro-European chancellor Kenneth Clarke was characteristically forthright. 'The public,' he said, 'were rather indifferent to this internal Conservative squabble over Europe, except they thought it made us look rather a shambles.' He immediately declared that he would stand as a leadership candidate and if elected would permit Conservative MPs a free vote over big European issues; they would be allowed to follow their conscience rather than the party whip. Europe, Mr Clarke argued, should be 'set aside' so that the party could 'unite around all the things on which it agreed'. But this proved wishful thinking. When the battle for the leadership got under way, the European issue was again to the fore.

The Euro-sceptics were not going to give up their chance of taking over the leadership and dominating the restructured party, and Lady Thatcher had no intention of staying out of the fight. There was no shortage of advice urging the Conservatives to look to a candidate who would unite rather than divide them on Europe, but all those in the frame had their cards marked on the European issue. As they had been for the duration of the previous Parliament, Conservatives on the right of the party were in no mood to compromise, but Mr Clarke was by far the most popular candidate overall and it looked as if he would benefit from the fact that the right wing could not agree on a candidate.

Some recent leading players were no longer in the race. Michael Portillo was now out of the reckoning, and Mr Heseltine decided he would not stand because of his heart attack four years previously and a recent bout of angina. Chris Patten, a centre-left favourite, was still governor of Hong Kong. All the candidates apart from Mr Clarke were against Britain joining a single currency. William Hague, at only thirty-six, was by far the youngest contender. He had been appointed to the cabinet as Welsh secretary in place of John Redwood, who now once again decided to contest the leadership. They were joined by the former home secretary Michael Howard, who was not considered likely to win because of his unpopularity with voters; and there was also Peter Lilley, but he was thought to be too colourless to have much of a chance.

Lady Thatcher hardly knew William Hague, although she had sat next to him at a party conference. She had also spoken to him on that famous occasion when he had made his name on television, at the age of sixteen, with an extraordinarily precocious speech at a previous party conference; he had wowed the hall in the manner of a young Harold Wilson. But when Lady Thatcher met him after he had declared his intention to run for the leadership, she was not very impressed. It is not clear why, except that he had disappointed some people on the Tory right by first agreeing to stand with Michael Howard, as his proposed deputy, and then pulling out and deciding to run on his own.

It was reported that Lady Thatcher and Lord Tebbit were poised to support John Redwood as the most suitable candidate of the right, but this did not happen. She decided not to come out openly for any of the contenders until after the first ballot – when it might have become clear which of them had the strongest chance of winning. As before in a leadership contest, Lady Thatcher was primarily concerned to stop the candidate of whom she most disapproved. Previously it had been Michael Heseltine; on this occasion it was Kenneth Clarke. Their old animosity over Europe and the part he had played in her downfall had not been forgiven. Her approach and that of her allies became known as ABC – anyone but Clarke.

At the first ballot two right-wing candidates, Michael

Howard and Peter Lilley, were knocked out of the race. Kenneth Clarke was only eight votes ahead of William Hague, who was seen as broadly from the centre. John Redwood did well to come third. A proposed deal among the right-wing candidates whereby whoever went on to the second round should be supported by the other two, failed to materialize. Mr Howard and Mr Lilley threw their weight behind Mr Hague and not Mr Redwood on the grounds that he was the only one who could stop Mr Clarke. The Redwood camp was extremely annoyed. 'This is all about rivalry and ambition,' one of Mr Redwood's supporters declared, not appreciating that he was stating the obvious.

As the second ballot approached, a poll of constituency chairmen was taken. The party in the country had no say in the election – it was still a contest decided by Conservative MPs – but in this unofficial survey Mr Clarke scored well ahead of Mr Hague. The former chancellor looked like the choice not only of the country at large, but also of Tory party members. The second ballot failed to settle the issue. Kenneth Clarke, with 64 votes, was just two votes ahead of William Hague, on 62. John Redwood came third with 38 votes, and he was immediately seen as the kingmaker. It seemed the winner would be the candidate he now supported.

The contest had already developed in a way that had become traditional in Tory leadership elections, with plenty of back-stabbing, deals and treachery, but there was then a dramatic move which took everyone by surprise. Kenneth Clarke and John Redwood announced they were forming an alliance whereby if Mr Clarke won, Mr Redwood would become his deputy. This was an astonishing deal across the internal party divide: the strongest pro-European would be linked to the freshly anointed champion of the Euro-sceptics. Always ready to come up with a parallel from history, some

Tory MPs dubbed this the Molotov–Ribbentrop Pact after the foreign ministers who negotiated the Nazi–Soviet alliance just before the outbreak of the Second World War.

To some undecided Tory MPs this was an obnoxious and unfair comparison. They could see that the Clarke–Redwood pact might be a way for the party to unite under new leadership. I certainly thought this might be a solution to their European problems. The first signs were promising, with some Euro-sceptics who had supported Mr Redwood clearly attracted to the idea. But I had underestimated the determination of Lady Thatcher and her allies. Her chief lieutenants acted quickly. The former prime minister was urged to watch twenty-four-hour television news in order to catch the formal announcement from Mr Clarke. She was dismayed. It looked as though ABC was doomed.

John Whittingdale, Lady Thatcher's former political secretary, had been re-elected to Parliament and was still operating as her go-between. One of William Hague's main supporters, Alan Duncan, rang Mr Whittingdale in some distress when the Clarke–Redwood alliance was announced. 'Will she come out for William?' he asked. Mr Whittingdale told me in an interview in 2003 that he replied, 'Well, I think actually this may change everything.' Mr Whittingdale spoke directly to Lady Thatcher. 'Clarke's going to win,' he told her. 'Redwood has done this extraordinary thing and people are buying it. The right is going over in sufficient numbers for Clarke to win.' Lady Thatcher told him, 'Right, I will come.' They agreed she should take a tour of the House of Commons, including the tea room, ending up with an appearance with William Hague before television cameras outside the St Stephen's entrance. It became the most memorable moment in the leadership contest. Lady Thatcher, who had not warmed to Mr Hague at the beginning of the campaign, now backed him with all the passion she could muster. To anyone who would listen she called out, 'William Hague, he's the man. Remember the name William Hague.' Mr Whittingdale's call had been one of many. Other right wingers, including Michael Howard and Peter Lilley, had begged her to intervene.

It was twenty years since Mr Hague had first met Lady Thatcher. She had been leader of the Opposition in 1977 when he made his speech to the Conservative party conference, and they had not talked much since that day. When I interviewed him in 2003 he recalled how at their first meeting Mrs Thatcher kept saying, 'We could be standing with another young Mr Pitt!' Mr Hague also remembers how she kept asking him if he had phoned his mother. 'She was very concerned about what my mother would think.' It is not surprising that when Lady Thatcher decided to take him under her wing in the leadership contest, this was hardly a relationship of equals.

Lady Thatcher had not been in the Commons tea room since resigning as an MP five years before; many of those present, including the large number of new Labour MPs, had only seen her on television. Mr Hague told me, 'It was as if Napoleon had walked in; every cup of tea stopped, the whole place froze.' Lady Thatcher made a point of not seeking special treatment and insisted on standing in the tea queue. 'She wanted to pay for the tea and carry the tray,' he said. They headed for the Conservative end of the room, where she wanted to meet any doubters. He told me, 'She was a missile that wanted to be directed at the right target. "What about him over there, is he voting for you?" she would ask. "Well, we're not sure, Margaret." "Right," she would say and go into that corner, handbag in hand. She was determined, you know.'

There were many Tory MPs not happy with the Clarke–Redwood alliance. Some of those on the centre left decided to switch their votes to William Hague, having previously supported Kenneth Clarke. They could not bring themselves to support an arrangement which would benefit the man who had stood against John Major. As usual, old scores were being settled. But when the result came in, few doubted the importance of the former prime minister's intervention. William Hague had beaten Kenneth Clarke by just twenty-two votes. It would have needed only a dozen Tory MPs to vote the other way for Mr Clarke to have won. The youngest Tory leader in modern times celebrated his victory with Lady Thatcher and the former cabinet ministers Michael Portillo and Michael Forsyth, who had both lost their seats in the general election. Mr Hague's message to his fellow MPs was succinct: 'The Conservative fightback starts here. I am determined to take our party back to unity, back to confidence and back to power. Join me in doing so.'

The next day the full extent of Lady Thatcher's victory became obvious. Her close friend and former colleague Lord Parkinson returned as party chairman, fourteen years after he had left Conservative Central Office. The right dominated the new shadow cabinet: Peter Lilley became shadow chancellor; Michael Howard was the new shadow foreign secretary; and John Redwood was appointed shadow trade and industry secretary. The new Conservative leadership was very much more to Lady Thatcher's liking than its predecessor. The long march of the Euro-sceptics from minority to majority on the Tory benches had finally been recognized. It was a heavy blow to the pro-Europeans and to those Tories who wished to see an end to the whole rancorous debate.

Kenneth Clarke declined to serve under Mr Hague, while Mr Major's other chancellor, Norman Lamont, was among those who came out strongly in favour of the new leader. He said that whereas Mr Major was 'instinctively of the left,' William Hague was definitely on the right, particularly over Europe. The *Sunday Times* described Mr Hague as 'Thatcher's heir'. Instead of being treated as a problem, Lady Thatcher now found herself being turned to for advice. 'When I was leader,' Mr Hague told me, 'she was very helpful and supportive – not demanding in any way. She didn't get into a huff if for a few months you didn't ask her for advice.' Sometimes Lady Thatcher was warned that Mr Hague would seek her opinion on some topic, often an issue of foreign affairs. When the call came through the former prime minister was well prepared. 'She would have articles and books ready. "Have you seen the article by so and so in the *Wall Street Journal*?" she might say. "This is very good; have you seen the thing in the *Spectator*?" She would give a lot of thought to what she was going to tell me.' Lady Thatcher would watch her protégé's performances on television, particularly at testing times such as when as leader of the Opposition he had to provide an instant response to a complicated budget statement. Mr Hague would be delighted to receive handwritten notes or cards covered on both sides with writing in blue ink. 'She wasn't trying to influence any policy particularly,' he said, 'but she was supportive.'

Just three weeks after his election victory Mr Blair also asked to see Lady Thatcher. They had a wide-ranging conversation, mostly covering foreign affairs, as part of Mr Blair's preparation for his first European summit and meetings with the American president Bill Clinton and the Russian president Boris Yeltsin. In the United States it is customary for a new president to seek advice from his predecessor, but when news of this meeting broke a few days later it was seen as a bold cross-party move by the new prime minister.

Mr Blair had promised that his 'big tent' approach would allow for a more relaxed view of party politics. For example, he made a former Conservative chief whip, Alastair Goodlad, Britain's high commissioner in Australia. But there were nevertheless rumblings among Labour left wingers that tea with Lady Thatcher was 'supping with the devil'. A senior civil servant was quoted as saying, 'For seven years Margaret Thatcher was almost a non-person in Downing Street; it is fascinating that a Labour government calls her in after three weeks in office.' Mr Blair and Lady Thatcher spoke for about an hour. They managed to agree on many points, though not on Europe. But even on this subject – where on the single currency, for instance, they were poles apart – Lady Thatcher appears to have stuck to the practical problems of how to deal with other European leaders. She was reported to have advised him to choose his ground carefully. 'Make up your mind what is important,' she was quoted as saying. 'Don't fight on ground which you cannot win.' John Whittingdale told me how flattered she felt to be asked to Number 10: 'She still missed being prime minister desperately, and the fact that the new prime minister had wanted to ask her advice meant a tremendous amount to her. She'd never vote Labour, but she didn't regard him in the same light as previous Labour leaders. She thought that he had accepted a lot of the things that she had tried to do. Blair charmed her.'

Mr Major largely kept out of the public eye as he prepared to write his memoirs and tried to recover from his time as prime minister. He once told me that it had taken him a year to get over the physical strain of the seven years he spent at Number 10. He was fearful historians would downplay his role: they might jump from Mrs Thatcher to Mr Blair without giving much attention to the part he had played, particularly over Europe. His opt-out from the single currency, the main object of his Maastricht negotiations, has stood the test of time. It became Mr Blair's policy, and despite the new prime minister's determination to be far more pro-European, like Mr Major he ended up out of step with France and Germany, but in his case over Iraq. But Mr Major's relations with Lady Thatcher did not improve. He held her responsible for many of the problems he had had to contend with, and he particularly disliked the way she shifted all the blame for ERM membership onto his shoulders. She had, after all, been prime minister at the time.

In public Lady Thatcher never showed the depth of her feelings towards Mr Major, but her husband Denis was not so inhibited. In his last interview, recorded for Channel Four the year before he died and transmitted not long after his death in 2003, he finally gave vent to his family's frustration and annoyance with his wife's successor. The interview was given to the Thatchers' daughter Carol, and this gave the programme the air of an authorized biography. This was clearly something he wanted to say, and he had no intention of being polite or diplomatic. He expressed what many Tories believe – that it would have been better if they had not won the 1992 election. He turned to his daughter, whom he called affectionately by her full name Carol Jane, and said, 'It would have been a very, very good thing if the next election after Margaret went we had lost. If Major had lost we wouldn't have the disaster we've got now . . .'

Speaking after the Tories' second defeat, in 2001, it is interesting how much blame Sir Denis heaped onto Mr Major personally, and how his wife, in his eyes, was utterly blameless. 'He was a ghastly prime minister,' he said. 'More people deserted our party and we have never recovered. And look what that bloody man [Tony Blair] did to us in the last election: total, total complete and utter defeat, disaster.' Sir Denis then summed up as only a true Thatcherite could: 'The whole situation in the Conservative party today springs from that night when they dismissed the best prime minister the country has had since Churchill.' As an exercise in pure emotion and loyalty, it takes a lot of beating.

28

The Mummy returns

IT IS AN INESCAPABLE FACT of political life that things
going well are far less worthy of comment than things going
badly. After the Conservative dramas of the 1990s it was
now Labour's turn to take centre stage, and Tony Blair's
honeymoon with the media was evident, to varying degrees,
for the whole of his first term. He was helped by a strong
economy. One of the ironies of Britain's removal from the
ERM was that the pound had been able to complete a highly
successful devaluation, made possible by a weakening of
inflationary pressures across the world; and by granting independence to the Bank of England, the government took the
troublesome issue of interest rates out of the political arena.
Labour were so pleased to be in power, after so long in
opposition, that the potential 'awkward squad' on the left of
the party were in no mood to complain. It was even possible
for the cautious new chancellor Gordon Brown to stick to the
Tory spending plans for his first two years, a feat which his
predecessor Kenneth Clarke thought the Conservatives would
not have matched if they had stayed in government.

Mr Blair took a firmly pro-European stance. Britain
accepted the Social Chapter of the Maastricht Treaty, an
option left open by Mr Major, but any move towards joining
the single currency was ruled out at least until after the next
election. At the same time a close alliance was formed with the
new American president Bill Clinton, who helped negotiate
the Good Friday Agreement in Northern Ireland in a contin-

uation of the policy started under Mr Major. Devolution led to the setting-up of the Scottish Parliament and the Welsh Assembly; and House of Lords reform began with the removal of the great majority of hereditary peers. British and American forces took military action in Kosovo which led to the removal of the Serbian leader Slobodan Miloševíc. This move was strongly supported by Lady Thatcher, who had campaigned vigorously against Mr Major's reluctance to use force. Mr Blair made no attempt to undo Mrs Thatcher's trade union reforms, and even Mr Major's botched privatization of the railways was allowed to stand.

Lady Thatcher was much happier with her role in public life. She had disliked being portrayed as a constant thorn in Mr Major's side, and she was pleased that her views on Europe were now broadly in line with those of the Conservative leadership. On the whole she managed to support William Hague, although she was not convinced he was ready for a move to Number 10. The former prime minister was nevertheless flattered to be asked to play an important part in the Conservative election campaign in 2001. Three months before the campaign started it was agreed that she would carry out a tour of marginal seats and make a major speech in Plymouth. According to a Conservative party official, the location appealed to Lady Thatcher because of its long naval history and its historical association with the defeat of the Spanish Armada. At first she was reluctant to play such a significant part in the campaign for fear she would again be criticized for taking attention away from the Conservative leader, but the deal was agreed very amicably with Mr Hague over a whisky in her study at Chesham Place. He had come to the conclusion that, as in his leadership campaign, it would be good to have Napoleon on his side.

Those running the Conservative campaign seemed pleased with the arrangement, which was not announced until after the election had been called for 7 June. 'It has been the Tories' best-kept secret,' one senior official boasted. 'Lady Thatcher is still one of our biggest hitters.' Now that so many of the party's favourites – the pro-Europeans – had retired from the race, it was not a large field. Inappropriate words from a nameless official did not help. A spokesman for Lady Thatcher said she did not want to be accused of 'trying to dictate the domestic political agenda'.

Given the paucity of well-known names on the Conservative side – and the lack of an experienced personality to lead them – it was perhaps not surprising that for about a third of the campaign Lady Thatcher was hardly out of the headlines. In one week it was calculated that she was the fourth most frequently quoted politician in the national newspapers – after the three main party leaders there was no one else to beat her – but the campaign in general did not generate much interest. With the opinion polls indicating another Labour landslide, there was little sense of excitement and, in the event, the turnout went below 60 per cent for the first time in modern history.

For a politician who was now seventy-five and had been dismissed by her own party years before, Lady Thatcher was still a remarkable phenomenon. The most striking aspect of Labour's campaign was a poster depicting Mr Hague's bald head covered by a wig modelled on Lady Thatcher's hair. The message was simple: he did not have a political personality of his own; he had to rely on hers. Large crowds gathered wherever she appeared, with many people keen just to see her irrespective of their political views. A mother urged forward her ten-year-old with the words, 'She was PM, one of the greatest; you won't know what that means but touch her.' Even some journalists appeared to fall under Lady Thatcher's spell. A *Sunday Times* correspondent described her 'almost imperial progress' across southern England. 'I note one strange and wonderful thing about all those who meet her,' he wrote, 'they bow instinctively out of respect.' He even likened her to Elizabeth I.

I took a more jaundiced view of Lady Thatcher's election tour. It seemed to demonstrate how weak the Conservatives were that they should have to rely on a former leader who would play no formal part in running the country – if by any chance they were to win. The broadcasters were tied to the usual rules of balance and her appearances were treated as an important part of the coverage allotted to the Conservatives, but it was not often to their advantage. Lady Thatcher appeared to confirm the impression of a party whose members were on average well over sixty years old and which was finding it extremely difficult to connect with younger voters.

To Lady Thatcher's audience of a thousand mostly elderly Tories, packed into a theatre in Plymouth, this would have seemed like media carping. They had come to see their superstar and, after a blast of triumphal martial music, she did not disappoint. They gave her a much warmer reception than the one they accorded Mr Hague, who followed immediately afterwards; and they reserved their biggest cheer for his praise of the former prime minister. There was even a joke. 'It's more than a decade since I was in the front line of politics,' Lady Thatcher told them. 'That's why I'm back . . . and you knew I was coming. On my way here I passed a cinema with the sign, "The Mummy Returns".' It got a good laugh, but Tory campaign experts were not amused. The film told the story of a pharaoh's mummified body coming back to life in the British Museum and going on the rampage. Even if voters did not make that connection, the inevitable headline – THE MUMMY RETURNS – was just what party officials were trying to avoid. They did not want to give the impression she was back in charge.

Of more serious concern was that Lady Thatcher once

again managed to give publicity to the party's differences on Europe. Although she was faultless in her praise for William Hague, describing him as 'cool and gritty', she ignored his carefully constructed compromise on the single currency. In order to try to unite the two main factions of the Tory party, he had decided to rule out Britain joining the euro in the lifetime of the next Parliament, if they won the election. It may seem a small enough concession, but the pro-Europeans cherished the fact that the party had not ruled out joining the euro for ever. The policy had more or less held throughout the election campaign and in Lady Thatcher's prepared speech she stuck to party policy, but after attacking Tony Blair for being prepared to lead Britain by the nose into the single currency, she added an impromptu line: 'I would never be prepared to give up our own currency.' For Lady Thatcher the greatest issue of the election was whether Britain remained a free independent nation state or was subsumed in a federal Europe. 'There are no half measures, no third ways and no second chances. Too many powers have already passed from our Parliament to the bureaucracy in Brussels. We must get them back. Above all we must keep the pound.' She ended with a dramatic flourish: 'We have sixteen days to shift opinion and to shake this rotten government to the core.'

Increasingly, Lady Thatcher appeared to be advocating renegotiation of Britain's position, which pro-Europeans argued would lead to the end of British membership of the EU. Mr Hague was conscious of the danger of alarming business people whose livelihoods depended on Britain's continuing membership, and on the same day as Lady Thatcher's Plymouth speech he had stressed that Britain would 'always' be in the EU. He was not advocating any policy which amounted to withdrawal. Europe was not the only issue on which Lady Thatcher disagreed with the Tory leadership during the campaign. She criticized them for putting a precise total of £8 billion on their promised tax cuts. In her only interview during the run-up to the election she also said she had no wish to see 'what they call a multicultural society'.

For the first part of the campaign Mr Hague gave enormous prominence to defeating the government on the issue of the single currency. No speech would go by without him declaring how many days there were left to 'save the pound'. When I went to see him campaigning at Bristol docks, there was a small crowd gathered round him and his wife Ffion as they tried to stem the Labour tide. By this time I was political editor of ITN and was preparing a report for *News at Ten*. I was anxious to ask Mr Hague why he was concentrating so much on this issue when all the opinion polls showed it was low on people's priorities. Public services, particularly health and education, were at the top. A man in the crowd told me he found Mr Hague's tactic puzzling; he was much more concerned about education. For most people Tony Blair's promise to hold a referendum on the euro ensured it was not a key issue at this election. On this occasion Mr Hague insisted to me that he was concentrating on other issues as well.

As the campaign progressed, it became clear that Labour was heading for another victory, and questions were asked at Tory Central Office about the wisdom of being so interested in Europe and so concerned about the question of asylum seekers. Was this right-wing agenda really what the public wanted and had Lady Thatcher not damaged the cause by criticizing the idea of a multicultural society? With a week to go before polling day, Mr Hague appeared to change course. Under attack from some shadow cabinet members for allowing Lady Thatcher to play too large a role in the campaign, he made a deliberate pitch for the centre ground. He told an audience in Bradford, 'It has never mattered to me whether people are Muslim, Christian, Hindu, Sikh, Jewish, White, Black or Asian. As far as I am concerned we are all as British as each other.' To emphasize the point, he referred to One Nation Tories, those whom Lady Thatcher had deliberately picked out for criticism in her Keith Joseph Memorial Lecture. Mr Hague said, 'The Conservative commitment to one nation means that we will govern for all the people of Britain. The next Conservative government will be committed to rooting out racism and bigotry.'

The day before this speech Lady Thatcher had annoyed some of those in Tory Central Office by using an article in the *Daily Telegraph* to warn that a second landslide for Labour would create an 'elective dictatorship'. A shadow cabinet minister was quoted as saying, 'My heart sank when I heard the BBC's news bulletins were leading with Mrs Thatcher accusing Blair of dictatorship. I thought people will think, 'That's rich coming from her. She's in danger of hijacking us.' One of the problems for the Tories was that more newspapers than ever before had decided to back Labour. *The Times, Sunday Times, Daily Express* and *Sunday Express* all switched to Labour, having supported Mr Major in 1997. Even the normally diehard *Daily Mail* felt unable to endorse Mr Hague. Almost all the newspapers had now declared against the Conservatives. The *Mail* said it understood why so many voters remained 'resolutely unimpressed' by the 'timid, incoherent' Tories. The *Financial Times*, for the third election in succession, came out in favour of Labour.

ELECTION NIGHT 2001 provided some of the least exciting television of modern times. I was with Jonathan Dimbleby discussing events on ITV but we had little drama to keep us going. Like a tennis player, Jonathan ate a large number of bananas during the programme to keep up his energy levels. He was certainly on top of all the issues and handled the whole affair with great aplomb, but only twenty seats, outside Northern Ireland, changed hands. After days of rehearsals, it was rather an anti-climax. Ruefully, I remembered watching Jonathan's father Richard Dimbleby, during his coverage of the knife-edge election of 1964, breaking off to announce that the Russian leader Nikita Khrushchev had been deposed, and then later that China had just exploded its first atomic bomb.

Unfortunately, ours was a quiet night, and we were unable to prevent large numbers of viewers heading for bed. They knew from the exit poll at the start of the programme that Mr Blair was safe in Number 10. The change in the number of seats held by the major parties was the smallest since 1910. Mr Blair was re-elected with another landslide majority of 167, after a swing from Labour to the Conservatives of only 1.8 per cent. The majority was just two less than in 1997, and the Conservatives had just one more MP. In those seats held by the Tories until 1997 and with large ethnic minorities, the proportion of those voting Conservative dropped by 3 per cent. Labour, in general, seemed to increase its support among affluent voters.

Tory pro-Europeans, who had kept a low profile during the election, were quick to blame the party's shift to the right for the disastrous result. Chris Patten, former party chairman and now a European commissioner, said that the Euro-sceptics had done 90 per cent of Mr Blair's work for him. They had rendered the Tories unelectable with their 'diet of unpopular populism' and rejection of mainstream Tory values. 'They helped to destroy the Major government. They have dominated the last four years in the Conservative party. The pro-Europeans have not been included, and we have seen the result yesterday.' The former deputy prime minister Michael Heseltine took the same line. He was scornful about Lady Thatcher's part in the campaign. 'I'm amazed,' he said, 'that anyone believed she would win the party votes in this election, not least because her intervention on the euro helped to blow William Hague's position out of the water.'

But when the inevitable battle got under way for the party leadership – Mr Hague announced his resignation the day after the election – there was little sign that the result would lead to the Tories closing ranks. Lady Thatcher emerged from her Belgravia home to say that obviously the election result had been very disappointing. 'But, my friends,' she told a television crew, 'make no mistake; the Conservative party will be back.' Back, it seemed, to all the old arguments. There was, though, a new electoral system, brought in by Mr Hague. First, MPs had a chance to vote, and when they had whittled the choice down to two candidates, the party at large was allowed to have its say on the basis of one member, one vote.

Kenneth Clarke announced that once again he would be standing. Another of the obvious candidates, Michael Portillo, had dramatically changed his public persona. Having once been a Thatcher arch-loyalist and the standard-bearer of the right, he had returned to Parliament in a by-election as a more caring, more inclusive Conservative. He admitted to having had homosexual experiences as a young man, and made it clear he now supported a more liberal social policy. For Lady Thatcher his political shift was more important than what he had got up to as a young man. The search was therefore on for a new standard-bearer, with the Maastricht rebel and later shadow defence secretary, Iain Duncan Smith, quickly becoming favourite to fill that role.

There were two other candidates for the leadership, Michael Ancram and David Davis, but they were knocked out in the first round. In the second round Kenneth Clarke came first with 59 votes, with Iain Duncan Smith on 54, and Michael Portillo just one vote behind on 53. Only two candidates could go forward to the party membership vote, so Mr Portillo's bid for the leadership was over. The result effectively put him out of front-line politics; his journey from the right to the centre left had brought him nowhere. If only one MP had switched from Mr Duncan Smith to Mr Portillo he would have had a chance at the leadership.

As had happened so often before, the key issue seemed to be which of the candidates had the support of Lady Thatcher, and there had been a crucial mix-up the weekend before the MPs' vote. A report in the *Sunday Telegraph*, based I am assured on good evidence, suggested that Mr Portillo had her endorsement. The story was headlined THATCHER SAYS PORTILLO IS THE RIGHT LEADER, but it seems that the evidence was out of date. Within hours Lady Thatcher had issued a denial: 'This story is plain wrong,' she said. 'I do not hold the views attributed to me and I am not backing Michael Portillo against Iain Duncan Smith.' Lady Thatcher was furious at this attempt, as she saw it, to use her to boost Mr Portillo's flagging campaign. Her angry denial may have been just enough to tip the election against him.

When the campaign got under way for the membership ballot, Lady Thatcher made sure that there was no misunderstanding about her position. Her commitment to ABC, anyone but Clarke, remained unchanged. In private she complained of not being sure whether he was a real Conservative, so pro-European and centre left was he. Surveys of party members suggested the result would be close. With Mr Clarke the more popular candidate with the general public, the strongly Eurosceptic Iain Duncan Smith was keen to boost his chances with a Thatcher endorsement. It came, without reservation.

Lady Thatcher fired her broadside at Mr Clarke in a letter to the *Daily Telegraph*, the paper most read by party members. She wrote, 'Ken Clarke has many qualities. But I have no doubt that Iain Duncan Smith would make infinitely the better leader. I fail to understand how Ken could lead today's Conservative party to anything other than disaster. He is at odds with the majority of its members on too many issues. He appears to be an even keener enthusiast for the euro than is the prime minister, let alone the chancellor. He seems to view with blithe unconcern the erosion of Britain's sovereignty in Europe.' Lady Thatcher went on to say how his leadership would expose the party split on Europe, accusing Mr Clarke of 'old-fashioned views, which have had their day'. She also took a swipe at his record: 'It would have been reassuring to hear from Ken Clarke about some of the mistakes which in 1997 led the Conservative party to the greatest defeat in its history. After all, he – not Iain Duncan Smith – was one of those who made them.' Kenneth Clarke, of course, had been chancellor when the election was called in 1997.

When the ballot was taken, Iain Duncan Smith won easily with around 60 per cent of the vote. It is impossible to say how much Lady Thatcher's intervention affected the result, but it had certainly been an enormous help to his campaign. Among the party faithful she was still a considerable figure; her reputation and influence within the Conservative party were far greater than anyone else's. It is also true that the majority of the party, many of whom were retired, were Euro-sceptic, and therefore not at all keen on Kenneth Clarke. With a big turnout and a clear majority Iain Duncan Smith could certainly claim a mandate for his leadership. For Lady Thatcher it would be the last time that she had a decisive effect on the outcome of a Conservative leadership election. Soon there was the first public hint of problems over her health. It was announced that she would not be attending the party conference in the autumn for fear she might overshadow the new leader, but friends of the former prime minister were quoted as saying that her memory was not as strong as it had been and she intended to retire from public life 'within a year'.

In March 2002 it was announced that Lady Thatcher had been ordered by her doctors to stop working for health reasons after a series of small strokes. She was seventy-six. Expressing her 'great regret' Lady Thatcher had agreed to retire from speaking in public. Denis Thatcher used to say that she would repeat phrases without realizing that was what she was doing. I saw her at a dinner later that year to celebrate the publication of her third book, *Statecraft*, a survey of foreign affairs. Before the event she signed copies and seemed in good health, but she only said 'Thank you' after the speeches in her honour. She was having serious trouble with her memory; after so many years in which it had provided much of her intellectual strength, it could no longer be relied on. When I spoke to her former press secretary and close friend Sir Bernard Ingham in the autumn of the following year he told me he still continued to make regular visits to her office. He believed they were for her a 'release from boredom'. He added, 'Even though the immediate memory is gone, her mind is exercised.'

Iain Duncan Smith was forced to resign in 2003 by his fellow MPs, who had come to believe he was incapable of delivering the revival they longed for. A straightforward, decent man with an attractive wife, he was neither an exceptional orator nor did he interview particularly well on television. He also suffered from a persistent throat problem, which made it hard for him to convey the necessary conviction during prime minister's questions in the Commons. As leader he had decided to play down the issue of Europe – ironically the issue which had most endeared him to his fellow Conservatives – and tried to concentrate on issues with more public appeal. But the strategy failed to shift the opinion polls, which showed the Conservatives had still not recovered from the position they held before the pound was thrown out of the Exchange Rate Mechanism in 1992, more than ten years earlier. Tory MPs dropped Mr Duncan Smith in favour of that old stalwart of the right Michael Howard, and it was perhaps not surprising that some newspapers published suggestions that

Lady Thatcher was in favour of the move. It seemed that no change in the leadership was possible without an intervention from the former prime minister.

But, as it happened, there was no other candidate and Mr Howard was elected unopposed. When Lady Thatcher attended a dinner in Westminster organized by the right-wing 92 Group in December 2003, she was the guest of honour and was given a very warm reception. She did not speak, but her spokesman said, 'It's taken for granted that she completely supports Mr Howard and is delighted he is leader. She is an old friend and believes he possesses lots of experience and talent for the job.' Since John Major had resigned in 1997, there had been three Conservative leaders, each in turn described as Thatcher's heir. Mr Howard was the first one who could be sure that she would not intervene if she thought his leadership was not up to scratch. The Thatcher period in British politics was finally over.

When Lady Thatcher's old friend and former president of the United States Ronald Reagan died, aged ninety-three in June 2004, she attended the memorial service in Washington along with many world leaders. A ten-minute eulogy she had managed to record on videotape some months earlier, to spare her frail health, was played at the service. Before he succumbed to Alzheimer's disease ten years before, he had asked her to carry out this final act. In the eulogy, she said, 'We have lost a great president, a great American, and a great man. And I have lost a dear friend.' The most poignant of her comments came right at the end: 'We here still move in twilight. But we have one beacon to guide us that Ronald Reagan never had. We have his example. Let us give thanks today for a life that achieved so much for all of God's children.'

29

'I am an ism'

ANY ASSESSMENT OF Lady Thatcher's career has to come to terms with the fact that she created such a distinctive approach to politics it became known as Thatcherism. It is unusual in Britain for a politician to be honoured in this way. In the post-war period the broad consensus of the two main parties over the NHS and the welfare state in general came to be known as Butskellism. But this stemmed from the names of two politicians: the Conservative R. A. B. Butler, known as Rab, and the Labour leader Hugh Gaitskell – two of the 'best prime ministers we never had'. It was also no more than a description – and perhaps not much more than a joke – of what had happened in British politics. It did not pretend to be a guide to further action. No one proudly labelled them-selves Butskellite in the way many insisted on being called Thatcherite.

In France it is far more common for politicians to give labels to their politics and their followers. President Chirac has his Chiraciens and supporters of the former president Giscard D'Estaing expect to be referred to as Giscardiens. In some cases such labels have taken on a wider significance, and have transferred to other contexts. An obvious example arises from the political impact of Charles de Gaulle. Gaullism conveys to us a clear nationalistic outlook; it is closely associated with his struggle to rid France of the shame of its defeat by Germany in 1940, while Pétainism is a convenient way of describing the politics of those like Marshal Pétain who collaborated. But even Britain's greatest politician of the twentieth century, Winston Churchill, never gave birth to an ism.

As part of the celebrations to mark her seventieth birthday in 1995, Lady Thatcher agreed to be interviewed by her journalist daughter Carol. It was extraordinary how at key points in her career the Thatcher family turned themselves into a cottage industry, not by weaving their own cloth, but by keeping journalistic tasks in house. Speaking to a close relative did not seem to inhibit the former prime minister, nor make her sound any less formal. She had been out of office for five years and was no longer a member of the House of Commons. The public had been able to appreciate for themselves what government was like without her forceful presence, and her image had improved now that she was out of the front line. She told her daughter, 'I've always had a natural passion for politics and a natural interest in history and a natural passion to get things right for the future, and I have brought about colossal changes. That's why I'm an ism . . . It is recognition that we didn't just govern from day to day – we had principles, we had purpose, we had action, and we had perseverance.'

Thatcherism had indeed become firmly established as a political term. As on so many other issues, Lady Thatcher partly had her opponents to thank. The label proved as useful to her enemies as it was to her friends. For many of her Labour opponents it was convenient to be able to dismiss controversial aspects of government policy simply by describing them as Thatcherism. No more explanation was needed; it was as easy to understand as the demonstrators who shouted, 'Maggie, Maggie, Maggie; out, out, out.' Lady Thatcher herself was not above the use of political shorthand to express what she felt about complicated issues. She found her own slogan of 'No, no, no' a tempting way to deal with the intricate details of European politics. The problem with the Thatcherism label was when it was given far more significance; when it was used to describe a political creed, or indeed a philosophy which aspired to be universal.

Lady Thatcher appreciated some of the dangers of using the term as if it was an ideology or some kind of doctrine. In a speech to an academic seminar at Hofstra University, New York in March 2000, she made a distinction between the description of her politics implied by the term Thatcherism, and the big isms of the twentieth century – communism, socialism, nazism and fascism. In her view these were related but their effects varied. 'Communism accounted for approaching one hundred million deaths,' she said. 'It enslaved the East, while its first cousin socialism impoverished much of the West. Nazism – that other brand of socialism – and its tamer forebear fascism killed about twenty-five million.' Lady Thatcher argued that all these ideologies promoted the idea that the state had the right, indeed the duty, to act like God. 'And the results were devilish.' She accepted that some isms, though, were benign, and she mentioned the advantages of liberalism, individualism and free enterprise capitalism. Then she came to her main point: 'I don't regard Thatcherism as an ism in any of these senses. And if I ever invented an ideology, that certainly wasn't my intention.'

Lady Thatcher admitted that as well as having a certain view of human nature – that people flourished without too much regulation and without too big a role for the state – she was also a practical politician. Thatcherism sprang from its time. In the 1970s, she argued, Britain was beset by restrictive practices, trade union militancy, penal taxes and poor profits from low investment and productivity. She believed that by the middle of that decade, which happened to be the moment she became leader of the Conservative party, the high point of British socialism had been reached, and there was a real threat to liberty from any further increase in state power. She argued that Thatcherism had been a practical answer to those problems, but it could still be applied in other circumstances because the need for a 'free economy and a free society' was always present. Many of Lady Thatcher's supporters are still content to accept her description of what happened, but some of them would go further. For Thatcher loyalists the phrase so often used about Churchill is relevant to her as well: she 'saved the country'. But even if you accept that this happened and was the result of her period in office, how much was it due to her, to her kind of leadership, and how much was it due to the body of ideas which came to be lumped together as Thatcherism?

Across the political spectrum there is a recognition that many of Mrs Thatcher's reforms during the 1980s have stood the test of time. When I spoke to Tony Blair in the garden of Number 10 in the summer of 2002 he accepted that Mrs Thatcher had a 'very defined political philosophy'. It involved rolling back the state, curbing trade union power and putting greater emphasis on the individual. It was an inevitable reaction against the welfare state and a public sector 'which had become very large – a vested interest which was out of touch'. He told me Mrs Thatcher had made changes to the structure of British industry which were clearly successful. Where she failed, in his view, was in being reluctant to invest in public infrastructure – public services, hospitals and schools; and he also complained about 'an indifference towards social division, because she felt people should stand on their own two feet'.

That summer I also interviewed Gordon Brown, in the chancellor's office at the Treasury. He too accepted that some of the changes brought in under Mrs Thatcher had produced long-term benefits. 'I think,' he told me, 'the relationship between the state and the private sector had to change. Britain had to change.' Even John Prescott offered grudging praise for the achievements of the Thatcher years – in a speech in New York in 1996. He said, 'Thatcherism challenged the traditional thinking of Britain and some of that needed to be done.' But he disapproved of the way she had undermined public services. When Labour came to power in 1997 little attempt was made to reverse the radical changes made by Mrs Thatcher, particularly privatization. No industries were taken back into public ownership; no attempt was made to stop council house sales; and there was almost no attempt to restore what used to be called trade union 'rights' over secondary picketing, the use of compulsory strike ballots and the 'closed shop'. Even the railways were not brought back into public ownership, despite strong support for this in opinion polls. Other discredited former Labour policies including direct attempts to control prices and incomes were not even considered. On the issue of nuclear weapons, which had taken up so much of the energies of Labour in opposition, there was no modification to existing policy.

When I interviewed John Major in the spring of 2003 he was keen to clear up some of the myths about Thatcherism. 'The first thing to make clear,' he said, 'is that strictly speaking it isn't Thatcherism.' He believes the influential Conservative thinker and cabinet minister Sir Keith Joseph should take some of the credit, as should Mrs Thatcher's chancellors Sir Geoffrey Howe and Nigel Lawson. 'Thatcherism is a mixture of Josephism, Howeism and Lawsonism; they manufactured the bullets and Margaret fired them. And of the three of them, the principal architect, ironically, is probably Geoffrey Howe. Many of the market reforms people think of as Thatcherism came from Geoffrey Howe when he was chancellor and Nigel Lawson was financial secretary. And it was they who persuaded Margaret of what came to be known as Thatcherism. She was not the progenitor of an ism, not the only begetter of an ism, she was the voice of the ism.' Many of those who worked with Mrs Thatcher in government are keen to point out that she was far from being the consistent ideologue of legend, always driving her views forward in the same direction. She was, Mr Major told me, 'infinitely more pragmatic' than her reputation suggests. 'Her oratory was often unremitting and unbending, but what she actually did was not.'

Michael Portillo, who served her loyally for many years and was for a time her chosen heir, was surprisingly frank in his interview with me about the limits of Thatcherism in practice. Both her supporters and her enemies contributed to some of the myths about the potency and consistency of her approach. Mr Portillo told me, 'She had very strong views; and because she liked to create enemies, a lot of people have made her the source of all the ills in their lives. So they think she destroyed the manufacturing industry; she was cruel to miners' families; she believed in no social benefits and destroyed the health service. It's all nonsense, but that is the myth that has been built up around her.' Mr Portillo believes she contributed to this myth by the way she often spoke about her policies. 'But the rhetoric and reality were so different. No wonder people thought she'd cut the health service down to nothing, because she kept talking about public spending cuts – health spending went up. No wonder they felt the welfare state had been dismantled, because to listen to her you might have thought so – but of course welfare spending went up. The fantastic irony was that the Conservatives demonstrated in office all the priorities that were the opposite of the ones they expressed to the public. Welfare spending and health spending went up; spending on defence and the police went down.'

Another part of the Thatcher rhetoric has also distorted the picture. Her frustration with some of the policies and attitudes which came out of the Treasury and the Foreign Office is well known, but Mr Portillo argues that although she loved to appear combative, in practice she would often wait and prepare the ground before acting. Her initial decision not to take on the miners in 1981 is often cited. She waited two years until she was convinced she could beat the miners' union and their leader Arthur Scargill with large stockpiles of coal and tough policing. Mr Portillo said, 'I remember someone saying her name is Margaret, caution Hilda, caution, caution Thatcher; the rhetoric was very clear-cut, but very often the action was much more circumspect.' Mr Portillo believes that in many ways the Thatcher governments, despite their radical claims, were conventional in practice. This, he believes, partly explains why Mrs Thatcher was prepared to go along with the pro-European designs of the Foreign Office, how she could be persuaded to sign obviously integrationist measures such as the Single European Act and why she accepted the need for Britain to join the European Exchange Rate Mechanism. 'She was never,' Mr Portillo says, 'interested in revolution; she wanted to make sure she was the embodiment of the British state.'

Lord Wakeham, who served in cabinets under Mrs Thatcher and Mr Major, told me she changed her mind far more than people imagine. She would often express a view at the beginning of a meeting only to find herself opposed by other members of the cabinet. Sometimes she would back down and accept a policy even if, Lord Wakeham said, 'her emotions' were against it. She was then likely to couple her agreement with a warning to the cabinet minister behind the policy: 'You'd better be right.' Lord Wakeham believes this was her way of protecting herself from complaints from the right wing of the party. She was, in effect, saying to the cabinet minister involved, 'Don't kid yourself you've got my heart and soul behind it; you've got my reason and my rational decision.' It also gave her the chance to say to her friends and close supporters, 'Of course, left to myself I would have been a bit more radical.' It is not surprising that those looking for consistency in the actions of her governments may not always be rewarded. They were far less ideological than the term Thatcherism would suggest. One of her constant concerns was to further the political aims of her party, and that was why she was always worried about the effects of policies on 'our people'. One of the reasons she was prepared to join the ERM was that in the short term the move would bring down interest rates; memories of her father's shop in Grantham meant she was all too aware of the effect of high interest on small businesses. She favoured council house sales – and in 1974 pegging the mortgage rate – partly because these measures would encourage people to buy their own homes, and property owners were 'our people'.

Margaret Thatcher was above all a practical politician. She was skilful in linking her policies to general ideas about liberty and free enterprise, but this did not amount to a rigid set of rules. There were no tablets of stone; there was no Thatcherite bible. Particularly during her later years in office, this gave her a remarkably free hand in deciding which policies were given her blessing. She hated communism but famously managed to get on with the Soviet leader Mikhail Gorbachev – so much so that she worried about the effect on the Soviet Union of the unification of Germany and gave this as one of her reasons for initially opposing it. She was strongly in favour of privatization but baulked at selling off the Royal Mail, and during her time in office the Conservatives did not take British Rail into the private sector. She made no move to privatize the BBC.

Mrs Thatcher complained bitterly about the size of the public sector, but the state's share of national output did not go down significantly over her period in office. She was totally committed to fighting inflation, but when she left office the annual rate was again in double figures. She was opposed to moves towards a federal Europe but signed the Single European Act and agreed to British membership of the ERM. On Northern Ireland she was a convinced unionist, but she still signed the Anglo-Irish agreement, which for the first time gave the Irish Republic a formal say in the affairs of the province. Her ultimately pragmatic approach to politics was evident in many areas: she strongly supported grammar schools but as education secretary gave the green light to the introduction of more comprehensive schools than any minister before or since, and when she was prime minister made no attempt to reintroduce selection via the eleven-plus.

Chris Patten, who came to disagree with her most strongly about Europe, worked closely with her for many years and often contributed to her speeches at party conferences. He became something of a hate figure on the Tory right, but for many Conservatives he is 'the best prime minister we never had'. He told me, 'I think it's ridiculous to regard Thatcherism as a coherent political philosophy. Her attitude certainly had roots in a belief in the market, in a distrust of the public sector, in a passionate belief that cutting taxes released people's energy. She was also passionately anti-communist, and one of the few institutions she believed in was the armed forces. But I don't think that you can point to her record in government as a seamless whole, or the steady, carefully planned working out of a philosophical strategy. I think Thatcherism was whatever Margaret Thatcher did, day to day, week to week.' Mr Patten is also cautious about relying too much on Mrs Thatcher's historical perspective. 'Her version of history was entirely one – and she didn't know much history actually – in which Americans had arrived twice in the last century to save Europe from totalitarianism, from civil war. She was much more at home in America, where her brisk, right-wing views were very close to an American audience. She conjured up for Americans the high points of the transatlantic relationship: Winston, the Cold War, the works.'

MANY PEOPLE I have spoken to, who were in a position to judge, agree that when she left office the views she expressed became less balanced or, according to some of her critics, more extreme. Margaret Thatcher was never again able to call on the skills and expertise of the civil servants who had become expert at turning her views on policy into practical plans for government. Inevitably, those who surrounded her after she left Number 10 held opinions which she was likely to share; she could no longer count on the wide range of views she had drawn on while in office. Although some of her most able advisers, such as Lord Powell and Sir Bernard Ingham, continued to see her regularly, they could not hope to reproduce the Rolls-Royce service provided in Downing Street. Those who caught Lady Thatcher's eye often had particular reasons to court her company. On Europe particularly even some of her closest friends and supporters acknowledge that the range and quality of the advice she received declined. Lord Powell told me how her view on the Maastricht Treaty had changed. To begin with she was impressed by Mr Major's negotiating skill. 'Her initial reaction was quite favourable; she thought he had done rather well to get opt outs, and so on. Her view hardened, partly as result of some very intensive lobbying by very hard-line Euro-sceptics, and partly because being Thatcher she read the whole text from beginning to end, and there were a lot of undesirable things in it.' Lord Powell says that Lady Thatcher tried to articulate her beliefs in the speeches she made. 'I think they did have some broad philosophical influence,' he told me, 'but it was not what she had focused her whole life upon.'

In Lord Powell's eyes, after she left office Lady Thatcher became a powerful symbol. 'Part of people's vision of her, particularly in Eastern Europe and Russia, was of the great heroine of the Cold War, who had together with Reagan brought about its end.' Being a woman increased her impact and her influence; Lord Powell believes the fact she was a woman was 'very, very important'. She also became a symbol of a changed Britain. 'She was the person who had broken the trade unions, who had brought down tax from ludicrous levels, and who had got rid of nationalized industry.' But the more Lady Thatcher enjoyed this extraordinary political afterlife, the harder it became for those who had to succeed her. They were forced to deal with the political realities she had adapted to in the past, while she was free to argue her position without the constraints of office. Her attitude to Europe began to diverge considerably from the position she had taken in Number 10. In later years she argued for a renegotiation of Britain's membership which seemed tantamount to withdrawal. Her former political secretary Stephen Sherbourne believes that there was also a personal reason for her concentration on this issue: 'It gave her a stick with which to beat John Major and the government; and it was her way of punishing those who had ousted her.'

There have been many attempts to define Thatcherism, most notably by Shirley Robin Letwin, an academic and, as it happens, the mother of the Conservative politician Oliver Letwin. In her book *The Anatomy of Thatcherism* she makes a brave attempt to make a case for it to be taken seriously as an ism. She accepts, though, that Thatcherism cannot be treated as 'an eternal truth'; she argues that its concern is with action. 'Thatcherism has not got what it takes to be a theory. Mrs Thatcher herself never had the time, aptitude or inclination to act as her own theorist.' Lord Hurd gave me a succinct version of how he saw Thatcherism: 'I think that Margaret Thatcher was converted in the early seventies to the set of ideas associated with Keith Joseph at that time, which were basically market-based. You could deal with most of the problems by decreasing the power of the state, letting the market decide things; and that was on the whole the right way to run, not just Britain, but the world. When she became leader she began to place on that foundation her personality, her way of doing things, her way of saying things, and all these together came to be called Thatcherism. I think there was a fundamental set of ideas, which she wasn't wholly devoted to, and which she often diverged from in practice.'

One of the reasons the argument over the nature of Thatcherism is important is that it helps to explain some of the problems faced by her successors. If it had been a coherent political philosophy, Mr Major and his government would have had a clear path to follow if they chose to do so. But on all sorts of issues, including trying to reach a settlement in Northern Ireland and the details of the privatization of the railways, there was no Thatcherite rule book they could turn to. Thatcherism was far more dependent on a single personality than any normal ism. It was indeed hard to see how there could be Thatcherism without Thatcher. Conservative politicians might ask the question, 'What would Margaret Thatcher do in these circumstances?' But the answer might not come very readily; and to make matters more difficult for those who followed her as leader, the supreme arbiter of what was, or was not, an article of the true faith was still alive. Lady Thatcher could always say, or hint through friends, that they were not following her principles or practice. They were besmirching her legacy. She had a strange power of veto over whether any Conservative party policy fitted into the most powerful myth of modern British politics. Thatcherism had become a personality cult.

Most of her realistic policy objectives had been achieved by the time Mrs Thatcher left office. Essentially, Thatcherism is a description of the government-led reforms in Britain during the 1980s. To talk of a Thatcher 'project' makes a good deal of sense, in the same way that Tony Blair used to talk about the New Labour project. This parallel is particularly relevant. From early on in his time in Downing Street, people began to talk about Blairism, consciously making the comparison with Thatcherism. Mr Blair even tried to give it some philosophical basis, taking part with Bill Clinton and other political leaders of the centre left in seminars devoted to what they called the Third Way. But like Thatcherism this had a way of slipping out of their fingers when they tried to nail it down. Opponents called it Blurism.

For a philosophy to have validity it must not be restricted by time or place. Political philosophies, no matter how impressive those who inspire them may be, have to pass far more rigorous tests than political projects, however ambitious and radical. On this basis it is not surprising that Winston Churchill did not have an ism named after him; he was a brilliant practical politician at his best when he inspired the country in the fight against Hitler. Calling this Churchillism would have achieved nothing. In the far less dangerous, less critical period of the 1980s and '90s it was convenient to describe the politics of Margaret Thatcher as Thatcherism. But this was not a universal creed or even a description of how politics should be practised; and now that Labour have left in place most of the Thatcher reforms, its relevance to everyday political argument has quickly faded. Thatcherism as an all-purpose label has passed its sell-by date. Politics has moved on.

30

The fatal legacy

CHRIS PATTEN'S off-the-cuff remark at a party that Lady Thatcher had 'destroyed the Conservative party' helped to determine the theme for this book. But after speaking to him only briefly I needed to work out the full implications of his accusation. It is a serious charge and I have been keen to weigh the evidence. To argue that Lady Thatcher left a 'fatal legacy' is an easier task. Wrong intent does not have to be proved; we merely have to describe the problems she left to her successors and determine the extent to which they were fatal. Someone leaving a bequest is not responsible for what those who inherit do with the money. An important part of the Thatcher legacy is there for all to see: the Conservatives were fatally wounded in electoral terms. A political generation of ambitious Tories have been denied office. The most impressive vote-winning machine in Europe – as it was once described – has gone. There may be a new dawn, but the party which emerges will not be the same as the old one.

According to the unwritten British constitution – that is to say the way our politics ought to work – the prime minister and the cabinet are collectively responsible for the decisions made in the name of the government. Neither civil servants, foreign powers or greedy speculators are expected to take the blame if things go wrong, although in practice many reasons are advanced as to why those formally held responsible should be allowed off the hook. But some matters – and without doubt that includes the decision to join the ERM – cannot be put casually to one side. It would have been possible for Mrs Thatcher to tell her new chancellor John Major that she had not changed her mind, and that Britain should stay out of the ERM. I find Mr Major's argument that in this situation he would not have resigned but would have obeyed her instructions very persuasive indeed. Douglas Hurd's contention that she had simply been 'worn down' over this issue by senior members of the government and by her two previous chancellors may well be true, but that does not release her from the responsibility.

The ERM decision and the political fallout when the pound was ejected were the key reasons why Mr Major lost authority and why the public ceased to believe in his government's economic competence. Another, more inspired, prime minister might have been able to restore confidence and conceivably win the following election, although the government's small parliamentary majority – and a resurgent Labour party – would have made that very unlikely. Much would have depended on the European issue, and it appears that a solution which could hold the Conservative party together simply did not exist. The more the Euro-sceptics were satisfied, the more the pro-Europeans would have been disaffected. Lady Thatcher has to take the blame for undermining Mr Major, not just over Europe but over a wide range of issues; and she had of course played a large part in ensuring he was there in the first place. Without her strong support, he might have been left in the whips' office where, some of his critics suggest, his considerable talents might have been better employed.

The way the politics of the Conservative party and the composition of its leadership changed during this period was greatly affected by Lady Thatcher. Many of her early battles were fought against the old Tory establishment, who may have been more open to constructive compromise and less earnest about political theory, but were also snobbish and unfairly suspicious of Lady Thatcher, not least because she was a woman. It is sometimes said that the most important difference between them was that they talked about Conservative principles, while she put them into practice. For many, her period in office is one of the most impressive achievements in the history of the Conservative party. Her influence continued long after she left Downing Street. The Conservatives became distinctly more Euro-sceptic and distinctly more ideological. Lady Thatcher's battle honours include victories for John Major, William Hague and Iain Duncan-Smith, who all made it to the top as a result of her help; and also defeats for Michael Heseltine, Kenneth Clarke and Michael Portillo, who all failed to become leader as a direct consequence of her intervention.

Mrs Thatcher found it very difficult to admit that in the short term, after she had been dismissed, the fortunes of the Conservative party improved. Although the European issue was crucial in her removal, her declining electoral appeal was the deciding issue for most Tory MPs. The poll tax had proved her undoing. But it was also true that the public had grown bored with her after eleven years of almost non-stop publicity. Seeing Mr Major's more consensual, less aggressive brand of Conservatism begin to take hold irritated her and undoubtedly increased the tension between them. She was more strident in defence of her ism the more she felt it might be passing into history. She fastened on to the European issue because she wanted to remain relevant, and, in her view, if that created her problems with Mr Major that was something they would both have to live with. Her sense of loyalty had been greatly diminished by the manner of her removal.

It would all have been much easier if Mrs Thatcher had been able to find an alternative to politics as a subject for most of her thoughts. She had few other interests and rejected any suggestion that she should retire. It was not in her nature. Six months after she resigned she paid a rare visit to the Royal Opera House at Covent Garden, but did not enjoy the performance of *Carmen* even though she was in the comfort of the royal box. The ROH general director, Jeremy Isaacs, found her distinctly unenthusiastic; after years of high-powered activity she found it very difficult to wind down. When it came to the big political issues of the day she simply could not resist getting involved, and visitors to her office often noticed how she used the Ceefax news service on television to keep up with the latest news. A restless, wounded former prime minister who still felt perfectly fit was hardly likely to keep out of the public eye, and there was an enormous demand for her opinions not just in Britain but abroad.

According to those in a position to know, there was no decline in her intellectual capabilities for a long time after she left office. As party chairman in the two years before Mr Major was defeated in the 1997 election, Sir Brian Mawhinney was in regular touch with Lady Thatcher; he talked to her in great detail about the political issues of the day. When I spoke to him in the summer of 2004 I asked him about the problems which were beginning to affect Lady Thatcher, particularly her loss of memory. Had there been any sign of this in the period when he had worked with her? 'Not at all,' he replied emphatically. 'She was very interested in what was going on; she was well abreast of events. She had a good memory, and her insights were succinct.' I think it would be a mistake to believe that declining health was a factor in her approach to important issues. She maintained such a high profile for so long because she was capable of doing so; and when she could not perform to her usual high standards in public, the decision was taken that she should retire.

It was only after Mrs Thatcher had left office in 1990 that she was able to appreciate the full intensity of the public response to her – as an individual and not just as the holder of the most important office in the country. Being treated as a superstar and guarded round the clock hardly encourages a balanced view of one's role in the world. In such an atmosphere it is much easier to imagine that you do embody an ism and that you are usually right in all your political judgements. Lady Thatcher's stardom was an awful burden on Mr Major. He was endlessly compared with her, almost always to his disadvantage. Thatcherism became a personality cult. It did not offer Mr Major a clear path through the practical political dilemmas he faced.

For Lady Thatcher, it is only fair to say that little was done to help her come to terms with the blow she had suffered by being dismissed from office. It would have been quite different, if like James Callaghan, she had been removed at a general election. The fact that she could have stayed in office but for the votes of her MPs and the lack of support among her cabinet was very difficult for the Conservative party as a whole to come to terms with, let alone Lady Thatcher herself. Relations with Mr Major would have improved if he had routinely praised her work, perhaps at the beginning of important speeches on policy. But he could not bring himself to do that. He was desperately keen to establish his own distinctive position; as his former press secretary Sir Christopher Meyer put it: 'He would have been happier if she had not existed.' Another who worked closely with Mr Major says that he has been 'scarred for life' as a result of his experiences at Number 10.

Chris Patten worked very closely with both Lady Thatcher and Mr Major. I interviewed him in 2003 in Westminster, at the headquarters of the European Commission in London, some time after our encounter at the party in west London. Speaking formally now, on the record, he explained how Lady Thatcher had 'wrecked' the Conservative party. Referring to the way she had initially supported Mr Major, he said, 'She blessed him as her philosophical successor, which was a huge surprise to anybody who knew his views, and at the same time dealt him a completely duff hand.' While acknowledging her successes as a prime minister he commented, 'Part of the price that was paid for her style of government was to wreck the Conservative Party for ten, fifteen years, whatever.' Mr Patten is convinced she could have acted in a far more positive way after she left office. 'I think that she encouraged the suicidal element in the Conservative party and in the media. I think she should have thrown buckets of cold water over people like Charles Moore [editor of the *Daily Telegraph*] and discouraged the more rabid commentators of the right. The curiosity about Margaret is [that] she became more radical and fundamentalist out of office than she had been in. Most politicians when they leave active politics become mellower and see both sides of the argument.' Lady Thatcher's actions, in his view, helped to prolong 'the nervous breakdown' the Conservatives suffered over the European issue.

John Major is also convinced that the party's desperate struggle over this issue could have been avoided, but he believes some disagreement was inevitable. He told me, 'I don't think it is just Margaret. It is the issue of Europe as well. The Conservative party is a constitutional party. For us the loss of any sovereignty, the transfer of any sovereignty, is a particularly painful business. We've had "ultras" on Europe from the onset of the debate on the Common Market. It became a much bigger problem after the 1992 election because the big majority disappeared and pragmatic, broadly pro-European Tories retired and were replaced by less pragmatic Tories, a number of whom were violently anti-European.' When I asked Mr Major whether this battle had had to be so 'incredibly divisive' he was unequivocal. 'Of course it didn't,' he replied. 'In previous years it hadn't been so divisive, but the fact that we had no majority led people to believe they could change the policy. Normally in the Conservative party dissent is not respectable. The constituencies don't like it.'

Mr Major believes that Lady Thatcher took such a strong view on Europe because with a largely Euro-sceptic press and a large section of the party holding the same view, it gave her an attractive platform. Her circle of advisers encouraged her; and there was the flattery of those who said, 'What a shame you are not still there – you were right.' When I put to Mr Major the view of some Euro-sceptics that Mrs Thatcher had put country before party, he could hardly have been more dismissive: 'I've never heard such nonsense.' He argued that whatever internal differences they may have had, the policies of the Conservative party were far closer to Lady Thatcher's views than those of the Labour party. 'The reality of the matter is that for all our differences the Conservative party were closer to Margaret's view; and it was hardly logical to put in power a Labour party that was far more integrationist. Where was the logic in that? There was no sense in destroying the government that was closest to their view.' The split over Europe, according to Mr Major, left 'a legacy of bitterness'. It made the Conservatives 'unelectable'.

ALLIES OF LADY THATCHER, of course, take an entirely different view. In my interview with Lord Tebbit, he said she had only acted in the way she had because Mr Major 'was pursuing the policies that he was'. It was also 'his attitude of wanting to distance himself all the time from the Thatcher period'. The most interesting point Lord Tebbit made was the extent to which some Tories were prepared to put up with a Labour government. Speaking in 2003, he told me that Tony Blair had become the 'worst prime minister of my lifetime', but in the run-up to the 1997 election there had been a lack of enthusiasm in fighting for Mr Major, and that view had been shared by Lady Thatcher. 'A lot of us thought that Blair can't be that bad.' The argument over Europe, Lord Tebbit agrees, made matters more difficult, 'but that was the choice which John Major made by his decision to go against his own party on Europe'. Lord Tebbit is convinced that Mr Major should take the blame. 'The party was against Maastricht. The party was against the single currency and the party had realized that ERM stands for Eternal Recession Mechanism. So you couldn't blame those of us who supported the party for sounding a bit unenthusiastic about Major.'

The former chancellor and Euro-sceptic Lord Lamont accepts that Lady Thatcher played a significant role in encouraging the Tory rebellion over Europe. 'They thought, Lady Thatcher, one of the greatest prime ministers of this country, agrees with us. So obviously it gave them legitimacy and confidence.' He believes there were faults on both sides in the way Mr Major and Lady Thatcher treated each other. 'I think she felt the people who were running the government were all in short trousers, and weren't up to it. I think she probably shouldn't have said as much as she did. But on the other hand I think the prime minister was oversensitive about it.' On the broader question of the split over Europe, he rejects comparisons with the internal dispute which rocked the Labour party in the early 1980s over the issue of unilateral nuclear disarmament. 'Unilateralism,' he told me in 2003, 'was wrong; it was irrational. Opposition to the single currency is rational, well-grounded and felt by the majority of people in this country. The Conservative party has paid a price in terms of office, but it has also gained a prize: it has won the argument, converted the country, and has a gridlock on the single currency issue today.'

But the polling evidence suggests that the public may not have been swayed very much by the long struggle of the Tory Euro-sceptics. The electorate seems to have decided very early on that they were against Britain joining a single currency, and their views did not alter much as the debate raged within the Conservative party. From 1991 until the end of the period covered by this book, according to opinion polls carried out by Mori, there was always a large majority against Britain joining the euro. Of those prepared to express an opinion, support never rose above 40 per cent, and opposition never fell below 60 per cent. Although the Euro-sceptics and pro-Europeans often behaved as if opinion was on a knife-edge, and they were fighting for the future of their country, the mood of the voters always appeared remarkably settled. As careers at Westminster soared and crashed with the twists and turns of this complicated debate, on the issue itself the public were largely unmoved.

Iain Duncan Smith, who became Conservative leader in 2001, agrees with the Mori findings that the arguments over Europe did not sway public opinion. 'As a general subject,' he told me in 2003, 'it doesn't sway their vote. As a specific issue, if they are about to enter the single currency, that is different. But I had to get the party to understand that what we said didn't much change their voting pattern.' He agreed that most people believed, more than ten years after Mrs Thatcher was ousted, that the Tories were still obsessed and obsessive about Europe, and this he was trying to change. 'Let's just treat it like any other issue,' he told me in an interview carried out a few months before Tory MPs decided they could not win under his leadership. 'We will resolve the issue over Europe in the way we have resolved every other issue. We will try to get a collective view about this, and calm down.'

It is ironic that the politician calling for the Conservative party to calm down about Europe was a Maastricht diehard whose career had flourished as a result of his Euro-scepticism. Another Tory who became famous as a result of his opposition to the Maastricht Treaty is not prepared to see the issue dwindle in importance. Bill Cash is unapologetic about his role in undermining Mr Major's leadership; he is convinced it was a battle for principle, not party advantage. If there had been no rebellion over Maastricht, he believes, the Conservative party would have become increasingly devoted to European integration. He told me, 'The Conservative party would actually lose its natural reason for existence, which is to support the democratic right of the British people to govern themselves. You have to fight the battles when they actually occur, and when they are matters of principle.' He disputes the suggestion that they should have let the Maastricht bill go through the Commons: 'It's no good saying "Oh, well, if we'd allowed it to go through we could have retrieved the situation." That would have been fool's gold.'

Retired prime ministers have the luxury of not having to worry about fighting elections or smoothing over the hurt feelings of senior colleagues; they simply have to fight for their reputations. But where they do exercise power, they should expect to be judged in much the same way as if they were in office. Lord Wakeham may well be right when he argues that Lady Thatcher did not consider she was actively undermining John Major – she was merely promoting herself and her own ideas; but in the world in which she operated for so many years, that distinction is not accepted. Politics is primarily concerned about the effects of an action; inferences are then drawn as to who should be held responsible. It is not enough to say that someone did not mean to hurt anyone else. Politicians show their skill by working out in advance what the effects of their actions will be; and they are judged accordingly. While the Tories suffered the consequences of Lady Thatcher's fatal legacy, Tony Blair was basking in the advantages of his Tory inheritance. Lady Thatcher's favourite words – choice, opportunity, competition – were hijacked by New Labour; and who could be keener than Mr Blair on promoting the need for strong armed forces and the importance of law and order? Much of the Thatcher legacy was alive and well, even if a large part of it had proved fatal to the Conservatives.

IN JULY 2004, for the first time, my wife Mary and I were invited to a Buckingham Palace garden party. This was indirectly because I was that year's president of the Johnson Society, based in Dr Johnson's home town of Lichfield. In my inaugural speech, at a dinner in the town hall, I had described how the great man had attempted to become one of the first ever parliamentary reporters – by making up most of the speeches himself. In those days reporters were not given access to the House of Commons. At the dinner we were introduced to the lord lieutenant of Staffordshire, who kindly suggested to the Palace that we should be invited to the garden party. It turned out to be a strange and moving occasion. There were no speeches and almost all of the thousands of guests were unknown to us; maybe there were a lot of presidents of literary societies, but we could not be sure. The Queen and the Duke of Edinburgh were on display; the sun shone, and there was plenty of cakes and tea.

'Hello, Mr Sergeant,' said a tall, well-built man in a grey suit whom I immediately took to be a police protection officer; over the years I have come to recognize their distinguishing features. They are always very fit, and keep glancing around at the crowd. He was pleased with what he had to say to me: 'Do you know that Lady Thatcher is here?' He pointed to the VIP tent in the distance, and as we hurried over to take a look, he shouted after me, 'Perhaps you could finish that interview with her . . .' He was of course referring to my encounter with her on the steps of the embassy in Paris. My requests for interviews with Lady Thatcher had been turned down over the previous two years. Her daughter Carol had told me personally she was not well enough to talk to me. But I was keen to see her, even from afar.

Mary spotted her first in a small group at one end of the marquee. 'Look, can't you see? It's the way she's standing.' I had to get closer, and then the unmistakable shape of the former prime minister came into focus. She was wearing a light summer outfit with a hat, and a matching handbag, clasped firmly as usual in her left hand. She looked very good for seventy-eight: slim and perfectly balanced on her high heels. Her chin jutted out in a characteristic pose. She was speaking in an animated fashion to the outgoing secretary general of NATO, the Labour peer Lord Robertson. We were too far away to get any idea of what they might be saying, but it made a cheering scene. For thirty years I had followed her closely and this was perhaps the last time I would see her. And what were my feelings towards her? I looked on her as you might on a famous film star, with familiarity, and a good deal of awe.

Index

Adams, Gerry 324
Alexandria 261
Anatomy of Thatcherism, The (Letwin) 357
Ancram, Michael 342
Anglo-Irish agreement 354–5
Anti-Federalist League 228
Archer, Lord Jeffrey 62, 142, 155,
   205–6, 307, 320
Argentina 21, 22
Armstrong, Robert 49
Ashdown, Paddy 146, 223
asylum seekers 339
Attlee, Clement 12, 18, 162–3, 166

Baker, James 181
Baker, Lord Kenneth 83, 100, 139, 174,
   236, 243, 257, 293, 319
Baldwin, Stanley 195
Bank of England 15, 334
Beckett, Margaret 300
Bell, Martin 324
Benn, Tony 22, 30, 88, 228, 265, 274
Bennett, Alan 141
Berkeley, Humphrey 113–15
Berlin Wall, fall of 84–5
Black Watch (cruise ship) 1–2, 5–6, 11
Black Wednesday 250, 251–4, 255, 256,
   257, 258, 279, 280
Blair, Tony 37, 234
   benefits from Tory inheritance
     369–70
   Blairism 358–9
   European policy 332, 334, 338
   Iraq crisis 15, 16, 24–5, 48, 183, 241

'modernization' of Labour party
   314–15
and Mrs Thatcher
   believes she would have won in
     1992 222–3
   compared with 13–14, 321
   her influence on 302–3
   on her resignation 143
   interviewed about 9, 12, 14–18,
     23–5, 28–9, 302, 350
   relationship with 16, 331–2
relationship with Gordon Brown 41,
   64, 299
relationship with media 12–13, 334
strains of office 14, 15
wins 1997 election 323
wins 2001 election 341
wins leadership contest 299–302
Body, Sir Richard 287
Bosnia 289, 306
Bournemouth 102, 103, 104, 105
Bowman, Dame Elaine Kellet 145
Boyson, Sir Rhodes 244
Brighton bomb 126, 143, 185
British Rail 354
Brittan, Leon 21, 47–8, 316
Brown, Gordon
   as chancellor of the exchequer 334
   on Mrs Thatcher's achievements 350
   as prospective leader of Labour party
     299, 300
   relationship with Tony Blair 41, 64,
     299
   as shadow chancellor 249
Bruges 74–5, 191, 192

Bruges Group 75, 189, 197
Brunei, sultan of 187
Brunson, Michael 281
BSE 324
Bush, George 17, 116, 158, 181–2, 183, 289
Bush, George W. 183
Butler, R. A. B. 347
Butler, Sir Robin 139
Butskellism 347

Cairo 260, 261
Callaghan, Lord James 13, 18, 32, 67, 119, 143, 146, 194–5, 258–9, 310
Cammell Laird 44–5, 135
Campaign for Nuclear Disarmament 44
Campbell, Alastair 13, 37
Cannes 312
Carlisle, John 256
Carrington, Lord Peter 10, 33, 153
Cartiss, Michael 268–9
Cash, Bill 277, 278, 282, 319–20, 368–9
Castle, Lady Barbara 30, 53–4
Chirac, Jacques 347
Churchill, Winston 145–6
Churchill, Sir Winston S. 10, 18, 27, 93, 137, 162, 194, 197, 260, 267, 348, 350, 359
Clark, Alan 118–19, 133, 293
Clarke, Charles 178
Clarke, Kenneth 130, 131, 132–3, 137, 252, 262
    as chancellor of the exchequer 279, 306, 312, 319, 334
    as contender for leadership 266, 280, 297, 325, 326, 327–30, 342–4, 362
    declines to serve under Hague 330
    as education secretary 175
    as home secretary 236
    interviewed about Mrs Thatcher 127, 194
    relationship with Mrs Thatcher 193, 280, 326, 343–4, 362
Clarke–Redwood alliance 327–8, 329
Clause 4 314

Cleese, John 106
Clinton, Bill 16, 302, 303, 331, 334, 359
Coates, Gwen 165–6, 168, 172
Cockfield, Lord Arthur 52–3, 56–7
Cole, John 87, 108
Collins, Tim 291
communism 349, 354
Community Charge *see* poll tax
Conference on Security and Cooperation in Europe 116–17
Conservative Central Office 158, 232, 321, 338, 339
Conservative party
    cliques and factions 238
    conferences
        1990 102, 103, 104–5
        1991 204–7
        1992 256–7
        1993 288, 289–91
        1994 304
        1995 315–16
        1996 320
    divided over Europe 75, 105, 140, 148, 180–1, 190, 208, 228, 239, 244, 262–3, 265, 275–6, 283, 320–1, 324, 344, 365–6, 368
    divisions weaken British politics 8
    elections
        1979 31–2
        1997 320–1, 322–5
        2001 335–41
        leadership 8, 86, 113–15, 117–18, 122–3, 142, 156, 325–30, 342–4
    and Mrs Thatcher
        cause of ideological rift in 238–9
        hasn't got over her downfall 7
        her legacy to 360, 365–6, 369, 370
        newspapers declare against (2001) 340
Conservative Way Forward group 189, 304
council house sales 351, 354
Council Tax 180
Crawford, Cynthia 125

Currie, Edwina 142, 169–71
customs dues 35

Daily Telegraph 343
Dardanelles campaign 93
Davis, David 156, 342
de Gaulle, Charles 163, 347
Delors, Jacques 73–4
Denmark, Maastricht referenda 242, 243,
    268, 274, 279, 283
devaluation 99, 254, 258, 334
devolution 15, 335
Dewar, Donald 231, 298
Dimbleby, Jonathan 340–1
Dimbleby, Richard 341
Downing Street Years, The (Thatcher) 285,
    288–9, 291, 292–5
Drum, Kitty 165
Dublin 36
Duncan, Alan 328
Duncan Smith, Iain 368
    as Conservative party leader 344
    as contender for leadership 342–4,
        362
    forced to resign 151, 345
    as rebel MP 264–5, 319
Dykes, Hugh 275

East Germany 247
Eastbourne by-election 1990 106
Economist, The 189, 287–8
Ecu, hard 108–9, 112
Edinburgh, Prince Philip, Duke of 370
Edinburgh summit 305
Egypt 260–1
El Alamein, Battle of 260, 261
electoral system, British 238
Elizabeth II, Queen 102–3, 130, 145,
    242, 315, 370
Elizabeth, the Queen Mother 143
Euro-sceptics 54, 73, 74–5, 101, 109,
    180, 217, 238, 242, 324, 325, 328,
    330, 341, 344, 361, 367–8
    call for Major to resign 285, 297, 319
    and ejection from ERM 254, 256
    in House of Lords 244, 280

and Maastricht Treaty 211, 218–19,
    240, 243, 249, 283, 356
    open rebellion over 257, 262,
        265, 266–9, 275–9, 281–2,
        365–6
    Referendum Party 233, 315, 321
    want single currency ruled out 311
European Assembly 53, 55
European Commission 9, 57, 63, 73, 74,
    241
European Communities (Amendment)
    Bill 276, 277
European Court 56, 59, 63, 319
European Economic Community
    Britain joins 30, 31, 68
    budget 34–6, 37
    other members' emotional attachment
        to 35
European Foundation 319–20
European Monetary System 67
European Parliament 55, 80–1
European Union 26, 52–3, 199–200,
    210, 240, 338
    presidency of 106–7
Exchange Rate Mechanism 68, 71–3,
    78–9, 81, 92, 111, 245, 247–57,
    259, 292, 332–3, 367
    Britain's entry 60, 97–100, 101, 103,
        104–5, 176, 353, 354, 360–1
    pound ejected from 175, 246, 253–4,
        324, 334, 345, 361

Fahd, King of Saudi Arabia 182
Falkland Islands 21–2, 24–5, 36
fascism 349
Field, Frank 135–6, 173–4
Finchley constituency 141, 225
Finland, devaluation 251
Fontainebleau 37
Foot, Michael 228, 310
Ford, Mrs Henry 185
Forsyth, Michael 319, 330
Fowler, Sir Norman 290
France
    protectionism 56
    referendum on Maastricht 251, 256

G7 173–4
Gaddafi, Colonel 96
Gaitskell, Hugh 298, 310, 347
Gallipoli 93, 260
Galtieri, General 22
Garel-Jones, Tristan 87, 119, 216
Genscher, Hans-Dietrich 85
Germany
    high interest rates in 247, 251
    reunification of 85, 96, 247, 354
Gilmour, Lord Ian 22
Gingrich, Newt 315
Giscard d'Estaing, Valéry 347
Goldsmith, Sir James 233, 315, 320
Good Friday Agreement 334
Goodlad, Alastair 331
Gorbachev, Mikhail 5, 69, 76, 85, 116,
    354
Gorman, Teresa 287
Gould, Philip 15
Gow, Ian 106
Grantham, Lincolnshire 26–7, 28, 354
Greig, Gordon 156
Guardian 141
Gulf War 1991 179–81, 221
Gulf War, Second 2003 183
Gummer, John 133–4, 146, 156,
    199–201

Hague, Ffion 339
Hague, William
    becomes leader of Conservative party
        330
    as contender for leadership 325–6,
        327, 328–30, 362
    relationship with Mrs Thatcher 264,
        326, 329, 330–1, 335, 338
    damaged by 341
    resigns as leader 342
    on single European currency 338,
        339
    supports Major's leadership bid 156
Hamilton, Neil 324
Hampson, Keith 86
handbags 3, 4, 17, 49, 124, 211
Hanover 73

Hanrahan, Brian 176
HarperCollins 187
Hattersley, Roy 230
Hatton, Derek 90–1
Haymarket Press 41–2, 50
Healey, Denis 65
Heath, Sir Edward 42, 115, 116, 164,
        173, 205, 207, 262–3
    on European issue 30–1, 192, 214
    relationship with Mrs Thatcher 29,
        32, 34, 115, 193, 226, 236,
        271–2, 311
Heseltine, Anne 49
Heseltine, Lord Michael
    appearance 40
    contends leadership 4, 51, 103–4,
        112, 116, 117, 118, 122, 129,
        136, 143, 147, 149–54, 209,
        266, 325, 326, 362
    as deputy prime minister 314
    as environment secretary 174,
        179–81
    personal wealth 150
    and poll tax 174, 180, 197
    position on Europe 176, 219, 252,
        268, 319
    relationship with John Major
        179–80, 313
    relationship with Mrs Thatcher
        40–51, 63, 291, 293, 316, 320
        interviewed about 41–3, 50, 341
        role in her downfall 40, 86, 102,
            124, 125, 139, 149, 151,
            153
    resigns from cabinet 49–50
    speech at 1991 conference 205,
        206–7
    as trade and industry secretary 235,
        236
    Westland Affair 46–50, 206, 239
Hislop, Ian 141
Hofstra University, New York 349
Hogg, Sarah 191
Home, Sir Alec Douglas 114, 115, 163,
        173
House of Commons, smallness of 7

House of Lords, reform of 335
Howard, Anthony 113–14
Howard, Michael 28, 133, 156, 167, 217, 237, 276, 329
  becomes Conservative leader 10, 151, 345–6
  as contender for leadership 326–7
  as shadow foreign secretary 330
Howe, Lord Geoffrey 153, 214
  as chancellor of the exchequer 20, 66
  and Exchange Rate Mechanism 72–3, 79, 81, 98, 100, 103
  as foreign secretary 68, 171
  as leader of the House of Commons and deputy prime minister 82, 97, 102–3
  position on Europe 30, 107
  relationship with Mrs Thatcher 63, 64–8, 69, 70, 82, 92–3, 103, 108, 293
  and her downfall 102, 111–12
  influence on 'Thatcherism' 351
  resignation 110–12, 116, 117, 140, 209, 246
Hunt, David 153
Hurd, Lord Douglas
  as contender for leadership 132–3, 142, 143, 152, 154–5, 156, 171, 266
  as foreign secretary 85, 174–5, 182–3, 211–12, 236, 312
  interviewed about Mrs Thatcher 10, 58, 70, 273, 361
  position on Europe 176, 240–1, 243, 252, 257, 268, 277
  relationship with Mrs Thatcher 186–7
  on 'Thatcherism' 357–8
Hussein, Saddam
  invasion of Kuwait 17, 131, 158, 175, 181–3
  supply of arms to 324

individualism 349, 350
inflation 99, 105, 111, 116, 140, 250, 334, 354

Ingham, Sir Bernard 3, 6–7, 13, 37, 47, 69, 117–18, 122, 123, 124, 134, 139, 203, 225, 236, 345, 356
interest rates 98, 99, 100, 101, 105, 151, 245, 247–8, 249, 251, 252, 253, 255, 256, 259, 334, 354
IRA 106, 143
Iraq
  crisis 2003–4 15, 16, 24–5, 48, 183, 241
  invasion of Kuwait 17, 131, 158, 175, 181, 289
Ireland
  Anglo-Irish agreement 354–5
  supports Maastricht in referendum 244
Isaacs, Jeremy 363
Italy
  devaluation 251
  presidency of European Union 106–7

Japan 285–8
Jay, Peter 176, 177
Jenkin, Bernard 266
Jenkins, Lord Roy 30, 208
Johnson, Lyndon B. 163
Johnson, Paul 266–7, 318–19
Johnson Society 370
Joseph, Sir Keith 316, 340, 351, 357

Kaletsky, Anatole 255
Kaufman, Gerald 22
Keays, Sara 59
Kennedy, John F. 163
Kerr, Sir John 215–16
Khrushchev, Nikita 341
Kinnock, Neil 72, 91, 145, 146, 162, 178, 214, 221–2, 223, 228–9, 230–1, 234, 235, 249, 310
Kohl, Helmut 73, 76, 77–8, 85, 94, 107, 116, 182, 191, 197, 247, 253, 288
Konrad Adenauer Foundation 191
Kosovo 15–16, 24, 335
Kuwait, invasion of 17, 131, 158, 175, 181–3, 289

Labour party
  death of John Smith 297–9
  divisions in 22, 24, 208, 228, 238,
    239
  forced to change by 1992 election
    234
  landslide victories 1997 and 2001 8,
    322, 336, 341
  manifesto 1979 19–20
  manifesto 1983 22
  position on Europe 36–7, 227–8, 334
  Sheffield Arena rally 1992 230–1
  Tony Blair elected leader 300–2
Lamont, Lord Norman
  calls for his resignation over Black
    Wednesday 258–9
  as chancellor of the exchequer
    175–6, 216–17, 219, 248, 250,
    252–3, 254, 256, 257
  contends leadership 312
  loses seat in 1997 324
  as Major's campaign manager 155–6,
    159
  on Mrs Thatcher's role in Tory
    rebellion 367
  sacked 279
  and single European currency 242–3
  support for William Hague 330
Lawson, Dominic 94
Lawson, Lord Nigel 111, 153
  as chancellor of the exchequer 63,
    64, 71–3, 79–80, 91, 97, 98,
    255, 292
    resigns 82–4, 140, 152, 175–6
  opposition to single European
    currency 214
  relationship with Mrs Thatcher 68–9,
    71–3, 79–80, 92–3, 97, 100,
    293
    influence on 'Thatcherism' 351
Letwin, Oliver 357
Letwin, Shirley Robin 357
Liberal Democrats 106, 228, 246, 278
Lilley, Peter 167, 237, 243, 274–5, 329
  as contender for leadership 326, 327
  as shadow chancellor 330

Luff, Peter 318
Luxembourg 52, 54, 55

Maastricht 214–15
Maastricht Treaty 228, 239–45, 251,
    255, 256, 260–1, 270, 272
  calls for referendum on 219, 242,
    244, 245, 273–4, 280
  Conservatives split over 219–20,
    240–5, 262–9, 283, 367–9
  debate prior to 210–14
  Labour position on 228, 334
  legislation 240–2, 244–5, 249, 254,
    257, 262–3, 275, 276, 277,
    278, 280–1
  negotiation of opt out clauses
    215–19, 356
  Single European Act precursor to 54,
    63
  votes on 262–9, 281–2
McAlpine, Lord 232, 233, 310
McGregor, John 129
McKay, Lord 139
Macleod, Iain 114
Macmillan, Harold 12, 39, 114, 163
Major, John
— *character and attributes*
  ambition and determination 172
  cautious 284
  charm and use of tactile gestures
    42, 61, 167–8, 172, 198,
    308
  image 162, 164–5, 295, 304–5
  reads body language 196
  sensitive nature 196, 367
  strengths 236
  temper tantrums 286
— *earlier career*
  becomes MP 167
  as Mrs Thatcher's chancellor 64, 84,
    97, 102, 108–9, 112, 156, 171,
    292
  as Mrs Thatcher's foreign secretary
    82, 156, 171–2
  rise to power at Westminster 168–9
  as a whip 292–3, 361

— *and Europe* 178–9, 191–2, 197,
          210–11, 214, 278, 287–8
at odds with members of own party
          239, 242, 243–5, 256, 274–6,
          282, 287, 305, 307, 308,
          365–6, 367, 369
'bastards' conversation 282, 284
comment on Euro-sceptics in cabinet
          282, 284
confidence motions 281, 305
considers resignation 254, 259, 267,
          285–6, 314
and Exchange Rate Mechanism
          97–9, 101, 104, 176, 245, 250,
          253–4, 292, 332–3, 361
federalism 240, 241, 268
Maastricht Treaty 215–20, 241,
          243–5, 260–9, 274–6, 281,
          332
Rome summit 1990 177–8
single European currency 211,
          212–14, 217, 241, 288,
          311–12, 319, 332
Social Chapter 214, 217, 241
— *leadership election* 1990
as contender 102, 105–6, 132–3,
          136, 142, 143, 152–3, 154–60
wins ballot 159–60
— *personal life*
affair with Edwina Currie 142,
          169–71
background 102, 164, 165–7
— *as prime minister*
abandons failed Thatcher policies
          202
abolishes poll tax 189–90, 222
attempts to unify party 314–16
'back to basics' speech 171, 291–2,
          308, 324
bunker mentality sets in 307–8
chooses cabinet 173–6
collapse of economic policy 254, 256,
          258, 279, 283, 324, 361
Conservative conference 1991 207
Conservative conference 1993 291–2
Conservative conference 1996 320

disappointment to Thatcherites
          192–3
establishes own position 161–2, 235,
          364
Gulf War 1991 181–3
hindered by small majority 13, 237,
          305, 307, 361, 365
IRA mortar attack on 14
leadership challenge 1995 312–14
loses 1997 election 320–1
loses trust of the electorate 283–4,
          303, 324, 361
Northern Ireland policy 324, 335,
          358
physical strain of office on 332
relationship with George Bush 182
relationship with media 178, 196,
          260, 285–7, 291, 306–7
relationship with Michael Heseltine
          179–80, 313, 314
relationship with Norman Lamont
          252, 254, 259, 279, 330
sterling crisis 250–1, 252–6, 258
style of leadership 163, 178–9,
          198–9, 253, 270–1, 284, 362
tribute to John Smith 297, 298
visits Egypt 260–1
visits Japan 285–8
visits Poland 303
visits South Africa 303–4
wins 1992 election 222–3, 227,
          228–9, 231–3
— *relationship with Mrs Thatcher* 136,
          168–9, 171–2, 197–8, 224,
          293, 317, 320, 332–3, 362,
          364–5
attempts to improve 316, 320
compared to 283–5, 304–5, 364
considers offering her cabinet post
          173–4
criticized in her memoirs 288–9,
          292–5
as her chancellor 84, 97, 100, 108–9
as her foreign secretary 82, 171–2
interviewed about 9, 60–3, 98–100,
          351–2

Index

Major, John (*cont.*)
    leadership undermined by 61, 62,
        188, 192–5, 196–7, 202, 204,
        225, 227, 233, 235–6, 306–8,
        316–19, 361, 365–6, 369
        on Europe 192, 213, 245, 257,
          263–4, 270–3, 311
    she questions his loyalty 293
    weighed down by her legacy 283–4,
        295, 303
— *since 1997 election*
    fears he will be overlooked by history
        332
    memoirs 234, 291, 332
    stands down as party leader 323
Major, Norma 159, 167, 170, 231, 298
Major, Tom 165–6
Mandelson, Peter 228
Mates, Michael 46, 47, 49, 51, 151–2
Maude, Francis 156, 219
Mawhinney, Sir Brian 315, 316, 320,
    363
Mayhew, Sir Patrick 48, 168
Meyer, Sir Anthony 86–7, 116
Meyer, Sir Christopher 306–8, 364
Mid-Staffordshire by-election 1990 91
Millar, Ronald 33
Milošević, Slobodan 15, 335
miners' strike 23, 352–3
Mitterand, François 76–7, 96, 107, 110,
    116
Moncrieff, Chris 217, 218
Montgomery, General 261
Monty Python 106
Moore, Charles 365
Moore, John 121
Morrison, Peter 118–19, 120–1, 123,
    156
Moscow 5, 69–71
Mosey, Roger 312

National Union of Mineworkers 23, 353
NATO 9
Naughtie, Ellie 11
Naughtie, James 11
Nazism 349

New Labour 24, 223, 234, 302, 358,
    369
Newbury by-election 278
Newsweek 235–6
1922 Committee 128, 319
92 group 153–4, 346
No Turning Back Group 197
Northern Ireland 324, 334, 354–5, 358

O'Donnell, Gus 286
opinion polls 91–2, 147, 154, 162, 223,
    226, 230, 231, 256, 266, 281, 303,
    307, 311, 320, 324, 336, 345
Opposition, importance of 8–9
Owen, David 67, 116

Parkinson, Lord Cecil 66, 129–30, 134,
    153, 189, 319
    in House of Lords 244, 280
    interviewed about Mrs Thatcher
        59–60, 126, 131, 221
    party chairman under Hague 330
Parris, Mathew 224–5
Path to Power, The (Thatcher) 310–11
Patten, Chris 91, 132, 167
    on Euro-sceptics 341
    as European commissioner 341
    as governor of Hong Kong 325
    interviewed about Mrs Thatcher
        92–3
    loses seat in Bath 231, 232–3
    Mrs Thatcher 'destroyed the
        Conservative party' 11, 360,
        364–5
    as party chairman 175, 205, 235
    on Thatcherism 355
Pétain, Marshal 347
Philip Morris 188
Poland 76, 303
poll tax 51, 88–93, 95, 103–4, 116, 140,
    151, 161–2, 173, 174, 179, 180,
    189–90, 222, 362
Pompidou, Georges 163
Portillo, Michael 315, 330
    as contender for leadership 313, 314,
        322–3, 325, 342–3, 362

interviewed about Mrs Thatcher
  66–7, 68, 134–5, 352–3
loses Enfield seat 322–3, 324–5
in Major's cabinet 237, 243, 275,
  319
Post Office 305
pound, the 101, 109, 216, 246, 248, 338
devaluation of 249–51, 254, 258
Powell, Lord Charles 37–8, 73, 77, 78,
  96, 171, 184, 191, 202, 209, 272,
  356
Powell, Jonathan 37
Prescott, John 300, 301, 350–1
Press Association 217
Prior, Jim 22
Private Eye 141
privatization 23, 69, 105, 140, 284, 305,
  335, 350, 354
proportional representation 238
Provisional Sinn Fein 324
Pym, Francis 8, 59, 68

QMV (qualified majority voting) 54, 56,
  58–9, 63

railways, privatization of 335, 354, 358
Raison, Timothy 168
Rawnsley, Andrew 165
Reagan, Ronald 38, 69, 76, 84, 346,
  356
Redwood, John 315, 318
contends leadership 312–14, 326,
  327–8
as shadow trade and industry secretary
  330
referendum on EEC membership 30
referendum (proposed) on joining the
  euro 212–13, 319, 338
referendum (proposed) on Maastricht
  219, 242, 244, 245, 273–4, 280
Referendum Party 233, 315, 321
Ridley, Nicholas 21, 91, 93–6, 104,
  192, 244, 292
Rifkind, Malcolm 132
Robertson, Lord 371
Rogaly, Joe 300

Rome
  Mrs Thatcher's first visits 33, 34
  summits 1990 107–9, 111, 176–8,
    190, 209, 210
Rome, Treaty of 26, 54, 107, 212
Roosevelt, Franklin D. 163
Royal Mail 305, 354
Rutlish Grammar School 166
Ryder, Richard 268

Scargill, Arthur 23, 353
Schlesinger, Dr Helmut 251
Schmidt, Helmut 36
Schultz, George 187
Scottish CBI 250
Scottish Parliament 335
Second World War 26–7
Serbia 15–16, 289, 306
Sergeant, John
  at Oxford 28
  childhood 27
  lectures on cruise ship 1–6, 11
  Mrs Thatcher hits with handbag
    (allegedly) 3, 4, 124
  professional coverage of Major
    260–2, 285–8, 312
  professional coverage of Mrs Thatcher
    5, 9, 18, 33–4, 69–71, 93,
    109–10, 122–4, 138–9, 140,
    144, 246, 371
Sergeant, Mary 2, 370, 371
Sergeant, Peter 2
Sheffield Arena, Labour rally at 230–1
Shepherd, Richard 218–19
Sherbourne, Stephen 28, 357
Sheridan, Tommy 89
Sikorsky 46, 47
Single European Act (1985) 52, 54–6,
    57–8, 59, 60, 62–3, 284, 353, 354
single European currency 55, 101,
    107–9, 175, 176, 211, 212–17,
    219, 228, 240, 241, 249, 251, 288,
    311–12, 319, 321, 324, 325, 332,
    334, 338, 339, 343–4, 367–8
Sissons, Peter 3, 123, 143
Sked, Alan 228

Skinner, Dennis 147
sleaze 292, 324
Smith, Ian 6
Smith, John 79–80, 83, 223, 229–30,
　　249, 256, 266, 301, 310
　death of 297–9
Smyth, Martin 145
Soames, Christopher 22
Social Chapter 214, 241, 278, 281, 334
Soros, George 248
South Africa 303–4
Spectator 94, 96
stalking horses 86
Statecraft (Thatcher) 345
Stock Exchange 147
Stokes, John 48
Strasbourg 53
Straw, Jack 143
Swan Hunter 44–5
Sweden, devaluation 251
Sykes, Paul 321

taxation 20–1, 229–30, 304, 339
Tbilisi 5
Tebbit, Margaret 143
Tebbit, Lord Norman 47, 81, 129, 144,
　　146, 227, 264, 275, 326
　as contender for leadership 143, 152–3
　as Euro-sceptic 213, 218, 242, 257,
　　320
　in House of Lords 244
　interviewed about Mrs Thatcher 43,
　　45–6, 58–9, 130, 209–10,
　　221–2, 366–7
　on John Major 169, 189–90
　as trade and industry secretary 44–6
Thatcher, Carol 186, 202, 232, 287,
　　333, 348, 370
Thatcher, Denis 27, 28, 122, 129, 160,
　　169, 185, 193, 202, 333, 345

THATCHER, LADY MARGARET
— *character and attributes*
　certain of her own judgement 209,
　　284
　changes of mind 353

femininity and 'sexy' side 18, 42
fine intellect and clarity of objective
　17, 23
following across the world 5, 137,
　303, 356
gift for shifting blame 63, 332–3
hands-on approach 198–9
image 37, 295, 304–5, 309, 320
loses her radiance 14–15
more pragmatic than her oratory 62,
　201, 284, 352–3
myths surrounding 352
political philosophy 350
practical politician 354–5
radical versus conservative nature 29,
　353
superstar status 364
survives on four hours sleep 125
symbolism of 356–7
well prepared 17
— *early career*
becomes leader of Conservative party
　29
election campaign 1979 32–3
junior member of Conservative party
　28
— *and Europe*
attitude to Germans 26–7, 78, 96,
　190–1, 208, 241
and British entry of EEC 30–1
as prime minister 26, 28, 32, 74–5,
　86, 108, 112
　decision to join ERM 60, 68, 71–3,
　　78–9, 81, 92, 93, 97–100,
　　255–6, 353, 354, 360–1
　and EEC budget 34–6, 37, 38
　elections to European Parliament
　　1989 80–1
　Rome summit 1990 107–9, 176,
　　177, 190, 209, 210
　and Single European Act 54–6,
　　57–60, 62–3, 353, 354
since leaving office
　anti-Maastricht campaign 244,
　　245, 262, 265, 266, 270,
　　273–4, 280

comments on exit from ERM
255–6, 257
donation to European Foundation
319–20
pursues debate 191, 192, 208–9,
211–12, 241–2, 255,
310–11, 357
views on federalism 74–5, 78, 108,
109, 111, 189, 190–1, 192,
208, 228, 289, 317, 319, 338,
344
views on single currency 107–9, 321,
332, 338, 343–4
— *personal life*
at Oxford 28
background 164
experience of Second World War
26–7, 208
health and memory problems 344–5,
346, 363
homes 185, 202
security problems 185, 294, 309, 364,
370
seventieth birthday party 315
— *as prime minister*
Anglo-American alliance 25, 38, 76,
355
attitude to the media 34, 178, 225–6
Conservative conference 1990 105–6
declining electoral appeal 362
early foreign policy 33
in Eastern Europe 76
economic policy 21
Falklands crisis 21–2
first term in office 20–2
and invasion of Kuwait 181, 182, 183
leadership challenge 1989 86–7, 116
leadership challenge 1990 112
election 'campaign' 117–19,
120–2, 123, 135
first ballot 3–4, 116–19, 122–4,
125–7, 152
miners' strike 23, 352–3
Northern Ireland policy 354–5
poll tax 51, 88–93, 173, 190, 362
second term in office 22–3

strength of her policies 19, 284, 350
visits Moscow 5, 69–71
Westland Affair 46–50
wins 1979 election 33
wins 1987 election 23, 25, 71
— *relationships*
with Douglas Hurd 186–7
with Edward Heath 29, 34, 115, 116,
192, 193, 226, 271–2, 311
with Francis Pym 8
with François Mitterand 76–7
with Geoffrey Howe 63, 64–8, 69,
70, 72–3, 79, 81–2, 92–3, 97,
100, 102–3, 108, 110–12, 293
with George Bush 17
with Helmut Kohl 73, 76, 77–8, 85,
191
with Iain Duncan Smith 342–4, 362
with John Major 168–9, 197–8, 317,
320, 332–3, 364
in 1992 election campaign 224,
225, 226–7, 235, 280
attempts to improve 316, 320
criticizes him in her memoirs
292–5
disillusioned with 202, 235, 306
endorses John Redwood challenge
on 313
as her chancellor 84, 97, 100,
108–9
as her foreign secretary 82, 171–2
possibility of cabinet post 173–4
questions his loyalty 293
reaction to his election victory
232–3, 234
supports his leadership bid 136,
157–60, 162, 193, 197,
361, 362, 364–5
undermines his leadership 61, 62,
188, 192–5, 204, 225, 233,
235–6, 283–4, 306–8,
316–19, 357, 361, 369
on Europe 192, 213, 245, 257,
263–4, 270–3, 311
with Kenneth Clarke 280, 326,
343–4, 362

THATCHER, LADY MARGARET (*cont.*)
  with Michael Heseltine 40–51, 63,
      125, 136, 181, 235, 291, 316,
      320, 326, 362
  with Michael Howard 345–6
  with Michael Portillo 313, 315,
      342–3, 362
  with Mikhail Gorbachev 69–71, 76,
      354
  with Nigel Lawson 63, 64, 68–9,
      71–3, 79–80, 81–4, 92–3, 97,
      100, 293
  with rank and file Tories 204
  with Ronald Reagan 38, 76, 346,
      356
  with Tony Blair 301, 310, 321,
      331–2
    influence on founding of New
        Labour 24
    supports over Kosovo 16–17, 24,
        335
  with William Hague 326, 328–31,
      335, 338, 362
    damage to 341
— *resignation* 4, 125–36, 137–48
  bewilderment over downfall 7, 131,
      141, 148
  chances of winning 1992 election
      221–3, 362
  leaves Downing Street 160
  reaction to 140–1, 143, 145–6,
      147–8, 187–8
  sense of betrayal 11, 134, 136, 138,
      139, 186, 197, 204, 209, 234,
      272, 357, 362
  valedictory address 146–7
— *since leaving office*
  comments on multicultural society 339
  complains her work is being undone
      235, 310–11, 358
  Conservative conference 1991
      204–5, 207
  Conservative conference 1993 290–1
  Conservative conference 1994 304
  Conservative conference 1995
      315–16

Conservative conference 1996 320
consultancies 188
continuing influence 4–5, 10–11,
    131, 188–9, 193–4, 344, 362
as destroyer of Conservative party
    11
and Gulf War 183, 221
in House of Lords 244, 245, 280
influence on 1997 leadership election
    325, 326, 328–30
involvement in 1997 election
    campaign 320–1
  comment on loss 323
involvement in 2001 election
    campaign 335–40
last attends Commons 224–5
lecture tours abroad 187–9, 225, 255,
    285, 294, 303, 313, 315
memoirs 187, 285, 288–9, 291,
    292–5, 310–11
more popular among Tory MPs 237
possibility of return to power 267,
    275
reforms consolidated by 1992 election
    victory 234
reforms not reversed by Labour 335,
    351, 359
sees herself as 'back-seat driver' 158
speeches 187–9, 190–1, 241, 270–1,
    337–8
  Keith Joseph Memorial Lecture
      1996 316–18
tries to adjust to 'normal' life 184–7
views become more extreme 356,
    365
views on Bosnia 289, 306
void in her life 202–3, 316, 362–3

Thatcher, Mark 68, 187, 202, 304
Thatcher Foundation 188, 309, 315
Thatcherism 66, 235–6, 347–50, 351,
    352, 355, 357–9
Thatchermania 294
Third Way 359
trade unions, curbing of 23–4, 74, 140,
    234, 235, 284, 301, 350351

Index

Truman, Harry 163
Turkey 93
Turnbull, Andrew 121–2
Twigg, Stephen 322

United States
    Anglo-American alliance 25, 38, 355
    support in Falklands War 22, 24

VAT 20–1, 35, 57, 180
veto, EC member states' right to 54
Vilnius 186

Wakeham, Lord John 126–9, 130, 131–2, 137, 179–80, 194, 353, 369
Walters, Professor Sir Alan 83–4, 97
Walters, Barbara 186
Watkins, Alan 113, 193
welfare state 347, 350, 352
Welsh Assembley 335

Westland Affair 46–50, 52, 149, 151, 206, 239
wets, the 22, 238, 282
whips' office 118, 119–20, 121, 168, 275
White, Lesley 309, 310
Whitelaw, Lord William 29, 42, 45–6, 82, 168, 257
Whittingdale, John 100, 106, 146, 185, 187, 263, 265–6, 272, 275, 276, 328, 329, 332
Wilson, Harold 30, 114, 146, 213, 259, 310, 326
winter of discontent 19, 20, 299–300
Winterton, Nicholas 242
Witchell, Nicholas 138
Wyatt, Woodrow 190, 307

Yeltsin, Boris 331
Young, Hugo 164–5
Younger, George 87, 121
Yugoslavia 289